lonely planet

Vienna

"All you've got to do is decide to go and the hardest part is over.

So go!"

TONY WHEELER, COFOUNDER – LONELY PLANET

CATHERINE LE NEVEZ, KERRY WALKER, MARC DI DUCA

Contents

HELEN CATHCART/LONELY PLANET ©

TRABANTOS/SHUTTERSTOCK ©

(left) **Haus des Meeres p92** Tropical forest on the site of a huge public aquarium.

(above) **Schönbrunn p159** Christmas market at the castle.

(right) **Kirche am Steinhof p168** Statue of an angel at Otto Wagner's church

GREG ELMS/LONELY PLANET ©

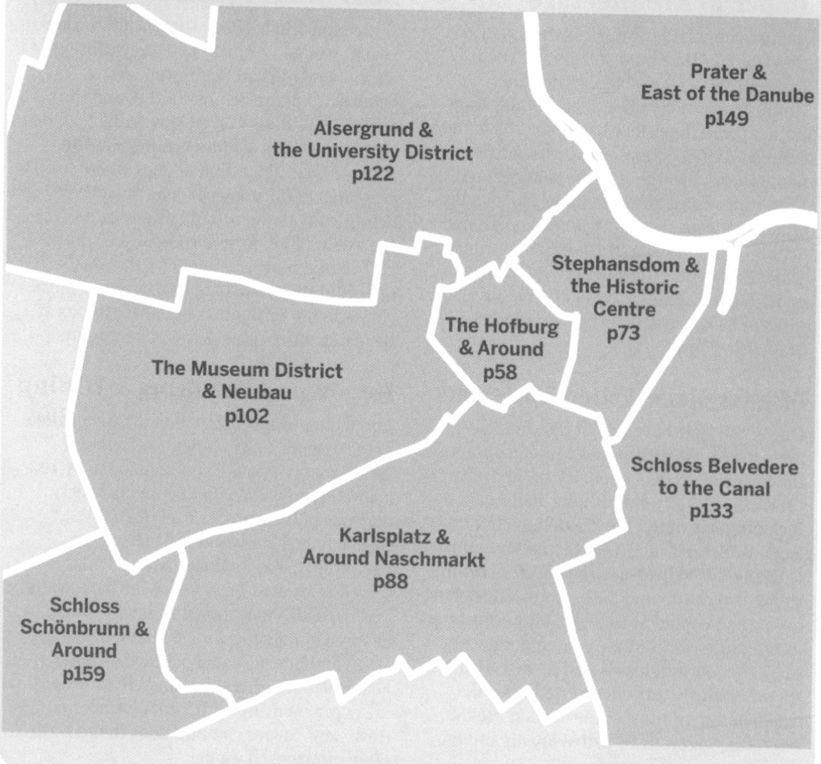

Welcome to Vienna

Baroque streetscapes and imperial palaces set the stage for artistic and musical masterpieces, alongside vibrant epicurean and design scenes.

Imperial Architecture

Vienna's imperial grandeur is the legacy of the powerful Habsburg monarchy. Their home for more than six centuries, the Hofburg palace complex, incorporates the Burgkapelle (Imperial Chapel) and the famed Spanish Riding School along with a trove of museums, including in the chandeliered Kaiserappartements (Imperial Apartments). Other immense palaces include the baroque Schloss Belvedere and Schloss Schönbrunn, while 19th-century splendours such as the neo-Gothic Rathaus (City Hall) line the magnificent Ringstrasse encircling the Innere Stadt (city centre).

Masterpiece-Filled Museums

One of the Habsburgs' most dazzling palaces, the Kunsthistorisches Museum, houses the imperial art collection. It's packed with priceless works by old masters, and treasures including one of the world's richest coin collections. Behind the Hofburg, the MuseumsQuartier has a diverse ensemble of museums, showcasing 19th- and 20th-century Austrian art at the Leopold Museum to often-shocking avant-garde works at the contemporary MUMOK. Meteorites, fossils and prehistoric finds fill the Naturhistorisches Museum, while exquisite furnishings at the applied-arts Museum für Angewandte Kunst are also among the artistic feasts in store.

Soul-Stirring Music

With a musical heritage that includes composers Wolfgang Amadeus Mozart, Joseph Haydn, Ludwig van Beethoven, Franz Schubert, Johann Strauss (father and son), Johannes Brahms and Gustav Mahler, among countless others, Vienna is known as the City of Music. Incredible venues where you can catch performances today include the acoustically renowned Musikverein, used by the Vienna Philharmonic Orchestra, the gold-and-crystal main opera house, the Staatsoper, and the multistage Konzerthaus. Music comes to life through interactive exhibits at the captivating Haus der Musik museum.

Renowned Drinking & Dining

The Viennese appreciation of the finer things in life extends to its opulent coffee-house 'living rooms' serving spectacular cakes; its beloved pub-like *Beisln* dishing up hearty portions of Wiener schnitzel, *Tafelspitz* (prime boiled beef) and goulash; elegant restaurants; and its fine Austrian wines served in vaulted *Vinothek* (wine bar) cellars, and in rustic vine-draped *Heurigen* (wine taverns) in the vineyards fringing the city. Local and international delicacies fill the heady Naschmarkt stalls, and creative chefs are experimenting with local produce and fresh new flavour combinations in innovative, often repurposed venues.

PFEIFFER/SHUTTERSTOCK ©

Why I Love Vienna

By Catherine Le Nevez, Writer

With its rambling palaces, winding cobbled lanes, grand *Kaffeehäuser* (coffee houses) and cosy wood-panelled *Beisln* (taverns), Vienna is steeped in history. Yet it's also at the cutting edge of design, architecture, contemporary art, and new directions in drinking and dining. What I love most about the city is that not only does it hold on to its traditions, it incorporates them in everything from high-fashion *Dirndls* (women's traditional dress) through to sweets made from resurrected recipes and third-wave coffee served at neo-retro-inspired cafes. Vienna's past is alive in its present, and, by extension, its future.

For more about our writers, see p256

Top: Statue of Johann Strauss in the Stadtpark (p134)

Vienna's Top 10

Schloss Schönbrunn *(p161)*

1 The magnificent rococo former summer palace and gardens of the Habsburgs are a perfect place to experience the pomp, circumstance and gracious legacy of Austria's erstwhile monarchs. A visit to 40 of the palace's lavishly appointed rooms reveals the lifestyle and the eccentricities of Europe's most powerful family. Beyond the palace, Schloss Schönbrunn Gardens invite a stroll past pseudo-Roman ruins, along bucolic paths winding through leafy woods and a stopover in the gardens' highlight, the Gloriette, with mesmerising views of the palace and city beyond.

Schloss Schönbrunn & Around

Kunsthistorisches Museum Vienna *(p104)*

2 The jewel in Vienna's artistic crown is its Kunsthistorisches Museum Vienna. As well as accumulating vassal lands, the Habsburgs assembled one of Europe's finest collections of art and artefacts. Housed inside a majestic neoclassical building, the highlight of this incredible cache is the Picture Gallery, an encounter with a vast and emotionally powerful collection of works by grand masters, such as Pieter Bruegel the Elder's evocative and 'industrial' *Tower of Babel* from the 16th century or the bright plenitude of Giuseppe Arcimboldo's *Summer*.

The Museum District & Neubau

1

CGE2010/SHUTTERSTOCK ©

2

ANTON_IVANOV/SHUTTERSTOCK ©

The Hofburg Palace (p60)

3 The imposing former wintering ground of the Habsburg monarchs for over 700 years not only has a fine collection of museums, it's also a living palace that today is home to the Austrian president, Austria's National Library and public offices (and is the temporary home of the Austrian Parlament; parliament). A leisurely stroll through the palace complex is an encounter with one gracious building, statue and square after another, taking in highlights such as the Swiss Courtyard, the grotesquely proportioned Heldenplatz and diminutive arches of the Outer Palace Gate.

Above: Dome of the Nationalbibliothek (p63).

The Hofburg & Around

Stephansdom (p75)

4 A Gothic reminder of another age, the Stephansdom is Vienna's heart and soul. The awe-inspiring cathedral lords over the city, topped by an intricately tiled roof, with its distinctive row of chevrons and Austrian eagle. Below the cathedral are the *Katakomben* (catacombs), with their eerie collection of the deceased; inside, a magnificent Gothic stone pulpit presides over the main nave; and rising above it to dizzying heights is the South Tower with its viewing stage offering dazzling views over town.

Stephansdom & the Historic Centre

Ringstrasse Tram Tour (p29)

5 For a spin around Vienna's architectural highlights, jump on a tram and travel along the Ringstrasse, one of Europe's most magnificent streets. This circular boulevard of imposing state buildings, palaces and majestic hotels was carved out of the space once occupied by fortifications protecting Vienna from Ottoman Turk attack in the 16th century. The monumental 19th-century masterpieces now rise up along the flanks, encircling most of the central Innere Stadt and separating the centre from the character-laden *Vorstädte* (inner suburbs).

Guided Tours & Walks

4

5
71
4090

Prater & Ferris Wheel *(p151)*

6 Rising above the beautiful green open spaces of the Prater, the 1897-built Riesenrad Ferris wheel, where Graham Greene sent his fictional character Harry Lime for a slow rotation in the 1949 film *The Third Man,* is a Viennese icon. A ride takes you high above the Prater, giving you a bird's-eye view of the city and the expanse of wooded parkland and meadows, which you can explore on inline skates, by bicycle or on a walk after hitting ground level.

Prater & East of the Danube

Schloss Belvedere *(p135)*

7 Living up to its Italianesque name 'beautiful view', this 18th-century palace and garden ensemble is deceptively close to Vienna's city centre while still creating a feeling of being worlds apart. Symmetrical, finely sculpted and manicured gardens overlooking Vienna's unfolding skyline connect two exquisite palaces dedicated to a who's who of Austrian art. Gustav Klimt's painting *The Kiss* is a highlight. The masterpieces on display are complemented by interiors so stately that they're worthy of a visit in their own right.

Schloss Belvedere to the Canal

6

Vienna Boys' Choir

(p46)

8 When Maximilian I founded the Wiener Sängerknaben (Vienna Boys' Choir) in 1498 he replaced castrati with young boys whose voices had not broken, creating the world's most celebrated choir. Today the celestial tones of this choir echo through the Burgkapelle (Imperial Chapel) of the Hofburg, where the choir performs classical music from Schubert, Mozart and other musical greats during Sunday Mass; it also stages an eclectic program of classical and contemporary music across town in MuTh, its own dedicated performing space.

☆ ***Entertainment***

Coffee Houses *(p35)*

9 Great works of art have been created in these 'living rooms' of the Viennese. Patronised by luminaries such as Mahler, Klimt, Freud, Trotsky and Otto Wagner in their day, Vienna's *Kaffeehäuser* (coffee houses) were added to the Unesco list of Intangible Cultural Heritage in 2011. Many retain their opulent original decor, and often specialise in a particular cake, such as the *Sacher Torte*, an iced-chocolate cake with apricot jam once favoured by Emperor Franz Josef, at Café Sacher. New-wave coffee houses are putting their own twist on the tradition.

Right: Café Sacher (p70)

Coffee Houses & Cake Shops

9

10

Beisln *(p31)*

10 A Viennese tradition, a *Beisl* is akin to a bistro pub, dishing up heaping portions of goulash, Wiener schnitzel, *Tafelspitz* (prime boiled beef) and other favourites along with wine and/or beer on unadorned tables in wood-panelled surrounds. In the warmer months, many *Beisln* open onto terraces or lantern-lit cobbled courtyards. Linger over a drink, enjoy the classic Austrian fare and soak up the unique atmosphere at stalwarts such as Griechenbeisl. These institutions have inspired a new breed of neo-*Beisln,* with an upmarket edge and often organic produce.

Above: Griechenbeisl restaurant (p83)

Eating

What's New

Digital Detox

'See Klimt. Not #Klimt' is the hashtag of Viennese initiative Unhashtag Vienna (www.unhashtag.vienna.info), aimed at luring travellers away from their smartphones and encouraging digital detox. The city's gardens, markets and coffee houses, such as institutions like Café Leopold Hawelka (p69), are just perfect for this.

Contemporary History Collections

Austria's first museum of contemporary history, the Haus der Geschichte Österreich, opened in the Hofburg in 2018. Starting from the mid-19th century and continuing to the present day, its evolving collection provides an insight into what makes the country tick. (p63)

Multisensory Illusions

Interactive exhibits at the 2018-opened Museum der Illusionen challenge your senses through a range of optical and spatial illusions, including a tunnel with spinning images on the walls that disrupt your balance. (p66)

Freud's Former Home

Devoted to the father of psychoanalysis, the compelling Sigmund Freud Museum, in his former home, underwent a makeover and expansion, and was set to reopen in spring 2020. (p125)

Socially Minded Tours

Get a unique perspective on Vienna with Shades Tours (p193), which runs guided circuits taking in the city's history, baroque architecture and hidden alleys, led by homeless guides. The organisation also provides support structures for those without homes.

Gallery-Hotel

New life has been breathed into the historic shell of Hotel Kunsthof, styled as a crossover between a gallery and a hotel, and incorporating modern art, striking light installations and designer furniture. (p190)

Art & Cocktails

Hybrid Melete Art Design Cocktails is at once an art gallery and a brilliant bar, and its creative craft cocktails are themed around its exhibitions. (p117)

Vegan Dining

Vienna is embracing the vegan trend, with a slew of homegrown enterprises spanning vegan ice-cream purveyors to burger restaurants such as Swing Kitchen. (p115)

Third-Wave Coffee

The reverential place of coffee houses in Viennese society has opened the door for a cornucopia of third-wave coffee specialists, such as J Hornig Kaffeebar (p117), using cutting-edge techniques to achieve a perfect brew.

Summer Beach

While it might be a long way from the coast, the beach now comes to Vienna at Tel Aviv Beach, with sand, DJs, cocktails and food. (p156)

For more recommendations and reviews, see **lonelyplanet.com/Vienna**

Need to Know

For more information, see Survival Guide (p213)

Currency

Euro (€)

Language

German

Visas

Generally not required for stays of up to 90 days; from 2021, non-EU nationals need prior authorisation under the new European Travel Information and Authorisation System (ETIAS) process for Schengen Area travel.

Money

ATMs are widely available. Credit cards are not always accepted in budget hotels or budget to midrange restaurants. Bars and cafes usually only accept cash.

Mobile Phones

You can use your mobile phone (*Handy* in German) in Austria provided it is GSM and tri-band or quad-band. Check with your service provider about using your phone in Austria.

Time

Central European Time (GMT/UTC plus one hour)

Tourist Information

Tourist Info Wien (Map p238; ☎01-245 55; www.wien.info; 01, Albertinaplatz; ⏰9am-7pm; 📶; 🚋D, 1, 2, 71 Kärntner Ring/Oper, Ⓤ Stephansplatz) Vienna's main tourist office.

Daily Costs

Budget: Less than €100

➡ Dorm bed: €25–30

➡ Cheap double per person: €40–65

➡ Self-catering or lunchtime specials: €7.50–12

➡ Free sights and cheap museums: to €8

➡ Happy hour: beer/wine €2–4, cocktails €4.50–7.50

Midrange: €100–180

➡ Hotel double per person: €65–110

➡ Two-course midrange meal with glass of wine: €25–35

➡ High-profile museums: €13

Top end: More than €180

➡ Upmarket hotel double per person: from €110

➡ Multicourse meal with wine: from €70

➡ Opera and theatre: from €40

Advance Planning

Three months before Reserve tickets for Staatsoper seating, Vienna Boys' Choir, the Spanish Riding School and major events.

One month before Make reservations for top-shelf restaurants; check upcoming events at www.wien.info and venue websites. Book accommodation in summer and during the Christmas market season.

One week before Check Falter (www.falter.at) for drinking and dining tips, and reserve a table in popular restaurants for weekend nights.

Useful Websites

Falter (www.falter.at) Eating, drinking and entertainment listings, and advice.

Vienna Webservice (www.wien.gv.at) Official Vienna city council website.

Österreich Werbung (www.austria.info) National tourism authority, with information on the capital and country.

WHEN TO GO

July and August are busy. April–June and September–October are ideal times to visit. November can be drizzly, while December–March often brings snow.

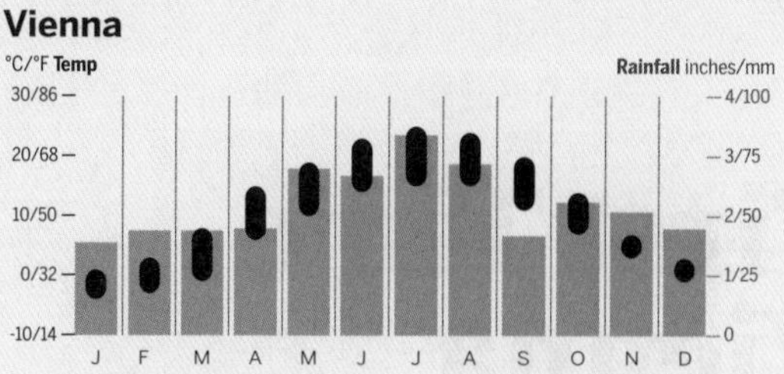

Arriving in Vienna

Vienna International Airport The City Airport Train leaves the airport every 30 minutes from 6.09am to 11.39pm, 365 days. The cheaper but slower S7 suburban train (€4.20, 37 minutes) also runs every 30 minutes from 5.18am to 12.18am from the airport to Wien-Mitte. It's €25 to €50 for a taxi.

Wien Hauptbahnhof Situated 3km south of Stephansdom, Vienna's gleaming main train station handles all international trains as well as trains from all of Austria's provincial capitals, and many local and regional trains. It's linked to the centre by U-Bahn line 1, trams D and O, and bus 13A. A taxi to the centre costs about €10. All stations are generally safe late at night and have good connections with the centre and suburbs.

For much more on **arrival** see p214

Getting Around

U-Bahn Fast, comfortable and safe. Trains run from 5am to midnight Monday to Thursday and continuously from 5am Friday through to midnight Sunday. Tickets are sold at machines or windows at stations. Validate tickets prior to boarding.

Tram Slower but more enjoyable. Depending on the route, trams run from around 5.15am to about 11.45pm. Buy tickets at kiosks or from the driver (more expensive). Validate tickets when boarding.

Bus Reliable, punctual, with several very useful routes for visitors. Most run from 5am to midnight; services can be sporadic or nonexistent on weekends. Buy tickets from the driver or a *Tabakladen* (tobacconist). Validate tickets on boarding.

Night Bus Especially useful for outer areas; runs every 30 minutes from 12.30am to 5am. Main stops are located at Schwedenplatz, Schottentor and Kärntner Ring/Oper.

For much more on **getting around** see p216

Sleeping

Vienna's lodgings cover it all, from luxury establishments where chandeliers, antique furniture and original 19th-century oil paintings abound and cutting-edge, statement-making design hotels to inexpensive youth hostels. In between are homey, often family-run *Pensionen* (guesthouses), many traditional, and less ostentatious hotels, plus a smart range of apartments.

Useful Websites

Lonely Planet (lonelyplanet.com/austria/vienna/hotels) Recommendations and bookings.

Hostelling International (www.hihostels.com) Global youth hostel organisation.

For much more on **sleeping** see p184

First Time Vienna

For more information, see Survival Guide (p213)

Checklist

- Make sure your passport is valid for at least six months past your arrival date.
- Arrange travel insurance and/or medical insurance.
- Inform your bank/credit-card company of your travel.
- Take copies of all important documents and cards, and store separately.
- Contact your mobile provider to enquire about roaming charges or getting an international plan.

What to Pack

- Comfortable walking shoes for exploration (with grip for ice in winter)
- Umbrella or rain jacket
- Decent shoes and jacket for going out – the Viennese dress up
- Day pack
- Electrical adaptor if needed

Top Tips for Your Trip

- Sightsee on foot in central Vienna. The Innere Stadt (inner city) is deceptively small and most places are a short walk from Stephansplatz.
- Save money by using a public-transport pass. It's easy to cross town on a U-Bahn or tram to explore outer neighbourhoods.
- Linger over a coffee and cake at one of 'Vienna's living rooms', its resplendent coffee houses, or over local specialities such as schnitzels, with a local wine or beer, in its cosy *Beisln* (bistro pubs).
- Catch a classical-music or opera performance for a true City of Music experience. Standing-room tickets start from just a few euros.

What to Wear

Winter can be cold and the ground icy, so several layers of warm clothing and good shoes are essential. In spring and summer the weather can be very changeable, so wear layers you can peel off and make sure you have a waterproof jacket for rain showers. The Viennese dress up well in the evening, but smart jeans are usually fine even for upmarket clubs and restaurants if combined with a good shirt or blouse. Pack a dress/suit if you're attending the opera.

Be Forewarned

Vienna is a very safe city and in general women and men will have no trouble walking around at night.

- Karlsplatz station and Gumpendorfer Strasse can be boisterous late in the evening.
- The Prater and Praterstern can get dodgy at night. Ausstellungsstrasse is best avoided due to sex workers and kerb-crawlers.
- The Gürtel has a sprinkling of red-light clubs: north of Westbahnhof along the Neubaugürtel has a high concentration (with fewer around Thaliastrasse), and directly south to Gumpendorfer Strasse can be seedy.
- S-Bahn and tram stops along Margareten and Wiedner Gürtel can be edgy.

Taxes & Refunds

Austria has a *Mehrwertsteuer* (MWST; value-added tax) of 20% on most items. It's always included in the price but listed separately on a formal receipt. Visitors from outside the EU can claim back around 13% for individual purchases over €75.01 when departing the EU; see www.globalblue.com for instructions. Vienna International Airport has refund desks; otherwise submit the paperwork by post.

Bargaining

Bargaining is a no-no in shops, although you can certainly haggle when buying secondhand. It's a must at the *Flohmärkte* (flea markets).

Tipping

Restaurants and cafes Tips are generally expected; round up smaller bills (to the nearest 50 cents or euro) when buying coffee or beer, and add 5% to 10% to the bill for full meals. Tip at the time of payment as one lump sum with the bill.

Taxis Drivers will expect around 10% extra.

Hotel porters and cloakroom attendants Tip a euro or two.

Shopping street Graben (p86)

Etiquette

The Viennese are fairly formal and use irony to alleviate social rules and constraints.

Greetings *Grüss Gott* or the less formal *Servus!* are the usual forms of greeting; *Guten Tag* is also common. Stick to the polite *Sie* (you) form unless you know someone well or are of a similar age in a young-ish scene. Never use *du* with shop assistants or waiters.

Acknowledgements When entering a breakfast room, it's usual to acknowledge others by saying *'Guten Morgen'* when you walk in and *'Auf Wiedersehen'* on leaving.

Telephone Give your name at the start of a telephone call, especially when making reservations. When completing the call, say *'Auf Wiederhören'* ('goodbye'; customary form on phone).

Language

In Vienna, the regional capitals and tourist areas (such as around lakes or in resorts), you'll find that many people speak English, especially in restaurants and hotels. In much of the countryside, however, it's a slightly different picture, and you should equip yourself with a few necessary phrases. Conductors on trains and many bus drivers know enough English to help with necessities. While English is widely spoken in Vienna, speaking even a few basic words of German is not only respectful but will make your visit much more rewarding. For language tips, see p222.

Top Itineraries

Day One

Stephansdom & the Historic Centre (p73)

Start your day at Vienna's heart, the **Stephansdom**, being awed by the cathedral's cavernous interior, Gothic stone pulpit and baroque high altar. For a bird's-eye view of Vienna, climb the **cathedral south tower** via 343 steps to the viewing platform. Or delve below ground into its ossuary, the **Katakomben** (catacombs). Spend the rest of the morning strolling the atmospheric narrow streets around the cathedral.

Lunch Deli food and a glass of wine at Zum Schwarzen Kameel (p83).

The Hofburg & Around (p58)

Make your way along **Graben** and Kohlmarkt to the **Hofburg**, where one of the ultimate pleasures is simply to wander through and soak up the grandeur of this Habsburg architectural masterpiece. Narrow it down to one or two of the museums here, such as the **Kaiserappartements**, which contain the Sisi Museum.

Dinner Restaurant Herrlich (p69): traditional but classy Viennese cuisine.

The Museum District & Neubau (p102)

Head into the cobblestoned Spittelberg district to enduring favourites such as old-school brewery **Siebensternbräu** and hip bars such as vintage-furnished **Liebling** or Parisian-styled **Le Troquet**.

Day Two

The Museum District & Neubau (p102)

Enjoy one of the city's best breakfasts at **Figar** before making your way to the **Kunsthistorisches Museum Vienna**, where you can plan on spending at least a whole morning in the thrall of its old masters.

Lunch Duck behind the MuseumsQuartier to hidden Glacis Beisl (p117) for fortifying classics such as schnitzels.

The Museum District & Neubau (p102)

The afternoon is a good time to change artistic direction and explore at least one of the museums in the MuseumsQuartier. The light, bright **Leopold Museum** has splendid Austrian art. **MUMOK** makes a complete contrast, with contemporary, often controversial works. The MuseumsQuartier has plenty of bars if you need a break, such as laid-back **Kantine**.

Dinner Motto am Fluss (p83) has a hip lounge ambience on the Danube Canal.

Stephansdom & the Historic Centre (p73)

Explore the Innere Stadt's illuminated streets and lively bar scene in the evening in the centre, sipping Austrian wines at **Vinothek W-Einkehr**, deliberating over dozens of varieties of gin in various taverns, or hitting architectural treasures such as **Zwölf Apostelkeller** or **Kruger's American Bar**.

RADU BERCAN/SHUTTERSTOCK ©

MUMOK (p111)

GREG ELMS/LONELY PLANET ©

Stephansdom pulpit (p75)

Day Three

Schloss Belvedere to the Canal (p133)

Divide your morning between Schloss Belvedere's magnificently landscaped French-style formal **gardens** and its galleries. The **Unteres Belvedere** (Lower Belvedere) has baroque state apartments and ceremonial rooms, and hosts some superb temporary exhibitions in its orangery, while a walk through **Oberes Belvedere** (Upper Belvedere) takes you through a who's who of Austrian art.

Lunch Meierei im Stadtpark (p146) for some of Austria's finest goulash.

Prater & East of the Danube (p149)

Make your way to the Prater, Vienna's playground of woods, meadows and sideshow attractions at the **Würstelprater**. The highlight here is the 19th-century **Riesenrad** Ferris wheel, famed for its role in 1949 film *The Third Man,* as well as the James Bond instalment *The Living Daylights* and art-house favourite *Before Sunrise.*

Dinner Fabulous vegan fare at Harvest (p154) in Leopoldstadt.

Prater & East of the Danube (p149)

Leopoldstadt is fast becoming one of Vienna's hippest districts, and there are an increasing number of cafes and bars popping up. Finish the evening at 18th-storey **Das Loft** for a cocktail accompanied by a sweeping panorama of the city.

Day Four

Schloss Schönbrunn & Around (p159)

Take an eye-popping tour of baroque extravaganza **Schloss Schönbrunn**, and stroll the French formal gardens, detouring to the **Gloriette**, with breathtaking views of the palace and city skyline beyond.

Lunch Browse the Naschmarkt (p92) for picnic supplies or stop at one of its sit-down restaurants.

Karlsplatz & Around Naschmarkt (p88)

Continue to another baroque jewel, the **Karlskirche**, and ride the lift into the dome for an up-close view of its stunning fresco by Johann Michael Rottmayr. Stop in for a glass of Austrian wine at Jakov's Weinkeller. Then head to **Secession** to see seminal works by members of the Vienna Secession including Klimt's 34m-long *Beethoven Frieze.*

Dinner Dine on local and/or organic produce at neo-*Beisl* Silberwirt (p95).

Karlsplatz & Around Naschmarkt (p88)

The Margareten (the 5th district) and Mariahilf (the 6th), both flanking the trickling Wien River, offer plenty of drinking and nightlife opportunities. Sip *Sekt* (sparkling wine) at **Sekt Comptoir**, enjoy a pint at **Café Rüdigerhof** and hit the dance floor at **Club U**.

If You Like...

Grand Architecture

Hofburg The Habsburgs' home from 1273 to 1918 exemplifies imperial splendour. (p60)

Schloss Belvedere Built for military strategist Prince Eugene of Savoy, the Belvedere now incorporates an art gallery. (p135)

Ringstrasse Ride a tram past this magnificent parade of 19th-century masterpieces. (p29)

Schloss Schönbrunn Of the palace's 1441 rooms, 40 are open to the public. (p161)

Great Works of Art

Kunsthistorisches Museum Vienna There are masterpieces in every room at Vienna's finest museum. (p104)

Leopold Museum A stunning collection of works with a strong focus on Egon Schiele, Oskar Kokoschka, Richard Gerstl and other expressionists. (p110)

MUMOK The Museum of Modern Art covers virtually all 20th- and 21st-century movements. (p111)

Schloss Belvedere The ensemble of galleries here focuses on the pantheon of Austrian artists from the Middle Ages to the present. (p135)

Kunsthalle Wien Showcases local and international artists in changing exhibitions. (p111)

Albertina Striking state apartments augmented by copies from the graphics collection and the outstanding Batliner Collection. (p66)

Ice skating at the Wiener Eistraum (p121)

Classical Music

Musikverein Used by the Vienna Philharmonic Orchestra, this concert hall has some of the world's best acoustics. (p100)

Staatsoper A performance at Vienna's famous opera house is unforgettable. (p100)

Konzerthaus Top-flight classical concerts are held at this multistage venue. (p147)

MuTh Listen to the angelic voices of the Vienna Boys' Choir at its dedicated home venue. (p157)

Haus der Musik Contains the Museum of the Vienna Philharmonic and imaginative interactive exhibitions. (p78)

Churches

Stephansdom Vienna's landmark Gothic cathedral soars above the city's rooftops. (p75)

Karlskirche Head up into the cupola for fresco close-ups at this baroque wonder. (p91)

Peterskirche This sublime church invites contemplation beneath a dome fresco painted by Rottmayr. (p79)

Franziskanerkirche The beauty of this church is its deceptive trompe-l'oeil dome. (p79)

Ruprechtskirche Believed to date from 740, this is Vienna's oldest church. (p78)

Getting Active

Donauinsel Vienna's artificial island is a favourite with water babies for swimming, boating and waterskiing. (p158)

Wienerwald These woods are a paradise for walkers and cyclists, and home to plenty of *Heurigen* (wine taverns). (p154)

Prater Forest trails lead through this central Viennese oasis. (p151)

Kletteranlage Flakturm The *Flakturm* (flak tower) housing the Haus des Meeres is a popular climbing spot for alpinists. (p101)

Therme Wien Austria's largest thermal baths have whirlpools, waterfalls and grotto-like pools. (p148)

Wiener Eistraum In winter skaters twirl on the ice outside the magnificent Rathaus at this picture-book-pretty rink. (p121)

Live Music & Clubs

Porgy & Bess Vienna's most popular jazz club has a velvety, refined atmosphere. (p86)

Arena Wien Rock, reggae, metal and more plays at this former slaughterhouse's outdoor and indoor stages. (p148)

Volksgarten ClubDiskothek Pavilion-housed venue in the Volksgarten with wide-ranging gigs, DJs and theme nights. (p70)

Flex Local and international DJs on the Danube Canal. (p40)

Markets

Naschmarkt Vienna's largest and most famous market is a feast for the senses. (p92)

Brunnenmarkt This fruit, vegetable and foodstuff market reflects its location in the Turkish district. (p126)

Karmelitermarkt Leopoldstadt's local flavour is in full swing at this ethnically diverse market. (p156)

For more top Vienna spots, see the following:

- Eating (p31)
- Drinking & Nightlife (p40)
- Entertainment (p44)
- Shopping (p48)
- Sports & Activities (p51)

Bio-Markt Freyung Pick up organic picnic ingredients at this Innere Stadt market. (p132)

Rochusmarkt A hive of activity in the Landstrasse district. (p145)

Flohmarkt Browse for bargains at this Viennese favourite, one of Europe's best flea markets. (p100)

Panoramas

Riesenrad Take in the quintessential Viennese panorama from the top of this historic Ferris wheel. (p151)

Gloriette Vienna shimmers in the distance from this viewpoint overlooking Schloss Schönbrunn. (p163)

Belvedere Gardens Linking Schloss Belvedere's upper and lower palace, these baroque gardens provide skyline, Stephansdom and Hofburg views. (p137)

Das Loft Views unfurl across the Danube Canal and over the Innere Stadt from this 18th-floor bar-restaurant. (p156)

Stephansdom South Tower Hiking up 343 steps rewards with an incredible view over the Innere Stadt's rooftops. (p76)

Naturhistorisches Museum Rooftop tours offer architectural close-ups and city panoramas. (p113)

Month By Month

TOP EVENTS

Wiener Festwochen, May to mid-June

Ostermärkte, March/April

Donauinselfest, June

Jazz Fest Wien, July

Christkindlmärkte, mid-November to late December

January

Although the first month of the year is one of the coldest in Vienna, it's also one of the least expensive and the city has a lively winter cultural scene.

Wiener Eistraum

From January through to early March the square in front of Vienna's Rathaus (City Hall) turns into a massive ice rink (p121).

February

Days remain short, dark and often snowy in February. But key attractions have few-to-no crowds and Vienna's famous coffee houses make wonderful refuges from the elements.

March

March brings the first taste of spring to the city; days start getting longer and some years it's warm enough to sit outdoors, though festivities are few.

April

Greenery emerges, flowers bloom and, in March or April, Easter signals the start of Vienna's tourist season. If planning on visiting in the summer, make sure to book accommodation from now. Layers (and an umbrella) are essential for the changeable weather.

Ostermärkte

Easter markets at locations including Am Hof (p48) and Schloss Schönbrunn (p48) herald the arrival of spring with traditional Easter decorations, floral and Easter-egg displays, handicrafts, food and drink stalls, and activities for kids. Markets typically take place in the two weeks leading up to Easter.

May

May is a lovely time in Vienna. Cycling is possible, Danube cruises are frequent and it's warm enough to consider an excursion to the Wachau.

June

The summer solstice (between 20 and 22 June) means warm days segue into lingering, balmy nights. Festivals take place Vienna-wide, and visitors start flocking to the city.

☆ Wiener Festwochen

A wide-ranging program of theatre productions, concerts, dance performances and visual arts from around the world, the month-long Wiener Festwochen takes place at various venues city-wide.

☆ Donauinselfest

Held over three days in late June, the free Donauinselfest (p45) on Donauinsel (Danube Island) features a feast of rock, pop, folk and country performers, attracting three million onlookers.

Regenbogen Parade

Part of Vienna's two-week-long Pride festivities, mid-June's Regenbogen Parade (p219) attracts some 150,000 people on the Ringstrasse.

July

School holidays start at the beginning of July. Temperatures – and visitor numbers – soar and Vienna's *Schanigärten* (pavement cafes and courtyard gardens) come into their own.

Jazz Fest Wien

From late June to mid-July, Vienna swings to jazz, blues and soul flowing from the Staatsoper and a number of clubs across town during Jazz Fest Wien (p45), with many free concerts on outdoor stages.

Musikfilm Festival

Free screenings of operettas, operas and concerts take place outside the Rathaus from late June to early September during the Musikfilm Festival (p46).

August

Locals leave the city for the countryside and beyond, and many smaller shops, restaurants and bars close for the *Sommerpause* (summer break). Major museums and attractions stay open, and visitors fill the city.

ImPulsTanz

Vienna's premier avant-garde dance festival, ImPulsTanz attracts an array of internationally renowned troupes and newcomers between mid-July and mid-August at theatres across Vienna.

September

Autumn is in the air in September. Temperatures fall, schools go back after the long holidays, businesses reopen after the *Sommerpause* and crowds tail off at museums.

Vienna Contemporary

Held over five days in late September, Vienna Contemporary is Austria's prime contemporary art fair, with over 100 galleries and institutions from 27 countries in attendance.

October

***Goldener Oktober* sees the sun reflect the golden brown leaves of autumn. In a good year you can sit outside, but days become shorter and nights can get chilly.**

Lange Nacht der Museen

On the first Saturday of October, scores of museums in Vienna open their doors to visitors between 6pm and 1am during the Lange Nacht der Museen.

Viennale

Austria's best film fest, the two-week Viennale Film Festival (p46), features fringe and independent films from around the world, with screenings across the city.

November

Vienna can be grey and wet in November and although you can't expect to spend much time outdoors, it's an ideal time to embrace the *Beisl* (small tavern or restaurant), coffee-house and cultural scenes.

Wien Modern

The month-long Wien Modern music festival features modern classical and avant-garde at more than two dozen venues Vienna-wide.

December

December is an enchanting month to visit Vienna. Festive lights twinkle, decorations garland the city, and magical *Christkindlmärkte* (Christmas markets) sell delightful toys and other quality gifts, along with warming *Glühwein*.

Christkindlmärkte

Vienna's much-loved Christmas market season runs from around mid-November to Christmas Eve. Magical Christkindlmärkte (p48) in streets and squares have stalls selling wooden toys, festive decorations and traditional food and drink such as *Würstel* (sausages) and *Glühwein*.

Silvester

The Innere Stadt becomes one big party zone for Silvester, with outdoor concerts and loads of fireworks in the crowded streets.

With Kids

Vienna is a wonderfully kid-friendly city. Children are welcomed in all aspects of everyday life, and many of the city's museums go out of their way to gear exhibitions towards children. Children's servings are typically available in restaurants, and, when kids need to burn off energy, playgrounds are plentiful.

Museums

Exhibits especially well suited to children include the following:

Haus der Musik (p78) Has lots of practical exhibits for almost all ages to promote an understanding of music.

Naturhistorisches Museum (p113) Has a superb anthropology section where you can have a photo of yourself taken as a prehistoric human and delve into forensics. Check for schedules for its *Nacht im Museum* (Night at the Museum) program, where kids (who must be accompanied by adults) can get a torch (flashlight) tour and bed down overnight (BYO sleeping bags).

Technisches Museum (p165) Has lots of hands-on exhibits to promote the understanding of science and technology.

The MuseumsQuartier has a couple of spaces created especially for kids:

Zoom (p112) Exhibitions and programs of hands-on arts and crafts (from eight months to 14 years old).

Dschungel Wien (p120) Children's theatre with dance and occasional English performances.

Playgrounds & Open Space

You'll find plenty of playgrounds scattered across the city.

Jesuitenwiese (p152) In the Prater – along Hauptallee, about 1.5km east of Praterstern – is a good playground with a Wild West theme.

Wasserspielplatz Donauinsel (p158) Where toddlers can paddle and kids can dart across water on flying foxes and cross suspension bridges.

MuseumsQuartier (p110) Has a sand pit from about May to September, as well as various events throughout the year.

Wiener Eistraum (p121) Open-air winter ice rink with a special area for children.

Schloss Schönbrunn

The splendid Schloss Schönbrunn palace will enchant children.

Kindermuseum (Children's Museum; p164) Here kids can dress up as princes and princesses, as well as check out exhibitions of natural science, archaeology and toys.

Marionetten Theater (p168) Performances of *The Magic Flute* and *Aladdin* take place at the palace's puppet theatre. Some shows are in German and others in English.

Irrgarten (p163) Good fun maze for everyone, while the labyrinth playground is designed for kids, with 14 playing stops for climbing, crawling and educational exploration.

Tiergarten (p164) Kids will love visiting the world's oldest continuously operating zoo, which is home to some 712 species including giant pandas and Siberian tigers.

NEED TO KNOW

Public Transport Free for children under six years; half-price on single tickets under 15 years.

Restaurants Nappy (diaper) changing facilities are rare. Dedicated kids' menus are also uncommon but children's servings are usually on offer.

Hotels Cots (cribs) usually available. Children under 12 staying in their parents' room often receive discounts.

Breastfeeding in Public Fine.

Like a Local

With its monumental palaces and clip-clopping horse-drawn Fiaker carriages, Vienna could be a film set. But behind the scenes you'll find Viennese locals hanging out in up-and-coming neighbourhoods, lingering at cool cafes, canalside beaches and Schanigärten (pavement terraces), and hiking in the woods and vineyards that fringe the city.

HELEN CATHCART/LONELY PLANET ©

ne and cheese platter at *Heurigen* (wine tavern) Sirbu (p41)

Navigating Like a Local

The 23 Wiener *Bezirke* (Vienna districts) spiral out clockwise from the centre like a snail shell (although in some instances leapfrog position). The Innere Stadt (city centre) sits at the centre, encircled by the Ringstrasse.

Every address in Vienna begins with the district number, starting with 01 for the Innere Stadt (inner city), with street numbers starting closest to the city. The district number is easily identifiable by the middle two digits of its four-digit post code, so for example 1010 is the 01 (Innere Stadt).

Each of the *Bezirke* has its own style and character. Within or straddling these districts, you'll often find smaller neighbourhoods, such as the romantic, cobblestoned Spittelberg, 07, behind the MuseumsQuartier, and the foodie favourite Freihausviertel on the edge of the 04 and 05 districts.

VIENNA DISTRICTS

Vienna's districts clockwise from the centre.

NO	DISTRICT NAME
01	Innere Stadt (city centre)
02	Leopoldstadt
03	Landstrasse
04	Wieden
05	Margareten
06	Mariahilf
07	Neubau
08	Josefstadt
09	Alsergrund
10	Favoriten
11	Simmering
12	Meidling
13	Hietzing
14	Penzing
15	Rudolfsheim-Fünfhaus
16	Ottakring
17	Hernals
18	Währing
19	Döbling
20	Brigittenau
21	Floridsdorf
22	Donaustadt
23	Liesing

Drinking & Dining Like a Local

In the chilly winter months, the city's famous *Kaffeehäuser* (coffee houses) come into their own as Vienna's 'living rooms', and cosy wood-panelled *Beisln* (bistro pubs) and wine bars (many with candlelit vaulted cellars) are favourite places to retreat.

When the weather warms up, everything spills outdoors to the *Schanigärten*. Unlike *Gastgärten* (beer gardens), *Schanigärten* set up on public property such as pavements and sometimes parking areas and squares according to inexpensive permits issued by authorities, which are valid from 1 March to 15 November. Actual opening dates depend on the weather each season.

Beach bars pop up along the waterfront in summer, such as Tel Aviv Beach (p156) and Strandbar Herrmann (p147). They're a great alternative for Viennese who don't join their fellow citizens decamping from the city to the Austrian lakes during the July/August *Sommerpause* (summer break), when many of the city's restaurants, bars and smaller shops shut down.

Heurigen (wine taverns) at vineyards within the greater city limits are also wonderful places to experience the local wines as well as hearty Viennese hospitality. Two of the best are Wieninger (p42), with a lantern- and candlelit vine-draped garden, wood-panelled interior and outstanding Austrian cuisine; and Zahel (p42), in a 250-year-old farmhouse with a heated garden house for winter.

Hanging out Like a Local

A fantastic introduction to local Viennese life is to take a local-led tour with Space and Place (p30). These edgy city walks are run by Brit-turned-Viennese Eugene Quinn, who'll reveal everything from Vienna's ugly side to visiting the city at midnight.

Great neighbourhoods away from the big-hitting tourist sights to start exploring include Leopoldstadt (02), which is becoming increasingly hip. Independent boutiques, galleries and retro cafes have all popped up in recent years, especially around Praterstrasse. The stretch of the Danube Canal here has been given a push with new graffiti art (now legal, so the quality is up).

Traditionally gritty Rudolfsheim-Fünfhaus (15) is gentrifying thanks to the arrival of third-wave coffee specialists and cafes attracting crowds of locals for brunch.

Another hotspot-of-the-moment is Yppenplatz (16), which is loaded with delis and boutiques. The square is at its liveliest during the Saturday morning Bauernmarkt.

In Neubau (07), Kirchengasse, Lindengasse, Neubaugasse and Zollergasse are filled with art, design and fashion ateliers and boutiques.

Near the chaotic, colourful Naschmarkt, artisan producers, delis, design stores and one-of-a-kind boutiques make for a tantalising wander in the Freihausviertel (04 and 05).

Celebrating Like a Local

A local favourite is the Summer Stage (p131), with concerts, food stalls and activities on Rossauer Lände on the Danube Canal, which takes place between 5pm and 1am from May to September.

Come winter, some of the more local village-like *Christkindlmärkte* include the Spittelberg Christkindlmarkt (p48) and the Schloss Schönbrunn Christkindlmarkt (p168).

Woodland Escapes

Places like the Prater (p151) are popular for *wandern* (walking) but to really get off the beaten track, join the Viennese heading to the Wienerwald, a 45km swath of forested hills bordering the capital from the northwest to the southeast.

Walks covered on the city council website (www.wien.gv.at/umwelt/wald/freizeit/wandern/wege) include some that lead into the forest. One of the best is Trail No 1, an 11km loop, which starts in Nussdorf (take tram D from the Ring) and climbs the vineyard-ribboned hill Kahlenberg (484m), with fantastic city panoramas. Afterwards, back in Nussdorf, rejuvenate at a *Heuriger* such as **Mayer am Pfarrplatz** (☎01-370 12 87; www.pfarrplatz.at; 19, Pfarrplatz 2, Nussdorf; ⊙4pm-midnight Mon-Fri, noon-midnight Sat & Sun; 🚌38A Fernsprechamt Heiligenstadt), where Beethoven lived in 1817.

For Free

Vienna offers a wealth of opportunities to experience the city for free, from strolls through the city streets soaking up the spectacular architecture to a number of free museums, exhibitions, public buildings, parks and churches, as well as fabulous free entertainment, festivals and events.

Free Museums & Exhibitions

Some museums are free for those under 19 years, and permanent exhibitions at the municipal museums run by the City of Vienna are free on the first Sunday of the month. If you're interested in modern or contemporary art, drop into any of the free private art galleries scattered throughout the Innere Stadt (city centre). Most stock a program with a useful map with listings of exhibitions and gallery locations.

The following places are free:

Dorotheum (p72) Sensational auction house packed with everything from paintings to furnishings and household objects.

Dokumentationsarchiv des Österreichischen Widerstandes (p82) Exhibition documenting the antifascist resistance movement under Nazi rule.

Schloss Belvedere Gardens (p134) Exquisitely laid out gardens between the Upper and Lower Belvedere palaces.

Schloss Schönbrunn Gardens (p163) Expansive gardens, manicured and adorned in some parts, but also with pleasant wooded parkland.

Hundertwasserhaus (p144) A building designed by the eccentric architect Friedensreich Hundertwasser (the interior is closed to the public).

Otto Wagner Buildings (p93) **& Naschmarkt** (p92) Also check out the Gürtel U-Bahn stations, designed by this architect who shaped so much of the city in the late 19th and early 20th centuries.

Free Public Buildings, Parks & Churches

The Ringstrasse is home to many spectacular buildings, including the Hofburg (p60) palace complex, which is free to wander (individual museums and attractions within the Hofburg incur admission fees). Other Ringstrasse highlights include the University Main Building (p124) and the Justizpalast (supreme court; p114).

Stephansdom (p75) The northern side-aisle is free to visit.

Rathaus (p114) Vienna's splendid City Hall has free guided tours.

Zentralfriedhof (p146) Beethoven, Brahms, Strauss and Schubert are among the luminaries buried at this cemetery.

Servitenkirche (p126) Wonderfully quiet church grounds and quarter around it.

Prater (p151) Vienna's park and woodland across the Danube Canal.

Donauinsel (p158) An island and recreation area in the middle of the Danube River.

Augarten (p153) Eighteenth-century parkland with paths and meadows.

Hietzinger Friedhof (p165) Burial place of Gustav Klimt, Otto Wagner and other notable Viennese.

Free Entertainment

Free festivals and events abound during summer, including rock, pop, folk and country performances at the Donauinselfest (p45), and opera, operettas and concerts at the Musikfilm Festival (p46). The spectacle of Vienna's pride parade, the Regenbogen Parade (p219), which translates to Rainbow Parade, is also free.

Winter freebies include wandering the city's enchanting Christmas markets, or Christkindlmärkte (p48). Spring and Easter brings Ostermärkte (p48) to the city's streets and squares.

You can often hear Djs spinning for free in bars, and sometimes at open-air spaces such as the MuseumsQuartier (p110).

Guided Tours & Walks

Vienna offers some great opportunities for guided exploration. Join a tour by bus, boat or on foot (perhaps on a specific theme), hop in a mini hot rod or aboard a Fiaker (horse-drawn carriage), jump on a tram tour, or tour a wine region outside town.

JORG HACKEMANN/SHUTTERSTOCK ©

Fiaker tour (p30)

Guided Walks

Vienna Tour Guides (www.wienguide.at; adult/child €17/8) An organisation of highly knowledgeable guides who conduct over 60 different guided walking tours (some in English) covering everything from *Jugendstil* (Art Nouveau) architecture to Jewish tradit ions in Vienna. Tours last roughly 1½ to two hours; some require a valid public-transport pass and extra euros for entrance fees into sights.

Vienna Walks & Talks (Map p252, B3; www.viennawalks.com; Third Man Tour adult/child €20/17.50) Offers the excellent 1½-hour Third Man Tour, based on the 1949 film, as well as many other options in both English and German.

3.MannTour (Map p240, G2; ☎01-4000 3033; www.drittemanntour.at; 01, Girardipark; tour adult/child €10/5; ⏰by reservation Thu-Sun May-Oct; UKarlsplatz) Follow in the footsteps of Orson Welles as Harry Lime in the famous chase scene of *The Third Man* on these atmospheric 45-minute tours of Vienna's 1830s-built former sewers, 25m beneath the city's streets, as clips from the black-and-white film are projected on the walls. English tours are available; check the schedule online. Kids must be aged 12 and above. Hardhats are provided; wear sturdy shoes and bring a jacket.

Bus Tours

Vienna Sightseeing Tours (☎01-712 46 83; www.viennasightseeing.at; tours €13-119; ⏰6.30am-6.30pm) Runs the Hop On Hop Off city tour and the tours by the affiliated Cityrama. The latter include hotel pick-ups and entrance fees.

Hop On Hop Off (Vienna Sightseeing Tours; Map p240, G2; ☎01-712 46 83; www.viennasightseeing.at; 01, Opernring 3-5; 24/48/72hr ticket €29/35/49; ⏰9.30am-8pm; 🚊D, 1, 2, 71 Kärntner Ring/Oper, UKarlsplatz) These hop-on, hop-off buses cover six routes with over 50 stops around Vienna. All buses depart from directly outside the Staatsoper. Tickets prepurchased online are 10% cheaper. The website has route maps.

Redbus City Tours (Map p238, E4; ☎01-512 40 30; www.redbuscitytours.at; 01, Kärntner Strasse 25; adult/child valid 24hr €25/17, 48hr €32/21; ⏰9am-7pm; 🚊D, 1, 2, 71 Kärntner Ring/Oper, UKarlsplatz) These hop-on, hop-off tours include a 1½-hour route covering the main sights in and around the Innere Stadt (inner city) and two-hour tours hitting all of the city's big sights. Buses leave from outside the Albertina.

Ringstrasse Tram Tour: Do-It-Yourself

Public trams are a cheap way to see the sights and enjoy a slice of everyday life in Vienna at the same time. This quintessential Vienna tram experience takes you past the city's palatial monuments.

Board tram 1 at Schwedenplatz (platform B) heading towards Stefan-Fadinger-Platz and immediately look out on the left for the Monument to the Victims of Fascism (p81) at the former Gestapo headquarters site.

On your left on the Ringstrasse will emerge Vienna's **Börse Palais** (Stock Exchange), a handsome structure bedecked in dusty brick with white trimmings, designed by renowned Ringstrasse architect Theophil von Hansen.

Pulling into Schottentor station you'll be accosted on your right by two stone-carved steeples reaching for the sky – the marvellous neo-Gothic Votivkirche (p125) is quite reminiscent of France's Chartres Cathedral.

When the spires of an arresting Flemish-Gothic edifice come into sight on the right, you will have reached the Rathaus (p114) and Rathausplatz.

The neoclassical facade of **Parlament**, Austria's parliament, with its majestic Greek pillars, will spill into view on the right, flanked by the **Athena Fountain** – the four figures lying at her feet represent the Danube, Inn, Elbe and Vltava, the four key rivers of the Austro-Hungarian Empire. The Parlament itself is closed for major renovations until at least 2024 (parliament temporarily sits in the Hofburg complex but it's not accessible to the public).

Ringstrasse Tram Tour

0 500 m
0 0.25 miles

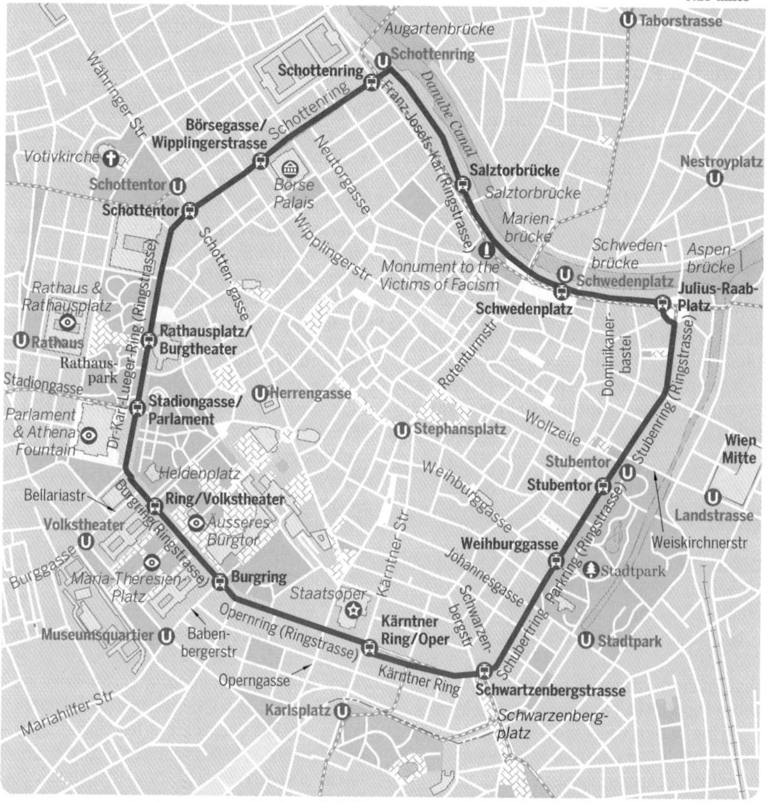

FIAKER IN VIENNA

Vienna's horse-drawn Fiaker carriages are an emblematic sight, and in 2016 the city took measures to address animal-welfare concerns. These include reducing service hours and stopping tours in 35°C-plus temperatures, and are well regulated.

You can learn more about the horses and their care on a Secrets of the Fiaker tour with **Riding Dinner** (☎0660 706 05 02; https://vienna.ridingdinner.com; Secrets of the Fiaker tour per person €25, dinner tours per carriage from €295), which includes a tour of the stables and a carriage ride.

A majestic testament to Austria's 1813 triumph over Napoleon in Leipzig, the **Äusseres Burgtor** (Outer Palace Gate) will loom into view on the left – the Roman gate leads the way to the Imperial Palace, the Hofburg (p60).

Directly opposite the Burgtor is **Maria-Theresien-Platz**, anchored by a statue of Empress Maria Theresia, the only female to ascend to the Austrian throne. Note the bundle of papers clasped in her left hand – these are the Pragmatic Sanctions of 1713, which made it possible for women to rule the empire.

The marvellous neo-Renaissance State Opera House, Staatsoper (p100), impresses the masses today, but when it was originally built the Viennese dubbed it 'the *Königgrätz* of architecture', likening it to the 1866 military disaster of the same name.

The final stretch of the tram route (tram 2) continues past Stadtpark (p134) back to the Danube Canal and Schwedenplatz.

Boat Tours

DDSG Blue Danube (Map p236, E3; ☎01-588 80; www.ddsg-blue-danube.at; 01, Schwedenbrücke; 1½hour tours adult/child €23/11.50; hours vary; 1, 2 Schwedenplatz, U Schwedenplatz) Boats cover a variety of cruise routes; some of the most popular include circumnavigating Leopoldstadt and Brigittenau districts using the Danube Canal and the Danube as their thoroughfare. Tours run year-round, weather permitting – check schedules online.

Wine Tours

Vienna Explorer (Map p236, C1; ☎01-890 96 82; www.viennaexplorer.com; 01, Franz-Josefs-Kai 45; tours Easter-Oct, bike rental 8.30am-6pm year-round; 1, 2 Schwedenplatz, U Schwedenplatz) This long-standing outfit has excellent bike tours in Vienna itself (three hours, adult/child €35/20) and further afield through the Wachau vineyards (10½ hours, €84/59), reached from Vienna by train to/from the town of Krems. Tours take in two wineries (with four to five tastings at each), and the Unesco World Heritage village of Dürnstein.

Other Tours

Fiaker Carriage Rides (20min/40min/1hr tour €55/80/110; 10am-9pm) These traditional-style carriages seating up to four passengers are an iconic way to see Vienna. Lines of horses, carriages and bowler-hatted drivers congregate at Stephansplatz, Albertinaplatz and Heldenplatz at the Hofburg. Short tours go through the old town, while long tours include the Ringstrasse.

Ring Tram (Map p236, E3; ☎01-712 46 83; www.wienerlinien.at; 01, Schwedenplatz, Platform C; adult/child €10/5; 10am-5.30pm; 1, 2 Schwedenplatz, U Schwedenplatz) You can do a DIY tour of the Ringstrasse (p29) by public tram but if you prefer a seamless tour with video screens and multilingual commentary, hop on the Ring Tram tour for a continuous 30-minute loop around the Ringstrasse (no stops). Tour tickets are valid for one unbroken trip, meaning you can't hop on and off.

Hot Rod City Tour (Map p236, D3; ☎01-660 87 73; www.hotrod-tour-wien.com; 01, Judengasse 4; 2hr tour per person €99-119; 10am-8pm; 1, 2 Schwedenplatz, U Schwedenplatz) If you've ever wanted to get behind the wheel of a mini hot rod, this is your chance. The low-to-the-ground one-person vehicles set off in convoy and cover a circuit of the city in 1½ hours, with Vienna's landmarks as a backdrop. Helmets, walkie-talkies and insurance are included in the price; you'll need a valid driver's licence (foreign licences accepted).

Space & Place (☎0680 125 43 54; www.spaceandplace.at; tours €10) For the inside scoop on Vienna, join Eugene's fun, quirky, English-language tours. The alternative lineup keeps evolving: from Vienna Ugly Tours, homing in on the capital's uglier architectural side, to Midnight Tours, showing you the city after dark. Tours typically last 2½ hours. See the website for dates and meeting points.

Eating

Dining in Vienna gives you a taste of the city's history, at its street stands sizzling up sausages, candlelit vaulted-cellar wine bars and earthy, wood-panelled Beisln (bistro pubs) serving goulash and Wienerschnitzel (breaded veal cutlet); its present, at hip cafes, multiethnic markets and international eateries; and its future, at innovative spaces with a wave of exciting chefs pushing in new directions.

The Dining Scene

Vienna has a lively and changing culinary scene. Traditional Austrian cuisine is taking on a lighter note, and new generations of chefs are turning to high-quality seasonal and local ingredients, coupled with the rapid uptake of new food ideas locally and from abroad.

Brunch continues to go from strength to strength in the Austrian capital, with retro-styled cafes serving breakfast until late into the afternoon. And craft cocktails and beers blur the line between a restaurant and bar.

The Viennese have also reaffirmed their love for traditional-style restaurants, in particular *Beisln,* dishing up heaping portions of Austrian favourites like Wiener schnitzel, *Tafelspitz* (prime boiled beef, served with radish) and *Gulasch* (goulash).

Today, eating out in Vienna lets you enjoy the best of both traditional and contemporary dining, with many places crossing effortlessly between the two.

HISTORY

Historically, classic Viennese cuisine has always thrived on foreign influences and change. Wiener schnitzel (a true Wiener schnitzel is made with veal) is rumoured – though hotly disputed today – to have originated from the recipe for Milanese crumbed veal cutlet brought back by Field Marshal Radtetzky in 1857. *Gulasch* comes from Hungary, but the dumplings served with it come from Czech regions. Interestingly, *Tafelspitz* was the favourite dish of Kaiser Franz Josef, but when foreign guests visited Schönbrunn Palace, he fed them French delights. Once they had left, he ate his Wiener schnitzel and *Tafelspitz* again.

The fastidious Viennese approach to coffee and the tradition of the *Kaffeehaus* (coffee house, where you can also eat a light meal) owes much to Ottoman Turks who brought their exotic elixir into Vienna's *Vorstädte (inner suburbs)* in 1683. This approach captures the essence of *die klassische Wiener Küche* (classic Viennese cuisine): pilfered by the Habsburgs wherever they reigned, localised at home, shoehorned into the imperial tradition and given new blood by the great culinary capitals abroad, like Paris – in this case, one of the relatively few places where the Habsburgs didn't actually rule – before being stylised in all its rich features for the contemporary table.

Beisln

Originating in the 18th century as inns offering local specialities, these cosy, down-to-earth, uniquely Viennese eateries are simple bistro pubs featuring wood panelling, plain tables, perhaps a ceramic oven and hearty local cuisine. Many have tables in cobbled courtyards or on pavement terraces in summer. The name *Beisl* is thought to be Jewish, from the Yiddish word *Bajiss,* meaning 'house'. Nowadays, marginally more expensive neo-*Beisln* are emerging, offering new takes on old recipes.

NEED TO KNOW

Opening Hours

Restaurants Generally 11am to 2pm and 6pm to 10pm or 11pm. Kitchens may stay open all day. Some places close on Sunday or Monday.

Cafes Typically 8am to midnight.

Beisln Usually 11am or noon to 11pm or midnight.

Price Ranges

Prices refer to a two-course meal, excluding drinks.

€ less than €15

€€ €15 – €30

€€€ over €30

Lunch Menu

Most restaurants have an inexpensive lunch special (*Mittagsmenü* or *Tagesteller*) for around €8 to €12.

Tipping

If the bill has been presented in a folder, you can leave the tip in the folder when you depart. It's also common to round up verbally by simply stating the amount and adding *'danke!'* or by saying *'das stimmt so'* (keep the change).

Reservations

Advance reservations are recommended for midrange restaurants and essential for high-end and/or popular places (several weeks for the most sought-after tables). Remember to state your last name at the start of a phone call.

Gedeck

Some restaurants charge €2 to €3 extra for the *Gedeck* (table setting), which includes bread and various sundries.

Mobile Phones

Switch off your phone, or at least the sound, in restaurants. Take calls away from your table.

Online Resources

Falter (www.falter.at) is Vienna's quintessential foodie guide.

Street Food & Markets

Würstel (sausages) are sold in up to a dozen varieties at *Würstelstände* (sausage stands) throughout the city. Sausages are served inside a bread roll hot-dog-style or sliced and accompanied by cut bread, and weighed down with sweet *(süss)* or hot *(scharf)* mustard *(Senf)*. As well as *Bratwurst* (fried sausage), you could try *Burenwurst* (the boiled equivalent), *Debreziner* (spicy) or *Käsekrainer* (infused with cheese).

The largest and best-known of Vienna's markets is the aromatic Naschmarkt (p92), which is laden with produce from all over Austria and the world, and lined with food 'stalls', including many fully fledged restaurants. Other fantastic markets include the Brunnenmarkt (p126), leading to Yppenplatz in Ottakring, and the Karmelitermarkt (p156), east of the Danube Canal.

Vegetarian & Vegans

Vegetarians will have no problem in Vienna, with generally at least one dish available at even the most traditional *Beisln*. Spurred by the locavore trend towards organic produce, vegetarian cuisine is now popular all over the city and copious cafes and restaurants have extensive offerings. There are also many exclusively vegetarian places in all price ranges, including Michelin-starred Tian (p83).

Vegan cuisine is also rapidly gaining a following: numerous places have at least some vegan options, and there are many vegan-only venues.

The Naschmarkt and other farmers markets offer lots of choices for vegetarian picnics, takeaway or sit-down meals.

How to Eat & Drink Like a Local

Meals A typical breakfast for the Viennese consists of a *Semmel* (bread roll) with jam, ham and/or cheese. Lunch is often the largest meal. In the evening, bread with cheese or ham and a beer or wine is usually eaten at home, although many Viennese enjoy a more substantial meal.

Where to Eat The main choices for a sit-down meal are a restaurant, *Beisl*, cafe or coffee house or a wine tavern, *Heuriger* (p41; wine tavern), on the outskirts of the city, with overflowing buffets of salads and pork, along with new wine.

Arriving In better establishments, a waiter will greet you and take your coat before showing you to a table. Once you're seated you'll have the chance to order a drink right away. The waiter is unlikely to return to take your order until you've closed your menu. In midrange and less formal places, it's usually fine to place your jacket over the back of your chair if you don't want to use the cloakroom.

Eating & Toasting Before starting to eat say *'Guten appetit!'* Before starting to drink, toast by clinking glasses while looking the person in the eye. Not to have eye contact is said to bring seven years of bad sex (you've been warned!). *'Zum Wohl'* ('to well-being') is the generic toast if you're drinking wine; *'Prost!'* ('Cheers!') if you're drinking beer.

Paying the Bill Many places don't accept credit cards. Tip 5% to 10% (or don't bother coming back) by rounding up the bill. If several of you are eating together, you will be asked *'Geht das zusammen oder getrennt?'* (Together or separately?). If paying separately, each diner pays the waiter and tips individually.

Cooking Courses

Pick up cooking tips (in English and German) from the following:

Vestibül (p117) Offers one-day Austrian cooking courses in English and German.

Wrenkh Cookery School (Map p236; ☎01-533 15 26; www.wrenkh-wien.at; 01, Bauernmarkt 10; ⏲per person from €48; ⓤStephansplatz) Austrian classics, international cuisines, and vegetarian and vegan classes; in English and German.

Vienna Cooking Tours (☎0699 1718 4761; www.viennacookingtours.at; 4hr market tour & cookery course €130; ⏲by reservation) Take a Naschmarkt tour before cooking (and eating) a three-course Austrian lunch.

Eating by Neighbourhood

Stephansdom & the Historic Centre (p82) Packed with options, especially around Stephansplatz and streets leading down towards the Danube Canal.

Karlsplatz & Around Naschmarkt (p94) Myriad food stalls and restaurants on Naschmarkt, and lots of options in Margareten and Mariahilf districts.

The Museum District & Neubau (p115) Some of the best eating in Vienna's *Vorstadt* districts, especially in and behind MuseumsQuartier.

Alsergrund & the University District (p128) Great markets, local eateries and student places close to the university campuses.

Schloss Belvedere to the Canal (p144) A handful of gems, otherwise limited; plenty of summer picnic spots.

Prater & East of the Danube (p154) Burgeoning dining scene, especially west of Karmeliterplatz and Taborstrasse, extending north towards Augarten.

VIENNESE SPECIALITIES

Vienna has a strong repertoire of traditional dishes. One or two are variations on dishes from other regions. Classics include the following:

Schnitzel Wiener schnitzel should always be crumbed veal, but pork is gaining ground in some places.

Goulash *Rindsgulasch* (beef goulash) is everywhere in Vienna but attains exquisite heights at Meierei im Stadtpark (p146).

Tafelspitz Traditionally this boiled prime beef swims in the juices of locally produced *Suppengrün* (fresh soup vegetables), before being served with *Kren* (horseradish) sauce.

Beuschel Offal, usually sliced lung and heart with a slightly creamy sauce.

Backhendl Fried, breaded chicken, often called *steirischer Backhendl* (Styrian fried chicken).

Zwiebelrostbraten Slices of roast beef smothered in gravy and fried onions.

Schinkenfleckerln Oven-baked ham and noodle casserole.

Bauernschmaus Platter of cold meats.

The undeniable monarchs of all desserts are *Kaiserschmarrn* (sweet pancake with raisins) and *Apfelstrudel* (apple strudel), but also look out for *Marillenknödel* (apricot dumplings) in summer.

Lonely Planet's Top Choices

Steirereck im Stadtpark (p147) Vienna's class act by the Wien River.

Lingenhel (p144) Deli-shop-bar-restaurant in a 200-year-old house serving seasonal treats.

Plachutta (p83) The ultimate place for Viennese *Tafelspitz*.

Griechenbeisl (p83) The history-soaked *Beisl* of your dreams.

Best by Budget

€

Bitzinger Würstelstand am Albertinaplatz (p68) Sausage stand opposite the opera.

Naschmarkt (p92) A snacker's fantasyland, Vienna's largest market teems with sit-down eateries.

Eis Greissler (p94) Organic ice cream with vegan options.

Mamamon (p128) Feisty Thai flavours.

€€

Motto am Fluss (p83) Ultimate restaurant, bar and cafe on the canal.

Said the Butcher to the Cow (p94) Phenomenal burgers and a hip gin bar.

Brezl Gwölb (p82) *Beisl* big on charm and Austrian home cooking.

Heunisch & Erben (p146) Contemporary wine bar with Mediterranean-accented cuisine.

€€€

Steirereck im Stadtpark (p147) Seasonal taste sensations at a two-Michelin-starred restaurant in Stadtpark.

Schnattl (p129) Elegant wood-panelled interior, seasonally changing menus and courtyard dining.

Meinl's Restaurant (p69) Exceptional quality through the seasons.

Best Beisln

Rustic

Beim Czaak (p83) Traditional as it gets.

Zum Alten Fassl (p95) Falco once lived above this woody *Beisl*, which has a regionally focused menu.

Haas Beisl (p95) Meaty menu and a genuinely local vibe.

Schank zum Reichsapfe (p155) Warm, wooden wine-tavern-style favourite.

Figlmüller (p82) Ever popular for its enormous schnitzels.

Contemporary

Silberwirt (p95) Atmospheric with an accent on organic and local grub.

Tancredi (p97) Pared-down interior, seasonal menu and garden for summer dining.

Amerlingbeisl (p117) Courtyard dining in the Biedermeier heart of Spittelberg.

Huth Gastwirtschaft (p83) Local favourite in an under-the-radar location.

Best Schnitzels

Figlmüller (p82) Bills itself as the home of the schnitzel.

Gasthaus Wickerl (p129) Warm wooden *Beisl* decor and sizzling schnitzels.

Huth Gastwirtschaft (p83) Serves a superb Wiener schnitzel with cranberry sauce and parsley potatoes.

Ubl (p95) *Beisl* dishing up four types of schnitzel, all cooked to thin, golden perfection.

Best Goulash

Meierei im Stadtpark (p146) Some speak of the world's best.

Soupkultur (p128) Soup specialist.

Haas Beisl (p95) Like *Oma* (grandma) made it.

Best Vegetarian & Vegan

Tian (p83) Michelin-starred vegetarian cuisine.

Harvest (p154) Vintage decor and superfresh veggie and vegan fare.

Tian Bistro (p116) Tian's laid-back younger sibling.

Hollerei (p167) Convivial veggie bistro near Schloss Schönbrunn.

Swing Kitchen (p115) Sensational vegan burgers.

Veganista (p116) All-vegan ice cream.

Cakes and pastries in the window of Demel (p70)

Coffee Houses & Cake Shops

Vienna's long-standing tradition of coffee houses and cake shops captures the spirit of Gemütlichkeit – that quintessential Austrian quality of cosiness and languid indulgence. Grand or humble, poster-plastered or chandelier-lit, this is where you can join the locals for coffee, cake and a slice of living history.

NEED TO KNOW

Prices

Expect to pay between €2 and €5 for a coffee, between €3 and €6 for a slice of cake, and around €9 for a main.

Opening Hours

Most open around 8am, and close between 7pm and midnight (earlier Sundays).

Meals

Many *Kaffeehäuser* serve *Frühstuck* (breakfast) and a moderately priced lunchtime *Tagesteller* (dish of the day). Dishes are invariably hearty.

Coffee at Landtmann's (p130)

Coffee Houses

Poet and playwright Bertolt Brecht once described Vienna as a small city built around a few coffee houses where the locals sit together and read papers. It's a simple observation but a perceptive one, for despite the overwhelming variety of coffee on offer, caffeine is secondary to the *Kaffeehaus* experience. In many ways coffee is but an entrance ticket to a world where you can meet friends, browse newspapers, play games, put the world to rights, reflect and linger undisturbed for hours. Many Viennese go misty eyed when you ask them about their favourite *Kaffeehaus,* affectionately dubbed Vienna's 'living rooms'.

HISTORY

It all started with some mystery beans. Back at the Battle of Vienna in 1683, when Polish-Habsburg allies sent the Ottoman invaders packing, the Turks, so the story goes, left sacks of precious coffee beans at the city gates as they beat a hasty retreat. There was much speculation as to what these beans were, with most surmising camel feed or dung. King John III Sobieski handed over the beans to his military officer, Jerzy Franciszek Kulczycki, who recognised their value, having encountered coffee during time spent in captivity in Turkey. Adding a dash of milk and sweetening the aromatic blend to Viennese tastes, he soon opened Vienna's first coffee house: the Hof zur Blauen Flasche. In coffee-house circles to this day, Kulczycki is considered something of a patron saint.

The Viennese were hooked and soon coffee houses began to pop up all over the city. By the late 18th century *Kaffeehäuser* were in vogue in high society, with composers such as Mozart and Beethoven giving public performances. They became places to meet, socialise and, on a practical level, warm up.

This boom continued in the 19th century thanks to the Habsburgs' insatiable appetite for coffee, cake and palatial surrounds. *Sacher Torte* was created for Prince Klemens Wenzel von Metternich in 1832 and swiftly became an imperial favourite. In the latter half of the century, grand coffee houses such as Landtmann, Central and Sperl opened their doors, setting a precedent with splendid interiors adorned with chandeliers, Thonet chairs and marble-topped tables.

At the turn of the century, coffee houses attracted the greatest artists, musicians, writers and radical thinkers of the age – Mahler, Klimt, Freud, Trotsky and Otto Wagner. The 1950s signalled the end of an era for many *Kaffeehäuser* – a period the Viennese call the *Kaffeehaussterben* (coffee-house death). Postwar, a new generation of Viennese had grown tired of the coffee house, which they saw as being antiquated and/or elitist. TVs and espresso bars also played a part in their closure. Luckily many of the best coffee houses survived and the tradition later revived.

Above: Cafe Schwarzenberg (p97)
Right: *Sacher Torte* at Café Sacher (p70)

JENS METSCHURAT/SHUTTERSTOCK ©

COFFEE-HOUSE CULTURE

In 2011 Vienna's coffee houses were added to the Unesco list of Intangible Cultural Heritage, which defines them as 'places where time and space are consumed, but only the coffee is found on the bill'. Indeed, life may rush ahead outside, but the clocks are stuck in 1910 in the *Kaffeehaus,* where the spirit of unhurried gentility remains sacrosanct. Neither time nor trend obsessed, coffee houses are like a nostalgic balm for the stresses of modern life; they are places where life dissolves into the warm simplicity of a good cup of coffee, impromptu conversation and nostalgic daydreaming.

While the echoes of the past can still be felt keenly in the marble splendour of stalwarts such as Central and Sperl, a growing number of coffee houses are ushering in a new age of creativity, including third-wave brewing techniques.

Another nod to the social importance of *Kaffeehäuser* is the Kaffeesiederball (www.kaffeesiederball.at), staged by the coffee-house owners at the Hofburg in February, one of the most glittering events on the ball calendar.

COFFEE DECODER

Ask for 'a coffee, please' and you may get a puzzled look. The following are fixtures on most menus:

Brauner Black but served with a tiny splash of cream; comes in *gross* (large) or *klein* (small).

Einspänner Strong coffee with whipped cream, served in a glass.

Verlängerter *Brauner* lengthened with hot water.

Mocca Sometimes spelled *Mokka* or *Schwarzer* – black coffee.

Melange The Viennese classic, half-coffee, half-milk and topped with milk froth or whipped cream, similar to a cappuccino.

Kapuziner With more milk than coffee and perhaps a sprinkling of grated chocolate.

Eiskaffee Cold coffee with vanilla ice cream and whipped cream.

Maria Theresia With orange liqueur and whipped cream.

Türkische Comes in a copper pot with coffee grounds and sugar.

ETIQUETTE

- In more formal coffee houses wait to be seated, otherwise take your pick of the tables.
- There's no dress code per se, but smart-casual wear is the norm at posh coffee houses.
- You're generally welcome to linger for as long as you please – waiters present the *Rechnung* (bill) when you ask for it.
- Some coffee houses have English menus, but failing that, you can sometimes choose from the counter.
- Viennese waiters are notoriously brusque, but a polite *Grüss Gott* (good day) and a smattering of German will stand you in good stead.
- Even in today's digital age, newspapers are freely available, often also in English.

Cake Shops

Forget schnitzel: if the sweet-toothed Viennese could choose one last meal on earth, most would go straight for dessert. The city brims with *Konditoreien* (cake shops), where buttery aromas lure passers-by to counters brimming with fresh batches of cream-filled, chocolate-glazed, fruit-topped treats. In these mini temples of three o'clock indulgence, pastries, cakes and tortes are elevated to a near art form.

Many cake shops also do a fine line in *Confiserie* (confectionery), producing their own sweets and chocolate. Sumptuous examples include Demel, one-time purveyor to the imperial and royal court, famous for its chocolate-nougat *Annatorte* and fragrant candied violets. The Viennese swear by the feather-light macaroons, chocolates and tortes at Oberlaa, while retro **Aïda** (www.aida.at; 13, Maxingstrasse 1; ⌚8.30am-6.30pm Mon-Fri, to 6pm Sat, 9am-6pm Sun; 🅤Hietzing) time warps you back to the 1950s with its delectable cakes and pink-kissed interior.

Top of the charts in Viennese cakes is *Sacher Torte.* Emperor Franz Josef was partial to this rich iced chocolate cake – its sweetness offset by a tangy layer of apricot jam – and it's still a favourite at Café Sacher today. *Esterházytorte,* a marbled buttercream and meringue torte, and flaky, quark-filled *Topfenstrudel* would also make the top 10. *Gugelhupf,* a ring-shaped marble cake; *Linzertorte,* a spiced tart filled with redcurrant jam; and good old apple strudel are as popular as ever, too.

Lonely Planet's Top Choices

Café Sperl (p98) The real-deal coffee house: history, good food, games and faded grandeur.

Café Central (p131) A drop of opulence in vaulted, marble surrounds.

Café Leopold Hawelka (p69) Viennese character exudes from the walls of this convivial coffee house.

Demel (p70) Decadent cakes that once pleased the emperor's palate.

Sperlhof (p156) Offbeat and arty 1920s haunt.

Supersense (p154) Retro-grand cafe in an 1898-built Italianate mansion.

Best Historic Coffee Houses

Café Sperl (p98) A blast of nostalgia and a game of billiards in this *Jugendstil* (Art Nouveau) beauty.

Café Central (p131) Trotsky and Lenin once played chess under the soaring vaults here.

Café Landtmann (p130) Mahler and Marlene Dietrich loved this old-world classic near the Burgtheater.

Café Leopold Hawelka (p69) Hundertwasser and Warhol once hung out at this warm, wood-panelled cafe.

Café Korb (p83) Freud's old haunt is now part gallery, part cafe.

Café Schwarzenberg (p97) Magnificent 1861-opened coffee house on the Ringstrasse.

Café Jelinek (p99) Warm, down to earth and full of regulars.

Kleines Café (p84) Boho flair in this dinky cafe on Franziskanerplatz.

Best Cakes & Sweets

Demel (70) Cakes and tortes fit for royalty.

Café Sacher (p38) King of the *Sacher Torte*.

Oberlaa (p38) Beautifully wrapped chocolates and macarons.

Bonbons Anzinger (p72) Specialises in the chocolate-covered *Mozartkugel* filled with pistachio marzipan and nougat.

Diglas (p85) Legendary *Apfelstrudel*.

Vollpension (p94) Intergenerational gem with a combined repertoire of 200 cake recipes.

Best Local Coffee Houses

Kaffee Alt Wien (p85) A dimly lit, arty haunt popular with students; located in the centre and has long hours.

Café am Heumarkt (p147) Old-school charmer near the Stadtpark.

Sperlhof (p156) Race back to the 1920s in this cafe with books, billiards and ping-pong.

Best New-Wave Cafes

Supersense (p154) Locally roasted coffee and a cool concept shop.

Balthasar (p157) Colourful spot serving tip-top espresso.

POC Cafe (p129) Seriously good coffee in lab-like surrounds.

J Hornig Kaffeebar (p117) Third-wave-coffee specialist.

Best Free Live Music

Café Bräunerhof (p71) Classical music from 3pm to 6pm on weekends.

Café Central (p131) A pianist plays from 5pm to 10pm daily.

Café Landtmann (p130) Live piano music tinkles from 8pm to 11pm Sunday to Tuesday.

Café Prückel (p86) Piano music plays from 7pm to 10pm on Monday, Wednesday and Friday in 1950s surrounds.

Diglas (p85) Bag a cosy booth to hear piano music from 7pm.

Drinking & Nightlife

In this city where history often waltzes with the cutting edge, the drinking scene spans vaulted wine cellars here since Mozart's day to boisterous beer gardens, boho student dives, and cocktail, retro and rooftop bars. And with over 700 hectares of vineyards within its city limits, a visit to a Heuriger (wine tavern) is a quintessential Viennese experience.

Vienna's Nightlife Hotspots

Vienna's wave of repurposed venues have their own distinctive flair and story to tell, such as former pet-grooming parlours, electrical shops and ruby-gold brothels that have been born again as bars. Also on the up are rooftop bars where you can take in skyline views while sipping a mojito. Retro cafe/bars with vintage-shop charm are in vogue, too, in a city that loves to time travel to a different era; many serve locally roasted coffee along with local wines. And given the Viennese appreciation of quality, craft beer bars, specialist gin bars and craft cocktail venues are all gaining a stronghold, with numerous new establishments.

Your options are limitless, but particularly lively nightlife stretches include Gumpendorferstrasse in Mariahilf, between Naschmarkt and Mariahilferstrasse, Schleifmühlgasse in the Freihausviertel south of Naschmarkt (Wieden district), and the more international *Bermudadreieck* (Bermuda Triangle) in the Innere Stadt's old Jewish quarter. The Gürtel ring road is great for DJs and live music in bar-club hybrids under the railway arches.

Summer in the City

With the advent of summer, many revellers descend on outdoor venues. The bars and shady courtyards at Altes AKH university attract plenty, as does the market square Yppenplatz in Ottakring and the Freihausviertel in Wieden. The reinvention of the Danube Canal as a bar strip has been a huge success; **Flex** (Map p246; www.flex.at; 01, Augartenbrücke; ⏲cafe 2pm-6am daily, club 11pm-6am Thu-Sat; 🚋1, 2 Schottentor, Ⓤ Schottenring) is a long-established location, but the likes of Strandbar Herrmann (p147), Tel Aviv Beach (p156) and Badeschiff (p87), pool by day, bar by night, have added an entirely new dimension to the waterway.

As spring ushers in summer, *Schanigärten* (courtyard gardens and pavement terraces) begin to pop up like wildflowers, luring the Viennese outdoors. There are around 3500 in total.

Intimate Clubbing

The Austrian capital's relatively small club scene still traverses the entire stylistic and musical spectrum, from chandelier-lit glamour to industrial-style grunge, with playlists skipping from indie through to house, electro, techno, R & B, reggae, metal and pop. Clubs invariably feature excellent DJs, with both homegrown and international talent working the decks.

Bombastic venues are rare creatures here and the vibe is kept intimate and friendly in small clubs, where dress codes and bouncers are often refreshingly relaxed. The borders between bars and clubs are often blurred, with DJs amping up the atmosphere as the night wears on. Indeed, what the clubs here often lack in size, they make up for with alternative flair or unique locations, whether you're partying poolside in a former sauna-turned-club in the Prater, under the arches on the Gürtel or in a 1950s-style pavilion in the Volksgarten.

Microbreweries

Venues where the beer is always fresh, the atmosphere jovial and families are welcome, Vienna's microbreweries make for a great night out. Most offer a healthy selection of beers brewed on the premises (and proudly display the shining, brass brewing equipment), complemented by filling Austrian staples. Punters spill out into their courtyard gardens in summer.

Outside the centre, **Fischer Bräu** (☎01-369 59 49; www.fischerbraeu.at; 19, Billrothstrasse 17; ⏰4pm-12.30am; Ⓤ Nussdorfer Strasse) brews a new beer every four to six weeks, and a *Helles* (light) lager all year round. Live music often plays in the rollicking beer garden on summer Sunday afternoons.

Grape & Grain

While wine is the chosen drink of the Viennese, beer also features heavily in the city's cultural make-up. Try the following:

Blauburgunder Complex, fruity Pinot Noir red.

Grüner Veltliner Strong, fresh white wine with hints of citrus and pear.

Riesling Fruity white wine with strong acidity.

Zweigelt Full-bodied red wine with intense cherry aromas.

Dunkel Thick dark beer with a very rich flavour.

Helles Lager with a bite – clear and lightly hoppy.

Pils Crisp, strong and often bitter Pilsner beer.

Märzen Red-coloured beer with a strong malt taste.

Zwickel Unfiltered beer with a cloudy complexion.

Schnäpse (schnapps) Fruit brandy; usually consumed after a meal.

Visiting Heurigen

Heurigen are rustic wine taverns mostly on the outskirts of the city serving young wine (and invariably serving traditional food), usually in a courtyard setting. *Buschenschenken* are a smaller variation open less often (usually in September), which bloomed after Joseph II decreed in 1784 that producers could sell their own wine from the vineyard without obtaining a licence.

Heuriger Wine The most important feature of any *Heuriger* is the wine, traditionally made by the owner and usually only a year old. *Sturm* (literally 'storm' for its cloudy appearance, perhaps even for its chaotic effects on drinkers) is yeasty because it is still fermenting. It's sold from around early September to the middle of October. A new vintage of bottled *Heuriger* wine is released each year on 11 November.

Heuriger Food & Ordering Traditionally, food is sold by the decagram (dag) in portions of 10 dag (100g), but increasingly a buffet meal is offered for a fixed price, from around €7.50 to €14 at

NEED TO KNOW

Opening Hours

Opening hours vary greatly, depending on whether the establishment serves food, and on the season, with longer hours in summer.

Bars & Pubs Anywhere from around 11am or about 4pm (or 5pm), to between midnight and 4am.

Clubs Generally between 10pm to around 4am; many only Thursday to Saturday.

Useful Websites

Falter (www.falter.at) Event and party listings.

Vienna Online (www.vienna.at) Keep track of club nights with this event calendar.

Tourist Info Wien (www.wien.info) Nightlife listings arranged by theme.

Drink Prices

- Standard beer prices range from €2 to €5, depending on the venue and location (central Vienna tends to be more expensive).
- A decent glass of local wine starts at around €2.
- Expect to pay at least €7 for a simple mixed drink and around €9 and up for a cocktail.

Club Entry

Entry prices can and do vary wildly – from nothing to €35 – and depend on who's on the decks. Many small, intimate clubs offer free entry at least once a week.

Tipping

For smaller bills (under €10) it is customary to round up and add another euro if need be; for larger tabs, 5% to 10% is customary.

simple places to about €18 to €35 at more upmarket establishments with greater choice. Typically, you'll find a selection of warm and cold foods, such as roast pork (in one or the other variety), blood sausage, meat loaf and a range of cured meats, lard and breads, pickled vegetables and salads (such as *Schwarzwurzelsalat;* black salsify salad) and potato salad. For dessert, strudel is on offer.

Where & When *Heurigen* are concentrated in and around winegrowing regions on Vienna's fringes. Many are only open part of the year. To avoid disappointment, confirm opening times with individual establishments before heading out.

Transport & Map Some *Heurigen* are up to 20 minutes' walk from the public transport stop: download the *Verkehrslinienplan für Wien* transport map (also showing streets in outer suburbs) for free at www.wienerlinien.at, or pick it up from any Wiener Linien service desk. Other *Heurigen* are located further out and require your own wheels.

TOP HEURIGEN

Wieninger (01-292 41 06; http://heuriger-wieninger.at; 21, Stammersdorfer Strasse 78, Stammersdorf; 5pm-midnight Fri, from 2pm Sat, noon-10pm Sun Apr–mid-Dec; 30A Freiheitsplatz) A hidden wonderland with a convivial local atmosphere, Wieninger has a magical lantern- and candlelit vine-draped garden and a cosy wood-panelled interior. Enjoy its light, fruity wines (mainly whites) alongside its extensive buffet laden with gourmet Austrian dishes augmented by seasonal specialities or its à la carte menu.

Zahel (01-889 13 18; www.zahel.at; 23, Maurer Hauptplatz 9; 4pm-midnight Mon-Sat; 60 Maurer Hauptplatz) One of the oldest *Heurigen* in Vienna, Zahel occupies a 250-year-old farmhouse. Its whites are considered some of Vienna's best, and Viennese and seasonal cuisine fills the buffet table. In addition to the timber-framed interior and terrace, there's a heated winter garden house. Cash only.

Sirbu (01-320 59 28; www.sirbu.at; 19, Kahlenberger Strasse 210; 4-11pm Mon-Fri, from 3pm Sat Apr-Oct;) Far-reaching views across Vienna's urban expanse extend from the terraces of this peaceful spot, which is marked by a small sign leading to the vine-draped rear garden adjoining the vineyards. Be sure to sample its award-winning Rieslings. A playground keeps kids occupied. Your own wheels are best as there's no nearby public transport.

Heuriger Huber (01-485 81 80; www.sissi-huber.at; 16, Roterdstrasse 5; 3pm-midnight Tue-Sat; 2, 10 Wilhelminenstrasse/Sandleitengasse) Riesling and Weissburgunder (Pinot blanc) are the main wines produced by this charming *Heuriger,* which is surrounded by a sprawling Mediterranean garden. Traditional dishes such as Styrian fried chicken with pumpkin-seed oil, and roast pork with sauerkraut and bread dumplings appear on its small but stellar menu.

Drinking & Nightlife by Neighbourhood

The Hofburg & Around (p69)Old-world wine taverns, intimate cocktail bars and drinks with Hofburg views in the Burggarten and Volksgarten.

Stephansdom & the Historic Centre (p84) Narrow lanes hide a mix of cellar bars, wine bars, pubs and serious cocktail bars.

Karlsplatz & Around Naschmarkt (p97) Boho hood crammed with clubs and retro and alternative bars, especially along Gumpendorferstrasse.

The Museum District & Neubau (p117) Arty bars with a spritz of culture and al fresco seating – hit Spittelberg for *Schanigärten* (pavement cafes).

Alsergrund & the University District (p129) Student pubs and all-night parties under the Gürtel viaduct.

Schloss Belvedere to the Canal (p147) Bars by the Danube Canal and the odd microbrewery.

Prater & East of the Danube (p155) Clubbing hotspot around Praterstern, rooftop haunts and relaxed cafe-bars around Karmelitermarkt.

Schloss Schönbrunn & Around (p167) A smattering of cafe-bars and clubs.

Lonely Planet's Top Choices

Vinothek W-Einkehr (p85) Superb Austrian wines.

Das Loft (p156) Map out Vienna from above at this supersleek lounge bar.

Loos American Bar (p70) Find a cosy alcove for a cocktail at Loos' 1908 classic.

Volksgarten ClubDiskothek (p70) Party in the park at this glam club near the Hofburg.

Palmenhaus (p70) Sip cocktails in this palm house with great outdoor seating overlooking Burggarten.

Best Waterside Bars

Strandbar Herrmann (p147) Lively 'beach' bar beside the Costa del Danube.

Motto am Fluss (p83) Inside the Wien-City ferry terminal with dazzling canal views.

Tel Aviv Beach (p156) Sun, sand and DJs each summer.

Best Wine Bars

Vinothek W-Einkehr (p85) Wines from all over Austria.

Achtundzwanzig (p129) Young, edgy but very serious about its wines.

Vis-à-vis (p85) Postage stamp of a wine bar tucked down a narrow passage.

Weinstube Josefstadt (p130) Atmospheric *Stadtheurigen* (city wine tavern) hiding in an oasis of a garden.

Villon (p70) The central district's deepest wine cellar has a light, modern ambience.

Sekt Comptoir (p96) Effervescent bar with Burgenland *Sekt* (sparkling wine) near the Naschmarkt.

Best Microbreweries

Siebensternbräu (p120) Cheery brewpub with hoppy beers and a warm-weather courtyard.

Wieden Bräu (p99) Helles, Märzen and hemp beers, plus summertime garden.

Salm Bräu (p147) Relaxed pick for home brews right by Schloss Belvedere.

Beaver Brewing (p130) Post-industrial, American-style craft brewery.

Best Cocktail Bars

Loos American Bar (p70) Mixology magic in this minimalist, Adolf Loos–designed bar.

Melete Art Design Cocktails (p117) Craft cocktails themed around changing art exhibitions.

Kruger's American Bar (p84) Sip a classic margarita in this 1920s, wood-panelled den.

Barfly's Club (p98) Terrific cocktails in an intimate setting.

Botanical Gardens (p130) Subterranean, nautical-themed bar.

Best Clubs

Volksgarten ClubDiskothek (p70) Popular house-spinning club.

Fluc (p156) Turbo-charged Praterstern club with an alternative edge.

Donau (p119) Tucked-away techno club with a friendly crowd.

Best Rooftop Bars

Das Loft (p156) Knockout skyline views from glass-clad bar on the 18th floor of the Sofitel.

Dachboden (p119) Big-top views of Vienna from the 25hours Hotel's rooftop bar.

Café Oben (p120) Landmark spot at this cafe atop Hauptbücherei Wien.

Sky Bar (p85) Vienna's most spectacular rooftop bar in the Innere Stadt.

Best LGBT Hangouts

Felixx (p98) A class act, complete with chandeliers.

Café Savoy (p99) The atmosphere of a traditional Viennese cafe plus a little pizzazz.

Mango Bar (p99) Perennially popular gay bar.

Best Schanigärten

Palmenhaus (p70) Slide into summer with DJ beats, barbecues and beers.

Volksgarten ClubDiskothek (p70) Drink in Hofburg views and summer vibes from this pavilion's tree-shaded garden.

Café Leopold (p119) A terrace perfect for soaking up Museums Quartier's cultural buzz.

Strandbar Herrmann (p147) Beloved urban beach bar.

Entertainment

From opera, classical music and theatre to live rock or jazz, Vienna provides a wealth of entertainment opportunities. The capital is home to the German-speaking world's oldest theatre, the Burgtheater, as well as the famous Wiener Sängerknaben (Vienna Boys' Choir) and the Vienna Philharmonic Orchestra, which performs in the acoustically superb Musikverein.

Opera

Vienna is a world capital for opera, and a stroll down Kärntner Strasse from Stephansplatz to the Staatsoper will turn up more Mozart lookalikes (costumed ticket sellers) than you can poke a baton at. The two main performance spaces are the Staatsoper, which closes in July and August, and Theater an der Wien (p100), which remains open during these months.

STAATSOPER TICKETS

As one of the world's premier venues, demand for Staatsoper (p100) tickets is high: book up to eight weeks in advance to be sure of getting a seating ticket. For some performances, one month or even in some cases a few days is sufficient. The chances of getting seats on the day at the *Abendkasse* (evening sales desk) or in the opera foyer are quite low for most performances. The best alternative in that case is a standing-room ticket.

The state ticket office, the **Bundestheaterkassen** (Map p240; ☎01-514 44 7880; www.bundestheater.at; 01, Operngasse 2; ⏰8am-6pm Mon-Fri, 9am-noon Sat & Sun; Ⓤ Stephansplatz), is located on Operngasse, on the west side of the Staatsoper. Tickets are available here for the Staatsoper two months prior to performance dates. Credit-card purchases can be made online or by telephone. The **Info unter den Arkaden** (Map p240; www.bundestheater.at; 01, Herbert-von-Karajan-Platz 1; ⏰9am-2hr before performance begins Mon-Fri, 9am-noon Sat Sep-Jun) branch is located on the Kärntner Strasse side of the Staatsoper.

Collecting Tickets Pick up tickets from the Bundestheaterkassen office using your ticket code. If you don't do this, the tickets must be collected at the *Abendkasse,* which opens one hour before the performance. If you use the 'print at home' option on the internet, you will be given a certain time period during which you must print your ticket.

Abendkasse Located inside the Staatsoper, it opens one hour prior to performances and sells the leftover contingent. Expect to queue for about 10 minutes here.

Staatsoper Foyer Sells tickets from 9am to two hours before performance Monday to Friday and 9am to noon Saturday.

Standing Room *Stehplätze* (room for 567 people) tickets are sold from an entrance on Operngasse, beginning 80 minutes before the performance (arrive two to three hours ahead). Tickets cost €4 for the *Parterre* (closest to the stage but without a view of the orchestra) and *Balcon* (balcony, but on the sides and sometimes with an obstructed view) to €10 for the *Galerie* (the best option, on the balcony with a full view of the stage). Cash only; limit of one ticket per person.

Cost Varies according to performance popularity and availability.

Binoculars Rental Costs €2.

Classical Music

Opportunities to listen to classical music in Vienna abound. Churches are a hub for recitals of Bach and Händel especially, but also great venues for all sorts of classical music recitals. Vienna's Philharmonic Orchestra is based in the Musikverein (p100).

Standing Room Prices are from €7.

Seating Cheapest is directly above the stage, with good views of the hall but not the orchestra. Everything up to €49 has partially obscured views, above €49 is with unimpeded views (ask when booking).

Return Tickets Although tickets are often sold out years ahead, tickets of those who are unable to attend a particular performance are returned and sold for between €15 and €101. Depending on whether the Musikverein or the Wiener Philharmoniker has organised the concert, returned tickets can be bought from the Musikverein itself (seven weeks or less before the concert) or from the **Wiener Philharmoniker Karten- und Ballbüro** (Map p240; ☎01-505 65 25; www.wienerphilharmoniker.at; 01, Kärntner Ring 12; ⊙box office 9am-3.30pm Mon-Fri & 1hr before performance Sep-Jun, 10am-1pm Aug, closed Jul) on the Monday before the performance or, for standing-room tickets, go to the ticket booking office at least one hour before the performance.

Rock & Jazz

Vienna's rock and jazz scene is lively, with a strong local list as well as international acts playing from the smallest bars to the largest arenas. See Falter (www.falter.at) for bands, venues and dates. The biggest bashes are the **Donauinselfest** (https://donauinselfest.at; ⊙late Jun) FREE and **Jazz Fest Wien** (www.viennajazz.org; ⊙late Jun–mid-Jul).

Theatre

The Burgtheater (p120), Volkstheater (p120), Theater in der Josefstadt (p132) and Akademietheater (p148) are Vienna's prime theatre addresses in an innovative and lively scene. Options for non-German speakers are generally limited to Vienna's English Theatre (p120) and the **Roncher** (Map p236; ☎01-588 85-111; www.musicalvienna.at; 01, Seilerstätte 9; tickets €20-99, standing room from €5; ⊙box office 2-6pm & 1hr before performance; 🚋2 Weihburggasse).

NEED TO KNOW

Opening Hours

Opera & Theatre Staatsoper (p100) has no performances in July and August. Theater an der Wien (p100) is open during these months.

Live Rock & Jazz Usually starts at 8pm or 9pm.

Advance Booking

Advance bookings are highly advisable for classical cultural offerings, but there are also plenty of opportunities to catch performances at short notice. High-profile acts aside, bookings for live rock and jazz are rarely required.

Ticket Organisations & Reservations

Bundestheaterkassen Official ticket office and exclusive outlet for the Staatsoper, Volksoper and Burgtheater.

Wien-Ticket Pavillon (Map p240; ☎01-588 85; www.wien-ticket.at; 01, Kärntner Strasse; ⊙10am-7pm; 🚋D, 1, 2, 71 Kärntner Ring/Oper, Ⓤ Karlsplatz) Charges anything from no commission up to a 12% levy. Tickets for all venues except the Staatsoper, Burgtheater and Volksoper.

Online Resources

Falter (www.falter.at) Weekly listings of all events.

Tourist Info Wien (www.events.wien.info/en) Lists upcoming events up to 18 months in advance.

Cinema

Both independent art-house films and Hollywood blockbusters are popular in Vienna. The websites (www.film.at) and **Falter** (www.falter.at) have listings. Some cinemas have discounted admission on Monday, Tuesday or Wednesday.

OF or *OV* following a film title means it will screen in the original language; *OmU* indicates the film is in the original language with German subtitles; and *OmenglU* and *OmeU* signify that it's in the original language with English subtitles.

VIENNA BOYS' CHOIR

Founded by Maximilian I in 1498 as the imperial choir, the Wiener Sängerknaben (Vienna Boys' Choir) is the most famous of its type in the world. The experience will be very different depending on where you see the performance. The most formal occasions are held in the Burgkapelle, where the focus is obviously on sacral music. Performances at other venues might range from pop through to world music. Regardless of the setting and style of the performance, the beauty and choral harmony of the voices remains the same.

Performances

The choir sings during Sunday Mass in the Burgkapelle (p61) in the Hofburg, but occasional concerts are also given during the week at other venues in Vienna and elsewhere. Sunday performances in the Burgkapelle are held from mid-September to June at 9.15am. Other venues where you can hear the choir include MuTh (p157), the choir's dedicated hall in Augarten, which hosts regular Friday afternoon performances.

The Vienna Boys' Choir website (www.wienersaengerknaben.at) has links to the venues alongside each performance date.

Tickets

Book tickets through the individual venue. Tickets for the Sunday performances at Burgkapelle cost €10 to €36 and can be arranged through the booking office (p157) by sending an email or fax. It's best to book about six weeks in advance.

For orders under €60, you pay cash when you pick up your tickets, which can be done from 11am to 1pm and 3pm to 5pm at the booking office of the chapel in the Schweizerhof of the Hofburg on the Friday before the performance. You can also pick them up between 8.15am and 8.45am on the Sunday, but this is less advisable as queues are long. If your order amounts to €60 or more, you will be sent the bank details for transferring the money. Credit cards and cheques aren't accepted. Seats costing €10 do not afford a view of the choir itself.

Tickets for a free *Stehplatz* (standing-room space) are available from 8.30am. Uncollected tickets are also resold on the day from 8am. The queues for these and for standing-room tickets are long, so arrive very early – around 7am – and be prepared to wait.

THE VIENNALE

Vienna's annual international film festival, the 'fringe-like' **Viennale** (www.viennale.at; ⏲late Oct-early Nov), is the highlight of the city's cinematic calendar. For two weeks from mid-October, public cinemas screen works ranging from documentaries to short and feature films.

Ticket sales commence on the Saturday before the festival begins. You can book by credit card, online or via a special hotline number that is published on the website once sales begin. Tickets can be picked up at any of the booths set up around town, such as the **Viennale main booth** (Map p240; www.viennale.at; 06, MuseumsQuartier, cnr Mariahilfer Strasse; ⏲10am-8pm; UMuseumsquartier).

OPEN-AIR CINEMA

Open-air cinema is hugely popular in Vienna when the weather warms up. The city hosts numerous such cinemas across town, the biggest of which is the **Musikfilm Festival** (www.filmfestival-rathausplatz.at; 01, Rathausplatz; ⏲late Jun-early Sep; D, 1, 2 Rathaus, URathaus) FREE from late June to September. Arena (p148) has open-air screenings over three weeks in August, and Kino wie noch nie (p157) has open-air screenings in July and August.

Lonely Planet's Top Choices

Staatsoper (p100) One of the world's foremost opera houses.

Musikverein (p100) Home of the Vienna Philharmonic Orchestra.

Hofburg Concert Halls (p71) The sumptuous Festsaal and Redoutensaal are regularly used for Strauss and Mozart concerts.

Radiokulturhaus (p147) Expect anything from odes to Sinatra and R.E.M. to evenings dedicated to Beethoven and Mozart.

MuTh (p157) The home of the Wiener Sängerknaben (Vienna Boys' Choir).

Konzerthaus (p147) Major venue in classical-music circles.

Best Classical Music

Staatsoper (p100) A sublime setting for opera productions.

Radiokulturhaus (p147) Venues here include the Grosser Sendesaal, home to the Vienna Radio Symphony Orchestra.

MuTh (p157) Catch concerts by the celestial Vienna Boys' Choir.

Burgkapelle (p61) The Vienna Boys' Choir also sings Sunday Mass in this chapel.

Konzerthaus (p147) Up to three simultaneous performances can be staged in the Konzerthaus' halls.

Orangery (p168) Regular classical concerts take place in Schloss Schönbrunn's orangery.

Best Rock & Jazz

Konzerthaus (p147) Ethnic music, rock, pop or jazz can also be heard in the Konzerthaus' hallowed halls.

Jazzland (p86) Long-standing venue covering all jazz styles.

Porgy & Bess (p86) Modern jazz plays at this 350-capacity club.

B72 (p131) Grungy venue with some great alternative acts.

Miles Smiles (p131) Intimate jazz club named after the great Miles Davis.

Café Carina (p132) Local bands play folk, jazz, rock and country at this tiny bar.

Best Theatre

Burgtheater (p120) One of the most important theatres in the German-speaking world.

Volkstheater (p120) Built in 1889, this is one of Vienna's largest and grandest theatres.

Akademietheater (p148) This 1920s-built theatre is the second venue of the highly esteemed Burgtheater.

Theater in der Josefstadt (p132) Ornate interior and traditional productions.

Marionetten Theater (p168) The puppets here delight kids and adults alike.

Best Cinema

Metro Kinokulturhaus (p86) Austria's national film archive has a restored cinema screening homegrown films.

Gartenbaukino (p86) Art-house films play to a 736-capacity crowd at this '60s timewarp.

Filmcasino (p100) Indie films from around the world plus shorts and documentaries from Asia and Europe.

Shopping

With a long-standing history of craftsmanship, this elegant city has recently spread its creative wings in the fashion and design world. Whether you're browsing for hand-painted porcelain in the Innere Stadt (inner city), new-wave streetwear in Neubau or epicurean treats in the Freihausviertel, you'll find inspiration, a passion for quality and an attentive eye for detail.

Markets

One of the true joys of shopping in Vienna is milling around its markets first thing in the morning and chatting to the producers.

Almost every district has at least one market selling fresh produce from Monday to Saturday, many reflecting the ethnic diversity of their neighbourhood. Some host *Bauernmärkte* (farmers markets) on Saturday mornings, where growers from the surrounding countryside travel to the big city to sell their wares: fresh vegetables, tree-ripened fruit, cured hams, free-range eggs, homemade schnapps and cut flowers. Do as the laid-back Viennese do and linger for banter and brunch at a market-side cafe or deli.

CHRISTMAS MARKETS

From around mid-November to late December the Christmas markets, or **Christkindlmärkte** (www.wien.info/en/shopping-wining-dining/markets/christmas-markets; ⏲mid-Nov–24 Dec), bring festive cheer into the city's squares, courtyards and cobbled lanes. Each has its own flair but all have *Glühwein* (mulled wine), *Maroni* (chestnuts) and twinkling trees. Annual dates and times are listed on www.wien.info.

Favourites include the following:

Rathausplatz (www.wienerweihnachtstraum.at; 01, Rathausplatz; ⏲mid-Nov–26 Dec; 🚋D, 1, 71 Rathausplatz/Burgtheater, ⓤRathaus) A whopper of a tree, 150 stalls and kid-pleasing activities from cookie-baking workshops to pony rides, all set against the atmospheric backdrop of the neo-Gothic Rathaus.

Schönbrunn (p168) Shop for nutcrackers, crib figurines and puppets at this handicraft market in the palace courtyard, with loads of events for the kids, and daily classical concerts at 6pm weekdays and 2pm weekends.

Spittelberg (www.spittelberg.at; 07, Spittelberggasse; ⏲mid-Nov–23 Dec; ⓤVolkstheater, Museumsquartier) The cobbled lanes of this Biedermeier quarter set the scene for this market, beloved of the Viennese, where stalls sell quality arts and crafts.

Stephansplatz (www.weihnachtsmarkt.at; 01, Stephansplatz; ⏲mid-Nov–26 Dec; ⓤStephansplatz) Christmas tree–style lights projected on Stephansdom's walls form a magical backdrop to this Christmas market.

EASTER MARKETS

Spring brings *Ostermärkte* (Easter markets) to Vienna. Along with Easter decorations and handicrafts, there are food and drink stalls, and kids' activities. Markets typically take place in the two weeks leading up to Easter.

Popular Easter markets:

Ostermarkt Hof (www.ostermarkt-hof.at; 01, Am Hof; ⏲Mar/Apr; ⓤHerrengasse) Stalls selling Easter decorations, arts, crafts and seasonal treats such as *Reindling* (yeast cake with raisins) fill Am Hof in the city centre.

Ostermarkt Schloss Schönbrunn (www.ostermarkt.co.at; 13, Schloss Schönbrunn; ⏲Mar/Apr; 👪; ⓤSchönbrunn, Hietzing) At Schloss Schönbrunn, Vienna's largest Easter market has over 70 stalls selling hand-painted eggs and other decorations to hang on your *Ostereierbaum* (Easter egg tree), along with handcrafted toys and ready-to-eat treats, plus live entertainment.

Trends

The Viennese have a love of life's fine details that extends to the way they shop, prizing quality, eye-catching details and an individual sense of style over identikit high streets and throw-away products. The city is full of ateliers and independent boutiques where regulars are greeted by name and designers can often be seen at work, whether adding the finishing touches to a shift dress, knitting chunky beanies from silky merino wool, or custom-making jewellery.

One of Europe's most dynamic, Vienna's contemporary fashion and design scene is fed by an influx of young up-and-coming creatives. This scene took root in the 7th district and has spread fresh new shoots everywhere from Praterstrasse in the 2nd to Yppenplatz in the 16th today. Social consciousness is key, with many shops placing the accent on fair-trade materials, and locally recycled or upcycled products – one person's junk becoming another's treasure is big.

Shopping Strips

Kärntner Strasse The Innere Stadt's main shopping street and a real crowd-puller.

Kohlmarkt A river of high-end glitz, flowing into a magnificent Hofburg view.

Neubau Track down the city's hottest designers along boutique-clogged streets like Kirchengasse, Lindengasse and Neubaugasse.

Mariahilfer Strasse Vienna's mile of high-street style, with big names and crowds.

Freihausviertel Lanes packed with homegrown fashion, design and speciality food stores, south of Naschmarkt.

Theobaldgasse Hole-in-the-wall shops purvey everything from fair-trade fashion to organic food.

NEED TO KNOW

Opening Hours

Most shops open between 9am and 6.30pm Monday to Friday and until 5pm on Saturday. Some have extended hours on Thursday (occasionally Friday) until around 8pm or 9pm.

Taxes

- *Mehrwertsteuer* (MWST; value-added tax) is 20% for most goods.
- Non-EU visitors can claim a MWST refund on purchases over €75.01. Ask shops to fill out a tax-refund cheque at the time of purchase, and get it stamped by border officials when you leave the EU.
- See www.globalblue.com for more details.

Useful Websites

Guided Vienna (www.guided-vienna.com) Pin down the city's hottest fashion and design by district.

Tourist Info Wien (www.wien.info) Takes a comprehensive look at shopping in Vienna by theme and neighbourhood.

Shopikon (www.shopikon.com/vienna/shopping-guide) Guide to Vienna's independent shops.

Shopping by Neighbourhood

The Hofburg & Around (p71) A nostalgic back-street romp reveals fine porcelain, hat shops and one of Europe's best auction houses.

Stephansdom & the Historic Centre (p86) Upper-crust Graben and Kohlmarkt fan into side streets hiding Austrian design stores, jewellers and confectioners.

Karlsplatz & Around Naschmarkt (p100) A picnic-basket banquet at the Naschmarkt and the Freihausviertel's idiosyncratic galleries, boutiques and speciality stores.

The Museum District & Neubau (p121) Vienna's creative trailblazer – streets ahead of other neighbourhoods when it comes to fashion and design.

Alsergrund & the University District (p132) Farm-fresh goods at Freyung Market, delis and chocolatiers in the ever-so-grand Palais Ferstel.

Prater & East of the Danube (p157) Karmelitermarkt and Praterstrasse have a growing crop of future-focused galleries, boutiques and design stores.

Lonely Planet's Top Choices

J&L Lobmeyr Vienna (p71) Exquisite homewares in lavish surrounds.

Zuckerlwerkstatt (p71) Resurrecting long-lost recipes to create sweets from Austrian sugar.

Henzls Ernte (p96) Garden veg and foraged herbs go into delectable spreads, sugars and salts.

Dorotheum (p72) Hammer time at this giant treasure chest of an auction house.

Gabarage Upcycling Design (p101) Reborn cast-offs become cutting-edge design.

Best Antiques & Crafts

Dorotheum (p72) One of Europe's largest auction houses.

feinedinge* (p101) Porcelain from the understated to the filigree.

Gmundner (p72) Over half of all Austrian households own at least one piece of Gmundner porcelain.

Best Design

Das Möbel (p118) Furniture on the cusp of cool at a try-before-you-buy cafe.

Österreichische Werkstätten (p72) A showcase for top-quality Austrian design.

Die Werkbank (p118) Design collective showcasing some of Vienna's most innovative creators.

Best Food & Drink

Staud's (p127) Wine jellies, apricot jams and chutneys.

Blühendes Konfekt (p101) Say it with a bouquet of chocolate-dipped herbs or candied flowers.

Unger und Klein (p87) The Austrian wine world uncorked.

Wald & Wiese (p86) Honey from Vienna's own rooftop apiaries.

Gegenbauer (p101) Prized oils and vinegars.

Best Fashion & Accessories

Runway (p121) Showcasing up-and-coming Austrian talent.

Ina Kent (p118) Silky soft leather bags made from vegetable-tanned leather.

Schau Schau (p87) Handcrafted eyewear beloved by celebs.

Mühlbauer (p121) In the hat business since 1903.

S/GHT (p119) Austrian and international designers are stocked at this ahead-of-the-curve shop.

Best Markets

Naschmarkt (p92) Hands down Vienna's best food market and street food.

Flohmarkt (p100) Fabulous flea market.

Karmelitermarkt (p156) Bag fresh produce and do brunch Viennese-style.

Brunnenmarkt (p126) As buzzing as a Turkish bazaar.

Bio-Markt Freyung (p132) Organic farm goodies.

Stall at Naschmarkt (p92)

Sports & Activities

Vienna steps between urban and outdoors without batting an eyelid. The Wienerwald to the west is crisscrossed with hiking and cycling trails, while the Danube, Alte Donau, Donauinsel and Lobau to the east offer boating, swimming, cycling and in-line skating. There are over 1200km of cycle paths, and the city is dotted with parks, some big (Prater), some small (Stadtpark).

Hiking & Walking

The Viennese are into *Wandern* (walking) and their vast backyard is perfect for hiking in woods, through meadows and along riverside trails. The green belt of the Wienerwald, on the western edge of Vienna, attracts walkers and cyclists, but the likes of the Prater (p151), with its lengthy tree-flanked trails, and the Lainzer Tiergarten (p166), a park to the west of Vienna where deer roam freely in woods of beech and oak, attract plenty of locals. Bordering the Danube, the Nationalpark Donau-Auen is a back-to-nature wilderness for walkers, and offers themed excursions such as birdwatching rambles. For those who want to go off-piste in summer, the **Lobau** (92B Lobgrundstrasse, S80 Lobau, Donaustadtbrücke) is an area of dense scrub, small lakes and woodland north of the Danube, in Donaustadt, with walking and cycling trails.

The Vienna Forestry Office maintains a number of local hiking paths, all of which are well signposted and accessible by public transport. Many include children's playgrounds, picnic tables and exceptional views en route. For a comprehensive list of local hiking trails in and around the Greater Vienna area, including detailed route descriptions and printable maps, go to www.wien.gv.at/en and type 'hiking' in the search field.

Cycling

Vienna is easily handled by bicycle. Around 1200km of cycle tracks cover the city, making it a breeze to avoid traffic, but not always pedestrians. Many one-way streets do not apply to cyclists; these are indicated by a bicycle sign with the word *ausgen* alongside it. Cycling routes lead through Vienna's parklands, along its waterways and the 7km path around the Ringstrasse. Popular cycling and in-line skating areas include the Donauinsel (Danube Island), the Prater and along the Danube Canal (Donaukanal).

Most bike- and skate-hire places are well informed and give local tips about where to head, including maps. Expect to pay around €29/50 per day for a standard/electric bike.

Over 120 Citybike Wien (p215) bike-share-scheme stands are located across the city. A credit card and €1 registration fee is required to hire bikes; just swipe your card in the machine and follow the multilingual instructions. The bikes are intended as an alternative to transport and can only be locked up at a bike station (unless you use your own lock). A lost bike will set you back €600.

Swimming

Swimming is the favoured summer pastime of the Viennese. The Donauinsel, Alte Donau and Lobau are often swamped with urbanites cooling off on hot summer days. Topless sunbathing is common, as is nude sunbathing, but only in designated areas; much of Lobau and both tips of the Donauinsel are FKK (*Freikörperkultur;* free body culture/ naked) areas.

There are also lidos run by the city, with open-air pools for swimming laps and lawns for sunbathing. Many also feature picnic

NEED TO KNOW

Planning Ahead

For most activities in Vienna, just turn up and you're good to go. It's worth prebooking guided walking and cycling tours a week or two in advance, especially in the high summer season, and the same goes for purchasing tickets for spectator sports.

Online Resources

Wein.at (www.wien.gv.at) A rundown of the main outdoor activities available in Vienna, from in-line skating to running, swimming and climbing.

Tourist Info Wien (www.wien.info) The inside scoop on activities in Vienna, from climbing halls to ice rinks, open-air swimming pools to jogging trails.

Fahrrad Wien (www.fahrradwien.at) Helps plan your cycling route.

Sporting Events

Argus Bike Festival (www.bikefestival.at) Trial shows, trick competitions and riders' parties, alongside workshops, exhibitions and other bike-focused fun. It's held on Rathausplatz over two days in late March.

Vienna City Marathon (www.vienna-marathon.com) Races through town in mid-April, starting at the Reichsbrücke and finishing at the Burgtheater.

areas, volleyball courts and slides for kids. They're open from 9am to around 7pm daily from May to mid-September and entry typically costs €5.90/2 for adults/children. For a full list of pools, visit www.wien.gv.at/english/leisure/bath.

Ice Skating

Most Viennese have ice skates collecting dust at the back of the wardrobe that are dragged out at least once over winter. Along with specialised ice-skating rinks, a number of outdoor basketball courts are turned into rinks during winter. For as little as €1 you can spend the whole day gliding around one of these temporary rinks: 08, Buchfeldgasse 7a; 16, Gallitzinstrasse 4; and 19, Osterleitengasse 14. Expect to pay around €8/5.50 per adult/child for skate hire. When it's cold enough, the Alte Donau is transformed into an ice-skater's paradise, with kilometres of natural ice.

Boating

The Alte Donau is the main boating and sailing centre in Vienna, but the Neue Donau, a long stretch of water separated from the Danube by the Donauinsel, also provides opportunities for boating, windsurfing and waterskiing. You can learn to sail or rent a boat at Hofbauer (p158).

Spectator Sports

The Stadthalle (p121) is a major player in hosting sporting events. Tennis tournaments (including the Austrian Open), horse shows and ice-hockey games are just some of the diverse events held here. The swimming pool is a major venue for aquatic events like races, water polo and synchronised swimming.

Krieau (Map p250; ☎01-728 00 46; www.krieau.at; 02, Nordportalstrasse 247; admission €5, box 1-6 people €40; Ⓤ Krieau, Stadion) is where Vienna's trotting racing events are held, and you can of course watch Lipizzaner stallions perform at the Spanish Riding School (p61).

Activities by Neighbourhood

The Hofburg & Around Home to the Spanish Riding School and sculpture-dotted parks.

Stephansdom & the Historic Centre Leap into the Badeschiff's pool by the Danube Canal.

The Museum District & Neubau Open-air ice skating in front of the illuminated Rathaus in winter.

Schloss Belvedere to the Canal Park life, ice skating and proximity to Vienna's best day spa.

Prater & East of the Danube Tops for activities in Vienna, with the Danube, lidos and a wildlife-crammed national park.

Schloss Schönbrunn & Around Palace gardens, parks and woodlands for walking.

Lonely Planet's Top Choices

Donauinsel (p158) Walk, cycle, swim, sail, boat or windsurf on this island in the Danube.

Wienerwald (p154) Tiptoe off the beaten trail to hike or mountain bike in these wooded hills.

Therme Wien (p148) Revive in the whirlpools, waterfalls and grotto-like pools of this thermal water wonderland.

Wiener Eislaufverein (p148) Get your skates on at the world's biggest open-air ice rink.

Prater (p151) Join the Viennese to jog, cycle and stroll in their best-loved park.

Best Hiking & Walking

Lobau (p51) Trails weave across this woody, lake-dotted floodplain, nicknamed Vienna's 'jungle'.

Wienerwald (p154) Don a pair of boots and head into Vienna's forested hills for a scenic day hike.

Nationalpark Donau-Auen (p150) Keep your eyes peeled for deer, kites and kingfishers on a back-to-nature ramble through these wetlands.

Prater (p151) Meadows, pockets of woodland and tree-lined boulevards are great for strolling.

Best Cycling

Wienerwald (p154) Roll through dappled woodlands or tear downhill on marked mountain-biking trails.

Donauinsel (p158) Pedal gently along the Danube, pausing for picnics, swims and cityscape views.

Prater (p151) The Prater's die-straight, chestnut-fringed Hauptallee is terrific for a city-centre spin.

Best Adrenaline Rush

Wienerwald (p154) Test your mettle on the woods' abundant mountain-bike trails.

Donauturm (p153) Feel the rush as you bungee jump from 152m, hitting speeds of 90km/h.

Kletteranlage Flakturm (p101) Scale the stark outside walls of the *Flakturm* (flak tower) in Esterházypark.

Best Lidos & Pools

Badeschiff (p87) Splash around with the cool kids in this ship-shape pool on the Danube.

Strandbad Gänsehäufel (p158) Summertime magnet, with a pool, activities and nudist area.

Strandbad Alte Donau (p158) Take a cooling dip in the river at this urban beach.

Therme Wien (p148) Thermal pools, slides, saunas and more.

Schönbrunnerbad (p168) Outdoor complex including an Olympic-size pool in the grounds of Schloss Schönbrunn.

Best Ice Rinks

Wiener Eislaufverein (p148) Glide across the ice at this gargantuan open-air skating rink.

Wiener Eistraum (p121) DJ beats put a swing in your skate at this open-air rink on Rathausplatz.

Alte Donau (p158) When it freezes, Viennese skaters head to this arm of the Danube.

Explore Vienna

DER·ZEIT·IHRE·KVNST·
DER·KVNST·IHRE·FREIHEIT·

VIENNA'S TOP SIGHTS

Left: Secession Hall (p93)

Neighbourhoods at a Glance

❶ The Hofburg & Around p58

Vienna's imperial splendour peaks in this part of the Innere Stadt (city centre), where horse-drawn carriages prance along curved, cobbled streets. Its centrepiece is the magnificent Hofburg palace complex, which brims with museums and world-famous attractions. Museums also abound in the streets north towards Stephansplatz.

❷ Stephansdom & the Historic Centre p73

Vienna's most distinctive landmark is Gothic cathedral Stephansdom. The oldest part of the city, with a tangle of cobbled lanes and elegant thoroughfares, this epicentral neighbourhood takes in the medieval Jewish quarter in the northwest, the stretch down to Danube Canal's southern bank and the areas northeast and east of Stephansplatz.

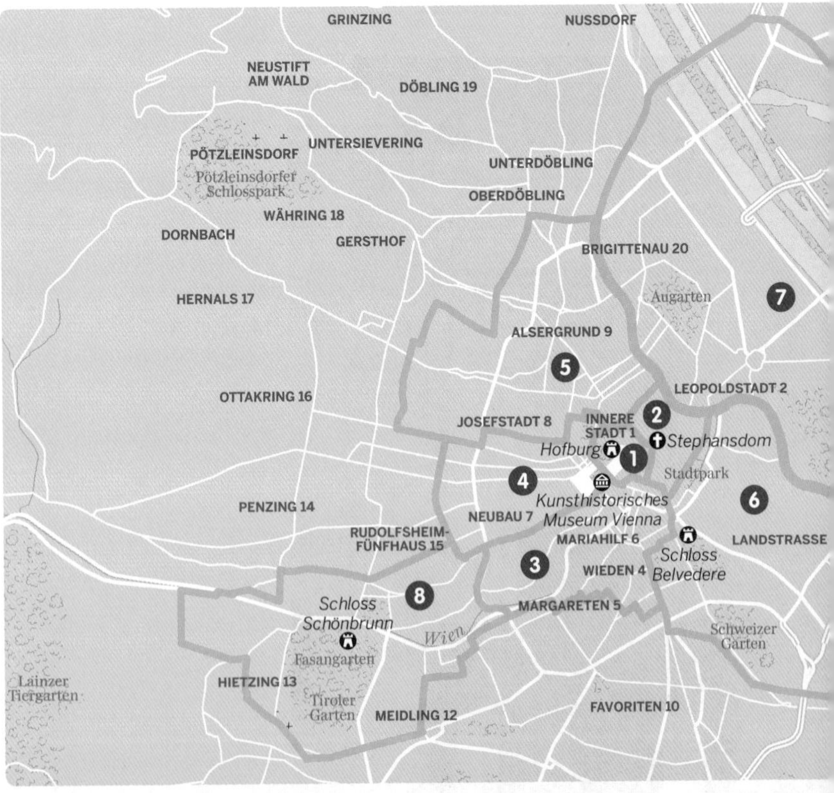

3 Karlsplatz & Around Naschmarkt p88

Fringing the Ringstrasse in the southeast corner of the Innere Stadt, this neighbourhood includes the city's sublime Staatsoper opera house, and extends south beyond Vienna's enormous market and food paradise, the Naschmarkt, into some of the city's most interesting Vorstädte (inner suburbs): Margareten, Mariahilf and Wieden. There's great eating, drinking and nightlife and a truly Viennese Vorstadt character.

4 The Museum District & Neubau p102

Attractions in this cultural neighbourhood include the incomparable Kunsthistorisches Museum Vienna (Museum of Art History), packed with old masters; the MuseumsQuartier's cache of museums, cafes, restaurants, bars and performance spaces; and the Renaissance-style Burgtheater, where premieres have included Mozart's and Beethoven's works. To the west, hip Neubau is an incubator for Vienna's vibrant fashion, art and design scenes.

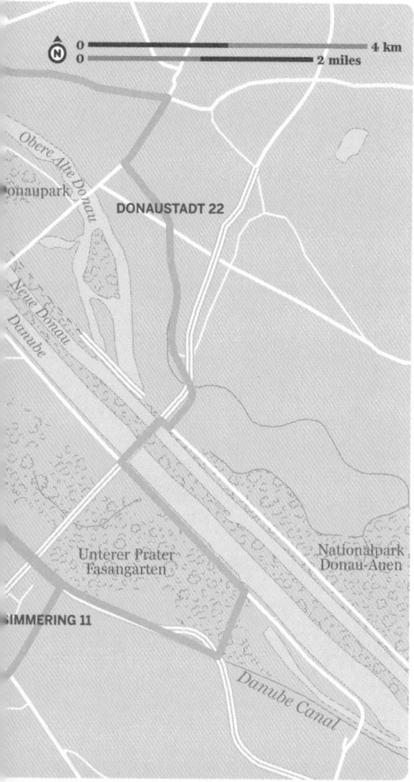

5 Alsergrund & the University District p122

Bookended by one of Europe's biggest universities, Alsergrund (9th district) spills south into Josefstadt (8th district), which moves to a similar groove and is scattered with low-key restaurants, cafes and shops. Further west lies the ethnically diverse Otta-kring (16th district).

6 Schloss Belvedere to the Canal p133

The crowning glory of this art-rammed neighbourhood is Schloss Belvedere and its gardens. Spread out across the neighbour-hood, other crowd-pullers include the kaleidoscopic KunstHausWien, as well as museums homing in on everything from military history to art fakes. Some cracking cafes, delis and restaurants have popped up recently, making breaks between sightseeing all the more pleasurable.

7 Prater & East of the Danube p149

Leopoldstadt, the city's Jewish quarter, is one of Vienna's hippest districts. The neighbourhood has graffiti art, beach bars by the Danube Canal and enticing new boutiques, restaurants, galleries and edgy cafes hiding down its sleepy backstreets. Its centrepiece is the Prater and further east is the Danube River and Danube Island recreation area.

8 Schloss Schönbrunn & Around p159

The palace dominates this well-to-do residential neighbourhood and the tight original village streets outside the palace's walls give way to a relatively suburban feel. The ensemble of suburbs adjoining the neighbourhood to the north – Fünfhaus, Rudolfsheim and Ottakring – also make for an interesting taste of everyday Viennese life.

The Hofburg & Around

Neighbourhood Top Five

❶ **Hofburg** (p60) Strolling through the monumental Hofburg palace complex, exploring courtyards like the Schweizerhof, and admiring the elegant gates, impressive squares, statues of the Habsburg rulers and monumental architecture.

❷ **Albertina** (p66) Viewing world-class graphic-arts exhibitions and the gallery's collection of original graphics by masters within luxurious palace rooms.

❸ **Kaiserappartements** (p60) Touring the Habsburg imperial apartments, the Sisi Museum, dedicated to Empress Elisabeth, and the Silberkammer (Silver Depot).

❹ **Spanish Riding School** (p61) Catching the famous white Lipizzaner stallions during a mesmerising equine ballet performance.

❺ **Neue Burg Museums** (p62) Revelling in the historical musical instruments, arms and armour, and ancient artefacts unearthed during Austrian archaeologists' excavations at Ephesus in Turkey.

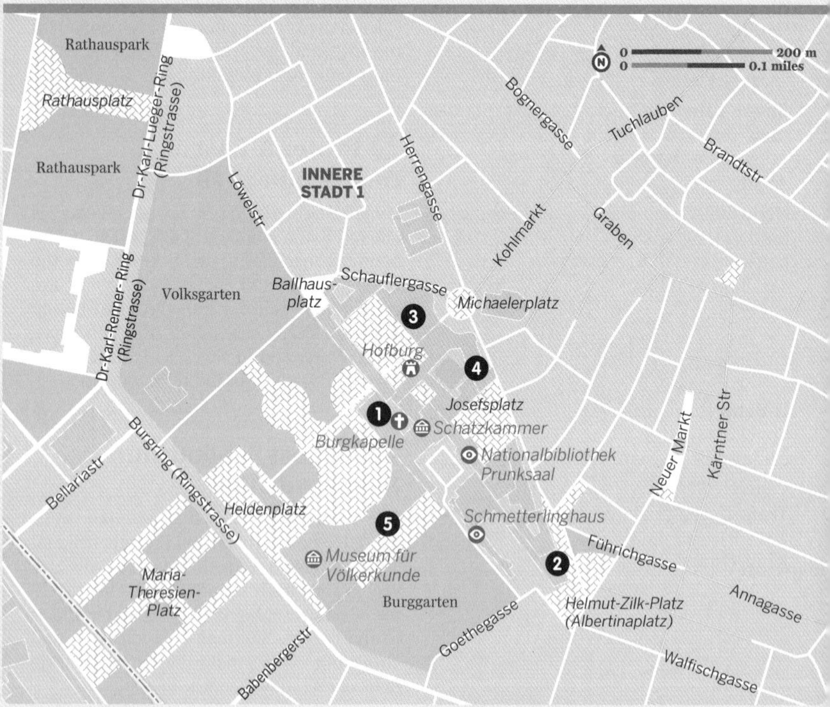

For more detail of this area see Map p238 ➡

Explore the Hofburg & Around

One of the most spectacular palace complexes in the Austrian capital, the Hofburg (p60) was the seat of the Habsburgs for some six and a half centuries. It can be easily approached from the MuseumsQuartier by crossing Maria-Theresien-Platz, but the the grandest place to start is at the gate on Michaelerplatz, where the Habsburgs used to enter. From here you can stroll from one end to the other in about an hour, with time to stop and admire the architecture. If you plan on visiting several museums, block your calendar for much of the day to see these comfortably. Although visitors are almost always walking through, it rarely feels crowded. Plan to spend at least another four hours taking in the most important sights around the Hofburg – the Albertina (p66) graphic-arts gallery, Kapuzinergruft (p66), where most of the Habsburg royal family are buried, and the Jüdisches Museum (p67). The neighbourhood has some good shopping as well as a handful of excellent eating and drinking options, with many more close at hand in the nearby MuseumsQuartier.

Local Life

Park Life This epicentral part of town has some of the prettiest parks in Vienna, with the Volksgarten flanking one side of the Hofburg and the Burggarten the other. Locals flock here in summer to picnic or simply relax.

Snack Life Join opera-going locals dressed in their finery, sipping champagne and tucking into sausages at open-air Bitzinger Würstelstand am Albertinaplatz (p68).

Nightlife A small but legendary collection of places for drinking or clubbing are here, ranging from coffee houses through to cocktail bars such as Loos American Bar (p70) to Volksgarten ClubDiskothek (p70).

Getting There & Away

U-Bahn Herrengasse (U3) and Stephansplatz (U1, U3) are closest to the Hofburg, but Museumsquartier (U2) can also be convenient for the Heldenplatz side of the palace complex.

Tram Useful for entering from Ringstrasse (D, 1, 2, 71 Ring/Volkstheater, Burgring and Kärntner Ring/Oper).

Lonely Planet's Top Tip

Although this neighbourhood is full of iconic sights, it's also a part of town that invites aimless strolling to soak up the atmosphere. The Hofburg is most impressive during the quiet hours of early morning or early evening, while the streets between the Hofburg and Stephansplatz, with lots of private art galleries, are best explored during business hours.

Best Places to Eat

- Bitzinger Würstelstand am Albertinaplatz (p68)
- Meinl's Restaurant (p69)
- Trześniewski (p68)

For reviews, see p68.

Best Places to Drink

- Blue Mustard (p69)
- Café Leopold Hawelka (p69)
- Loos American Bar (p70)
- Meinl's Weinbar (p69)
- Volksgarten ClubDiskothek (p70)
- Palmenhaus (p70)

For reviews, see p69.

Best Places to Shop

- J&L Lobmeyr Vienna (p71)
- Julius Meinl am Graben (p69)
- Zuckerlwerkstatt (p71)
- Dorotheum (p72)

For reviews, see p71.

NSAFONOV/SHUTTERSTOCK ©

TOP SIGHT
THE HOFBURG

Built as a fortified castle in the 13th century, the home of the Habsburg rulers from Rudolph I in 1279 until the Austrian monarchy collapsed under Karl I in 1918 is the ultimate display of Austria's former imperial power. Today the impressive palace complex contains the offices of the Austrian president, an ensemble of extraordinary museums and stately public squares.

Kaiserappartements

The Kaiserappartements were once the official living quarters of Franz Josef I (1830–1916) and Empress Elisabeth (1837–98; or Sisi, as she was affectionately named). The highlight is the **Sisi Museum** (adult/child €15/9, incl guided tour €18/10.50; ⏲9am-6pm Jul & Aug, to 5.30pm Sep-Jun), devoted to Austria's most beloved empress, which has a strong focus on the clothing and jewellery of Austria's monarch and a replica of her personal fitness room complete with rings and bars. Also here is a reconstruction of Sisi's luxurious Pullman coach. Many of the empress' famous portraits are also on show, as is her death mask, made after her assassination in Geneva in 1898.

Multilingual audio guides are included in the admission price. Guided tours take in the Kaiserappartements, the Sisi Museum and the adjoining **Silberkammer** (Silver Depot, Imperial Silver Collection; adult/child €15/9, incl guided tour €18/10.50; ⏲9am-6pm Jul & Aug, to 5.30pm Sep-Jun) - its largest silver service caters to 140 dinner guests.

DON'T MISS

- Strolling through the Hofburg
- Kaiserappartements
- Kaiserliche Schatzkammer
- Neue Burg Museums
- Haus der Geschichte Österreich
- Spanish Riding School

PRACTICALITIES

- Imperial Palace
- Map p238, D3
- ☎01-533 75 70
- www.hofburg-wien.at
- 01, Michaelerkuppel
- 🚋D, 1, 2, 71 Burgring, Ⓤ Herrengasse

Kaiserliche Schatzkammer

The **Kaiserliche Schatzkammer** (Imperial Treasury; Map p238; ☎01-525 24-0; www.kaiserliche-schatzkammer.at; 01, Schweizerhof; adult/child €12/free; ⏰9am-5.30pm Wed-Mon) contains secular and ecclesiastical treasures of priceless value and splendour – the sheer wealth of this collection of crown jewels is staggering. As you walk through the rooms you see a golden rose, diamond-studded Turkish sabres, a 2680-carat Colombian emerald and, the highlight of the treasury, the imperial crown. The wood-panelled **Sacred Treasury** has a collection of rare religious relics: fragments of the True Cross, the Holy Lance that pierced Jesus on the Cross, one of the nails from the Crucifixion, a thorn from Christ's crown and a piece of tablecloth from the Last Supper. Multi lingual audio guides cost €5 (the shorter highlight audio tour is free) and are very worthwhile.

Burgkapelle

The **Burgkapelle** (Royal Chapel; Map p238; ☎01-533 99 27; www.hofmusikkapelle.gv.at; 01, Schweizerhof; ⏰10am-2pm Mon & Tue, 11am-1pm Fri; 🚋D, 1, 2, 71 Burgring) originally dates from the 13th century. It received a Gothic makeover from 1447 to 1449, but much of this disappeared during the baroque fad. Its vaulted wooden statuary survived and is testament to those Gothic days. The Vienna Boys' Choir Mass (p46) takes place here every Sunday at 9.15am between September and June. The chapel is sometimes closed to visitors in July and August, so check ahead in those months.

Spanish Riding School

The world-famous **Spanish Riding School** (Spanische Hofreitschule; Map p238; ☎01-533 90 31-0; www.srs.at; 01, Michaelerplatz 1; tickets €27-225, standing room €13; ⏰hours vary) is a Viennese institution truly reminiscent of the imperial Habsburg era. This unequalled equestrian show is performed by Lipizzaner stallions formerly kept at an imperial stud established at Lipizza (hence the name). These graceful stallions perform an equine ballet to a program of classical music while the audience watches from pillared balconies – or from a cheaper standing-room area – and the chandeliers shimmer above.

There are many different ways to see the Lipizzaner. **Performances** are the top-shelf variant, and for seats at these you will need to book several months in advance. The website lists performance dates and you can order tickets online. As a rule of thumb, performances are at 11am on Sunday from mid-February to June and mid-August to December, with frequent additional performances on Saturday

VISITING THE IMPERIAL APARTMENTS

Entrance to the Kaiserappartements is via the Kaiserstieg staircase, after which you learn about the Habsburgs and the history of the Hofburg and you can look at a model of the complex. You then enter the Sisi Museum and afterwards the restored apartments of Empress Elisabeth and Kaiser Franz Josef I. The Silberkammer occupies another part of the Reichskanzeleitrakt (State Chancery Tract) of the building.

Empress Maria Theresia (1717–80) is immortalised in her robed, operatic glory in the middle of Maria-Theresien-Platz, but Empress Elisabeth, better known as Sisi, is the real darling of the Habsburg show in this part of town. The cult of Sisi knows no bounds in German-speaking countries, due in large part to the trilogy of films from the 1950s starring Austro-French actress Romy Schneider. Schneider embodied the empress so well that in the popular mind it often seems hard to distinguish Sisi as art and the empress in reality.

and occasionally other days of the week. For standing-room tickets, book at least one month in advance. During the summer break, it hosts special 'Piber meets Vienna' performances. Visitors to the **Morgenarbeit** can drop in for part of a session (morning training sessions; adult/child €15/7.50, 10am to noon mid-August to June).

One-hour **guided tours** (adult/child €18/9; 2pm, 3pm and 4pm Tuesday to Sunday), held in English and German, take you into the performance hall, stables and other facilities. A combined **morning training and tour** (adult/child €31/15) is another option. The visitor centre here sells all tickets.

Neue Burg Museums

One ticket covers entry to three **Neue Burg Museums** (Map p238; ☎01-525 24-0; www.khm.at; 01, Heldenplatz; adult/child €16/free; ⊙10am-6pm Fri-Wed, to 9pm Thu Jun-Aug, closed Wed Sep-May). The **Sammlung alter Musikinstrumente** (Collection of Ancient Musical Instruments) contains a wonderfully diverse array of instruments. The **Ephesos Museum** features artefacts unearthed during Austrian archaeologists' excavations at Ephesus in Turkey between 1895 and 1906. The **Hofjagd- und Rüstkammer** (Arms and Armour) museum contains ancient armour dating mainly from the 15th and 16th centuries. An audio guide costs €5.

THE WHITE HORSE IN HISTORY

The Lipizzaner stallion breed dates back to the 1520s, when Ferdinand I imported the first horses from Spain for the imperial palace. His son Maximilian II imported new stock in the 1560s, and in 1580 Archduke Charles II established the imperial stud in Lipizza (Lipica; today in Slovenia), giving the horse its name. Austria's nobility had good reason for looking to Spain for its horses: the Spanish were considered the last word in equine breeding at the time, thanks to Moors from the 7th century who had brought their elegant horses to the Iberian Peninsula. Italian horses were added to the stock around the mid-1700s (these too had Spanish blood) and by the mid-18th century the Lipizzaner had a reputation for being Europe's finest horses.

Over the centuries, natural catastrophe, but more often war, caused the Lipizzaner to be evacuated from their original stud in Slovenia on numerous occasions. One of their periods of exile from the stud in Lipica was in 1915 due to the outbreak of WWI. Some of the horses went to Laxemburg (just outside Vienna), and others to Bohemia in today's Czech Republic (at the time part of the Austro-Hungarian Empire).

When the Austrian monarchy collapsed in 1918, Lipica passed into Italian hands and the horses were divided between Austria and Italy. The Italians ran the stud in Slovenia, while the Austrians transferred their horses to Piber, near Graz, which had been breeding military horses for the empire since 1798 – at that time stallions were mostly crossed with English breeds.

The fortunes of these pirouetting horses rose and fell with the collapse of the Habsburg empire and advent of two world wars. When WWII broke out, Hitler's cohorts goose-stepped in and requisitioned the Piber stud in Austria and started breeding military horses and pack mules there. They also decided to bring the different studs in their occupied regions together under one roof, and Piber's Lipizzaner wound up in Hostau, situated in Bohemia. Fearing the Lipizzaner would fall into the hands of the Russian army as it advanced towards the region in 1945, American forces seized the Lipizzaner and other horses in Hostau and transferred them back to Austria.

Today, Piber still supplies the Spanish Riding School with its white stallions.

'olksgarten (p59)

Haus der Geschichte Österreich

Austria's first museum of contemporary history, the 2018-opened **Haus der Geschichte Österreich** (hdgö; House of Austrian History; Map p238; ☎01-534 10-805; www.hdgoe.at; 01, Heldenplatz; adult/child €8/free; ⏰10am-6pm Tue, Wed & Fri-Sun, to 9pm Thu; 🚋D, 1, 2, 71 Burgring) spans the period from the mid-19th century to the present. Exhibits, documents, photos and films cover political, cultural, economic and social history, including the First Republic's 1918 founding, Nazi occupation, migrations, protest culture, democracy and science. The evolving collection includes, for example, a football used in a 2018 friendly match against Germany, which Austria won. Guided tours in English lasting 1½ hours depart at 3pm on Saturdays (adult/child €4/free).

Nationalbibliothek Prunksaal

The **Nationalbibliothek** (National Library) was once the imperial library and is now the largest library in Vienna. The real reason to visit these esteemed halls of knowledge is to gaze on the **Nationalbibliothek Prunksaal** (Grand Hall; Map p238; ☎01-534 10; www.onb.ac.at; 01, Josefsplatz 1; adult/child €8/free; ⏰10am-6pm Fri-Wed, to 9pm Thu Jun-Sep, closed Mon Oct-May; 🚋D, 1, 2, 71 Burgring, ⓤHerrengasse). Commissioned by Charles VI, this baroque hall was the brainchild of Johann Bernhard Fischer von Erlach, who died the year the first brick was laid, and finished by his son Joseph in 1735. Leather-bound scholarly tomes line the walls, and the upper storey of shelves is flanked by an

TIPS FOR THE KAISERLICHE SCHATZKAMMER

Multilingual audio guides cost €5 (the shorter highlight audio tour is free) and are very worthwhile. A combined Schatz der Habsburger (Treasures of the Habsburgs) ticket, which includes the Kunsthistorisches Museum Vienna and Neue Burg, costs €22.

The Kaislerliche Schatzkammer dates back to the time of Ferdinand I (1503–64), who commissioned an antiquarian to take care of the collection. In the 18th century under Maria Theresia, the treasures were separated and reorganised, possibly to hide the sale of some treasures to finance the War of the Austrian Succession (1740–48). Under Hitler, all the imperial regalia from the Holy Roman Empire was transferred to Nuremberg, where it had previously been kept for about 400 years from 1424. It was returned to the Hofburg after WWII.

Roof detail on the Hofburg palace

elegantly curved wood balcony. Rare ancient volumes (mostly 15th century) are stored within glass cabinets, with pages opened to beautifully illustrated passages of text. A statue of Charles VI stands guard under the central dome, which itself has a magnificent fresco by Daniel Gran depicting the emperor's apotheosis.

Papyrusmuseum

Part of the Nationalbibliothek museum ensemble, along with the Esperantomuseum (p68) and Globenmuseum (p67), the **Papyrusmuseum** (Map p238; 01-534 10-425; www.onb.ac.at; 01, Heldenplatz; adult/child €5/free; 10am-6pm Tue, Wed & Fri-Sun, to 9pm Thu; D, 1, 2, 71 Burgring, U Herrengasse) displays an interesting collection of 200 fragments of ancient writing on papyrus from Egypt and also has inscriptions on other media, such as parchment and clay. One of its highlights is a fragment of musical notation on pottery depicting the choral ode from *Orestes,* a tragedy written by the Greek Euripides. An audio guide costs €3.

Schmetterlinghaus

Sharing the Habsburg's personal *Jugendstil* (Art Nouveau)glasshouse (1901) with the Palmenhaus (p70) bar in the **Burggarten** (Castle Garden; Map p238; www.bundesgaerten.at; 01, Burgring; 6am-10pm Apr-Oct, 7.30am-5.30pm Nov-Mar; D, 1, 2, 71 Burgring, U Museumsquartier) FREE, the **Schmetterlinghaus** (Butterfly House; Map p238; 01-533 85 70; www.schmetterlinghaus.at; 01, Burggarten; adult/child €7/4; 10am-4.45pm Mon-Fri, to 6.15pm Sat & Sun Apr-Oct, to 3.45pm Nov-Mar; D, 1, 2, 71 Burgring, U Karlsplatz) has hundreds of fluttering butterflies and a shop stocking a great range of butterfly paraphernalia. Its warm, humid air is especially welcome on chilly days.

HOFBURG PALACE COMPLEX

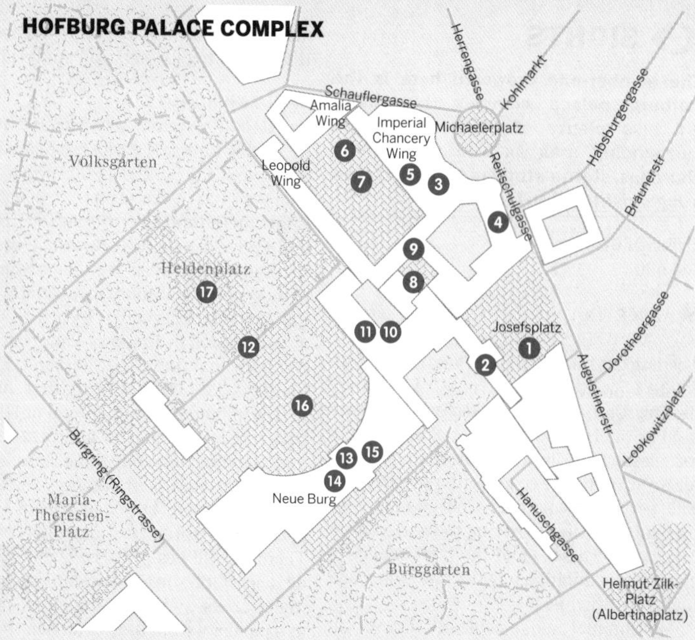

Palace Tour
The Hofburg

LENGTH ONE HOUR TO ONE DAY

The Hofburg is a jigsaw puzzle of monumental buildings. For the full effect, enter from Michaelerplatz, as the monarchs used to. First, though, admire the pretty square just to the south, 1 **Josefsplatz**, named after Joseph II and adorned with the equestrian monument to Emperor Josef II. Josefsplatz also serves as the entrance to the 2 **Nationalbibliothek Prunksaal** (p63).

Pass through the 3 **Michaelertor** and neobaroque Michaelertrakt. The Michaelerplatz side of the building is lined with statues of Hercules and evocative fountains depicting the Power of the Land and the Power of the Sea. On the left of the hall is the 4 **Spanish Riding School** (p61) and its visitor centre, on the right the 5 **Kaiserappartements** (p60).

Straight ahead, you reach the large courtyard 6 **In der Burg**, with a monument to 7 **Emperor Franz I**, the last in a long line of Holy Roman emperors after Napoleon brought about the collapse of the Reich in 1806.

The oldest part of the Hofburg is the 8 **Schweizerhof** (Swiss Courtyard), named after the Swiss guards who used to protect its precincts. This is reached via the Renaissance 9 **Swiss Gate**, which dates from 1553. The 13th-century courtyard gives access to the 10 **Burgkapelle** (p61) and the 11 **Schatzkammer** (p61).

Straight ahead is 12 **Heldenplatz** (Hero's Sq) and the 13 **Neue Burg**, built between the second half of the 19th century and WWI. The Neue Burg houses the three 14 **Neue Burg Museums** (p62) as well as the 15 **Haus der Geschichte Österreich** (p63). The balcony is where Hitler addressed a rally during his 1938 visit to Vienna after the *Anschluss*. Facing each other on Heldenplatz are monuments to 16 **Prince Eugene of Savoy** (closest to the Neue Burg) and 17 **Archduke Karl** (Charles of Austria). Pass through the Äusseres Burgtor (Outer Palace Gate) to the Ringstrasse.

SIGHTS

The number-one drawcard here is the Hofburg palace complex, but there are also plenty of museums in the surrounding area as well as splendid churches, statue-studded parks and even a *Jugendstil* butterfly house.

THE HOFBURG — PALACE

See p60.

★ALBERTINA — GALLERY

Map p238 (☎01-534 830; www.albertina.at; 01, Albertinaplatz 1; adult/child €16/free; ⊙10am-6pm Sat-Tue & Thu, to 9pm Wed & Fri; 🚋D, 1, 2, 71 Kärntner Ring/Oper, ⓤKarlsplatz, Stephansplatz) Once used as the Habsburgs' imperial apartments for guests, the Albertina is now a repository for an exceptional collection of graphic art. The permanent Batliner Collection – with over 100 paintings covering the period from Monet to Picasso – and the high quality of changing exhibitions make the Albertina highly worthwhile.

Multilingual audio guides (€4) cover all exhibition sections and tell the story behind the apartments and the works on display.

French impressionism and post-impressionism, as well as the works of the Swiss Alberto Giacometti, were the original focus of the Batliner Collection, but over time husband and wife benefactors Herbert and Rita Batliner added a substantial number of Russian avant-garde works to create a who's who of 20th-century and contemporary art: Monet, Picasso, Degas, Cézanne, Klimt, Matisse, Chagall, Nolde, Jawlensky and many more.

Tickets (but not the audio guides) are valid for the whole day, so you can nip out for lunch and return later to finish off a visit.

A branch of the Österreichisches Filmmuseum (p71) is located here.

MUSEUM DER ILLUSIONEN — MUSEUM

Map p238 (Museum of Illusions; ☎01-532 22 55; www.museumderillusionen.at; Wallnerstrasse 4; adult/child €12/8; ⊙10am-8pm; ⓤHerrengasse) Vienna's mind-bending Museum of Illusions, opened in 2017, confounds your senses through its 40 interactive optical illusions and installations. They include stereograms (3D pictures with 'hidden' objects), tilted rooms, mirages, a giant kaleidoscope, an infinity room, and a tunnel with spinning images on the walls that make it impossible to keep your balance (despite the central walkway not moving). It's fascinating for kids and adults alike.

KAPUZINERGRUFT — MAUSOLEUM

Map p238 (Kaisergruft; www.kapuzinergruft.com; 01, Tegethoffstrasse 2; adult/child €7.50/4.50, incl guided tour €10.50/7.50; ⊙10am-6pm Fri-Wed, from 9am Thu; ⓤStephansplatz) Beneath the **Kapuzinerkirche** (Church of the Capuchin Friars; Map p238; www.erzdioezese-wien.at; ⊙8am-6pm), the Kapuzinergruft is the final resting place of most of the Habsburg royal family, including Empress Elisabeth. Opened in 1633, it was instigated by Empress Anna (1585–1618). Her body and that of her husband, Emperor Matthias (1557–1619), were the first entombed in this impressive vault. A total of 149 Habsburgs are buried here, including 12 emperors and 19 empresses. Only three Habsburgs are notable through their absence. The last emperor, Karl I, was buried in exile in Madeira, and Marie Antoinette (daughter of Maria Theresia) still lies in Paris. The third is Duc de Reichstadt, son of Napoleon's second wife, Marie Louise, who was transferred to Paris as a publicity stunt by the Nazis in 1940. Also on display are rows of urns containing the internal organs of the Habsburgs. One of the many privileges of being a Habsburg was to be dismembered and dispersed after death: their hearts are in the Augustinerkirche in the Hofburg and the rest of their bodies are in the Kapuzinergruft.

English-language, hour-long guided tours take place at 3.30pm Wednesday to Saturday.

THEATERMUSEUM — MUSEUM

Map p238 (☎01-525 24 3460; www.theatermuseum.at; 01, Lobkowitzplatz 2; adult/child incl all exhibitions €12/free; ⊙10am-6pm Wed-Mon; 🚋D, 1, 2, 62, 71 Kärntner Ring/Oper, ⓤStephansplatz) Housed in the baroque Lobkowitz palace (1694), this museum has temporary exhibitions on Vienna's theatre history. It also displays Staatsoper's collection of portraits of operatic greats, costumes, stage designs and documents, spotlighting premieres and milestones like Herbert von Karajan's eight-year reign as director. Performing arts fans will also enjoy the occasional gem, such as ballerina Dame Margot Fonteyn's pointe shoe.

AUGUSTINERKIRCHE — CHURCH

Map p238 (Augustinian Church; ☎01-533 70 99; http://augustinerkirche.augustiner.at; 01, Augustinerstrasse 3; ⊙7.30am-5.30pm Mon, Wed & Fri, to 7.15pm Tue & Thu, 9am-7.30pm Sat & Sun; ⓤStephansplatz, Herrengasse) The real highlight of the 14th-century Gothic Augustinerkirche is not its pale, vaulted interior but the Herzgruft, a crypt containing silver urns with the hearts of 54 Habsburg rulers. The crypt is open on Sunday after the 11am Mass (celebrated with a full choir and orchestra) – turn up around 12.30pm. The church hosts regular evening classical music concerts; check schedules at http://hochamt.augustiner.at. Sometimes on a visit you can catch the choir practising. Many Habsburg weddings took place here.

JÜDISCHES MUSEUM MUSEUM

Map p238 (Jewish Museum; ☎01-535 04 31; www.jmw.at; 01, Dorotheergasse 11; adult/child incl Museum Judenplatz €12/free; ⏱10am-6pm Sun-Fri; Ⓤ Stephansplatz) Housed inside Palais Eskeles, Vienna's Jüdisches Museum showcases the history of Jews in Vienna, from the first settlements at Judenplatz in the 13th century to the present. Spaces devoted to changing exhibitions are complemented by its permanent exhibition covering 1945 to the present day; the highlight is the startling collection of ceremonial art on the top floor. Multimedia guides cost €4. Combined tickets to the Jüdisches Museum and Museum Judenplatz (p78) are valid for four days.

MICHAELERKIRCHE CHURCH

Map p238 (☎01-533 80 00; www.michaelerkirche.at; 01, Michaelerplatz; church free, crypt tours adult/child €7/3; ⏱7am-10pm Mon-Sat, from 8am Sun; Ⓤ Herrengasse) The Michaelerkirche dates from the 13th century. Its highlight is the burial crypt which you can see on 40-minute bilingual German/English tours at 11am and 1pm Monday to Saturday. Tours take you past coffins, some revealing occupants preserved by the rarefied air of the crypt. Concerts take place throughout the year; check the website for the program.

MINORITENKIRCHE CHURCH

Map p238 (Minorite Church; ☎01-533 41 62; www.minoritenkirche-wien.info; 01, Minoritenplatz; ⏱8am-6pm; Ⓤ Herrengasse) The Minoritenkirche is a 13th-century Gothic church that later received a baroque facelift. The stubby edifice was 'shortened' (ie partially destroyed) by the Turks in 1529. The most noteworthy piece inside is a mosaic copy of da Vinci's *Last Supper,* commissioned by Napoleon. Sunday services are held at 8.30am in German and 11am in Italian. The church is used for occasional classical concerts and choir recitals throughout the year – see the website's calendar for details.

GLOBENMUSEUM MUSEUM

Map p238 (☎01-534 10-425; www.onb.ac.at; 01, Herrengasse 9, 1st fl; adult/child €5/free; ⏱10am-6pm Tue, Wed & Fri-Sun, to 9pm Thu; 🚋D, 1, 2, 71 Burgring, Ⓤ Herrengasse) Part of the Nationalbibliothek collection of museums, along with the Esperantomuseum (p68) and Papyrusmuseum (p64), where admission covers all three and audio guides cost €3, this small museum situated inside a former palace (Palais Mollard) is dedicated to cartography. Among the collection of 19th-century globes and maps are some gems dating from the 16th century. Look for the globe made for Emperor Karl V by Mercator in 1541.

LOOS HAUS HISTORIC BUILDING

Map p238 (01, Michaelerplatz 3; Ⓤ Herrengasse) FREE Designed by Adolf Loos, this modernist gem put Franz Josef's nose seriously out of joint when it was completed in 1911. Its intentionally simple facade offended the emperor so deeply that he ordered the curtains to be pulled on all palace windows overlooking the building. Today it houses a bank.

HELMUT-ZILK-PLATZ SQUARE

Map p238 (Albertinaplatz; Ⓤ Stephansplatz, Karlsplatz) Wedged between the Staatsoper and the Albertina, this square stands out for its **Monument Against War & Fascism** (Mahnmal Gegen Krieg und Faschismus; Map p238; Ⓤ Stephansplatz, Karlsplatz) by Alfred Hrdlicka (1988). The series of pale, block-like sculptures has a dark, squat shape wrapped in barbed wire, representing a Jew

LOCAL KNOWLEDGE

ORNATE PUBLIC TOILETS

Built in 1905 by celebrated Czech-born, Vienna-based architect Adolf Loos (1870–1933) and still operating today, these opulent **public toilets** (Map p238; 01; €0.50; ⏱24hr; Ⓤ Stephansplatz) down a flight of steps below Graben were built as a showcase for a toilet manufacturer and retain their mahogany-panelled stalls with opaque-glass doors and exquisite tiling (the original chandeliers have been replaced with electric lighting). Admission is payable even if you're not using the facilities.

scrubbing the floor; poignantly, the greyish block originally came from the Mauthausen concentration camp.

MICHAELERPLATZ ROMAN RUINS — ROMAN SITE

Map p238 (01, Michaelerplatz; UHerrengasse) FREE Ringed by gorgeous architecture, Michaelerplatz is centred on Roman ruins that are reputed to have been a brothel for soldiers. This cobblestoned circular 'square' is a major pick-up point for tours by *Fiaker* (horse-drawn carriages).

ESPERANTOMUSEUM — MUSEUM

Map p238 (01-534 10-425; www.onb.ac.at; 01, Herrengasse 9, ground fl; adult/child €5/free; 10am-6pm Tue, Wed & Fri-Sun, to 9pm Thu; D, 1, 2, 71 Burgring, UHerrengasse) The oft-overlooked Esperantomuseum is mostly devoted to the artificial language created by Dr Ludvik Zamenhof in 1887. The first book in Esperanto, by Dr Zamenhof himself, features among interesting exhibits on artificial languages, such as language used in the *Star Trek* TV series and films. Tickets also include entry to the Nationalbibliothek's Globenmuseum (p67) and Papyrusmuseum (p64). An audio guide costs €3.

EATING

The dining scene is fairly limited (although there are some standouts), but improves closer to Stephansplatz. Alternatively, it's easy to skip across Maria-Theresien-Platz from the palace into the MuseumsQuartier.

★BITZINGER WÜRSTELSTAND AM ALBERTINAPLATZ — STREET FOOD €

Map p238 (www.bitzinger-wien.at; 01, Albertinaplatz; sausages €3.50-4.70; 8am-4am; D, 1, 2, 71 Kärntner Ring/Oper, UKarlsplatz, Stephansplatz) Behind the Staatsoper, Vienna's best sausage stand has cult status. Bitzinger offers the contrasting spectacle of ladies and gents dressed to the nines, sipping beer, wine or Joseph Perrier champagne while tucking into sausages at outdoor tables or the heated counter after performances. Mustard comes in *Süss* (sweet, ie mild) or *Scharf* (hot).

TRZEŚNIEWSKI — SANDWICHES €

Map p238 (www.trzesniewski.at; 01, Dorotheergasse 1; 1/8 sandwiches €1.40/8.40; 8.30am-7.30pm Mon-Fri, 9am-6pm Sat, 10am-5pm Sun; UStephansplatz) Trześniewski has been serving exquisite open-faced finger-style

COMBINATION MUSEUM TICKETS

There are lots of combined options for visiting the Hofburg and nearby museums.

Sisi Ticket (adult/child €34/21) Includes the Imperial Apartments, Sisi Museum and Silberkammer (Imperial Silver Collection) with an audio guide, as well as Schloss Schönbrunn and the Hofmobiliendepot (Imperial Furniture Collection).

Neue Burg Museums (adult/child €16/free) Includes the Neue Burg Museums' Sammlung Alter Musik Instrumente (Collection of Ancient Musical Instruments), Ephesos Museum and Hofjagd- und Rüstkammer (Arms and Armour) museum, and the Kunsthistorisches Museum Vienna.

Annual ticket Kunsthistorisches Museum Vienna (adult/child €44/25) Includes the Kunstkammer, Kunsthistorisches Museum Vienna, Neue Burg Museums, Kaiserliche Schatzkammer, Wagenburg, Schloss Ambras Innsbruck and Theatermuseum.

Schatz der Habsburger (Treasures of the Habsburgs; adult/child €22/free) Includes the Kunsthistorisches Museum Vienna, Neue Burg Museums and Kaiserliche Schatzkammer.

Masterticket (adult/child €24/free) Includes the Neue Burg Museums, Kunsthistorisches Museum Vienna and the Leopold Museum.

Die Kostbarkeiten des Kaisers (Treasures of the Emperors; adult/child €24/free) Includes the Kaiserliche Schatzkammer and Morgenarbeit (morning training sessions) at the Spanish Riding School.

Nationalbibliothek Universal-Wochenticket (€16.50) Includes entry to the Nationalbibliothek's Esperantomuseum, Globenmuseum and Papyrusmuseum, the Nationalbibliothek Prunksaal and the Literaturmuseum. Valid for seven days.

sandwiches since 1902. Choose from 22 delectable toppings incorporating primarily Austrian-sourced produce – chicken liver; smoked salmon and horseradish cream cheese; wild paprika and red pepper; egg and cucumber – on dark Viennese bread. This branch is the flagship of a now 11-strong chain in Vienna.

LE BOL — CAFE €

Map p238 (www.lebol.at; 01, Neuer Markt 14; dishes €4.50-15; 8am-11pm Mon-Sat, from 9am Sun; U Stephansplatz) French cafe Le Bol specialises in tartines (open-faced sandwiches) such as artichoke crème, basil and olive tapenade, brie with chicken and red onion, roast beef, and courgette, tomato and cabbage, along with a wide selection of baguettes, *croques madame* and *monsieur* (toasted sandwiches), and wonderful coffee and hot chocolate.

CAFÉ MOZART — CAFE €€

Map p238 (01-241 00-200; www.cafe-mozart.at; 01, Albertinaplatz 2; mains €14-32, cakes & pastries €4.50-8.50, mains €14-32; kitchen 8am-11.30pm, bar to midnight; wi-fi; U Karlsplatz) Opening to a covered terrace, 1794-established Café Mozart serves classic Viennese cakes including *Apfelstrudel* (apple strudel), *Esterhazy Torte* (layered almond cake), *Sacher Torte* (chocolate cake with apricot jam) and *Rehrücken* (chocolate-almond mousse dipped in dark chocolate). More substantial dishes span *Tafelspitz* (boiled beef) with creamed spinach potato salad to beef goulash with bread dumplings.

Breakfast is also served until 11.30am.

BIERHOF — AUSTRIAN €€

Map p238 (01-533 44 28; www.bierhof.at; 01, Haarhof 3; mains €11-25; 11.30am-10pm Mon-Sat, to 9pm Sun; wi-fi; U Herrengasse) A narrow passageway opens to a courtyard where shaded tables beneath the trees make a charming spot to dine on homemade classics like *Eiernockerl* (flour-and-egg dumplings), *Tiroler Gröstl* (pork, potatoes and bacon, topped with a fried egg), *Tiroler Leber* (liver dumplings with apple sauce and green beans) and *Wiener schnitzel* with parsley potatoes. The midweek lunch menu costs just €7.90.

★ MEINL'S RESTAURANT — INTERNATIONAL €€€

Map p238 (01-532 33 34 6000; www.meinlamgraben.at; 01, Graben 19; mains €27-39, 4-course menus €79; 8am-11pm Mon-Fri, from 9am Sat; wi-fi; U Stephansplatz) Meinl's combines cuisine of superlative quality with an unrivalled wine list and views of Graben. Creations at its high-end restaurant span calamari and white-truffle risotto, and apple-schnapps–marinated pork fillet with green beans and chanterelles. The providore, **Julius Meinl am Graben** (Map p238; 8am-7.30pm Mon-Fri, 9am-6pm Sat; U Stephansplatz), has a cafe and a sushi bar, and the cellar wine bar serves great-value lunch menus.

RESTAURANT HERRLICH — AUSTRIAN €€€

Map p238 (01-534 04-920; www.steigenberger.com; 01, Herrengasse 10; mains €14-36; noon-2.30pm Mon, noon-2.30pm & 6-10.30pm Tue-Fri, 7am-10.30pm Sat & Sun; U Herrengasse) Located inside the **Steigenberger Hotel Herrenhof**, the upmarket Herrlich focuses on a lighter style of Austrian cooking in a modern setting. It serves dishes such as Tyrolean mountain cheese ravioli with brown butter and sage, or pike perch with paprika foam and mushroom jelly on its changing, seasonal menus.

DRINKING & NIGHTLIFE

Aside from the neighbourhood's famous coffee houses, drinking venues tend to congregate around the edges of the neighbourhood, rather than in the centre, particularly the streets leading off Graben.

★ BLUE MUSTARD — COCKTAIL BAR

Map p238 (01-934 67 05; www.bluemustard.at; 01, Dorotheergasse 6-8; 5pm-2am Tue-Thu, to 4am Fri & Sat; wi-fi; U Stephansplatz) Backlit wood hand carvings of Stephansdom's Gothic windows and a wall-to-wall neon-lit map of Vienna make this one of the city's coolest bars. Sensational craft cocktails vary seasonally, and might include the Donau (absinthe, apricot schnapps, blueberry-infused gin and pineapple juice), the Sisi (Jägermeister, chocolate liqueur and cream) and the Habsburg (Goldschläger – cinnamon liqueur with gold leaf – triple sec, soda and lime).

★ CAFÉ LEOPOLD HAWELKA — COFFEE

Map p238 (www.hawelka.at; 01, Dorotheergasse 6; 8am-midnight Mon-Thu, to 1am Fri & Sat, 10am-midnight Sun; U Stephansplatz) Opened in 1939 by Leopold and Josefine Hawelka, whose son Günter and grandsons Amir and Michael still bake the house-speciality

CAKE WARS: THE SACHER TORTE

Eduard Sacher, the son of the *Sacher Torte* creator Franz Sacher, began working at Demel in 1934, bringing the original recipe and sole distribution rights with him. Between 1938 and 1963 legal battles raged between Demel and Café Sacher over the trademark and title. An out-of-court settlement gave Café Sacher the rights to the phrase 'Original Sacher Torte', and Demel the rights to decorate its torte with a triangular seal reading 'Eduard-Sacher-Torte'. Each cafe still claims to be a cut above the other; try both and decide.

Buchteln (jam-filled, sugar-dusted yeast rolls) to the family's secret recipe, this low-lit, picture-plastered coffee house is a slice of Viennese history. Artists and writers who hung out here have included Friedensreich Hundertwasser, Elias Canetti, Arthur Miller and Andy Warhol.

★LOOS AMERICAN BAR COCKTAIL BAR

Map p238 (www.loosbar.at; 01, Kärntner Durchgang 10; ⊙noon-4am; U Stephansplatz) Loos is *the* city centre spot in the Innere Stadt for a classic cocktail such as its signature dry martini, whipped up by talented mixologists. Designed by Austrian architect Adolf Loos in 1908, this tiny 27-sq-metre box (seating just 20 or so patrons) is bedecked from head to toe in onyx, marble, mahogany and polished brass, with space-enhancing mirrored walls.

★VOLKSGARTEN CLUBDISKOTHEK CLUB

Map p238 (www.volksgarten.at; 01, Burgring 1; ⊙9pm-6am Thu, from 11pm Fri & Sat Apr–mid-Sep; Tram D, 1, 2, 71 Ring/Volkstheater, U Museumsquartier, Volkstheater) Spilling onto the Volksgarten's lawns, these early-19th-century premises are split into three areas: the Wintergarten lounge bar with vintage 1950s furnishings and palms; Cortic Säulenhalle (column hall), hosting live music; and the hugely popular ClubDiskothek. Check the agenda online.

★PALMENHAUS BAR

Map p238 (☎01-533 10 33; www.palmenhaus.at; 01, Burggarten; ⊙10am-midnight Mon-Fri, from 9am Sat, 9am-11pm Sun; Tram D, 1, 2, 71 Burgring, U Karlsplatz, Museumsquartier) Housed in a beautifully restored *Jungendstil* palm house with high arched ceilings, glass walls and steel beams, looking through into the adjacent *Schmetterlinghaus* (butterfly house), the Palmenhouse opens onto a summer terrace facing the Burggarten. The relaxed ambience is ideal for a glass of wine or a coffee. DJs occasionally spin on weekend evenings.

CAFÉ SACHER COFFEE

Map p238 (www.sacher.com; 01, Philharmonikerstrasse 4; ⊙8am-midnight; Tram D, 1, 2, 71 Kärntner Ring/Oper, U Karlsplatz) With a battalion of waiters and an air of nobility, this grand cafe is celebrated for its *Sacher Torte,* a rich iced-chocolate cake with apricot jam once favoured by Emperor Franz Josef. For the full-blown experience, head to the opulent chandelier-lit interior. There's also a pavement terrace, and a 1920s-styled tearoom, Sacher Eck, next door serving the same menu.

DEMEL CAFE

Map p238 (www.demel.at; 01, Kohlmarkt 14; ⊙8am-7pm; Bus 1A, 2A Michaelerplatz, U Herrengasse, Stephansplatz) Within sight of the Hofburg, this elegant and regal cafe has a gorgeous rococo-period salon. Demel's specialities include the *Annatorte* (a calorie-bomb of cream and nougat) and the *Fächertorte* (with apples, walnuts, poppy seeds and plum jam). The window displays an ever-changing array of edible art pieces (ballerinas and manicured bonsai, for example).

KAFFEE RÖSTEREI HAWELKA COFFEE

Map p238 (www.hawelka.at; 01, Dorotheergasse 7; ⊙10am-6pm Tue-Sun; U Stephansplatz) Hawelka's headquarters in Vienna's southwest roasts beans that supply its famous Café Leopold Hawelka (p69) as well as this 2019-opened, contemporary cafe-shop with a full-length glass facade. Sip a coffee in-house on striped seating or buy beans to take away.

VILLON WINE BAR

Map p238 (www.villon.at; 01, Habsburgergasse 4; ⊙11am-11pm Mon-Sat; U Herrengasse, Stephansplatz) This 500-year-old wine cellar is sunk 16m deep into the ground. Spanning four levels, the interior is smart and modern, with light-coloured woods in the main room where you can order wine by the glass or bottle, accompanied by Parmesan cheese, bread, olives and Thun ham (a Viennese speciality).

ESTERHÁZYKELLER WINE BAR

Map p238 (☎01-533 34 82; www.esterhazykeller.at; 01, Haarhof 1; ⏲5-11pm; Ⓤ Stephansplatz, Herrengasse) Tucked in a quiet courtyard just off Kohlmarkt, this *Heurigen* (wine tavern) has an enormous rustic cellar – complete with medieval weaponry and farming tools – where excellent wine is served direct from the Esterházy Palace wine estate in Eisenstadt, as well as beer. The adjoining Esterházy Stüberl (restaurant; mains €10.90 to €26.90) opens from 11am to 11pm.

PASSAGE CLUB

Map p238 (☎01-961 66 77-0; www.club-passage.at; 01, Burgring 3, Babenberger Passage; ⏲11pm-6am Thu-Sat; 🚋D, 1, 2, 71 Burgring, Ⓤ Museumsquartier) Originally a pedestrian underpass, neon-lit Passage is the closest thing in Vienna to a megaclub. The music is loud (noise from the Ringstrasse traffic directly overhead is easily drowned out) and spans anything from early classics to house. Some nights have free admission; others incur a cover charge.

FLEDERMAUS CLUB

Map p238 (www.fledermaus.at; 01, Spiegelgasse 2; ⏲9pm-4am Wed-Mon; Ⓤ Stephansplatz) Fledermaus is among Vienna's most relaxed clubs in terms of decor and clientele. Its program runs the spectrum of musical styles from the 1950s to '90s and beyond, with each night dedicated to a particular movement or epoch. Some nights have free admission; other times there's a cover charge.

CAFÉ BRÄUNERHOF COFFEE

Map p238 (www.braeunerhof.at; 01, Stallburggasse 2; ⏲8am-10pm Mon-Sat, 10am-6pm Sun; Ⓤ Herrengasse, Stephansplatz) Little has changed in Bräunerhof from the days when Austria's seminal writer Thomas Bernhard (1931–89) frequented the premises. Classical music plays from 3pm to 6pm on weekends.

☆ ENTERTAINMENT

ÖSTERREICHISCHES FILMMUSEUM CINEMA

Map p238 (Austrian Film Museum; ☎01-533 70 54; www.filmmuseum.at; 01, Auginerstrasse 1; adult/child €10.50/6; ⏲film screenings Sep-early Jun; 🚋D, 1, 2, 71 Kärntner Ring/Oper, Ⓤ Karlsplatz) Situated inside the Albertina (p66), the Austrian Film Museum shows a range of films with and without subtitles in the original language, featuring a director, a group of directors or a certain theme from around the world in programs generally lasting a couple of weeks. Screenings are usually at 6.45pm; check the website for other times.

SHOPPING

This neighbourhood is bordered by the city's most upmarket shopping street, Graben, with a wealth of high-end fashion, accessories and homewares. Look out for generations-old establishments hidden down the side streets, including some sublime food shops.

★J&L LOBMEYR VIENNA HOMEWARES

Map p238 (www.lobmeyr.at; 01, Kärntner Strasse 26; ⏲10am-7pm Mon-Fri, to 6pm Sat; Ⓤ Stephansplatz) Reached by a beautifully ornate wrought-iron staircase, this is one of Vienna's most lavish retail experiences. The collection of Biedermeier pieces, Loos-designed sets, fine/arty glassware and porcelain on display here glitters from the lights of the chandelier-festooned atrium. Lobmeyr has been in business since 1823, when it exclusively supplied the imperial court.

★ZUCKERLWERKSTATT FOOD & DRINKS

Map p238 (www.zuckerlwerkstatt.at; 01, Herrengasse 6-8; ⏲10am-6pm Mon-Fri, 9am-5pm Sat; Ⓤ Herrengasse) 🍃 Long-lost recipes for traditional sweets and all-natural ingredients including Austrian sugar are used by this 'sugar workshop'. Its pillow-shaped striped silk candies, sugar drops, fruit jellies, lollipops, candy canes and boiled sweets are enticingly displayed in glass jars.

HOFBURG CONCERT HALLS

The Neue Hofburg's **concert halls** (Map p238; ☎01-587 25 52; www.hofburgorchester.at; 01, Heldenplatz; tickets €45-110; 🚋D, 1, 2, 71 Burgring, Ⓤ Herrengasse), the sumptuous Festsaal and Redoutensaal, are regularly used for Strauss and Mozart concerts, featuring the Hofburg Orchestra and soloists from the Staatsoper and Volksoper. Performances start at 8.30pm; tickets are available online. Seating is not allocated, so get in early to secure a good seat.

★STEIFF TOYS

Map p238 (www.steiff-galerie-wien.at; 01, Bräunerstrasse 3; ⌚10am-12.30pm & 1.30-6pm Mon-Fri, 10am-12.30pm & 1.30-5pm Sat; Ⓤ Stephansplatz) Founded in Germany in 1880, Steiff is widely regarded as the original creator of the teddy bear, which it presented at the 1902 Leipzig Toy Fair: an American businessman bought 3000, selling them under the name 'teddy bear' after US president Theodore ('Teddy') Roosevelt. Today its flagship shop is filled with adorable bears and other cuddly toys.

ROZET UND FISCHMEISTER JEWELLERY

Map p238 (www.rozetundfischmeister.at; 01, Kohlmarkt 11; ⌚10am-1pm & 2-6pm Mon-Fri, 10am-3pm Sat; Ⓤ Herrengasse) Founded in 1770, Rozet und Fischmeister supplied the imperial court, and is today run by the sixth generation of the same family. It uses time-honoured techniques to create exquisite jewellery, as well as silverware. Restoration, repairs and engraving can be arranged.

SCHELLA KANN FASHION & ACCESSORIES

Map p238 (www.schellakann.com; 01, Spiegelgasse; ⌚11am-6pm Mon-Fri, to 5pm Sat; Ⓤ Stephansplatz) Viennese women's fashion label Schella Kann shuns current trends, instead creating its own. Collections change seasonally; innovative designs have included silhouette-changing dresses, oversized coats and interchangeable fabric accessories.

BONBONS ANZINGER CHOCOLATE

Map p238 (www.bonbons-anzinger.at; 01, Tegetthoffstrasse 7; ⌚10am-6pm Mon-Sat, noon-4pm Sun; D, 1, 2, 71 Kärntner Ring/Oper, Ⓤ Karlsplatz) A jewel box of a chocolate shop, with a dazzling array of handmade truffles and pralines, Bonbons Anzinger has a tiny tearoom serving coffee, tea and hot chocolate, with a chocolate on the side. Its speciality is the *Mozartkugel*, a dark-chocolate–covered ball filled with pistachio marzipan and nougat.

DOROTHEUM ANTIQUES

Map p238 (www.dorotheum.com; 01, Dorotheergasse 17; ⌚10am-6pm Mon-Fri, 9am-5pm Sat; Ⓤ Stephansplatz) The Dorotheum is among the largest auction houses in Europe, and for the casual visitor it's more like a museum, housing everything from antique toys and tableware to autographs, antique guns and, above all, lots of quality paintings. You can bid at the regular auctions held here; otherwise just drop by and enjoy browsing.

LANZ CLOTHING

Map p238 (www.lanztrachten.at; 01, Kärntner Strasse; ⌚10am-6.30pm Mon-Fri, to 6pm Sat; Ⓤ Stephansplatz) *Tracht* (traditional Austrian clothing) fills the racks at Lanz. Browse for *Lederhosen*, *Dirndls* (women's traditional dress) and adorable kids' outfits. A tailoring service is available.

GMUNDNER CERAMICS

Map p238 (www.gmundner.at; 01, Bräunerstrasse 3; ⌚10am-6.30pm Mon-Fri, to 5pm Sat; Ⓤ Stephansplatz) Gmundner has been manufacturing ceramics by hand since 1492, and it's estimated over 50% of Austrian households own at least one piece. International shipping can be arranged.

OBERLAA FOOD & DRINKS

Map p238 (www.oberlaa-wien.at; 01, Neuer Markt 16; ⌚8am-8pm; Ⓤ Stephansplatz) This much-loved confectioner is famed for its 'LaaKronen' – brightly coloured macarons in flavours like pistachio, lemon and strawberry. It also sells chocolates, loose-leaf teas and homemade ice creams in summer. There are nine other branches around town.

ÖSTERREICHISCHE WERKSTÄTTEN GLASS

Map p238 (www.austrianarts.com; 01, Kärntner Strasse 6; ⌚10am-7pm Mon-Fri, to 6pm Sat; Ⓤ Stephansplatz) Established in 1945, Österreichische Werkstätten sells work made by Austrian companies and designed by Austrian designers. Look out for Kisslinger, a family glassware company since 1946, with Klimt- and Hundertwasser-styled designs; and the world-renowned Riedel wine glasses.

FREYTAG & BERNDT BOOKS

Map p238 (www.freytagberndt.com; 01, Wallnerstrasse 3; ⌚9.30am-6.30pm Mon-Fri, to 6pm Sat; 1A, 2A Michaelerplatz, Ⓤ Herrengasse) The ultimate place to inspire wanderlust, Freytag & Berndt has an extensive collection of guides and maps (many in English) to Vienna, Austria (including some superbly detailed walking maps) and destinations around the globe.

UNITED NUDE SHOES

Map p238 (www.unitednude-shop.at; 01, Herrengasse 6-8; ⌚10am-7pm Mon-Fri, to 6pm Sat; Ⓤ Herrengasse) Founded by Rem D Koolhaas (the nephew of star Dutch architect Rem Koolhaus) and seventh-generation English shoemaker Galahad Clark (of Clarks shoes), United Nude creates some of the most unusual (and postmodern) shoes you will ever see, much less wear.

Stephansdom & the Historic Centre

Neighbourhood Top Five

❶ **Stephansdom** (p75) Marvelling at the intricate details of the city's most famous landmark and Austria's best-known Gothic cathedral.

❷ **Haus der Musik** (p78) Conducting your own virtual orchestra and engaging with other interactive exhibits at this innovative music museum.

❸ **Literaturmuseum** (p77) Getting acquainted with Austria's literary luminaries and their seminal works, from the 18th century to the present day, at this museum dedicated to Austrian writing.

❹ **Museum Judenplatz** (p78) Viewing the excavated remains of the medieval synagogue that stood on this site and learning about Vienna's Jewish history.

❺ **Mozarthaus Vienna** (p77) Visiting Wolfgang Amadeus Mozart's only surviving Viennese home, where he composed *The Marriage of Figaro* during his 2½-year residency.

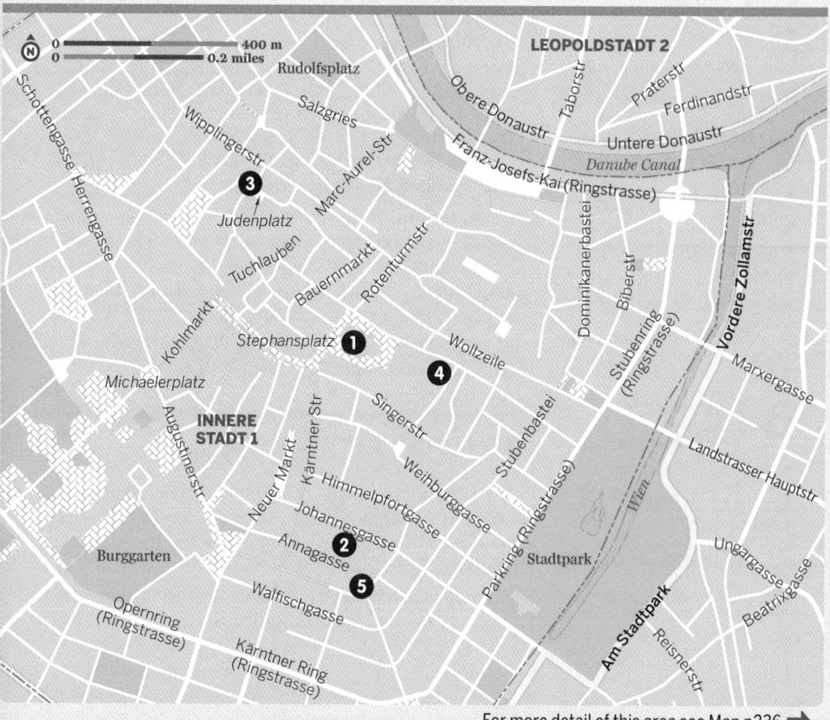

For more detail of this area see Map p236

Lonely Planet's Top Tip

The U-Bahn is handy for connecting to outlying neighbourhoods and crossing the historic centre, and the Ringstrasse trams are good for circumnavigating it, but public transport is limited within the centre itself. Taxis are plentiful but costly due to the plethora of one-way streets and slow-moving traffic, so it's best to explore on foot. Nothing is more than a 10- to 20-minute walk away, and the terrain is largely flat, with wide, smooth footpaths and pedestrian areas.

Best Places to Eat

- Plachutta (p83)
- Tian (p83)
- Griechenbeisl (p83)
- Wrenkh (p82)

For reviews, see p82.

Best Places to Drink

- Kruger's American Bar (p84)
- Needle Vinyl Bar (p84)
- Zwölf Apostelkeller (p84)
- Kleines Café (p84)

For reviews, see p84.

Best Places to Shop

- Wald & Wiese (p86)
- Schau Schau (p87)
- Altmann & Kühne (p87)

For reviews, see p86.

Explore Stephansdom & the Historic Centre

Vienna's entire Innere Stadt (inner city) is compact and easily walked – especially its core, the Stephansdom (p75) and historic-centre neighbourhood. The city's monumental cathedral makes an ideal starting point; plan to spend half a day exploring it in its entirety, including scaling the south tower's 343 steps for sweeping views over the Innere Stadt's rooftops.

After lunch, head to the Haus der Musik (p78) and Mozarthaus Vienna (p77) to discover the Austrian capital's incredible musical heritage. Other key sights here include the Museum Judenplatz (p78). Keep Vienna's iconic coffee houses on your radar along the way to rest up, rejuvenate and relax into Viennese life.

The historic centre gets very crowded in summer, making early evening one of the best times to stroll around and soak up the atmosphere. After dinner, late on a warm night, is ideal for a romantic stroll through the illuminated streets.

Local Life

Street Life Walking the historic centre's main streets in summer can sometimes give you the feeling of being on an ant trail. Take local side lanes like Blutgasse and duck into squares and courtyards along the way. Heiligenkreuzerhof (p81) is one of the prettiest. Streets around it, such as Sonnenfelsgasse, Schönlaterngasse and Dr-Ignaz-Seipel-Platz (p81), are also quieter parts of town, as are areas around Ruprechtskirche (p78), Maria am Gestade (p78), and the area between Judenplatz and Am Hof.

Canal Life In summer join locals relaxing along the banks of the Danube Canal, where you'll also find bars, restaurants and the city's oldest jazz club, Jazzland (p86).

Nightlife The historic centre is beautiful when lit up at night. Soak it up the way the Viennese do: on a leisurely evening stroll.

Getting There & Away

U-Bahn Stephansplatz (U1, U3) and Schwedenplatz (U1, U4) – and to a lesser extent Stubentor (U3), Herrengasse (U3) and Karlsplatz (U1, U2, U4) – are the main stops.

Tram Schwedenplatz (1, 2) and Kärntner Ring/Oper (1, 2, D, 71) are the most convenient stops.

MORFON MEDIA/SHUTTERSTOCK ©

TOP SIGHT
STEPHANSDOM

Soaring above the surrounding cityscape, Vienna's immense, filagreed Gothic masterpiece Stephansdom (St Stephen's Cathedral) – or Steffl (Little Stephen) as it's locally (and ironically) dubbed – symbolises the city like no other building. Highlights include the cathedral's spectacular main nave with its Gothic stone pulpit and baroque high altar, its *Katakomben* (catacombs), two towers and the cathedral treasures.

History

A church has stood on this site since the 12th century, reminders of which today are the Romanesque **Riesentor** (Giant Gate) and **Heidentürme** (Towers of the Heathens) at the entrance and above it. In 1359, at the behest of Habsburg Duke Rudolf IV, Stephansdom began receiving its Gothic makeover and Rudolf earned himself the epithet 'The Founder' by laying the first stone in the reconstruction.

Stephansdom: Inside & Out

From outside the cathedral, the first thing that will strike you is the glorious **tiled roof**, with its dazzling row of chevrons on one end and the Austrian eagle on the other.

Inside the cathedral, the magnificent Gothic **stone pulpit** takes pride of place, fashioned in 1515 by Anton Pilgrim (his likeness appears in the stonework). The **pulpit railing** is adorned with salamanders and toads, symbolising the battle of good against evil.

At the far end of the main nave, the baroque **high altar** shows the stoning of St Stephen. The chancel to its left has the winged Wiener Neustadt **altarpiece**, dating from 1447; the

DON'T MISS

- Main nave
- Gothic stone pulpit
- Baroque high altar
- Cathedral south tower
- Cathedral Pummerin (north tower bell)
- *Katakomben* (catacombs)

PRACTICALITIES

- St Stephen's Cathedral
- Map p236, C5
- www.stephanskirche.at
- 01, Stephansplatz
- adult/child incl audio guide or guided tour €6/2.50, all-inclusive ticket €14.90/3.90
- 9-11.30am & 1-4.30pm Mon-Sat, 1-4.30pm Sun, English tours 10.30am Mon-Sat
- U Stephansplatz

THE FIRST CHURCH

The first church built on the site of the cathedral was a Romanesque church consecrated in 1147. It was remodelled completely and consecrated again in 1263. Entering the cathedral today, you pass though the Riesentor, which dates from the early 13th century. The Heidentürme rise above this main portal. The name 'Riesentor', derived from the old German *rīsanan* (rising), reflects its deep, inward-sloping funnel shape.

Stephansdom is an unlikely El Dorado for animal lovers. The Riesentor is packed with basilisks as well as fearsome dragons and lions. Friedrich III's tomb (1513) has some rather hideous creatures (serpents, ugly eagles, lions and a goblin) on top, but you can't get close enough to see these. The zoological highlight, however, is the pulpit, with salamanders and toads, topped off by the pug-faced Fearless Dog, there to ward off evil.

right chancel has the Renaissance red-marble tomb of Friedrich III. Under his guidance the city became a bishopric (and the church a cathedral) in 1469.

Stephansdom Katakomben

The area around the cathedral was originally a graveyard. But with plague and influenza epidemics striking Europe in the 1730s, Karl VI ordered the graveyard be closed and henceforth Vienna buried its dead beneath Stephansdom in the Katakomben. Today, they contain the remains of countless victims, which are kept in a mass grave and a bone house. Also on display are rows of urns containing the internal organs of the Habsburgs. One of the many privileges of being a Habsburg was to be dismembered and dispersed after death: their hearts are in the Augustinerkirche in the Hofburg and the rest of their bodies are in the Kapuzinergruft. Entrance is allowed only on a tour.

Cathedral South Tower

When the foundation stone for the **south tower** (Südturm; Map p236; www.stephanskirche.at; 01, Stephansplatz; adult/child €5/2; ⏲9am-5.30pm; Ⓤ Stephansplatz) was laid in 1359, Rudolf IV is said to have used a trowel and spade made of silver. Two towers were originally envisaged here, but the Südturm grew so high that little space remained for the second; in 1433 the tower reached its final height of 136.7m. Today you can ascend the 343 steps to a small platform for one of Vienna's most spectacular views over the rooftops of the Innere Stadt; you don't need a tour ticket for the main nave.

Cathedral Pummerin

Weighing 21 tonnes, the **Pummerin** (Boomer Bell; Map p236; www.stephanskirche.at; 01, Stephansplatz; adult/child €6/2.50; ⏲9am-5.30pm; Ⓤ Stephansplatz) is Austria's largest bell and was installed in the 68.3m-high **north tower** in 1957. While the rest of the cathedral was rising up in its new Gothic format, work was interrupted on this tower due to a lack of cash and the fading allure of Gothic architecture. It's accessible only by lift (elevator); no need for a tour ticket for the main nave.

Dom- & Diözesanmuseum

The **Dom- & Diözesanmuseum** (Cathedral & Diocesan Museum of Vienna; Map p236; www.dommuseum.at; 01, Stephansplatz 6; adult/child €8/3; ⏲10am-6pm Wed & Fri-Sun, to 8pm Thu; Ⓤ Stephansplatz) is a treasure trove of religious art pieces spanning a period of more than 1000 years. Among the collection's extraordinary exhibits are the earliest European portrait – of Duke Rudolf IV (1360) – and two Syrian glass vessels (1280–1310), thought to be among the oldest glass bottles in the world.

SIGHTS

Stephansdom sits at the heart of this central neighbourhood, with sights fanning out all around it.

STEPHANSDOM CATHEDRAL

See p75.

★MOZARTHAUS VIENNA MUSEUM

Map p236 (☎01-512 17 91; www.mozarthausvienna.at; 01, Domgasse 5; adult/child €11/4.50, incl Haus der Musik €18/8; ⏰10am-7pm; ⓊStephansplatz) The great composer spent close to three happy and productive years at this residence between 1784 and 1787. Exhibits include copies of music scores and paintings, while free audio guides re-create the story of his time here. Mozart spent a total of 11 years in Vienna, changing residences frequently and sometimes setting up his home outside the Ringstrasse in the cheaper *Vorstädte* (inner suburbs) when his finances were tight. Of these, the Mozarthaus Vienna is the only one that survives.

The exhibition begins on the top floor, overlooking a narrow, closed-in inner courtyard, and covers the society of the late 18th century, providing asides into prominent figures in the court and Mozart's life, such as the Freemasons (to whom he dedicated a number of pieces). Coverage of Mozart's vices – his womanising, gambling and ability to waste excessive amounts of money – gives it an edge.

Retaining its original stucco ceilings, the middle floor concentrates on Mozart's music and his musical influences. It was in this house that he penned *The Marriage of Figaro*. A surreal holographic performance of scenes from *The Magic Flute* is in another room. The final floor has Mozart's bedroom and a few pieces of period furniture in glass cases to give a feel for the era.

★LITERATURMUSEUM MUSEUM

Map p236 (Literature Museum; www.onb.ac.at/museen/literaturmuseum; 01, Grillparzerhaus, Johannesgasse 6; adult/child €7/free; ⏰10am-6pm Tue, Wed & Fri-Sun, to 9pm Thu; ⓊStephansplatz) An 1844 Biedermeier building houses Austria's literature museum, which opened in 2015. It contains books, manuscripts, letters, photos, illustrations and personal effects (such as desks) from the country's most seminal authors, playwrights and poets, from the 18th century to the present day. The celebrated writers represented include Günther Anders, Ingeborg Bachmann, Peter Handke, Robert Menasse, Herta Müller and Hilde Spiel. You can also hear readings and quotes from the museum's 550 hours of audio recordings. Information leaflets are available in English.

GUIDED TOURS & MUSIC IN VIENNA'S CATHEDRAL

Multilingual audio-guide tour The most common option to take in the cathedral interior. Audio guides (adult/child cost €6/2.50) are available from 9am to 11.30am and 1pm to 4.30pm Monday to Saturday, and from 1pm to 4.30pm Sunday.

Guided tours in English & German English-language tours explain the background of the cathedral and walk you through its main interior features. The 30-minute tours leave at 10.30am Monday to Saturday (adult/child €6/2.50). The same guided tours in German leave at 3pm daily.

All-inclusive tour All-inclusive tours are partly with an audio guide, partly with a tour guide (adult/child €14.90/3.90). Tours take in the cathedral interior, *Katakomben*, south tower and north tower. Children aren't allowed to do it alone. Total time is 2½ hours; they're available from 9am to 5.30pm daily.

Evening roof-walk tours in English and German These 75-minute tours (adult/child €11/5) depart at 7pm every Saturday from July to September (weather permitting) and feature a brisk climb to the top of the south tower and a walk along the exterior rain gutter with close-up views of the roof and panoramas of the city.

Special events & Mass The website www.dommusik-wien.at has a program of special concerts and events, but the 10.15am Mass on Sundays (9.30am during the school holidays around July and August) is something special, as it's conducted with full choral accompaniment. Tickets are available online at www.kunstkultur.com.

HOLOCAUST-DENKMAL MEMORIAL

Map p236 (01, Judenplatz; UStephansplatz) Deliberately reminiscent of a bunker, the steel-and-concrete Holocaust-Denkmal (2000) is a memorial to the 65,000 Austrian Jews who perished in the Holocaust. Designed by British sculptor Rachel Whiteread, this 'nameless library' depicts books with their spines facing inwards, representing the lost knowledge of the Holocaust victims. It's inscribed with the names of Austrian concentration camps where the victims were murdered.

MARIA AM GESTADE CHURCH

Map p236 (☎01-533 95 94-0; www.redemptoristen.at; 01, Salvatorgasse 12; ⊙8am-7pm; UStephansplatz) Originally a wooden church built by Danube boatsmen around 880, Maria am Gestade (Maria on the Riverbank) was built in stone between 1394 and 1414, making it one of Vienna's few surviving Gothic structures. Compensating for steep ground, the nave was built narrower than the choir and with a slight bend. In 1805 Napoleon used it to store weapons and horses. The interior has a high vaulted Gothic ceiling and pretty stained glass behind a winged Gothic altar.

RUPRECHTSKIRCHE CHURCH

Map p236 (St Rupert's Church; ☎01-535 60 03; www.ruprechtskirche.at; 01, Ruprechtsplatz 1; ⊙10am-noon Mon & Tue, 10am-noon & 3-5pm Wed, 10am-5pm Thu & Fri, 11.30am-3.30pm Sat; 🚊1, 2 Schwedenplatz, USchwedenplatz) Vienna's oldest church is believed to date from 740. The lower levels of the tower date from the 12th century, the roof from the 15th century and the iron Renaissance door on the west side from the 1530s. In summer, its stone walls are clad in ivy. The interior is sleek and worth a quick viewing, with a Romanesque nave from the 12th century. Note that there are no public visiting hours on Sunday due to religious services.

★**MUSEUM JUDENPLATZ** MUSEUM

Map p236 (☎01-535 04 31; www.jmw.at; 01, Judenplatz 8; adult/child incl Jüdisches Museum €12/free; ⊙10am-6pm Sun-Thu, to 5pm Fri; 👪; UStephansplatz, Herrengasse) The main focus of Museum Judenplatz is on the excavated remains of a medieval synagogue

TOP SIGHT
HAUS DER MUSIK

The Haus der Musik explains the world of sound and music to adults and children alike in an amusing and interactive way (in English and German).

Floor 1 hosts the **Museum of the Vienna Philharmonic**. Find out about the history of the orchestra's famous New Year's concerts and listen to recent concert highlights. You can even compose your own waltz by rolling dice.

Floor 2, called the **Sonosphere**, has plenty of engaging instruments, interactive toys and touch screens. Among the activities here, you can experience sound production with oversized instruments such as a walk-in organ pipe.

Floor 3 covers classical composers who lived and worked in Vienna, including Mozart, Beethoven, Schubert, Haydn, Johann Strauss II, and Mahler. Each has their own dedicated room with music scores, personal documents and images. It's polished off with an amusing interactive video in which you conduct the Vienna Philharmonic Orchestra.

Floor 4 has the so-called **Virtostage**, in which your own body language and movements shape the music to create an opera.

DON'T MISS

- Sonosphere
- Virtual conductor
- The Vienna Philharmonic Orchestra concert footage

PRACTICALITIES

- Map p236, C7
- www.hausdermusik.com
- 01, Seilerstätte 30
- adult/child €13/6, incl Mozarthaus Vienna €18/8
- ⊙10am-10pm
- 👪
- 🚊2, 71 Schwarzenbergplatz, UKarlsplatz

that once stood on Judenplatz, with a film and numerous exhibits to elucidate Vienna's Jewish history. It was built in the Middle Ages, but Duke Albrecht V's 'hatred and misconception' led him to order its destruction in 1421. The basic outline of the synagogue can still be seen here. Combined tickets to the Museum Judenplatz and Jüdisches Museum (p67) are valid for four days.

STADTTEMPEL SYNAGOGUE

Map p236 (☎01-531 04-0; www.ikg-wien.at; 01, Seitenstettengasse 4; tours adult/child €5/free; ⊙guided tours 11.30am & 2pm Mon-Thu Apr-Oct, 11.30am Mon-Thu Nov-Mar; 🚊1, 2 Schwedenplatz, ⓤSchwedenplatz) Vienna's main synagogue, seating 500 people, was completed in 1826, after *Toleranzpatent* reforms by Joseph II in the 1780s granted rights to Vienna's Jews to practise their religion. This paved the way for improved standing for Jews and brought a rise in fortunes. Built in an exquisite Biedermeier style, the main prayer room is flanked by 12 ionic columns and is capped by a cupola. Security is tight; you'll need your passport to gain entry.

When it was built, only Catholic places of worship were allowed to front major streets, so the Stadttempel was built inside an apartment complex – because of this, it was the sole survivor of 94 synagogues in Vienna following the November Pogroms of 1938.

FRANZISKANERKIRCHE CHURCH

Map p236 (☎01-512 45 78 11; http://wien.franziskaner.at; 01, Franziskanerplatz; ⊙7am-8pm; ⓤStephansplatz) This Franciscan church is a glorious architectural deception. Outside it exudes the hallmarks of an early-17th-century Renaissance style, yet inside it is awash with gold and marble decorative features from the baroque era (about 100 years later). The high altar takes the form of a triumphal arch; hidden behind this is Vienna's oldest organ (1642), built by Johann Wöckherl. **Concerts** (€6) lasting 45 minutes take place at 2pm on Fridays from April to October.

UHREN MUSEUM MUSEUM

Map p236 (Clock Museum; ☎01-533 22 65; www.wienmuseum.at; 01, Schulhof 2; adult/child €7/free; ⊙10am-6pm Tue-Sun; ⓤHerrengasse) Opened in 1921 in the Hafenhaus, one of Vienna's oldest buildings, the municipal Uhren Museum's three floors are weighed down with an astounding 21,200 clocks and watches, ranging from the 15th century to a 1992 computer clock, with 700 on display at any one time. The collection of Biedermeier and belle époque models will, for most, steal the show. The peace and quiet is shattered at the striking of each hour.

PETERSKIRCHE CHURCH

Map p236 (Church of St Peter; www.peterskirche.at; 01, Petersplatz; ⊙7am-8pm Mon-Fri, 9am-9pm Sat & Sun; ⓤStephansplatz) One of the city's prettiest churches, the Peterskirche was built in 1733 according to plans of the celebrated baroque architect Johann Lukas von Hildebrandt. Interior highlights that make a visit highly worthwhile include a fresco on the dome painted by Johann Michael Rottmayr and a golden altar depicting the martyrdom of St John of Nepomuk. Regular organ recitals and concerts are also held here; check the program online.

NEIDHART-FRESKEN MUSEUM

Map p236 (☎01-535 90 65; www.wienmuseum.at; 01, Tuchlauben 19; adult/child €5/free; ⊙10am-1pm & 2-6pm Tue-Sun; ⓤStephansplatz) An unassuming house on Tuchlauben hides a remarkable decoration: the oldest extant secular frescos in Vienna. The small frescos, dating from 1407, tell the story of the minstrel Neidhart von Reuental (1180–1240), as well as life in the Middle Ages, in lively scenes. They were discovered when the house was set to be redeveloped into apartments in 1979. The artworks are in superb condition considering their age.

GRIECHENKIRCHE ZUR HEILIGEN DREIFALTIGKEIT CHURCH

Map p236 (Holy Trinity Greek Orthodox Church; ☎01-533 38 89; www.metropolisvonaustria.at; 01, Fleischmarkt 13; ⊙10am-3pm; 🚊1, 2 Schwedenplatz, ⓤSchwedenplatz) Built in 1861 at the behest of the Greek community, the interior of Vienna's main Greek Orthodox church is a glittering blaze of Byzantine designs. A ceiling fresco depicting the prophets surrounded by swirls of gold is augmented by a high altar of 13 panels – each of which features sparkling gilding – and a doorway to the inner sanctum.

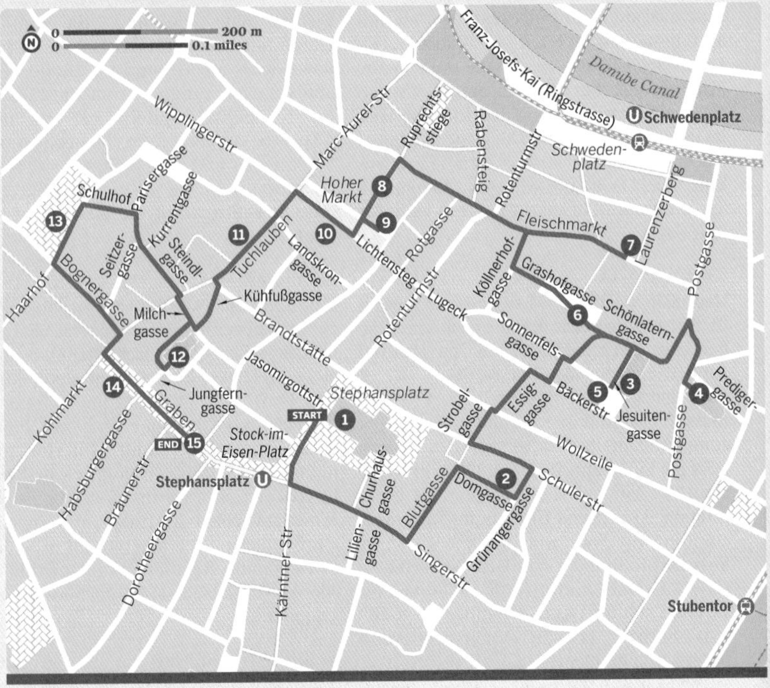

Neighbourhood Walk
The Historic Centre

START STEPHANSDOM
FINISH GRABEN
LENGTH 3KM; 90 MINUTES TO FIVE HOURS

Begin at Vienna's signature cathedral, **1 Stephansdom** (p75). After following a small section of Kärntner Strasse, you'll wind through the atmospheric backstreets to **2 Mozarthaus Vienna** (p77), where the great composer lived for almost three years.

A series of narrow lanes leads you down towards two fine baroque churches. The interior of the **3 Jesuitenkirche** (p81) is pure deception, with frescos creating the illusion of a dome, while the 1634 **4 Dominikanerkirche** (p81) is Vienna's finest reminder of the early baroque period of church building. The Jesuitenkirche is opposite the **5 Österreichische Akademie der Wissenschaften** (p81), housed in a university building dating from 1755.

During daylight hours, you can enter **6 Heiligenkreuzerhof** from the eastern side (at night time, enter it from Grasshofgasse). At Christmas, this lovely, tranquil courtyard is filled with traditional decorations. Busy **7 Fleischmarkt** (p81) is the heart of the traditional Greek quarter of Vienna, where the Greek merchants settled from the 18th century. Climb the stairs and enter the lively **8 Judengasse**, the centre of the traditional Jewish quarter. These days, Hoher Markt – Vienna's oldest square – is a busy commercial street. Highlights here include the art-nouveau **9 Ankeruhr**, a mechanical clock with historic figures marking the time as they pass over the clock face and the **10 Römer Museum** (p82), Roman ruins dating from the 1st to the 5th century. You'll then pass the remarkable **11 Neidhart-Fresken** (p79) mural and reach the most impressive church this side of Stephansdom, the **12 Peterskirche** (p79), with a golden altar.

Northwest of here, **13 Am Hof** (p81) is spiked by an impressive Mariensäule column. As you walk along Graben back towards Stephansplatz, pop into **14 Adolf Loos' Public Toilets** (p67), replete with mahogany-panelled stalls and exquisite tiling, then admire the 1693 gilded baroque **15 Pestsäule memorial** to Vienna's 75,000 plague victims.

MONUMENT TO THE VICTIMS OF FASCISM — MONUMENT

Map p236 (01, Morzinplatz; 1, 2 Schwedenplatz, U Schwedenplatz) On the site of the former Gestapo headquarters during the Nazi era at **Morzinplatz** (Map p236; 01; 1, 2 Schwedenplatz, U Schwedenplatz), this 1985 monument features the Star of David and the pink triangle, representing the Jewish and homosexual victims of the Nazis.

AM HOF — SQUARE

Map p236 (01; U Herrengasse) Before moving to the site of the Hofburg in the late 13th century, the ruling family the Babenbergs resided on this large square. Rising up in the centre is the **Mariensäule** (Mary's Column; 1667), dedicated to the Virgin Mary. Look out, too, for house **No 11**, where a gold-painted cannonball is a reminder of the 1683 Turkish siege. The former Jesuit monastery Kirche Am Hof (p81) occupies the southeast side; it's now the Croatian Catholic Church.

FLEISCHMARKT — STREET

Map p236 (01, Fleischmarkt; U Stephansplatz) Greek merchants settled around Fleischmarkt from about 1700, which gradually became known as the Griechenviertel (Greek quarter). Today it has some attractive art nouveau buildings, such as **No 14**, built by F Dehm and F Olbricht (1899), **No 7** (Max Kropf; 1899) – the childhood home of Hollywood film director Billy Wilder from 1914 to 1924 – and **Nos 1 & 3** (1910). The favourite meeting place of the Greek community was the Griechenbeisl (p83), Vienna's oldest *Beisl* (small tavern or restaurant) dating to 1447.

JESUITENKIRCHE — CHURCH

Map p236 (01-512 52 32-0; www.jesuitenkirche-wien.at; 01, Dr-Ignaz-Seipel-Platz 1; 7am-7pm Mon-Sat, 8am-7pm Sun; U Stephansplatz, Stubentor) Opposite **Dr-Ignaz-Seipel-Platz** (Map p236; 01; U Stephansplatz) is the Jesuitenkirche, formerly the university church, which dates from 1627. In 1703 this church received a baroque makeover by the Italian architect and painter Andrea Pozzo (1642–1709), who created its startling trompe-l'œ dome and other ceiling frescos. Walk beyond the 'dome' to visually destroy Pozzo's illusion. The **crypt** is the resting place of Austrian ethicist and author Johannes Schasching SJ (1917–2013); it's open from 2pm to 7pm on Sundays from September to July.

ÖSTERREICHISCHE AKADEMIE DER WISSENSCHAFTEN — HISTORIC BUILDING

Map p236 (Austrian Academy of Sciences; 01-515 81-0; www.oeaw.ac.at; 01, Dr-Ignaz-Seipel-Platz 2; 9am-5pm Mon-Fri; U Stubentor) FREE The Austrian Academy of Sciences opens to the public only for events, such as German-language seminars on the role of women in journalism on the eve of WWII. You can, however, visit the building it's housed in, the attractive **Alte-Uni** (Old Uni). Designed by Jean Nicolas Jadot de Ville-Issey and completed in 1755, it incorporates an ornate **Festsaal** (ceremonial hall) with elaborate ceiling frescos by Gregorio Guglielmi.

KIRCHE AM HOF — CHURCH

Map p236 (01-533 83 94; www.hkm-wien.at; 01, Am Hof; 8am-noon & 4-6pm Mon-Sat, 4-6pm Sun; U Herrengasse) Now the Croatian Catholic Church, this former Jesuit monastery on the southeast side of Am Hof (p81) has a baroque facade adapted from its fire-damaged Gothic predecessor. The hugely expansive nave is lined with white pillars and topped with gold badges. It was here in 1806 that a royal herald announced the end of the Holy Roman Empire, which had been ruled by the Habsburgs for about 500 years. Mass is held in Croatian. Opening hours can vary.

POSTSPARKASSE — MUSEUM

Map p236 (www.ottowagner.com; 01, Georg-Coch-Platz 2; 10am-5pm Mon-Fri; 1, 2 Schwedenplatz, U Schwedenplatz) FREE The marble-cased and metal-'studded' Post Office Savings Bank building is the *Jugendstil* (Art Nouveau) work of Otto Wagner, who oversaw its construction between 1904 and 1906, and again from 1910 to 1912. You can explore the back section of the building, where there's also a small **museum** with temporary exhibitions on design and a video section on the history of the building.

DOMINIKANERKIRCHE — CHURCH

Map p236 (Dominican Church; 01-512 91 74; 01, Postgasse 4; 7am-7pm; U Stubentor) Vienna's oldest baroque church (consecrated in 1634) is largely the work of Italian architects and artisans, with a spacious interior adorned with white stucco and frescos. The Dominicans first came to Vienna in 1226, when Leopold VI of Babenberg invited them to settle, but their earliest church burned down less than 50 years later. Its Gothic replacement was dismantled during the first Turkish siege in 1529 and its stone used to fortify the city walls.

DOKUMENTATIONSARCHIV DES ÖSTERREICHISCHEN WIDERSTANDES — MUSEUM

Map p236 (Documentation Centre of Austrian Resistance; ☎01-228 94 69-319; www.doew.at; 01, Wipplingerstrasse 5-8; ⏱9am-5pm Mon-Wed & Fri, to 7pm Thu; Ⓤ Stephansplatz) **FREE** Housed in the Altes Rathaus (Old City Hall), this centre documents the little-known antifascist resistance force that operated during the Nazi regime; some 2700 resistance fighters were executed by the Nazis and thousands more sent to concentration camps. The exhibition gives in-depth analysis of the Nazi doctrines on homosexuality, 'unworthy' citizens, concentration camps and forced labour, with photos and memorabilia detailing the time before and after the *Anschluss* (annexation).

RÖMER MUSEUM — MUSEUM

Map p236 (☎01-535 56 06; www.wienmuseum.at; 01, Hoher Markt 3; adult/child €7/free; ⏱9am-6pm Tue-Sun; Ⓤ Stephansplatz) This small expanse of Roman ruins dating from the 1st to the 5th century CE is thought to be part of the officers' quarters of the Roman legion camp at Vindobona. You can see crumbled walls, tiled floors and a small exhibition of artefacts here, along with a 3D film with English subtitles.

EATING

For a truly authentic Viennese experience, head to a *Beisl* (a small tavern, like a bistro pub). Those on the eastern fringes of the historic centre, and on and around Wollzeile and Himmelpfortgasse, offer the most local experience.

SIMPLY RAW BAKERY — VEGAN €

Map p236 (www.simplyrawbakery.at; 01, Drahtgasse 2; dishes €7-12; ⏱9am-6pm Mon-Sat; Wi-Fi; vegetarian; Ⓤ Herrengasse) At Simply Raw, superfoods, nuts, seeds, fruit, veggies and herbs are organic, everything is vegan, and nothing is cooked above 42°C to preserve the vitamin content. The vintage-style black-and-cream floor tiles, chandelier and striped feature wall form a charming backdrop for dishes like banana bread with homemade hazelnut-and-cocoa spread, avocado cake with vegan sour cream, and pumpkin and poppy-seed tart.

ZANONI & ZANONI — GELATO €

Map p236 (www.zanoni.co.at; 01, Lugeck 7; ice cream per 1/2/3/4 scoops €1.30/2.30/3.20/3.90; ⏱7.30am-midnight; Ⓤ Stephansplatz) Opening to a vast summer terrace, this Italian gelateria and pasticceria has 30 seasonal varieties of gelato, such as vanilla–poppy seed, blueberry–ricotta, strawberry and lemon, *biscotto*, tiramisu, and chocolate and apricot. It also has vegan ice creams, frozen yoghurts and diabetic-friendly dishes, including crêpes.

★ WRENKH — BISTRO €€

Map p236 (☎01-533 15 26; www.wrenkh-wien.at; 01, Bauernmarkt 10; mains €11.50-30; ⏱11am-10pm Mon-Sat; vegetarian; Ⓤ Stephansplatz) Wrenkh specialises in vegetables, like lentils in white-wine sauce with bread dumplings, roast sweet potato stuffed with goat's cheese, and pumpkin soufflé with pistachio pesto. It also creates some superb fish-based dishes (grilled mountain-stream trout with smoked-garlic potato salad) and meat options (dry-aged rib-eye with miso and aubergine crème). On weekdays, bargain-priced two-/three-course lunch menus cost €10.50/11.50.

BREZL GWÖLB — AUSTRIAN €€

Map p236 (☎01-533 88 11; www.brezl.at; 01, Ledererhof 9; mains €11-21.50; ⏱11.30am-midnight; Ⓤ Herrengasse) Hidden down an alley near Freyung, Brezl Gwölb has won a loyal following for its winningly fresh Austrian home cooking. Atmospherically lit by candles, with classical music playing in the background, the crypt-like cellar magics you back in time with its carvings, brick arches, wrought-iron lanterns and alcoves. No wonder the place overflows with regulars.

FIGLMÜLLER — AUSTRIAN €€

Map p236 (☎01-512 61 77; www.figlmueller.at; 01, Wollzeile 5; mains €13-20.50; ⏱11am-9.30pm; Wi-Fi; Ⓤ Stephansplatz) Vienna would simply be at a loss without Figlmüller. This famous *Beisl* has a rural decor and some of the biggest (on average 30cm in diameter) and best schnitzels in the business. Wine is from the owner's vineyard, but no beer is served. Its popularity has spawned a second location nearby on **Bäckerstrasse** (Map p236; ☎01-512 17 60; www.figlmueller.at; 01, Bäckerstrasse 6;

mains €13.50-22; 11am-9.30pm; Stephansplatz) with a wider menu (and drinks list).

HUTH GASTWIRTSCHAFT AUSTRIAN €€

Map p236 (01-513 56 44; www.zum-huth.at; 01, Schellinggasse 5; mains €12.90-18.90; noon-11pm; 2 Weihburggasse) One of several local neo-*Beisln* in this under-the-radar part of Innere Stadt, Huth serves superb Viennese classics such as Wiener schnitzel with cranberry sauce and parsley potatoes, *Selchfleisch* (smoked pork with sauerkraut) and desserts including *Topfenstrudel* (quark-filled strudel) in a high-ceilinged main dining room, vaulted brick cellar and a summer terrace.

ZUM SCHWARZEN KAMEEL EUROPEAN €€

Map p236 (01-533 81 25 11; www.kameel.at; 01, Bognergasse 5; restaurant mains €23.50-39, 5-course dinner menu €69, patisserie dishes €1.50-6.50; restaurant noon-2.30pm & 6-11pm daily, deli & patisserie 8am-8pm Mon-Sat; ; Herrengasse) Zum Schwarzen Kameel is an eclectic deli/patisserie/highbrow-wine-bar hybrid. Above all, it's worth a visit for the inventive cuisine in its wood-panelled upstairs restaurant: grilled lobster with truffled pea ragout, Styrian chicken with saffron risotto, or steak stuffed with blue cheese and grappa-soaked raisins served with roast artichokes. Downstairs, the patisserie serves open-faced sandwiches and steaming soups.

MOTTO AM FLUSS INTERNATIONAL €€

Map p236 (01-252 55 10; www.mottoamfluss.at; 01, Franz-Josefs-Kai 2; restaurant mains €12.50-29, cafe dishes €5-12.50; restaurant 11.30am-2pm & 6-11.30pm Mon-Fri, 6-11.30pm Sat & Sun, cafe 8am-midnight daily, bar 6pm-4am daily; ; 1, 2 Schwedenplatz, Schwedenplatz) Located inside the Wien-City ferry terminal, with dazzling views of the Danube Canal, Motto am Fluss' restaurant serves Austro-international cuisine with quality organic meats, fish such as Donau trout, and vegetarian and vegan options. Its upstairs cafe does great all-day breakfasts, cakes and pastries, and its bar is a superbly relaxed hang-out for Austrian wines, beers and house-creation cocktails.

CAFÉ KORB AUSTRIAN €€

Map p236 (www.cafekorb.at; 01, Brandstätte 9; dishes €4.50-11.20, mains €13-20; 8am-midnight Mon-Sat, 10am-midnight Sun; ; Stephansplatz) Sigmund Freud's former hangout is first and foremost a coffee house, but its top-notch Austrian menu places it in the realm of a *Beisl*. The food is classic – including three house-speciality schnitzels, several varieties of *Würstel* (sausages), and a famous, flaky apple strudel – and the crowd eclectic and offbeat.

★GRIECHENBEISL AUSTRIAN €€

Map p236 (01-533 19 77; www.griechenbeisl.at; 01, Fleischmarkt 11; mains €17-29; 11.30am-11.30pm; ; 1, 2 Schwedenplatz, Schwedenplatz) Dating from 1447, and frequented by Beethoven, Brahms, Schubert and Strauss among other luminaries, Vienna's oldest restaurant has vaulted rooms, wood panelling and a plant-fringed front garden that's lovely in summer. Every classic Viennese dish is on the menu, along with three daily vegetarian options.

BEIM CZAAK BISTRO €€

Map p236 (01-513 72 15; www.czaak.com; 01, Postgasse 15; mains €12-24; 4-11pm Mon-Sat; 1, 2 Schwedenplatz, Schwedenplatz) In business since 1926, Beim Czaak retains a genuine and relatively simple interior, entered via the restaurant's tree-shaded, ivy-clad courtyard garden. Classic Viennese meat dishes dominate the menu, with longtime favourites including schnitzels (gluten-free variations available), Tafelspitz (prime boiled beef), beef goulash with bacon and shredded dumplings, and fried Styrian chicken. Midweek lunch menus cost €10.50.

★PLACHUTTA AUSTRIAN €€€

Map p236 (01-512 15 77; www.plachutta-wollzeile.at; 01, Wollzeile 38; mains €19-27.20; 11.30am-11.15pm; Stubentor) If you're keen to taste *Tafelspitz*, you can't beat this specialist wood-panelled, white-tableclothed restaurant. It serves no fewer than 13 varieties from different cuts of Austrian-reared beef, such as *Mageres Meisel* (lean, juicy shoulder meat), *Beinfleisch* (larded rib meat) and *Lueger Topf* (shoulder meat with beef tongue and calf's head). Save room for the Austrian cheese plate.

★TIAN GASTRONOMY €€€

Map p236 (01-890 46 65; www.tian-restaurant.com; 01, Himmelpfortgasse 23; 4-/6-/8-course lunch menus €89/109/127, 8-course dinner menu €127; 6-9pm Tue, noon-2pm & 6-9pm Wed-Sat; ; 2 Weihburggasse, Stephansplatz) Christian Holper's chandelier-lit, lounge-style restaurant takes 100% vegetarian cuisine to Michelin-starred heights using regionally sourced produce, including from Tian's own garden. Menus are zero choice, but might feature tomato and white-raspberry soup, porcini risotto with spruce shoots, and green-almond quinoa with broccoli. Only an eight-course menu is served of an evening. Wine pairings are available. Book well ahead.

KONSTANTIN FILIPPOU GASTRONOMY €€€

Map p236 (☎01-512 22 29; www.konstantinfilippou.com; 01, Dominikanerbastei 17; 3-/4-course lunch menu €37/49, 6-/8-course dinner menu €145/185; ⏲noon-2pm & 6.30-10.30pm; 🚊1, 2 Schwedenplatz, Ⓤ Schwedenplatz) With two Michelin stars to its name, this minimalist restaurant helmed by Austrian-Greek chef Konstantin Filippou is one of Vienna's top tables. Seafood is the speciality: Salzkammergut crayfish and cauliflower crumble; Lake Constance Arctic char with an anchovy crust, pickled horseradish and cucumber foam; and catfish strudel with sweetcorn beurre-blanc sauce are among the highlights of its multicourse menus.

ARTNER STEAK €€€

Map p236 (☎01-503 50 34; www.artner.co.at; 01, Franziskanerplatz 5; mains €19-28; ⏲noon-11pm Mon-Sat; 📶; Ⓤ Stephansplatz) A double-height wall of wine bottles (including vintages from the owners' vineyard) links Artner's ground-floor wood-panelled dining room and romantic vaulted brick cellar. Locally reared, dry-aged Austrian steaks are its signature; there are also Austrian dishes like *Tafelspitz*. Tables set up on the square opposite in the shadow of the Renaissance-style Franziskanerkirche in summer. Service is outstanding.

DRINKING & NIGHTLIFE

The historic centre is a hub for everything from cutting-edge cocktail bars and craft-beer bars to relaxed *Vinothek* (wine bars) and pubs with leafy beer gardens. There are also some lively student haunts, particularly the hub of bars around the area Viennese locals call the *Bermudadreieck* (Bermuda Triangle), between Schwedenplatz, Morzinplatz and the corner of Seitenstettengasse and Judengasse.

★KRUGER'S AMERICAN BAR BAR

Map p236 (www.krugers.at; 01, Krugerstrasse 5; ⏲6pm-3am Mon-Thu, to 4am Fri & Sat, 7pm-2am Sun; 🚊D, 1, 2, 71 Kärntner Ring/Oper, Ⓤ Stephansplatz) Retaining original decor from the 1920s and '30s, this dimly lit, wood-panelled American-style bar is a legend in Vienna, furnished with leather Chesterfield sofas and playing a soundtrack of Frank Sinatra, Dean Martin et al along with contemporary jazz. Cocktails such as highballs, fizzes, daiquiris and Collinses come in classic versions and creative spin-offs (eg Pisco Collins, lychee daiquiri).

★NEEDLE VINYL BAR BAR

Map p236 (www.needlevinylbar.com; 01, Färbergasse 8; ⏲11am-1am Mon-Sat, 2pm-1am Sun; 📶; Ⓤ Herrengasse) Retro-styled Needle Vinyl Bar has bare-brick walls, mismatched furniture, light fittings made from vintage gramophones, and a vinyl library of jazz, blues and rock to browse before giving the bar staff your requests. Designed like a vinyl record, the drinks list covers classic cocktails, local wines and Vienna-brewed beers. The bar's retractable glass frontage slides wide open in warm weather.

ZWÖLF APOSTELKELLER PUB

Map p236 (Twelve Apostle Cellar; ☎01-512 67 77; www.zwoelf-apostelkeller.at; 01, Sonnenfelsgasse 3; ⏲11am-midnight; Ⓤ Stephansplatz) Occupying a vast, dimly lit tri-level cellar dating back to the Romanesque and Gothic period, Zwölf Apostelkeller has a spirited atmosphere bolstered by traditional *Heuriger* (wine-tavern) ballads from 7pm daily. In addition to outstanding local wines there's also a good choice of schnapps and beer, and a menu of traditional dishes (schnitzel, suckling pig, *Tafelspitz*) made from all-Austrian ingredients.

KLEINES CAFÉ CAFE

Map p236 (01, Franziskanerplatz 3; ⏲10am-2am; 🚊2 Weihburggasse, Ⓤ Stubentor) Designed by architect Hermann Czech (b. 1936) in the 1970s, Kleines Café has a bohemian atmosphere reminiscent of Vienna's heady *Jugendstil* days. True to its name, it's tiny inside, but the wonderful summer outdoor seating on a cobbled square overlooking the baroque Franziskanerkirche is among the best in the Innere Stadt.

FENSTER CAFÉ
COFFEE

Map p236 (www.fenster.cafe; 01, Fleischmarkt 9; 8am-4pm Mon-Fri, 9am-5pm Sat & Sun; 1, 2, 31 Schwedenplatz, U Schwedenplatz) Tucked down a cobbled lane, this cute hole-in-the-wall cafe is riding the third-wave coffee movement with ease. Place your order through the *Fenster* (window) for a classic espresso (made with freshly ground beans) or specialities like 'marshmallowcino' (cappuccino with marshmallow fluff). It accepts payment by card only (no cash).

★VINOTHEK W-EINKEHR
WINE BAR

Map p236 (0676 408 28 54; www.w-einkehr.at; 01, Laurenzerberg 1; 4-10pm Tue-Sat; 1, 2, 31 Schwedenplatz, U Schwedenplatz) There are just 15 seats inside this contemporary wine bar and another eight on the summer terrace, so the action often spills onto the pavement (you can also reserve a table). All of the wines here are Austrian, from prestigious viticulture regions including Blaufränkischland and Neusiedler See in Burgenland, and Carnuntum, Wagram and Weinviertel in Lower Austria.

SKY BAR
ROOFTOP BAR

Map p236 (www.steffl-vienna.at/de/skybar; 01, Kärntner Strasse 19; 4.30pm-2am Mon-Wed, 3pm-2am Thu & Fri, noon-2am Sat,; ; U Stephansplatz) A heart-stopping glass lift whisks you up to the top floor of the **Steffl** (Map p236; www.steffl-vienna.at; 01, Kärntner Strasse 19; 10am-8pm Mon-Fri, 9.30am-6pm Sat; U Stephansplatz) department store to take in the Innere Stadt's best panoramas from the bar and open-air terrace. One (or more) of its 350 cocktails makes a great accompaniment. Live music plays from Monday to Friday. From breakfast through to dinner, it operates as a cafe and restaurant.

1516 BREWING COMPANY
MICROBREWERY

Map p236 (www.1516brewingcompany.com; 01, Schwarzenbergstrasse 2; 10am-2am; 2 Schwarzenbergstrasse, U Karlsplatz) Copper vats and bare-brick walls create an industrial backdrop at this locally loved venue, which brews beers from malted wheat, rye and rice, including unusual varieties such as Heidi's Blueberry Ale. The awning-shaded terrace gets packed in summer. Arrive early for a good seat when it screens international football (soccer) games.

VIS-À-VIS
WINE BAR

Map p236 (01-512 93 50; www.weibel.at/visavis01.html; 01, Wollzeile 5; 4-10.30pm Tue-Fri, 3-10.30pm Sat; U Stephansplatz) Tucked down an atmospheric passage, this tiny wine bar only seats 10 people, but it makes up for it with over 350 wines on offer (with a strong emphasis on Austrian drops) and charcuterie.

KAFFEE ALT WIEN
CAFE

Map p236 (www.kaffeealtwien.at; 01, Bäckerstrasse 9; 9am-2am; ; U Stephansplatz) Low-lit and full of character, Alt Wien is a classic dive attracting students and arty types. It's a one-stop shop for a lowdown on events in the city – every available wall space is plastered with posters advertising shows, concerts and exhibitions. The goulash is legendary and perfectly complemented by dark bread and beer.

DIGLAS
CAFE

Map p236 (01-512 57 65; www.diglas.at; 01, Wollzeile 10; 8am-10.30pm Mon-Fri, 9am-10.30pm Sat & Sun; U Stephansplatz) Classic coffee house Diglas has crimson booths, timber-panelled walls hung with black-and-white photographs, vaulted ceilings, an extensive range of coffee and an elegant, venerable clientele. The reputation of Diglas' cakes precedes it, and the *Apfelstrudel* is unrivalled, as are the seasonal apricot or plum dumplings. Live piano music fills the room from 7pm.

WINE TASTING

The Innere Stadt has some great *Vinothek* – one of the best is **Enrico Panigl** (Map p236; www.enrico-panigl.at; 01, Schönlaterngasse 11; 6pm-4am Mon-Sat, to 2am Sun; U Stephansplatz). Tucked down a narrow passage off Lugeck, this rustic, dark-timber-furnished venue with a vaulted ceiling is one of Vienna's best-kept wine secrets, with 40 rotating Austrian, Italian and Hungarian wines available by the glass and bottle. For a more modern ambience, head for **Wein & Co** (Map p236; www.weinco.at; 01, Jasomirgottstrasse 3-5; 9am-10pm Mon-Wed, 9am-midnight Thu-Sat, 11am-10pm Sun; ; U Stephansplatz), which is attached to a comprehensive wine shop.

HISTORIC GRABEN

Today Vienna's most elegant shopping street, **Graben** (Map p236; 01; Ⓤ Stephansplatz) began life as a ditch dug by the Romans to protect Vinodoba. In 1192 Leopold V filled in the ditch and built a defensive city wall that ended at Freyung, financed by the ransom paid by arch-rival Richard the Lionheart – at that time, kept under lock and key in a castle near Dürnstein, on the Danube.

CAFÉ PRÜCKEL COFFEE

Map p236 (www.prueckel.at; 01, Stubenring 24; ⏲8.30am-10pm; 📶; Ⓤ Stubentor) Unlike other Viennese cafes with sumptuous interiors, Prückel features an intact 1950s design. Intimate booths, strong coffee, diet-destroying cakes and Prückel's speciality – its crispy, flaky apple strudel served with cream – are all big drawcards. Live piano music plays from 7pm to 10pm on Mondays, Wednesdays and Fridays.

WHY NOT? GAY

Map p236 (www.why-not.at; 01, Tiefer Graben 22; ⏲10pm-4am Fri & Sat; 📶; Ⓤ Herrengasse) Why Not? is a fixture of Vienna's gay scene. The small club quickly fills up with mainly young guys; there are three bars and a dance floor. Cover charges vary depending on the event.

☆ ENTERTAINMENT

JAZZLAND LIVE MUSIC

Map p236 (☎01-533 25 75; www.jazzland.at; 01, Franz-Josefs-Kai 29; cover €11-20; ⏲7pm-1am Mon-Sat mid-Aug–mid-Jul, live music from 9pm; 🚋1, 2, 31 Schwedenplatz, Ⓤ Schwedenplatz) Buried in a 500-year-old cellar beneath Ruprechtskirche (p78), Jazzland is Vienna's oldest jazz club, dating from 1972. The music covers the whole jazz spectrum, and features both local and international acts. Past performers have included Ray Brown, Teddy Wilson, Big Joe Williams and Max Kaminsky. Arrive early as it doesn't take reservations.

METRO KINOKULTURHAUS CINEMA

Map p236 (☎01-512 18 03; www.filmarchiv.at; 01, Johannesgasse 4; film tickets €8.50, exhibition tickets €7.50, combined ticket €13; ⏲3-9pm; Ⓤ Stephansplatz) Part of the Austrian Film Archive, with a collection that includes 200,000 films, two million photographs and stills, 50,000 programs and 16,000 posters, the Metro Kinokulturhaus is a showcase for exhibitions. The restored cinema here was first converted for screenings in 1924 and retains its wood panelling and red-velvet interior; it shows historic and art-house Austrian films (in German).

GARTENBAUKINO CINEMA

Map p236 (☎01-512 23 54; www.gartenbaukino.at; 01, Parkring 12; tickets €9-12.50; 🚋2, Ⓤ Stubentor, Stadtpark) With an interior dating from the 1960s, this cinema seats a whopping 736 people, and is packed during Viennale Film Festival (p46) screenings. Its regular screening schedule is filled with art-house films, often in their original language (including English) with German subtitles.

PORGY & BESS JAZZ

Map p236 (☎01-512 88 11; www.porgy.at; 01, Riemergasse 11; ⏲performances from 7pm; Ⓤ Stubentor) The program here features top-range modern jazz from around the globe; book ahead for popular acts. The dimly lit interior has a capacity of 350, and the vibe is velvety and very grown-up.

🛍 SHOPPING

Graben is Vienna's most elegant shopping street, with fashion boutiques, department stores and other high-end establishments. Intersecting it, Kärntner Strasse is also a major shopping thoroughfare. The small surrounding laneways contain venerable shops selling sweets, jewellery and more. For up-and-coming designs head to Wollzeile.

★ WALD & WIESE FOOD

Map p236 (www.waldundwiese.at; 01, Wollzeile 19; ⏲10am-6.30pm Mon-Fri, to 5pm Sat; Ⓤ Stephansplatz) 🍃 Some 5000 bee colonies and 600 beekeepers harvest honey within Vienna's city limits, including on the rooftops of the Rathaus, Staatsoper, Kunsthistorisches Museum Vienna, Secession and several hotels. The fruits of their labour are sold at this specialist honey boutique, which also sells honey-based beverages including mead, honey-and-whisky liqueur and grappa, along with beeswax candles, hand creams, toothpaste, royal jelly…

SCHAU SCHAU
FASHION & ACCESSORIES

Map p236 (☎01-533 45 84; www.schau-schau.at; 01, Rotenturmstrasse 11; ⏰10am-6pm Mon-Sat; UStephansplatz) Austrian and global celebrities – Beyoncé include – head to this one-off boutique for stunning sunglasses and prescription eyewear. It was founded in the late '70s by Peter Kozich, who handcrafts frames from natural materials including buffalo horn, gold, platinum and various woods. Designs can be made to order.

ALTMANN & KÜHNE
CHOCOLATE

Map p236 (www.altmann-kuehne.at; 01, Graben 30; ⏰9am-6.30pm Mon-Fri, 10am-5pm Sat; UStephansplatz) This small, charming shop is the flagship of century-old chocolatier Altmann & Kühne, which produces handmade chocolates and sweets. It's located behind a modernist facade designed by Josef Hoffmann, a founding member of the visual arts collective Wiener Werkstätte. Hoffmann also designed the interior as well as the iconic packaging: miniature hat boxes, luggage trunks, glass cabinets, bookshelves and baroque buildings.

CUISINARUM
HOMEWARES

Map p236 (www.cuisinarum.at; 01, Singerstrasse 14; ⏰9.30am-6.30pm Mon-Fri, to 6pm Sat; UStephansplatz) Everything you need to cook Austrian cuisine is here: specialised cookware such as a *Spätzle Sieb* (a metal press to make *Spätzle* noodles); pots, pans and casserole dishes from Austrian manufacturer Riess; Austrian cookbooks (in English and German); and cookie cutters and cake moulds in Viennese designs.

VOM FASS
FOOD & DRINKS

Map p236 (www.vomfass-wien.at; 01, Brandstätte 5; ⏰10am-6.30pm Mon-Fri, to 6pm Sat; UStephansplatz) Austrian specialities filling the shelves of this gourmet shop include Styrian pumpkin-seed oil, blueberry balsamic vinegar, Alpine herbal liqueurs from Tyrol, spiced walnut liqueur from Upper Austria, and smoked salt from Salzkammergut, as well as wines from around the country.

SO AUSTRIA
DESIGN

Map p236 (www.so-austria.at; 01, Lugeck 3a; ⏰10am-7pm Mon-Fri, to 6pm Sat; UStephansplatz) Founded by two South Tyroleans with a passion for Austrian home and fashion accessories, this high-quality shop only sells goods handcrafted in Austria: hand towels, tea towels, bags, shoes, jewellery, sculptures, hats, scarves and clothing.

UNGER UND KLEIN
WINE

Map p236 (www.ungerundklein.at; 01, Gölsdorfgasse 2; ⏰4pm-midnight Mon-Fri, 5pm-midnight Sat; 🚋1, 2 Schwedenplatz, USchwedenplatz) Unger und Klein's small-but-knowledgeable wine collection spans the globe, but the majority of its labels come from Europe, including the best of Austrian wines – from expensive boutique varieties to bargain-bin bottles. It doubles as a small, laid-back wine bar, with a good selection of wines by the glass; Friday and Saturday evenings get crowded.

SPORTS & ACTIVITIES

ÖTK
CLIMBING

Map p236 (Österreichischer Touristenklub; ☎01-512 38 44; www.oetk.at; 01, Bäckerstrasse 16; per climb €6.90, equipment hire €1.50, lesson per hour from €25; ⏰climbing hall 10.30am-10pm Mon, 9am-10pm Tue-Fri, 1-10pm Sat & Sun; UStephansplatz) Founded in 1869, the ÖTK is Austria's second-oldest (and third-largest) Alpine club. Its glass-roofed interior courtyard has aclimbing wall reaching 15m in height. The adjacent shop sells climbing and outdoor gear such as clothing, footware and camping equipment. It also organises climbing, via ferrata, abseiling, mountain-biking and hiking trips further afield (English guides can be arranged).

BADESCHIFF
SWIMMING

Map p236 (www.badeschiff.at; 01, Danube Canal; adult/child €6.50/2; ⏰9am-8pm May-Sep; 🚋1, 2 Schwedenplatz, USchwedenplatz) Swim on (not in!) the Danube. Floating on the bank of the Danube, between Schwedenplatz and Urania, this 28m-long lap pool has multiple decks with sun loungers and an open-air football pitch on the platform suspended above. It doubles as a bar at night; in winter the pool closes and the ship is a bar and restaurant only. Both the bar and kitchen are open year round, with drinks available until 1am and food until 10pm.

The ship's hold contains a bowling alley and dance floor where DJs spin regularly.

Karlsplatz & Around Naschmarkt

Neighbourhood Top Five

❶ **Karlskirche** (p91) Catching the lift up to this mesmerising church's elliptical copper dome for a view of the incredible frescos by Johann Michael Rottmayr.

❷ **Staatsoper** (p90) Reliving operatic highs with a guided tour of this resplendent gold-and-crystal-adorned opera house.

❸ **Secession** (p93) Contemplating the sensuous shapes, gold mosaics and mythological symbolism of Klimt's *Beethoven Frieze* at the 1897-designed exhibition centre of the Vienna Secession-movement artists.

❹ **Naschmarkt** (p92) Breathing in the heady aromas of spices, olives, oils, vinegars, cheeses, hams, sausages and much more while snacking your way from stall to tantalising stall.

❺ **Akademie der Bildenden Künste** (p92) Viewing Bosch's riveting triptych, *The Last Judgment* altarpiece.

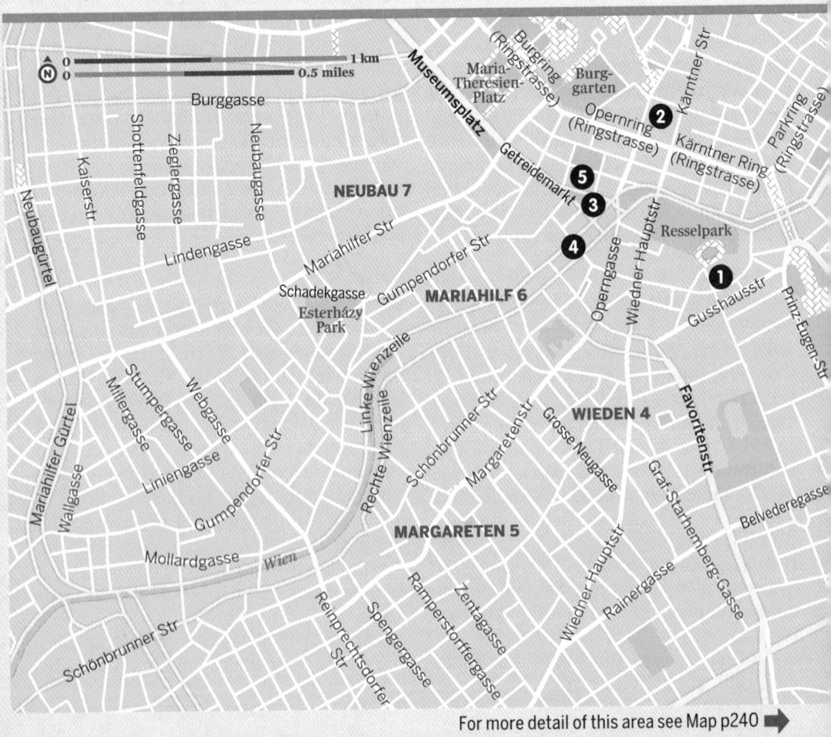

For more detail of this area see Map p240 ➡

Explore Karlsplatz & Around Naschmarkt

Spreading south of the Opernring is Vienna's cultured 4th district, Wieden. Here days can be spent gazing upon the baroque frescos that dance across the Karlskirche, Otto Wagner's art nouveau buildings and Klimt's sensual friezes. Nights lift the curtain on high-calibre opera and classical music in some of the world's finest concert halls. Wander west and within minutes you swing from gilded opulence to the multilingual buzz, street-food sizzle and market-stall banter of the Naschmarkt. Stroll south of here to the easygoing Freihausviertel and Vienna suddenly shrinks to village scale, with arty cafes, ateliers and food shops run by folk with genuine passion.

North of Wieden is 6th-district Mariahilf. Give the high-street throngs on Mariahilfer Strasse the slip and you soon find yourself in quintessentially Viennese backstreets, home to speciality shops and old-school *Beisln* (bistro pubs). On the cutting edge of the city's nightlife and design scene is Gumpendorfer Strasse.

Wedged between Wieden and Mariahilf in the 5th district is Margareten, with few heavyweight sights but strong local flavour, particularly around the increasingly fashionable Margaretenplatz.

Local Life

Shopping Life Follow the hungry Viennese to the Naschmarkt (p92) for a world of street food, and scout out delis, design stores and one-of-a-kind boutiques in the artsy Freihausviertel and around Margaretenplatz.

Cafe Life Great cafes in this neighbourhood range from boho Café Jelinek (p99) to starkly contemporary Café Drechsler (p95).

Nightlife Hang out with a young and up-for-it crowd on Gumpendorfer Strasse, crammed with bars, cafes and lounge-style restaurants, or find a more laidback scene around Schleifmühlgasse.

Getting There & Away

U-Bahn Karlsplatz is well connected to all corners of Vienna, served by the U-Bahn lines U1, U2 and U4. The U4 line to Kettenbrückengasse is handy for Naschmarkt and the Freihausviertel, while the U3 line (Zieglergasse, Neubaugasse etc) is useful for reaching Mariahilfer Strasse. Pilgramgasse (U4) is the most central stop for Margareten, and Taubstummengasse (U1) for Wieden.

Tram Key routes include trams 1 and 62, which stop at Karlsplatz and pass through Wieden.

Lonely Planet's Top Tip

It's a pleasure simply to wander the backstreets of the Freihausviertel, just south of Naschmarkt. One of the neighbourhood's most elegant streets is Mühlgasse, lined with late-19th-century houses with Juliet balconies and ornate doors in the *Jugendstil* (Art Nouveau) style. Numbers 26 and 28 are fine examples.

Best Places to Eat

- Naschmarkt (p92)
- Vollpension (p94)
- Said the Butcher to the Cow (p94)
- Entler (p95)
- Eis Greissler (p94)

For reviews, see p94.

Best Places to Drink

- Café Schwarzenberg (p97)
- Kaffeefabrik (p96)
- Café Sperl (p98)
- Rafael's Vinothek (p98)
- Café Rüdigerhof (p98)

For reviews, see p97.

Best Shopping

- Flohmarkt (p100)
- Gegenbauer (p101)
- Beer Lovers (p101)
- Käseland (p101)
- Blühendes Konfekt (p101)

For reviews, see p100.

KONSTANTIN TRONIN/SHUTTERSTOCK ©

TOP SIGHT
STAATSOPER

Few concert halls can hold a candle to the neo-Renaissance Staatsoper, Vienna's foremost opera and ballet venue. Even if you can't snag performance tickets (p100), you can get a taste of the architectural brilliance and musical genius that have shaped this cultural bastion on a guided tour.

Built between 1861 and 1869 by August Siccard von Siccardsburg and Eduard van der Nüll, the Staatsoper initially revolted the Viennese public and Habsburg royalty and quickly earned the nickname 'stone turtle'. Despite the frosty reception, it went on to house some of the most iconic directors in history, including Gustav Mahler, Richard Strauss and Herbert von Karajan.

Guided tours take in highlights such as the **foyer**, graced with busts of Beethoven, Schubert and Haydn and frescos of celebrated operas, and the **main staircase**, watched over by marble allegorical statues embodying the liberal arts. The **Tea Salon** dazzles in 22-carat gold leaf, the **Schwind Foyer** captivates with 16 opera-themed oil paintings by Austrian artist Moritz von Schwind, while the **Gustav Mahler Hall** is hung with tapestries inspired by Mozart's *The Magic Flute*. You'll also get a behind-the-scenes look at the **stage**, which raises the curtain on over 300 performances each year.

DON'T MISS

- Foyer
- Tea Salon
- Gustav Mahler Hall

PRACTICALITIES

- Map p240, G2
- www.wiener-staatsoper.at
- 01, Opernring 2
- tour adult/child €9/4
- D, 1, 2, 62, 71 Kärntner Ring/Oper, U Karlsplatz

TOP SIGHT
KARLSKIRCHE

Rising imperiously above Resselpark is Vienna's baroque magnum opus: the Karlskirche. Crowned by a 72m-high copper dome, the church was built between 1716 and 1739 as thanks for deliverance from the 1713 plague. The edifice bears the hallmark of prolific Austrian architect Johann Bernhard Fischer von Erlach, while the interior swirls with the vivid colours of Johann Michael Rottmayr's frescos.

In the flower-strewn **Resselpark**, a pond centred on a **Henry Moore sculpture** (*Hill Arches;* 1973) reflects the splendour of the church like a celestial mirror. Your gaze is drawn to the neoclassical portico, the spiralling pillars, which are modelled on Trajan's Column in Rome and embellished with scenes from the life of St Charles Borromeo, as well as cross-bearing angels from the Old and New Testaments intricately carved from white marble. The pediment reliefs depict the suffering of Vienna's plague victims.

Inside, a lift (elevator) soars up into the elliptical cupola for a close-up of Johann Michael Rottmayr's **frescos** of the glorification of St Charles Borromeo. Look for tongue-in-cheek Counter-Reformation details, such as angels setting fire to Martin Luther's German bible. The **high altar** panel, which shows the ascension of St Charles Borromeo, is a riot of golden sunrays and stucco cherubs.

DON'T MISS

- Cupola frescos
- High altar panel
- Facade view from Resselpark

PRACTICALITIES

- St Charles Church
- Map p240, H3
- www.karlskirche.at
- 04, Karlsplatz
- adult/child €8/4
- 9am-6pm Mon-Sat, noon-7pm Sun
- U Karlsplatz

SIGHTS

Most of this neighbourhood's key sights centre around Karlsplatz, including the Karlskirche (p91) and Secession gallery as well as the vibrant Naschmarkt. A short stroll north, the glorious Staatsoper (p90) abuts the historic centre.

STAATSOPER NOTABLE BUILDING

See p90.

KARLSKIRCHE CHURCH

See p91.

NASCHMARKT MARKET

Map p240 (www.wien.gv.at; 06, Linke & Rechte Wienzeile; ⏲6am-7.30pm Mon-Fri, to 5pm Sat; Ⓤ Karlsplatz, Kettenbrückengasse) Vienna's famous market and eating strip (p94) began life as a farmers market in the 18th century, when the fruit market on Freyung was moved here. Interestingly, a law passed in 1793 said that fruit and vegetables arriving in town by cart had to be sold on Naschmarkt, while anything brought in by boat could be sold from the docks.

The fruits of the Orient poured in, the predecessors of the modern-day sausage stand were erected and sections were set aside for coal, wood and farming tools and machines. Officially, it became known as Naschmarkt ('munch market') in 1905, a few years after Otto Wagner bedded the Wien River down in its open-topped stone and concrete sarcophagus. This Otto Wagnerian horror was a blessing for Naschmarkt, because it created space to expand. A close shave came in 1965 when there were plans to tear it down – it was saved, and today the Naschmarkt is not only the place to shop for food but has a flea market (p100) each Saturday.

AKADEMIE DER BILDENDEN KÜNSTE MUSEUM

Map p240 (Academy of Fine Arts; www.akbild.ac.at; 01, Schillerplatz 3; adult/child €12/free; ⏲10am-6pm Wed-Mon; 🚋D, 1, 2 Kärntner Ring/Oper, Ⓤ Museumsquartier, Karlsplatz) Founded in 1692, the Akademie der Bildenden Künste is an often-underrated art space. Its gallery concentrates on Flemish, Dutch and German painters, including important figures such as Hieronymus Bosch, Rembrandt, Van Dyck, Rubens, Titian, Francesco Guardi and Lucas Cranach the Elder. The supreme highlight is Bosch's macabre triptych of *The Last Judgment* altarpiece (1504–08), depicting the banishment of Adam and Eve on the left panel, and the horror of Hell in the middle and right panels. Audio guides cost €2.

WIEN MUSEUM MUSEUM

Map p240 (www.wienmuseum.at; 04, Karlsplatz 8; Ⓤ Karlsplatz) The Wien Museum covers Vienna's history from Neolithic times to the 20th century, putting the city and its personalities in a meaningful context. It's closed completely for extensive renovations until 2022. In the meantime, some of the collections will be on display in thematic exhibitions at the Wien Museum MUSA (p125), while others will tour internationally.

THIRD MAN MUSEUM MUSEUM

Map p240 (www.3mpc.net; 04, Pressgasse 25; adult/child €8.90/4.50, guided tour incl admission €10; ⏲2-6pm Sat, guided tours 2pm Wed; Ⓤ Kettenbrückengasse) Fans of this quintessential 1948 film about Vienna (voted best British film of the 20th century by the British Film Institute) will enjoy the posters, paraphernalia and the other 3000-plus objects on show here. Stills illustrate the work of Australian cinematographer Robert Krasker, who received an Oscar for his work on this movie. The museum covers aspects of Vienna before and after 'Harry Lime Time' as well as the film itself. Guided 75-minute tours take place in English. Cash only.

HAUS DES MEERES MUSEUM

Map p240 (House of the Sea; www.haus-des-meeres.at; 06, Fritz-Grünbaum-Platz 1; museum adult/child €18.90/8.60, viewing platform €5; ⏲9am-6pm Fri-Wed, to 9pm Thu; Ⓤ Neubaugasse) The 'House of the Sea' offers an interesting glimpse into the world of giant fish, reptiles and creepy-crawlies. Aim to visit during feeding time: sharks are fed at 10.30am Monday, 3pm Wednesday and 3.30pm Fridays, while a staff member hops into the shark tank at 6pm Thursday. Piranhas go into a frenzy at 3pm Tuesday, as do reptiles at 7pm Thursday and 10am Sunday. A 192-step exterior staircase leads to the 9th-floor viewing platform.

HAYDNHAUS MUSEUM

Map p240 (www.wienmuseum.at; 06, Haydngasse 19; adult/child €5/free, 1st Sun of month free;

⌚10am-1pm & 2-6pm Tue-Sun; ⓤZieglergasse) Joseph Haydn (1732–1809) lived in Vienna during the heady times of Napoleon's occupation, and this exhibition at his last residence focuses on Vienna as well as London during the late-18th and early-19th centuries. An Austrian composer prominent in the classical period, he is most celebrated for his 104 symphonies and 68 string quartets. The small garden here is modelled on Haydn's. Audio guides cost €4.

OTTO WAGNER BUILDINGS NOTABLE BUILDING

Map p240 (06, Linke Wienzeile & Köstlergasse; ⓤKettenbrückengasse) A problem zone due to flooding, the Wien River needed regulating in the late-19th century. At the same time, Otto Wagner had visions of turning the area between Karlsplatz and Schönbrunn into a magnificent boulevard. The vision blurred and the reality is a gushing, concrete-bottomed creek and a couple of attractive Wagner houses on the Linke Wienzeile.

Majolika-Haus at No. 40 (1899) is the prettiest as it's completely covered in glazed ceramic to create flowing floral motifs on the facade. The second of these *Jugendstil* masterpieces is a corner house at **No. 38** (1899), with reliefs from Kolo Moser and shapely bronze figures from Othmar Schimkowitz. Nearby is a third house, simpler than these, at **Köstlergasse 3** (1899) and, finally, you can put Wagner's functionality to the test by descending into his **Kettenbrückengasse U-Bahn station** (1899).

SCHUBERT STERBEWOHNUNG MUSEUM

Map p240 (www.wienmuseum.at; 04, Kettenbrückengasse 6; adult/child €5/free; ⌚10am-1pm & 2-6pm Wed & Thu; ⓤKettenbrückengasse) Here, in his brother's apartment, Franz Schubert spent his dying days (40 to be precise) in 1828. While dying of either typhoid fever or syphilis (his exact cause of death is unknown), he continued to compose, scribbling a string of piano sonatas and his last work, 'Der Hirt auf dem Felsen' (The Shepherd on the Rock). Schubert's Death Apartment is fairly bereft of personal effects but does document these final days with some interesting knick-knacks and sounds.

TOP SIGHT SECESSION

In 1897, 19 progressive artists turned from the mainstream Künstlerhaus artistic establishment to form the Vienna Secession. Among their number were Gustav Klimt, Josef Hoffmann, Kolo Moser and Joseph Olbrich. Olbrich designed their new exhibition centre, combining sparse functionality with stylistic motifs. The building has a delicate golden dome of intertwined laurel leaves that deserves better than the description 'golden cabbage' accorded it by some Viennese.

The 14th exhibition (1902) held here featured the *Beethoven Frieze*, by Klimt, based on Richard Wagner's interpretation of Beethoven's ninth symphony. This 34m-long work was intended as a temporary display, little more than an elaborate poster for the main exhibit, Max Klinger's *Beethoven* monument. Now the star exhibit, the frieze has occupied the basement since 1983.

Inspired by Greek mythology, the frieze is bewitching. The yearning for happiness finds expression in ethereal, female figures floating across the walls, a choir of rapturous, flower-bearing angels, and the arts personified as curvaceous, gold-haired nudes who appear to grow like trees. These are juxtaposed by the hostile forces, whose serpent-haired gorgons and beastly portrayals of sickness, madness and death caused outrage in 1902.

DON'T MISS

- *Beethoven Frieze*
- The dome
- Rotating exhibitions of contemporary art

PRACTICALITIES

- Map p240, F2
- www.secession.at
- 01, Friedrichstrasse 12
- adult/child €9.50/6
- ⌚10am-6pm Tue-Sun
- ⓤKarlsplatz

EATING

In a neighbourhood that's the home turf of Vienna's best food market, it's not surprising that there are some fantastic places to eat here in all price categories, both at the Naschmarkt itself and in its nearby streets.

★NASCHMARKT — MARKET €

Map p240 (www.wien.gv.at; 06, Linke & Rechte Wienzeile; 6am-7.30pm Mon-Fri, to 5pm Sat; ; UKarlsplatz, Kettenbrückengasse) Stretching 500m along Linke Wienzeile between the U4 stops of Kettenbrückengasse and Karlsplatz, this is Vienna's biggest and best market. The western (Kettengasse) end has meats, fruit and vegetables (including exotic varieties), spices, wines, cheeses, olives, Indian and Middle Eastern specialities, and kebab and felafel stands. Altogether, there are 123 fixed stalls, including numerous sit-down restaurants.

Temporary stalls such as farmers' stands are allocated another 35 places. The market peters out at the eastern end to stalls selling Indian fabrics, jewellery and trashy trinkets. A Flohmarkt (p100), or flea market, sets up on Saturdays.

★VOLLPENSION — CAFE €

Map p240 (www.vollpension.wien; 04, Schleifmühlgasse 16; dishes €5-10; 7.30am-10pm Mon-Sat, 8am-8pm Sun; ; UKarlsplatz) This white-painted brick space with mismatched vintage furniture, tasselled lampshades and portraits on the walls is run by 15 *Omas* (grandmas) and *Opas* (grandpas) along with their families, with over 200 cakes in their collective repertoire. Breakfast (eg avocado and feta on pumpernickel bread) is served until 4pm; lunch dishes include a vegan goulash with potato and tofu. Cash only.

EIS GREISSLER — ICE CREAM €

Map p240 (www.eis-greissler.at; 06, Mariahilfer Strasse 33; 1/2/3/4/5 scoops €1.60/3/4.30/5.30/6; 11am-8pm; UMuseumsquartier) The inevitable queue makes Eis Greissler easy to spot. Locals flock here – whatever the weather – for ice cream made from organic milk, yoghurt and cream from its own farm in Lower Austria. Vegans are well catered to with soy and oat milk varieties. All-natural flavours vary seasonally but might include goat's cheese, pumpkin-seed oil, cinnamon, pear or marzipan.

HEISSE UND KALTE WURSTWAREN — FAST FOOD €

Map p240 (06, Naschmarkt Stand 47; dishes €3-4.50; 11am-6pm Tue-Fri, 8am-3pm Sat; UKettenbrückengasse) Heisse und Kalte Wurstwaren is a long-standing fixture in the Naschmarkt, serving *Bratwurst* (fine pork and beef German sausage), *Burenwurst* (coarse bacon and beef sausage), *Debreziner* (Hungarian pork and paprika sausage), *Käsekrainer* (cheese-filled sausage) and *Bosna* (veal, pork and marjoram sausage). You can order them either in a bread roll, or chopped and topped with sauce to eat using toothpicks.

URBANEK — DELI €

Map p240 (04, Naschmarkt Stand 46; dishes €5.50-13; 9am-6.30pm Mon-Thu, 8am-6.30pm Fri, 7.30am-4.30pm Sat; UKarlsplatz) Stepping inside Urbanek is to enter a world of cured meats in all their different varieties – smoked, salted, cooked or raw. The atmosphere is rarefied but relaxed as you enjoy a glass of wine and perhaps delicately cut slices of Mangalitza pig – a breed prized for its delicious ham. The roast beef is organic, and the selection of cheeses outstanding.

NASCHMARKT DELI — CAFE €

Map p240 (www.naschmarkt-deli.at; 04, Naschmarkt Stand 421-436; dishes €5-14; 7am-midnight Mon-Sat; UKettenbrückengasse) Amid the enticing stands at Vienna's famous market, Naschmarkt Deli serves breakfast (Turkish, English or Prosecco) until 4pm. Sandwiches, falafel, big baguettes and chunky lentil soups fill out the menu; DJs play from 5.30pm.

★SAID THE BUTCHER TO THE COW — BURGERS €€

Map p240 (01-535 69 69; www.butcher-cow.at; 01, Opernring 11; burgers €12-20.50, steaks €28.50-39; kitchen 2-10pm Tue & Wed, to 11pm Thu-Sat, bar 5pm-1am Tue & Wed, to 2am Thu-Sat; ; D, 1, 2, 71 Kärntner Ring/Oper, UKarlsplatz) Not only does this wildly popular hang-out have a brilliant name, it serves knock-out brioche-bun burgers (chicken teriyaki with wasabi mayo; black tiger prawns with bok choy; black-bean patty with lotus root), chargrilled steaks and house-speciality cheesecakes. Better yet, it moonlights as a gin bar with 30 gin varieties and seven different tonics.

ENTLER AUSTRIAN €€

Map p240 (☎01-504 35 85; www.entler.at; 04, Schlüsselgasse 2; mains €14-28.50; ⊙5-10pm Tue-Sat; 📶; 🚋1, 62 Mayerhofgasse) While the setting beneath a vaulted ceiling is traditional, the cuisine here is cutting edge. Reinventions of Austrian classics include *Bergkässe* (hard cow's cheese) and black-truffle soup, pork medallions stuffed with apricots and smoked ham, roast hare strudel, and, for dessert, a walnut mousse sphere with hazelnut ice cream and candied hazelnut shards.

UBL AUSTRIAN €€

Map p240 (☎01-587 64 37; 04, Pressgasse 26; mains €12-24; ⊙noon-2pm & 6-10pm Wed-Sun; UKettenbrückengasse) The menu at this much-loved *Beisl* is loaded with Viennese staples, such as *Wiener Rindsgulasch* (Viennese beef goulash), *Schweinsbraten* (roast pork) and four types of schnitzel, and is enhanced with seasonal cuisine throughout the year. You could do worse than finish the hefty meal off with a stomach-settling plum schnapps. The tree-shaded garden is wonderful in summer.

WALDVIERTLERHOF AUSTRIAN €€

Map p240 (☎01-586 35 12; www.waldviertlerhof.at; 05, Schönbrunner Strasse 20; mains €8-18; ⊙10am-11pm Mon-Sat; 📶; UKettenbrückengasse) Rambling over a series of cavernous, timber-furnished rooms and a table-filled courtyard sheltered by a retractable awning, Waldviertlerhof is a local institution well off the tourist track. Its staunchly traditional menu features *Kalbsleber* (calf's liver with parsley potatoes), *Kalbskopf* (baked veal's head), *Karpfenfilet* (poppy seed–crusted carp) and enormous portions of *Rindsgulasch* (beef goulash). The two-course lunch menu costs €8.20.

MILL AUSTRIAN €€

Map p240 (☎01-966 40 73; www.mill32.at; 06, Millergasse 32; mains €11-21; ⊙4-11pm Mon & Fri, 11.30am-2.30pm & 4-11pm Tue-Thu, 11am-4pm Sun; UWestbahnhof) This bistro, with a hidden courtyard for summer days, feels like a local secret. Scarlet-painted brick walls and wooden floors create a warm backdrop for seasonal dishes such as sweet-potato goulash or Styrian chicken salad drizzled in pumpkin-seed oil. Sunday is an all-you-can-eat brunch buffet (€19).

SILBERWIRT AUSTRIAN €€

Map p240 (☎01-544 49 07; www.silberwirt.at; 05, Schlossgasse 21; mains €9-18; ⊙noon-midnight; 👪; UPilgramgasse) This atmospheric neo-*Beisl* offers traditional Viennese cuisine, mostly using organic and/or local produce. A meal might begin with Waldviertel sheep's cheese salad with walnuts and poppy seeds, followed by trout with parsley potatoes and almond butter, and *Palatschinken* (pancakes) with homemade apricot jam. A dedicated kids' menu appeals to little appetites. In summer, dine in the tree-shaded garden.

HAAS BEISL AUSTRIAN €€

Map p240 (☎01-586 25 52; 05, Margaretenstrasse 74; mains €9-25; ⊙11am-11pm Tue-Sat, 11.30am-9pm Sun; UPilgramgasse) Warm and woody, this traditional Margareten *Beisl* is absolutely genuine and a great place to enjoy hearty food in a very local atmosphere. Classics such as *Tafelspitz* (boiled beef), *Rindsgulasch* (goulash and dumplings) and *Krautfleckerl* (hand-rolled noodles with peppered roast cabbage) are prepared the way your Austrian *Oma* (grandmother) might have done them. Two-course midweek lunch menus cost €7.90.

ZUM ALTEN FASSL AUSTRIAN €€

Map p240 (☎01-544 42 98; www.zum-alten-fassl.at; 05, Ziegelofengasse 37; mains €9-17.50; ⊙11.30am-3pm & 5pm-midnight Mon-Fri, 5pm-midnight Sat, noon-3pm & 5pm-midnight Sun; UPilgramgasse) With its private garden amid residential houses and polished wooden interior, this well-kept *Beisl* is a great spot to sample the Viennese favourites and regional specialities, such as *Eierschwammerl* (chanterelles) and *Blunzengröstl* (a potato, bacon, onion and blood sausage fry-up). When it's in season, *Zanderfilet* (fillet of zander) is the chef's favourite. Midweek lunch menus cost €6.80 to €7.80.

CAFÉ DRECHSLER CAFE €€

Map p240 (www.cafedrechsler.at; 06, Linke Wienzeile 22; mains lunch €9.50-12.50, dinner €12.50-14.90; ⊙8am-midnight Mon-Sat, 9am-midnight Sun; 📶🌶; UKettenbrückengasse) A giant decoupage of ripped posters covers one wall at lively Drechsler. It's especially popular at

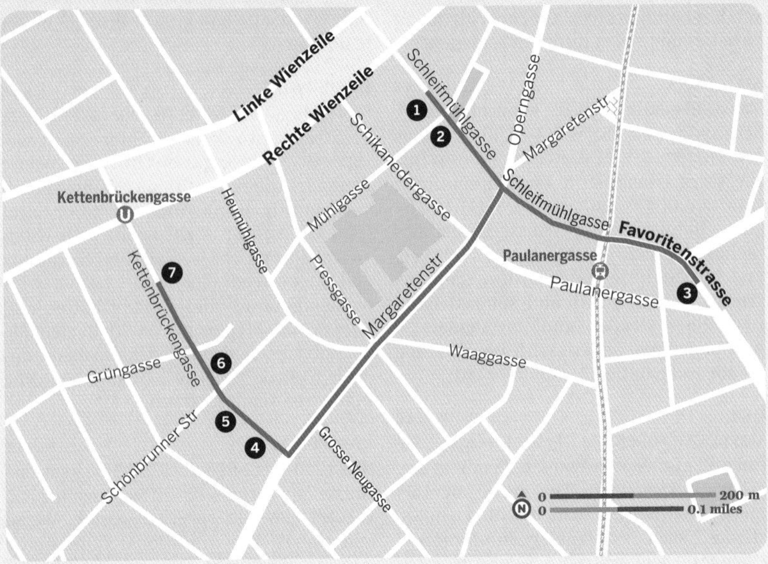

Local Life
Epicure Tour of the Freihausviertel

Once home to impoverished artisans, today the Freihausviertel has been revitalised: its attractive lanes harbour boho cafes, speciality food stores and some of Vienna's most exciting new galleries, ateliers and boutiques. After browsing Vienna's gourmand's fantasyland, the Naschmarkt, continue your spin through the district with this food-and-drink tour.

1 Austrian Bubbly

Raise a toast at **Sekt Comptoir** (Map p240; www.sektcomptoir.at; 04, Schleifmühlgasse 19; 5-11pm Mon-Thu, 3-11pm Fri, noon-11pm Sat; U Kettenbrückengasse) over a glass of *Sekt* (sparkling wine) produced at its own vineyard in Burgenland. Located near the Naschmarkt, shoppers often spill onto the sidewalk here. It's a great place to stock up on bottles to take home, too.

2 Literary Lunch

Browse cookbooks filled with recipes from around the world at **Babette's** (Map p240; www.babettes.at; 04, Schleifmühlgasse 17; 10am-7pm Mon-Fri, 10.30am-5pm Sat Sep-Jul, 11am-6pm Mon-Fri, 10am-3pm Sat Aug; U Kettenbrückengasse) and from noon to 2.30pm on weekdays taste international lunch specials (such as curry) prepared in its open kitchen with own-brand spices and fresh Naschmarkt produce. It also runs evening cookery classes (in German).

3 Cutting-Edge Coffee

Burgenland-roasted beans brewed using state-of-the-art espresso machines are the hallmark of contemporary, whitewashed cafe-shop **Kaffeefabrik** (Map p240; www.kaffeefabrik.at; 04, Favoritenstrasse 4-6; 8am-6pm Mon-Fri, 11am-5pm Sat; U Taubstummengasse). Stop in for a caffeine hit (with organic Austrian milk or nondairy alternatives), or pick up a bag of beans to take home.

4 Sugar & Spice

At **Henzls Ernte** (Map p240; www.henzls.at; 05, Kettenbrückengasse 3; 1-6pm Tue-Fri, 9am-5pm Sat; U Kettenbrückengasse), you might see the Henzl family drying, grinding and blending their home-grown and foraged herbs and spices with sugar and salt. Specialities include sloe-berry salt, lavender sugar, wild-garlic pesto and green-tomato preserve.

5 Farm Fresh

Farmers' store **Helene** (Map p240; www.bauernladenhelene.at; 05, Kettenbrückengasse

Artisanal cheeses

7; ⏲8am-6pm Tue-Fri, to 3pm Sat; Ⓤ Kettenbrückengasse) has a smorgasbord of quality fresh regional produce. You'll find Joseph Brot vom Pheinsten organic loaves from the Waldviertel, chestnut, larch and acacia honeys from Lower Austria, and wine and chilli jam from Burgenland.

6 Regional Cheeses

All-organic Austrian cheeses made by small artisan dairies around the country are the speciality of **Käseschatztruhe** (Map p240; www.kaeseschatztruhe.at; 04, Kettenbrückengasse 10; ⏲10am-6.30pm Wed-Fri, 9am-2.30pm Sat; Ⓤ Kettenbrückengasse). Among the varieties here are Froihof's soft sheep cheeses from Styria, Ziegenliese's semihard goat's cheeses from Burgenland, and Plangger's *Höhlentaler* (similar to Emmental) from Tyrol.

7 Just Desserts

At chocolatier and patisserie **Fruth** (Map p240; www.fruth.at; 04, Kettenbrückengasse 20; ⏲11am-7pm Tue-Fri, 9am-5pm Sat; Ⓤ Kettenbrückengasse), Eduard Fruth creates edible works of art. Delicacies include strawberry tartlets, rich truffles, featherlight eclairs, and chocolate flavoured with chilli, chestnut and cranberry.

brunch for poached eggs (with truffle aoili or spicy avocado), pancakes and French toast. Beyond Austrian dishes, lunch and dinner menus make international forays, from Indian masala curry to Thai papaya salad. Cocktails include a Ho-gu (Prosecco, limoncello, elderberry syrup, mint and soda).

UMARFISCH SEAFOOD €€

Map p240 (☎01-587 04 56; www.umarfisch.at; 06, Naschmarkt Stand 76-79; mains €19-29; ⏲10am-11pm Mon-Sat; Ⓤ Karlsplatz) One of the best fish restaurants in Vienna, Umarfisch serves seafood from the Mediterranean and beyond at its large Naschmarkt stall. Choose between whole fish, mussels in white-wine sauce and giant shrimps fried in herb butter along with wines from the Wachau. The midweek lunch menu ($14.90) is a bargain.

There's a second stall at Naschmarkt stand 38-39.

TANCREDI AUSTRIAN €€

Map p240 (☎01-941 00 48; www.tancredi.at; 04, Grosse Neugasse 5; mains €14-25; ⏲11.30am-2.30pm Mon, 11.30am-2.30pm & 6-11pm Tue-Fri, 6-11pm Sat; Ⓤ Taubstummengasse) An extensive range of Austrian wines complements the expertly prepared seasonal fare at this welcoming spot with warm, pastel-yellow walls, stripped-back wooden floors, fittings from yesteryear and an umbrella-shaded garden. On weekdays, lunch menus cost €9.80 to €16.80. The entrance is on Rubengasse.

DRINKING & NIGHTLIFE

Pubs, bars, cocktail specialists and clubs – as well as cafes that turn into nightlife hotspots – are especially prevalent around Naschmarkt (p92) and Theobaldgasse. This neighbourhood is home to one of Vienna's liveliest gay scenes, with drinking and nightlife hangouts scattered throughout the area.

★CAFÉ SCHWARZENBERG CAFE

Map p240 (www.cafe-schwarzenberg.at; 01, Kärntner Ring 17; ⏲7.30am-midnight Mon-Fri, 8.30am-midnight Sat & Sun; 📶; 🚊2, 71 Schwarzenbergplatz) One of the last grand Viennese coffee houses on the Ringstrasse, this 1861 beauty has chandelier-lit vaulted ceilings, wood-panelled walls, marble tables and studded leather seats. Secessionist architect and designer Josef Hoffmann was among its patrons and it still draws a local crowd for its coffee, international newspapers, flaky *Warmer Topfenstrudel* (warm cheese-curd strudel) and sublime *Sacher Torte*.

★CAFÉ SPERL — COFFEE

Map p240 (www.cafesperl.at; 06, Gumpendorfer Strasse 11; ⏲7am-10pm Mon-Sat, 10am-8pm Sun, closed Sun Jul & Aug; 📶; Ⓤ Museumsquartier, Kettenbrückengasse) With its gorgeous *Jugendstil* fittings, grand dimensions, cosy booths and unhurried air, 1880-opened Sperl is one of the finest coffee houses in Vienna. The must-try is *Sperl Torte,* an almond-and-chocolate-cream dream. Grab a slice and a newspaper, order a coffee (from some three dozen kinds) and join the people-watching patrons. A live pianist plays from 3.30pm to 5.30pm on Sundays.

RAFAEL'S VINOTHEK — WINE BAR

Map p240 (06, Naschmarkt Stand 121; ⏲10am-8pm Mon-Fri, to 6pm Sat; Ⓤ Kettenbrückengasse) Over 450 different wines from all over Austria are stocked at this Naschmarkt *Vinothek*. Many are available to drink at its wine-barrel tables by the glass or bottle, accompanied by cheese and charcuterie platters in a chaotically sociable atmosphere.

CAFÉ RÜDIGERHOF — CAFE

Map p240 (05, Hamburgerstrasse 20; ⏲9am-2am; Ⓤ Kettenbrückengasse, Pilgramgasse) Rüdigerhof's facade is a glorious example of *Jugendstil* architecture, and the '50s furniture and fittings inside could be straight out of an *I Love Lucy* set. The atmosphere is homey and familiar, and the shaded wraparound garden huge. Hearty Austrian fare – huge schnitzels, spinach *Spätzle* (noodles), goat's cheese strudel – is way above average. On Saturday mornings it fills with Naschmarkt shoppers.

JUICE DELI — JUICE BAR

Map p240 (www.juicedeli.at; 06, Mariahilfer Strasse 45, Shop 20, Raimundhof; ⏲8.30am-6pm Mon-Fri, 10am-5pm Sat; 📶; Ⓤ Neubaugasse) 🍃 Tucked in a courtyard reached via a narrow alleyway leading off Mariahilfer Strasse, this locavore spot uses regionally sourced, seasonal organic fruit, vegetables and herbs in its cold-pressed juices and smoothies such as mango and banana with handmade almond milk. It also has detox water varieties (lemongrass and mint, or ginseng). Plastic packaging is shunned in favour of glass bottles.

BARFLY'S CLUB — COCKTAIL BAR

Map p240 (www.barflys.at; 06, Esterházygasse 33; ⏲6pm-2am Mon-Thu, to 4am Fri & Sat, 8pm-2am Sun; Ⓤ Neubaugasse, Zieglergasse) This sophisticated low-lit bar is famous for its extensive cocktail list and intimate ambience, which attracts a regular crowd of journalists and actors. It's decorated with photos of Ernest Hemingway, Fidel Castro, Che Guevara, Marilyn Monroe, plus the Rat Pack, whose music plays in the background. Drinks aren't cheap, but they're among the city's best.

JAKOV'S WEINKELLER — WINE BAR

Map p240 (04, Rechte Wienzeile 25-27; ⏲11am-10pm Mon-Fri, to 11pm Sat; Ⓤ Kettenbrückengasse) Wine barrels double as tables outside Jakov's (a favourite with stallholders from the nearby Naschmarkt) with more seats inside at the wooden bar. Wines from Burgenland, Styria and Lower Austria's Weinviertel are specialities; there are also Hungarian reds and delicate Italian whites. Try them by the glass along with charcuterie and cheese platters, or pick up bottles to go.

FELIXX — GAY

Map p240 (www.felixx-bar.at; 06, Gumpendorfer Strasse 5; ⏲10am-2am Sun-Thu, to 3am Fri & Sat; Ⓤ Museumsquartier) Chandeliers, mini-disco balls, striped wallpaper and leather lounges make this one of Vienna's classiest gay bars. Themed events might include 'girl bands' or 'retro' with '70s and '80s music; check the online calendar for the week's agenda. Its on-site cafe is especially popular for Sunday's 'drag brunch'.

ZWEITBESTER — BAR

Map p240 (www.zweitbester.at; 04, Heumühlgasse 2; ⏲11.30am-1am Mon-Fri, 10am-2am Sat, 10am-midnight Sun; 📶; Ⓤ Kettenbrückengasse) Bang in the heart of the Freihausviertel, Zweitbester hosts DJ nights as well as fun events such as table-football championships and a summer street festival. There's a pavement terrace for imbibing on summer nights.

ALT WIEN

COFFEE

Map p240 (www.altwien.at; 04, Schleifmühlgasse 23; 10am-6pm Mon-Fri, to 4pm Sat; Kettenbrückengasse) The enticing aroma of coffee wafts from Alt Wien. It roasts organic, fair-trade beans in Vienna's 23rd district, from where it's delivered each day, and sells its blends and accessories here. Sip a cup at the little bar on-site.

WIEDEN BRÄU

MICROBREWERY

Map p240 (www.wieden-braeu.at; 04, Waaggasse 5; 11.30am-midnight Sep-late Dec & early Jan-Jun, 4pm-midnight Sat & Sun Jul & Aug; ; Taubstummengasse) *Helles, Märzen* and *Radler* beers are brewed year-round at this upbeat microbrewery, and there are a few seasonal choices, including a ginger beer and hemp beer. All are brewed in keeping with the 1516 German Purity Law and are matched with Austrian dishes such as schnitzel and goulash. Retreat to the garden in summer.

EBERT'S COCKTAIL BAR

COCKTAIL BAR

Map p240 (www.eberts.at; 06, Gumpendorfer Strasse 51; 7pm-2am Tue-Sat; Neubaugasse, Kettenbrückengasse) Expert bartenders shake things up: all the mixologists here double as instructors at the bartending academy next door. The cocktail list is novel-esque, the vibe stylish, modern minimalism, the tunes jazzy to electronic, and on weekends you'll barely squeeze in.

CAFÉ JELINEK

COFFEE

Map p240 (www.steman.at; 06, Otto-Bauer-Gasse 5; 9am-10pm; ; Zieglergasse) With none of the polish or airs and graces of some other coffee houses, this shabbily grand cafe is Viennese through and through. The wood-burning stove, picture-plastered walls and faded velvet armchairs draw people from all walks of life with their cocoon-like warmth. Join locals lingering over freshly roasted coffee, cake and the daily newspapers.

CAFÉ SAVOY

GAY

Map p240 (www.savoy.at; 06, Linke Wienzeile 36; 10am-1am Mon-Thu, 10am-2am Fri, 9am-1am Sat, 9am-1am Sun; ; Kettenbrückengasse) Café Savoy is an established gay haunt with the ambience of a traditional cafe (its massive mirrors are the second largest in Europe after Versailles). The clientele is generally very mixed on a Saturday – mainly due to the proximity of the Naschmarkt – but at other times it's filled with men of all ages.

ROXY

CLUB

Map p240 (www.roxyclub.org; 04, Faulmanngasse 2; 11pm-4am Fri & Sat; D, 1, 2 Kärntner Ring/Oper, Karlsplatz) This seminal Viennese venue still manages to run with the clubbing pack, and sometimes leads the way. DJs from Vienna's electronica scene regularly guest on the turntables and most nights it's hard to find a space on the small dance floor. Expect a crowded, but very good, night out. Cash only.

PHIL

BAR

Map p240 (https://phil.business.site; 06, Gumpendorfer Strasse 10-12; 5pm-1am Mon, 9am-1am Tue-Sat, 9am-midnight Sun; ; Museumsquartier, Kettenbrückengasse) A retro bar, book and record store, Phil has a relaxed-as-it-gets vibe and attracts a bohemian crowd happy to hang out on kitsch furniture like your grandma used to own. TVs from the '70s, DVDs, records and books are for sale, as is all the furniture.

CLUB U

CLUB

Map p240 (www.club-u.at; 01, Künstlerhauspassage; 9pm-4am; ; Karlsplatz) Club U occupies one of Otto Wagner's **Stadtbahn Pavillons** on Karlsplatz. It's a small, student-favourite bar-club with regular DJs and a wonderful outdoor seating area overlooking the pavilions and park. Happy hour runs from 9pm to 11pm.

MANGO BAR

GAY

Map p240 (www.why-not.at; 06, Laimgrubengasse 3; 10pm-6am Fri & Sat; Kettenbrückengasse) Mango attracts a young gay crowd with good music, friendly staff and plenty of mirrors to check out yourself and others. There are three bars, a dance floor and a darkroom. It's often the place where the party continues for those who don't want the night to end.

ENTERTAINMENT

The Staatsoper is the biggest show in town, but this neighbourhood is also home to the Musikverein (where the Vienna Philharmonic Orchestra performs), the prestigious Theater an der Wien (p100), and a slew of cinemas including many art-house venues.

★STAATSOPER — OPERA

Map p240 (☎01-514 44 7880; www.wiener-staatsoper.at; 01, Opernring 2; tickets €14-287, standing room €4-10, tour adult/child €9/4; D, 1, 2, 62, 71 Kärntner Ring/Oper, UKarlsplatz) The glorious Staatsoper is Vienna's premier opera and classical-music venue. Productions are lavish, formal affairs, where people dress up accordingly. In the interval, wander the foyer and refreshment rooms to fully appreciate the gold-and-crystal interior. Opera is not performed here in July and August, though tours (p90) still take place. Tickets can be purchased up to two months in advance.

★MUSIKVEREIN — CONCERT VENUE

Map p240 (☎01-505 81 90; www.musikverein.at; 01, Musikvereinsplatz 1; tickets €15-105, standing room €7-15; box office 9am-8pm Mon-Fri, to 1pm Sat Sep-Jun, 9am-noon Mon-Fri Jul & Aug; UKarlsplatz) The opulent Musikverein holds the proud title of the best acoustics of any concert hall in Austria, which the Vienna Philharmonic Orchestra embraces. The lavish interior can be visited by 45-minute guided tour (in English; adult/child €8.50/5) at 1pm Tuesday to Saturday. Smaller-scale performances are held in the Brahms Saal. There are no student tickets.

THEATER AN DER WIEN — THEATRE

Map p240 (☎01-588 85-111; www.theater-wien.at; 06, Linke Wienzeile 6; tickets €5-165; box office 10am-6pm Mon-Sat, 2-6pm Sun; UKarlsplatz) The Theater an der Wien has hosted some monumental premiere performances, including Beethoven's *Fidelio,* Mozart's *The Magic Flute* and Johann Strauss II's *Die Fledermaus*. These days, besides staging musicals, dance and concerts, it's re-established its reputation for high-quality opera.

Student tickets go on sale 30 minutes before shows; standing-room tickets are available one hour prior to performances.

BURG KINO — CINEMA

Map p240 (☎01-587 84 06; www.burgkino.at; 01, Opernring 19; tickets €8-9.50; D, 1, 2 Burgring, UMuseumsquartier) The Burg Kino shows *The Third Man,* Orson Welles' timeless classic set in post-WWII Vienna, at least three times a week in English without subtitles. Most other screenings, from Hollywood blockbusters to art-house releases from around the world, are in their original languages, sometimes with German or English subtitles.

FILMCASINO — CINEMA

Map p240 (☎01-587 90 62; www.filmcasino.at; 05, Margaretenstrasse 78; tickets €9.50-10.50; UKettenbrückengasse) An art-house cinema of some distinction, Filmcasino screens an excellent mix of Asian and European documentaries and avant-garde short films, along with independent feature-length films from around the world. Its '50s-style foyer is particularly impressive.

SHOPPING

Food shops proliferate here, particularly around the eastern side of the Naschmarkt (p94). This neighbourhood also has some of the city's most exciting design boutiques and studios. Vienna's longest shopping street, Mariahilfer Strasse, is lined with shopping centres and high-street stores, as well as a handful of one-off boutiques.

★FLOHMARKT — MARKET

Map p240 (Flea Market; 05, Linke Wienzeile; 6.30am-2pm Sat; UKettenbrückengasse) One of the best flea markets in Europe, this Vienna institution adjoining the Naschmarkt's southwestern end brims with antiques and *Altwaren* (old wares). Some 400 stalls hawking books, clothes, records, ancient electrical goods, old postcards, ornaments, carpets, you name it, stretch for several blocks. Arrive early, as it gets increasingly packed, and be prepared to haggle.

★GEGENBAUER
FOOD & DRINKS

Map p240 (www.gegenbauer.at; 06, Naschmarkt Stand 111-112; ⏲9am-6pm Mon-Fri, to 5pm Sat; ⓊKarlsplatz) Some of the world's finest chefs use the oils and vinegars from this cornerstone of the Naschmarkt. At his Vienna distillery, Erwin Gegenbauer makes over 70 different vinegars from fruits and vegetables such as asparagus, fig, melon, tomato, as well as beer, along with balsamic varieties from grapes (some aged in oak casks) and 20 flavoured oils.

BEER LOVERS
DRINKS

Map p240 (www.beerlovers.at; 06, Gumpendorfer Strasse 35; ⏲11am-8pm Mon-Fri, 10am-5pm Sat; ⓊKettenbrückengasse) A wonderland of craft beers, this emporium stocks over 1000 labels from at least 125 different breweries in more than 70 styles, with more being sourced every day. Tastings are offered regularly, and cold beers are available in the walk-in glass fridge and in refillable growlers. It also stocks craft ciders, small-batch liqueurs and boutique nonalcoholic drinks such as ginger beers.

KÄSELAND
CHEESE

Map p240 (www.kaeseland.com; 06, Naschmarkt Stand 172-174; ⏲9am-6pm Mon-Fri, 8am-6pm Sat; ⓊKarlsplatz, Kettenbrückengasse) Cheese aficionados find it nearly impossible to tear themselves away from this venerable Naschmarkt stand, which has been in this spot for four decades. Over 100 Austrian cheeses (prized Lüneberg, Montafoner Sauerkäse and Tiroler Graukäse included) are piled high alongside hand-picked varieties from Switzerland, Italy and Hungary. Vacuum packing is available.

BLÜHENDES KONFEKT
FOOD

Map p240 (☎0660 341 1985; www.bluehendes-konfekt.com; 06, Schmalzhofgasse 19; ⏲10am-6.30pm Wed-Fri, by reservation Mon & Tue; ⓊZieglergasse, Westbahnhof) Violets, forest strawberries and cherry blossom, mint and oregano – Michael Diewald makes the most of what grows wild and in his garden to create confectionery that fizzes with seasonal flavour. Peek through to the workshop to see flowers and herbs being deftly transformed into one-of-a-kind bonbons and minibouquets that are edible works of art. Cash only.

★GABARAGE UPCYCLING DESIGN
DESIGN

Map p240 (www.gabarage.at; 04, Schleifmühlgasse 6; ⏲10am-6pm Mon-Thu, 7pm Fri, 11am-5pm Sat; ⓊTaubstummengasse) Recycled design, ecology and social responsibility underpin the quirky designs at Gabarage. Old bowling pins become vases, rubbish bins get a new life as tables and chairs, advertising tarpaulins morph into bags, and traffic lights are transformed into funky lights.

TEUCHTLER RECORDS
MUSIC

Map p240 (☎01-586 21 33; www.schallplatten-ankauf-wien.com; Windmühlgasse 10; ⏲1-6pm Mon & Fri, 10am-1pm Sat; ⓊNeubaugasse) Film fans will recognise Teuchtler Records from Richard Linklater's classic 1995 Vienna homage *Before Sunrise* – the promotional poster still hangs prominently above the till. It jostles for pride of place amongst autographed headshots of jazz stars, punk-rock record posters and vintage gramophone players. This is a musical cave of wonders covering everything from the Beatles to rare opera recordings.

FEINEDINGE*
CERAMICS

Map p240 (www.feinedinge.at; 04, Margaretenstrasse 35; ⏲10am-6pm Mon-Sat; ⓊKettenbrückengasse) Sandra Haischberger's exquisite handmade porcelain reveals a clean, modern aesthetic. Her range of home accessories, tableware and lighting is minimalist, but often features sublime details, such as crockery in chalky pastels, filigree lamps that cast exquisite patterns, and candle holders embellished with floral and butterfly motifs.

SPORTS & ACTIVITIES

KLETTERANLAGE FLAKTURM
CLIMBING

Map p240 (☎01-585 47 48; www.flakturm-klettern.at; climbing incl gear per hour €37; ⏲2pm-dusk Apr-Oct; ⓊNeubaugasse) The stark outside walls of the *Flakturm* (flak tower) in Esterházypark are used for climbing exercises organised by the Österreichischer Alpenverein (Austrian Alpine Club). Over 30 routes (gradients four to eight) climb to a maximum height of 34m.

The Museum District & Neubau

Neighbourhood Top Five

❶ **Kunsthistorisches Museum Vienna** (p104) Throwing yourself head first into the artistic vortex of the Museum of Art History, a whirl of Habsburg treasures from Egyptian tombs to rare-breed Raphael, Dürer and Caravaggio masterworks.

❷ **MuseumsQuartier** (p110) Checking Vienna's cultural pulse during an art-packed day at this vast ensemble of museums, cafes, restaurants and bars inside the Hofburg's former imperial stables.

❸ **Naturhistorisches Museum** (p113) Encountering the dinosaurs and prehistoric divas at the Museum of Natural History.

❹ **Rathaus** (p114) Revelling in the neo-Gothic riches of the City Hall on a free guided tour.

❺ **Burgtheater** (p114) Taking a behind-the-scenes tour of Vienna's magnificent theatre, which has staged premieres by Mozart and Beethoven, among others, throughout its illustrious history.

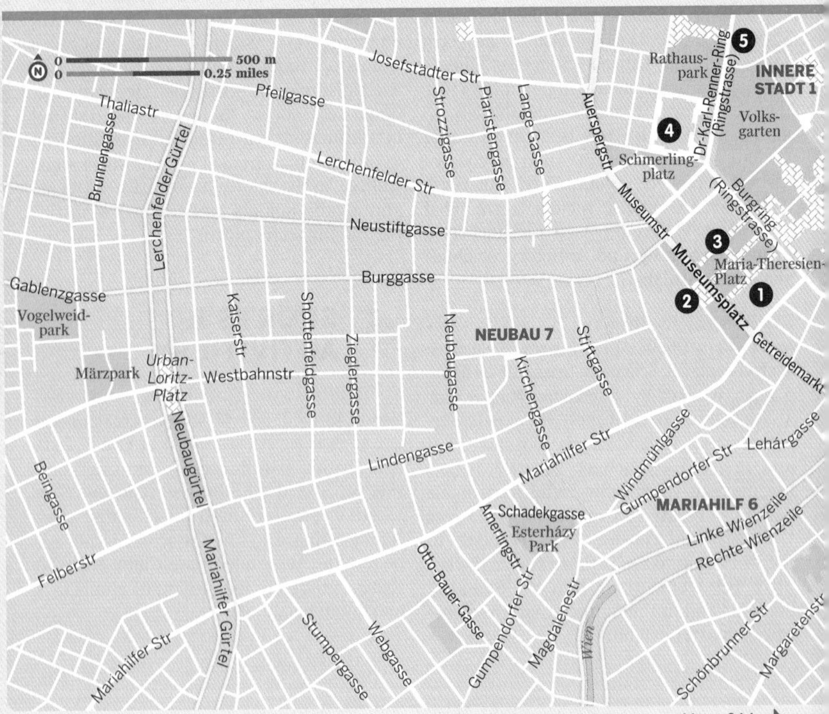

For more detail of this area see Map p244

Explore the Museum District & Neubau

The Museum District and Neubau walk a fine line between Habsburg history and modernity. The baroque imperial stables have cantered into the 21st century with their transformation into the MuseumsQuartier (p110), a colossal complex of on-the-pulse bars, cafes, boutiques and museums, including the Leopold (p110), the proud holder of the world's largest Schiele collection. Hang out in the courtyards here in summer and the creativity in the air is palpable.

Just around the corner on Maria-Theresien-Platz is the Kunsthistorisches Museum Vienna (p104), an epic and exhilarating journey through art, where Rubens originals star alongside Giza treasures. Its architectural twin is the neoclassical Naturhistorisches Museum (p113) opposite.

When you've had your fill of art and culture, keep tabs on Vienna's evolving fashion and design scene with a mosey around Neubau's backstreet studios and boutiques. After dark, the live-wire clubs and bars tucked under the Gürtel arches, slightly west, are where the young Viennese go to party.

Local Life

Schanigärten Life Join the locals toasting summer at a flurry of *Schanigärten* (pavement cafes and courtyard gardens), including Amerlingbeisl (p117) in Spittelberg, and Kantine (p116) and Café Leopold (p119) in the MuseumsQuartier.

Design Life Mill around Kirchengasse, Lindengasse, Neubaugasse and Zollergasse, where artists and creatives put a fresh spin on Viennese fashion and design.

Brunch Life Grazing over brunch at local hotspots like Figar (p115) or Liebling (p115).

Getting There & Away

U-Bahn Useful U-Bahn stops include Museumsquartier (U2 line) and Volkstheater (U2 and U3). The U3 Neubaugasse and Zieglergasse stops, and the U6 stops Burggasse Stadthalle and Thaliastrasse are best for accessing Neubau.

Tram Trams D, 1 and 71 travel around the Ringstrasse, stopping at Rathausplatz/Burgtheater and Parlament en route. The No. 49 line trundles from Ring/Volkstheater through Neubau, with handy stops including Siebensterngasse and Westbahnstrasse/Neubaugasse.

Lonely Planet's Top Tip

Time your visit to catch one of the neighbourhood sights' guided tours. Gallery tours that are covered in the admission price include those at the Kunsthalle Wien at 3pm and 4pm on Saturday and Sunday, and the MUMOK at 4pm on Saturday. Free guided tours of the neo-Gothic Rathaus take place at 1pm on Monday, Wednesday and Friday. Palais Epstein, housing the Austrian national parliament administrative offices, also has free tours by appointment on Saturday.

Best Places to Eat

- Tian Bistro (p116)
- Vestibül (p117)
- Liebling (p115)
- Figar (p115)

For reviews, see p115.

Best Places to Drink

- Melete Art Design Cocktails (p117)
- J Hornig Kaffeebar (p117)
- Espresso (p117)
- Café Leopold (p119)

For reviews, see p117.

Best Shopping

- Die Werkbank (p118)
- Das Möbel (p118)
- S/GHT (p119)

For reviews, see p121.

TOP SIGHT
KUNSTHISTORISCHES MUSEUM VIENNA

The Habsburgs built many bombastic palaces but, artistically speaking, the Kunsthistorisches Museum Vienna is their magnum opus. Occupying a neoclassical building as sumptuous as the art it contains, the museum takes you on a time-travel treasure hunt – from classical Rome to Egypt and the Renaissance. If your time's limited, skip straight to the old master paintings in the Picture Gallery.

Picture Gallery

The Kunsthistorisches Museum Vienna's vast Gemäldegalerie (Picture Gallery) is by far and away the most impressive of its collections. Devote at least an hour or two to exploring its feast of old masters.

Dutch, Flemish & German Painting

First up is the **German Renaissance**, where Lucas Cranach the Elder stages an appearance with engaging Genesis tableaux like *Paradise* (1530) and *Fall of Man* (aka *Adam and Eve;* 1537). The key focus, though, is the prized Dürer collection. Dürer's powerful compositions, sophisticated use of light and deep feeling for his subjects shine through in masterful pieces like *Portrait of a Venetian Lady* (1505), the spirit-soaring *Adoration of the Trinity* (1511) and the macabre *Martyrdom of the Ten Thousand* (1508).

Rubens throws you in the deep end of **Flemish baroque** painting next, with paintings rich in Counter-Reformation themes and mythological symbolism. The monumental *Miracles of St Francis Xavier* (1617), which used to hang in Antwerp's Jesuit church, the celestial *Annunciation* (1610), the *Miracles of St Ignatius* (1615–20) and the *Triptych of*

DON'T MISS

- Dutch Golden Age paintings
- Italian, Spanish & French collection
- Kunstkammer
- Offering Chapel of Ka-ni-nisut

PRACTICALITIES

- KHM, Museum of Art History
- Map p244, H4
- www.khm.at
- 01, Maria-Theresien-Platz
- adult/child incl Neue Burg museums €16/free
- 10am-6pm Fri-Wed, to 9pm Thu Jun-Aug, closed Mon Sep-May
- U Museumsquartier, Volkstheater

St Ildefonso (1630) all reveal the iridescent quality and linear clarity that underscored Rubens' style. Mythological masterworks move from the gory, snake-riddled *Medusa* (1617) to the ecstatic celebration of love in *Feast of Venus* (1636).

In 16th- and 17th-century **Dutch Golden Age** paintings, the desire to faithfully represent reality through an attentive eye for detail and compositional chiaroscuro is captured effortlessly in works by Rembrandt, Ruisdael and Vermeer. Rembrandt's perspicuous *Self-Portrait* (1652), showing the artist in a humble painter's smock, Ruisdael's palpable vision of nature in *The Large Forest* (1655) and Vermeer's seductively allegorical *The Art of Painting* (1665), showing Clio, Greek muse of history, in the diffused light of an artist's studio, are all emblematic of the age.

Keenly felt devotional works by Flemish baroque master **Van Dyck** include *The Vision of the Blessed Hermann Joseph* (1630), in room XXIII, in which the Virgin and kneeling monk are bathed in radiant light, and *Virgin and Child with Saints Rosalie, Peter and Paul* (1629), in room XIV. An entire room (X) is given over to the vivid depictions of Flemish life and landscapes by Flemish Renaissance painter **Pieter Bruegel the Elder**, alongside his biblical star attraction, *The Tower of Babel* (1563).

Italian, Spanish & French Painting

The first three rooms here are given over to key exponents of the **16th-century Venetian** style: Titian, Veronese and Tintoretto. High on your artistic agenda here should be Titian's *Nymph and Shepherd* (1570), elevating the pastoral to the mythological in its portrayal of the futile desire of the flute-playing shepherd for the beautiful maiden out of his reach. Veronese's dramatic depiction of the suicidal Roman heroine *Lucretia* (1583), with a dagger drawn to her chest, and Tintoretto's *Susanna and the Elders* (1556), watched by two lustful power brokers, are other highlights.

Devotion is central to Raphael's *Madonna of the Meadow* (1506) in room III, one of the true masterpieces of the **High Renaissance**, as it is to the *Madonna of the Rosary* (1607), a stirring Counter-Reformation altarpiece by **Italian baroque** artist Caravaggio in room V. Room VII is also a delight, with compelling works like Giuseppe Arcimboldo's anthropomorphic paintings inspired by the seasons and elements, such as fruit-filled *Summer* (1563), *Winter* (1563) and *Fire* (1566). Look out, too, for Venetian landscape

GUIDED TOURS

For more insight, pick up a multilingual audio guide (€5) near the entrance. The KHM runs 30-minute guided tours in English (€4); tours of the Picture Gallery and Kunstkammer take place at 4pm on Sunday, and the Egyptian, Near Eastern and Antiquities collections at noon on Sunday. There are also regular guided tours in German. See www.khm.at for details.

As you climb the ornate main staircase of the Kunsthistorisches Museum Vienna, your gaze is drawn to the ever-decreasing circles of the cupola, and marble columns guide the eye to delicately frescoed vaults, roaring lions and Antonio Canova's mighty statue of *Theseus Defeats the Centaur* (1805). Austrian legends Hans Makart and the brothers Klimt have left their hallmark between the columns and above the arcades – the former with lunette paintings, the latter with gold-kissed depictions of women inspired by Greco-Roman and Egyptian art.

Kunsthistorisches Museum Vienna

HALF-DAY TOUR OF THE HIGHLIGHTS

The Kunsthistorisches Museum Vienna's scale can seem daunting; this half-day itinerary will help you make the most of your visit.

Ascend the grand marble staircase, marvelling at the impact of Antonio Canova's *Theseus Slaying the Centaur*. Turn right into the Egyptian and Near Eastern Collection, where you can decipher the reliefs of the ❶ **Offering Chapel of Ka-ni-nisut** in room II. Skip through millennia to Ancient Rome, where the intricacy of the ❷ **Gemma Augustea Cameo** in room XVI is captivating. The other wing of this floor is devoted to the Kunstkammer Wien, hiding rarities such as Benvenuto Cellini's golden ❸ **Saliera** in room XXIX.

Head up a level to the Picture Gallery, a veritable orgy of Renaissance and baroque art. Moving into the East Wing brings you to Dutch, Flemish and German Painting, which starts with Dürer's uplifting

Gemma Augustea Cameo
Greek & Roman Antiquities, Room XVI
Possibly the handiwork of imperial gem-cutter Dioscurides, this sardonyx cameo from the 1st century CE shows in exquisite bas-relief the deification of Augustus, in the guise of Jupiter, who sits next to Roma. The defeated barbarians occupy the lower tier.

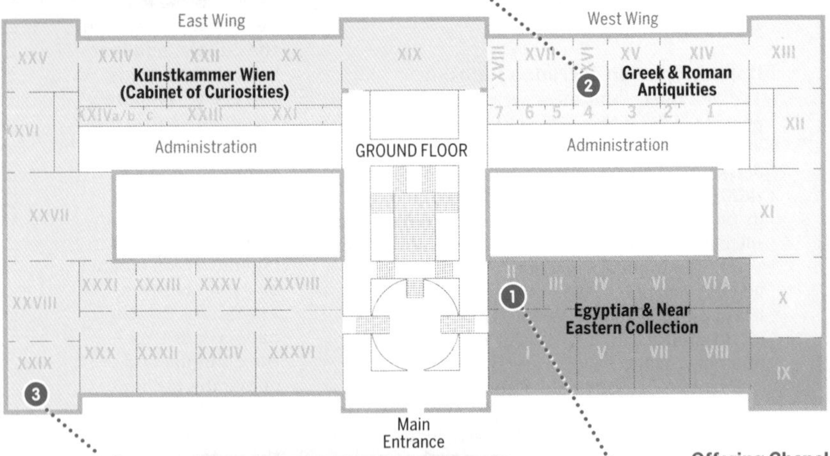

Saliera
Kunstkammer Wien, Room XXIX
Benvenuto Cellini's hand-wrought gold salt cellar (1543) is a dazzling allegorical portrayal of Sea and Earth, personified by Tellus and trident-bearing Neptune. They recline on a base showing the four winds, times of day and human activities.

Offering Chapel of Ka-ni-nisut
Egyptian & Near Eastern Collection, Room II
Reliefs and hieroglyphs depict the life of high-ranking 5th-dynasty official Ka-ni-nisut, together with his wife, children and entourage of mortuary priests and servants. This 4500-year-old tomb chamber is a spectacular leap into the afterlife.

4 **Adoration of the Trinity** in room XV, takes in meaty Rubens and Rembrandt works en route, and climaxes with Pieter Bruegel the Elder's absorbingly detailed 5 **The Tower of Babel** in room X. Allocate equal time to the Italian, Spanish and French masters in the halls opposite. Masterpieces including Raphael's 6 **Madonna of the Meadow** in room 4, Caravaggio's merciful 7 **Madonna of the Rosary** in room V and Giuseppe Arcimboldo's 8 **Summer** in room 7 steal the show.

TOP TIPS

➡ Pick up an audio guide and a floor plan in the entrance hall to orient yourself.

➡ Skip to the front of the queue by booking your ticket online.

➡ Visit between 6pm and 9pm on Thursday for fewer crowds.

➡ Flash photography is not permitted.

The Tower of Babel
Dutch, Flemish & German Painting, Room X
The futile attempts of industrial souls to reach godly heights are magnified in the painstaking detail of Bruegel's *The Tower of Babel* (1563). Rome's Colosseum provided inspiration.

Madonna of the Meadow
Italian, Spanish & French Painting, Room 4
The Virgin Mary, pictured with infants Christ and St John the Baptist, has an almost iridescent quality in Raphael's seminal High Renaissance 1506 masterpiece, set against the backdrop of a Tuscan meadow.

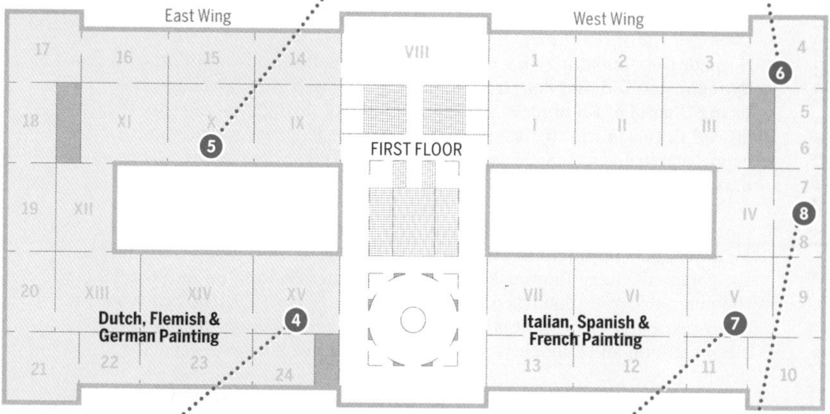

Adoration of the Trinity
Dutch, Flemish & German Painting, Room XV
Dürer's magnum-opus altarpiece was commissioned by Nuremberg merchant Matthäus Landauer in 1511. Angels, saints and earthly believers surround the Holy Trinity, while Dürer hides in the bottom right-hand corner.

Madonna of the Rosary
Italian, Spanish & French Painting, Room V
Caravaggio's trademark chiaroscuro style brings depth, richness and feeling to this 1607 masterpiece. Holding infant Jesus, the Madonna asks St Dominic to distribute rosaries to the barefooted poor who kneel before her.

Summer
Italian, Spanish & French Painting, Room 7
Italian court painter Giuseppe Arcimboldo's *Summer* (1563) was a hit with the Habsburgs. The most striking of his four seasons cycle, this masterwork celebrates seasonal abundance in the form of a portrait composed of fruit and vegetables.

painter Canaletto's *Schönbrunn* (1761), meticulously capturing the palace back in its imperial heyday.

Of the artists represented in the rooms dedicated to **Spanish, French and English** painting, the undoubted star is Spanish court-painter Velázquez. Particularly entrancing is his almost 3D portrait of *Infanta Margarita Teresa in a Blue Dress* (1651–73), in room XII, a vision of voluminous silk and eight-year-old innocence. English painter Sir Joshua Reynolds' studied *Portrait of a Young Lady* (c 1760–5) and French painter Jean-Marc Nattier the Younger's *Princess Maria Isabella of Parma* (1758) are both in room XIII.

Kunstkammer

Imagine the treasures you could buy with brimming coffers and the world at your fingertips. The Habsburgs did just that, filling their *Kunstkammer* (cabinet of art and curiosities) with an encyclopaedic collection of the rare and the precious: from narwhal-tusk cups to table holders encrusted with fossilised shark teeth. Its 20 themed rooms containing 2200 artworks open a fascinating window on the obsession with collecting curios in royal circles in Renaissance and baroque times.

The biggest crowd-puller here is Benvenuto Cellini's allegorical *Saliera* (salt cellar), room XXIX, commissioned by Francis I of France in 1540, which is exquisitely hand-crafted from rolled gold, ivory and enamel. Among the Kunstkammer's other top-drawer attractions are the wildly expressive, early-17th-century ivory sculpture *Furie* (Master of the Furies), the serenely beautiful *Krumauer Madonna* (1400), a masterpiece of the Bohemian Gothic style, and Gasparo Miseroni's lapis lazuli *Dragon Cup* (1570), a fiery beast glittering with gemstones.

Egyptian & Near Eastern Collection

Decipher the mysteries of Egyptian civilisations with a chronological romp through this miniature Giza of a ground-floor collection, beginning with **predynastic** and **Old Kingdom** treasures. Here the exceptionally well preserved **Offering Chapel of Ka-ni-nisut** spells out the life of the high-ranking 5th-dynasty official in reliefs and hieroglyphs. The Egyptian fondness for adornment finds expression in artefacts such as a monkey-shaped kohl container and fish-shaped make-up palette.

Stele, sacrificial altar slabs, jewellery boxes, sphinx busts and pharaoh statues bring to life the **Middle Kingdom** and **New Kingdom**. The Egyptian talent for craftsmanship shines in pieces like a turquoise ceramic hippo (2000 BC) and the gold seal ring of Ramses X (1120 BC). The **Late Period** dips into the land of the pharaohs, at a time when rule swung from Egypt to Persia. Scout out the 3000-year-old *Book of the Dead of Khonsu-mes,* the polychrome mummy board of Nes-pauti-taui and Canopic jars with lids shaped like monkey, falcon and jackal heads.

Stone sarcophagi, gilded mummy masks and busts of priests and princes transport you back to the **Ptolemaic** and **Greco-Roman** period. In the **Near Eastern** collection, the representation of a prowling lion from Babylon's triumphal Ishtar Gate (604–562 BC) is the big attraction.

Greek & Roman Antiquities

This rich Greek and Roman repository reveals the imperial scope for collecting classical antiquities, with 2500 objects traversing three millennia from the Cypriot Bronze Age to early medieval times.

Cypriot and Mycenaean Art catapults you back to the dawn of Western civilisation, 2500 years ago. The big draw here is the precisely carved votive statue of a man wearing a finely pleated tunic. Among the muses, torsos and

Kunsthistorisches Museum and Maria-Theresien-Platz

mythological statuettes in **Greek Art** is a fragment from the Parthenon's northern frieze showing two bearded men. The arts flourished in **Hellenistic** times, evident in exhibits like the *Amazonian Sarcophagus,* engraved with warriors so vivid you can almost hear their battle cries. In **pre-Roman Italy**, look for sculptures of Athena, funerary crowns intricately wrought from gold, and a repoussé showing the Titans doing battle with the gods.

The sizeable **Roman** stash includes the 4th-century AD *Theseus Mosaic* from Salzburg, a polychrome, geometric marvel recounting the legend of Theseus. You'll also want to take in the captivating 3rd-century AD *Lion Hunt* relief and the 1st-century AD *Gemma Augustea,* a sardonyx bas-relief cameo. Early medieval showstoppers include the shimmering golden vessels from the **Treasure of Nagyszentmiklós**, unearthed in 1799 in what is now Romania.

Kunstschatzi Cocktails

Sipping a cocktail under the Kunsthistorisches Museum Vienna's dome, illuminated with dazzling projections, is unforgettable. The museum organises monthly Kunstschatzi cocktail evenings (7pm to 11pm Tuesday; €16, not including museum admission), during which DJs work the decks and the Picture Gallery remains open all evening. Check schedules and prebook online.

COIN COLLECTION

A piggy bank of gigantic Habsburg proportions, this coin collection covers three halls and three millennia on the 2nd floor (rooms I, II and III). The 2000 notes, coins and medallions on display are just a tiny fraction of the Kunsthistorisches Museum Vienna's 700,000-piece collection.

The coin collection's first hall presents medals of honour, first used in Renaissance Italy around 1400, and showcases gold and silver House of Habsburg wonders. The second hall travels through monetary time, from the birth of the coin in Lydia in the 7th century BC to the 20th century. Look out for classical coins, like the stater embellished with a lion head, in circulation under Alyattes, King of Lydia (610–560 BC), and Athenian coins featuring the goddess Athena and her owl symbol. The third hall stages one-off exhibitions.

TOP SIGHT
MUSEUMSQUARTIER

Baroque heritage and the avant-garde collide at the MuseumsQuartier, one of the world's most-ambitious cultural spaces. Spanning 90,000 sq metres, this ensemble of museums, cafes, restaurants, shops, bars and performing-arts venues occupies the former imperial stables designed by Fischer von Erlach in 1725. You can't see it all in a day, so exploring selectively is the way to go.

Leopold Museum

The **Leopold Museum** (Map p244; www.leopoldmuseum.org; adult/child €14/10; ⏲10am-6pm Fri-Wed, to 9pm Thu Jun-Aug, closed Mon Sep-May) is named after Rudolf Leopold, a Viennese ophthalmologist who, on buying his first Egon Schiele (1890–1918) for a song as a young student in 1950, started to amass a huge private collection of mainly 19th-century and modernist Austrian artworks. In 1994 he sold the lot – 5266 paintings – to the Austrian government for €160 million (sold individually, the paintings would have made him €574 million), and the Leopold Museum was born. Café Leopold (p119) is located on the top floor.

The Leopold has a white limestone exterior, open space (the 21m-high glass-covered atrium is lovely) and natural light flooding most rooms. Considering Rudolf Leopold's love of Schiele, it's no surprise the museum contains the world's largest collection of the painter's work: 41 paintings and 188 drawings and graphics. Among the standouts are the ghostly 1911 *Self-Seer II (Man and Death)*, the mournful *Mother with Two Children* (1915) and the 1912 caught-in-the-act *Cardinal and Nun (Caress)*.

Other artists well represented include Albin Egger-Lienz, with his unforgiving depictions of pastoral life, Richard Gerstl and Austria's third-greatest expressionist, Oskar

DON'T MISS

- Schiele collection at the Leopold Museum
- Viennese Actionism at the MUMOK
- Cafe life in the courtyard in summer

PRACTICALITIES

- Museum Quarter; MQ
- Map p244, G4
- ☎01-523 58 81
- www.mqw.at
- 07, Museumsplatz
- ⏲information & ticket centre 10am-7pm
- 🚊49 Volkstheater, Ⓤ Museumsquartier, Volkstheater

Kokoschka. Of the handful of works on display by Klimt, the unmissable is the allegorical *Death and Life* (1910), a swirling amalgam of people juxtaposed by a skeletal grim reaper. Works by Adolf Loos, Josef Hoffmann and Otto Wagner are also on display.

MUMOK

The dark basalt edifice and sharp corners of **MUMOK** (Museum Moderner Kunst, Museum of Modern Art; Map p244; www.mumok.at; adult/child €12/free; 2-7pm Mon, 10am-7pm Tue, Wed & Fri-Sun, 10am-9pm Thu) are a complete contrast to the MQ's historical sleeve. Inside, MUMOK is crawling with Vienna's finest collection of 20th- and 21st-century art, centred on Fluxus, nouveau realism, pop art and photorealism. The best of expressionism, cubism, minimal art and Viennese Actionism is represented in a collection of 9000 works that are rotated and exhibited by theme – but take note that sometimes all the Actionism is packed away to make room for temporary exhibitions. Viennese Actionism evolved in the 1960s as a radical leap away from mainstream art, in what some artists considered to be a restrictive cultural and political climate. Artists like Günter Brus, Hermann Nitsch and Rudolf Schwarzkogler aimed to shock with their violent, stomach-churning performance and action art, which often involved using the human body as a canvas. Not only did their work shock, some artists were even imprisoned for outraging public decency. Other well-known artists represented throughout the museum – Pablo Picasso, Paul Klee, René Magritte, Max Ernst, Alberto Giacometti, Dorit Margreiter and Yto Barrada – are positively tame in comparison. Check the program before visiting with children to ensure exhibits are suitable.

Kunsthalle Wien

The **Kunsthalle** (Arts Hall; Map p244; 01-521 890; www.kunsthallewien.at; adult/child €8/free; 11am-7pm Tue, Wed & Fri-Sun, to 9pm Thu;) is a collection of exhibition halls used to showcase local and international contemporary art. Its high ceilings, open planning and functionality have helped the venue leapfrog into the ranks of the top exhibition spaces in Europe. Programs, which run for three to six months, rely heavily on photography, video, film, installations and new media. Weekend visits include one-hour guided tours in English and German. The Saturday tours (Halle 1 at 3pm, Halle 2 at 4pm) focus on a theme, while Sunday tours (same times) give an overview.

CHILDREN'S THEATRE

Dschungel Wien (p120) covers the entire spectrum, from drama and puppetry to music, dance and narrative theatre. There are generally several performances daily in German and occasionally in English; see the website for details. Adults pay children's prices for matinee performances.

The MuseumsQuartier's courtyards host a winter and summer program of events, from film festivals to Christmas markets, literary readings to DJ nights; see the website www.mqw.at for details. Their cafe terraces hum with life in the summer.

DANCE

Tanzquartier Wien (Map p244; 01-581 35 91; www.tqw.at; 07, Museumsplatz 1; tickets €10-57; box office 10am-4.30pm mid-Jul–Aug, 9am-7.30pm Mon-Fri, 10am-7.30pm Sat Sep–mid-Jul; U Museumsquartier, Volkstheater) is Vienna's first dance institution. It hosts an array of local and international performances with a strong experimental nature. Students receive a €10 discount on advance tickets. Unsold tickets (€5) go on sale 15 minutes before showtime.

MUSEUMSQUARTIER COMPLEX

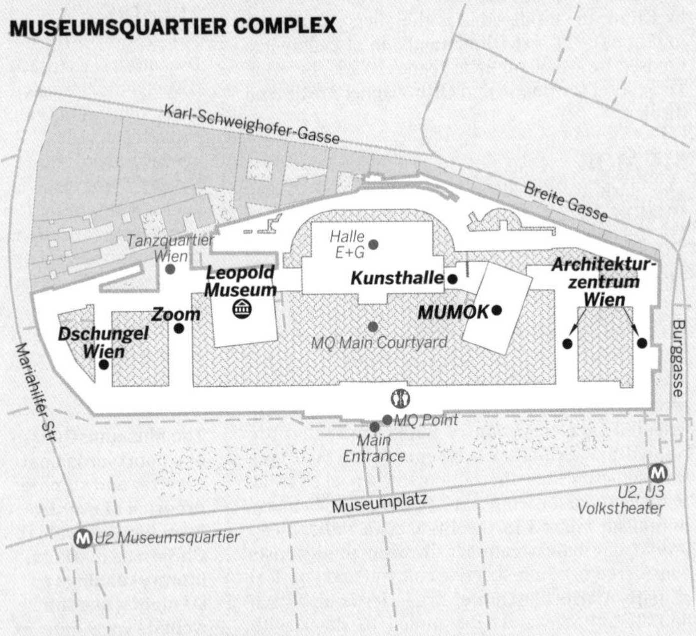

Architekturzentrum Wien

The **Architekturzentrum Wien** (Vienna Architecture Centre; Map p244; ☎01-522 31 15; www.azw.at; adult/child €9/2.50; ⊙architecture centre 10am-7pm, library 10am-5.30pm Mon, Wed & Fri, to 7pm Sat & Sun) collectively encompasses three halls used for temporary exhibitions, a library and a cafe. Exhibitions focus on international architectural developments, and change on a regular basis. Check the online calendar and book ahead for regular walking tours through Vienna (in English and German) organised by the centre, covering various architectural themes.

Zoom

Kids love this hands-on **children's museum** (Map p244; ☎01-524 79 08; www.kindermuseum.at; exhibition adult/child €6/free, activities child €5-7, accompanying adult €6; ⊙Tue-Sun; 👪), an arts-and-crafts session with lots of play thrown in. Budding Picassos have the chance to make, break, draw, explore and be creative in the 'Atelier'. 'Exhibition' stages a new exhibition every six months, while 'Ocean' appeals to tots with its mirrored tunnels, grottoes and ship deck for adventure play that stimulates coordination. For children aged eight to 14, there is an animated film studio and the future-focused Lab Club. Check schedules on the website. Activities last one to 1½ hours; reserve at the ticket office or online.

TOP SIGHT
NATURHISTORISCHES MUSEUM

Vienna's astounding Naturhistorisches Museum covers four billion years of natural history in a blink. With its exquisitely stuccoed halls and eye-catching cupola, this late-19th-century building is the identical twin of the Kunsthistorisches Museum Vienna which sits opposite. Among its minerals, fossils and dinosaur bones are one-of-a-kind finds like the miniscule 25,000-year-old Venus of Willendorf and a peerless 1100-piece meteorite collection.

DON'T MISS

- Meteorite collection
- Venus of Willendorf and Fanny of Galgenberg
- Dinosaurs in room 10
- Rooftop tours

PRACTICALITIES

- Museum of Natural History
- Map p244, G3
- www.nhm-wien.ac.at
- 01, Maria-Theresien-Platz
- adult/child €12/free, planetarium extra €5/3, rooftop tours €8
- ⌚9am-6.30pm Thu-Mon, to 9pm Wed, rooftop tours in English 3pm Fri, Sat & Sun Apr-Dec, 3pm Sun Jan-Mar
- Ⓤ Volkstheater

Ground Floor: Meteorites, Dinosaurs & Prehistoric Finds

The ground floor leads in with a treasure chest of minerals, fossils and gemstones, with star exhibits like the 115kg chunk of smoky quartz from Switzerland's Tiefen Glacier, a 6.2kg platinum nugget from the Urals and the dazzling 'Blumenstrauss' **gemstone bouquet** which Maria Theresia gave to Emperor Franz I in 1760.

Room 5 blasts you into outer space with the world's largest **meteorite** collection, featuring such beauties as the Martian meteorites Chassigny that landed in France in 1815; Tissint, which fell in Morocco in 2011; and the iron Cabin Creek meteorite, which landed in Arkansas in 1886.

For kids and **dinosaur** fans, the big-hitters hang out in room 10 on the ground floor. On a raised platform loom the skeletons of a diplodocus, iguanodon and a 6m-tall animatronic replica of an allosaurus. Keep an eye out, too, for the skeleton of an *Archelon ischyros*, the largest turtle ever.

Rooms 11 to 13 spell out **prehistory** in artefacts, with curiosities such as the coat of a woolly mammoth and Neanderthal tools. Highlights include the Stone Age Venus of Willendorf, just 11cm tall, and 32,000-year-old Fanny of Galgenberg, one of the world's oldest female statuettes, named after famous Viennese dancer Fanny Elssler (1810–84).

Occupying rooms 14 to 15, the **anthropological collection** brings to life hominid evolution and themes such as bipedalism and brain development at hands-on stations. You can determine the gender, age and cause of death of a virtual skeleton at the CSI table, take and email a prehistoric photo of yourself, and spot the difference between Neanderthals and *Homo sapiens* by touching skulls.

Room 16 has a 62-seat digital **planetarium** with a 8.5m dome. Its 45-minute films span 'the Earth to the Universe' to 'Live to the Stars: Journey Through the Night'. Shows are in German, with multilingual audio guides.

First Floor: Zoology

The 1st floor is a taxidermist's dream. Spotlighting zoology and entomology, the collection slithers, rattles, crawls, swims and swings with common, endangered and extinct species, from single-cell organisms to large mammals. Showstoppers include a 1.4m-wide giant clam in room 23, a Galapagos giant tortoise in room 28, two-toed sloths, found in 1831 in Brazil, in room 33, and a fin-whale skeleton in room 34.

Rooftop Tours

Panoramic rooftop tours take you onto the building's roof to view the ornate architecture up-close; children under 12 aren't allowed.

SIGHTS

The trophy sights in this neighbourhood are concentrated on the eastern side of Museumsplatz.

KUNSTHISTORISCHES MUSEUM VIENNA — MUSEUM

See p104.

MUSEUMSQUARTIER — MUSEUM

See p110.

NATURHISTORISCHES MUSEUM — MUSEUM

See p113.

BURGTHEATER — THEATRE

Map p244 (☎01-514 44 4140; www.burgtheater.at; 01, Universitätsring 2; tours adult/child €7/3.50; ⏲English tours 3pm daily Jul & Aug, 3pm Fri-Sun Sep-Jun; 🚋D, 1, 71 Rathausplatz/Burgtheater) This stately Renaissance-style theatre (p120) sits with aplomb on the Ringstrasse. Designed by Gottfried Semper and Karl von Hasenauer and completed in 1888, it was restored to its pre-WWII glory in 1955. The theatre company dates to 1741, making it Europe's second oldest. If the walls could talk, they'd tell of musical milestones like the premiere of Mozart's *The Marriage of Figaro* (1786) and Beethoven's *First Symphony* (1800). For a behind-the-scenes look at this magnificent theatre, join a 50-minute guided tour.

HOFMOBILIENDEPOT — MUSEUM

Map p244 (Imperial Furniture Collection; ☎01-524 33 57; www.hofmobiliendepot.at; 07, Andreasgasse 7; adult/child incl audio guide €10.50/6.50, incl 1hr guided tour €12.50/7.50; ⏲10am-6pm Tue-Sun; UZieglergasse) The Habsburgs stashed away the furniture not displayed in the Hofburg, Schönbrunn, Schloss Belvedere and their other palaces at the Hofmobiliendepot. A romp through this regal attic of a museum, covering four floors and 165,000 objects, provides fascinating insight into furniture design, with highlights such as a display of imperial travelling thrones, Emperor Maximilian's coffin and Empress Elisabeth's neo-Renaissance bed from Gödöllő Castle. One of the more underrated museums in the city, it's included in the Sisi Ticket (p68).

JUSTIZPALAST — HISTORIC BUILDING

Map p244 (☎01-521 52-0; www.justiz.gv.at; 01, Schmerlingplatz 11; ⏲7.30am-3.30pm Mon-Fri; 🚋46 Schmerlingplatz, UVolkstheater) Completed in

TOP SIGHT
RATHAUS

The crowning glory of the Ringstrasse boulevard's 19th-century architectural ensemble, Vienna's neo-Gothic City Hall was completed in 1883 by Friedrich von Schmidt of Cologne Cathedral fame and modelled on Flemish city halls. From the fountain-filled **Rathauspark**, where Josef Lanner and Johann Strauss I, fathers of the Viennese waltz, are immortalised in bronze, you get the full effect of its facade of lacy stonework, pointed-arch windows and spindly turrets.

For an insight into the Rathaus' history, take the free guided tour that leads through the **Arkadenhof**, one of Europe's biggest arcaded inner courtyards, and the barrel-vaulted **Festsaal** (Festival Hall), which hosts the Concordia Ball in June. Look for the reliefs of composers Mozart, Haydn, Gluck and Schubert in the orchestra niches. In the **Stadtsitzungsaal** (Council Chamber), a 3200kg-heavy, flower-shaped chandelier dangles from a coffered ceiling encrusted with gold-leaf rosettes and frescoes depicting historic events such as the foundation of the university in 1365. Other tour highlights include the **Stadtsenatssitzungssaal** (Senate Chamber), the **Wappensäle** (Coat of Arms Halls) and the **Steinsäle** (Stone Halls).

DON'T MISS

- Rathauspark
- Arkadenhof
- Festsaal
- Stadtsitzungsaal

PRACTICALITIES

- City Hall
- Map p244, G1
- ☎01-502 55
- www.wien.gv.at
- 01, Rathausplatz 1
- admission free
- ⏲tours 1pm Mon, Wed & Fri Sep-Jun, 1pm Mon-Fri Jul & Aug
- 🚋D, 1, 2, 71 Rathausplatz/Burgtheater, URathaus

1881, the Justizpalast is home to the supreme court. It's an impressive neo-Renaissance building that – as long as you're not being dragged in wearing handcuffs – is also interesting inside. The 23m-high central hall is a majestic ensemble of staircase, arcades, glass roofing and an oversized statue of Justitia poised with her sword and law book. To enter, you pass through airport-style security; bring photo ID.

PALAIS EPSTEIN NOTABLE BUILDING

Map p244 (☎01-401 10 2400; www.parlament.gv.at; 01, Dr-Karl-Renner-Ring 1; ⏲tours by reservation 10.30am & 1.30pm Sat; 🚊D, 1, 2, 71 Ring/Volkstheater, ⓊVolkstheater) FREE Designed by Theophil Hansen, the same architect who created the plans for the **Österreichisches Parlament** (Austrian parliament) next door, Palais Epstein houses Austrian national parliament administrative offices and the glass atrium rises an impressive four floors. The only way to see inside is by taking a free one-hour guided tour in English and German through its hallowed halls and visit its *bel étage* (1st-floor) rooms. Tour times can vary.

HAUPTBÜCHEREI WIEN LIBRARY

Map p244 (www.buechereien.wien.at; 07, Urban-Loritz-Platz 2a; ⏲11am-7pm Mon-Fri, to 5pm Sat; ⓊBurggasse-Stadthalle) Vienna's central city library straddles the U6 line, its pyramid-like steps leading up to the enormous main doors, which are two storeys tall. At the top of the library is the Café Oben (p120), which has far-reaching views to the south.

EATING

Spittelberg's warren of narrow lanes and the streets fanning west of the MuseumsQuartier, between Burggasse and Mariahilfer Strasse, are packed with restaurants, cafes and bars, many of which offer inexpensive lunch menus.

LIEBLING CAFE €

Map p244 (☎01-990 58 77; www.facebook.com/liebling1070; 07, Zollergasse 6; dishes €3.50-11; ⏲kitchen 9am-10pm, bar 9am-2am Mon-Thu, to 4am Fri & Sat, to midnight Sun; 📶✎; ⓊNeubaugasse) No sign hangs above the door at Liebling, whose distressed walls, stripped-back floorboards and mishmash of flea-market furniture create a cool, laid-back vibe. Settle in for breakfast (until 4pm), sip fresh-squeezed juices, and lunch on wholesome daily specials like spinach-feta strudel or pumpkin and pine-nut wraps, topped off with chocolate-lavender cake. By night the bar is rocking. Cash only.

NIGHT AT THE NATURHISTORISCHES MUSEUM

If you're keen to re-create a *Night at the Museum* experience, book a **Nacht im Museum**. Adults (€200) receive a gala dinner, torch/flashlight tour of the permanent collections and champagne on the roof terrace before bedding down next to the dinosaurs and receiving a breakfast bag the following morning. Children (€75) must be accompanied by an adult, and also get a torch/flashlight tour. Films (included) screen in the planetarium. Bring your own sleeping bag. Check dates and make reservations on the museum's website or at its shop.

FIGAR CAFE €

Map p244 (☎01-890 99 47; http://1070.figar.net; 07, Kirchengasse 18; breakfast €4.50-9.50, mains €10-16; ⏲kitchen 8am-10.30pm Mon-Fri, 9am-10.30pm Sat & Sun, bar to midnight Sun-Wed, to 2am Thu-Sat; 📶; 🚊49 Siebensterngasse, ⓊNeubaugasse) Splashed with a street-art-style mural, this neighbourhood favourite serves mighty breakfasts until 4pm, from Working Class Hero (sausage, mushrooms, homemade baked beans, spinach and skewered roast cherry tomatoes) to Exquisite (Viennese Thum ham, chorizo, Emmental and scrambled eggs), plus yoghurt, muesli, porridge and pastries. At night it morphs into a craft cocktail bar with a soundtrack of house music.

SWING KITCHEN VEGAN €

Map p244 (www.swingkitchen.com; 07, Schottenfeldgasse 3; dishes €5-9; ⏲11am-10pm; 📶✎; ⓊZieglergasse) 🍃 Eco-minded Swing Kitchen calculates that its all-organic vegan burgers use 93% less land, 85% less water, 96% less grain, 95% less energy and produce 92% less greenhouse emissions than meat-based burgers. Its four varieties include a vegan schnitzel Vienna burger and Swing Burger with smoky barbecue sauce. Fries and onion rings are cooked in vegetable oil; there are also salads.

VEGANISTA ICE CREAM €

Map p244 (www.veganista.at; 07, Neustiftgasse 23; 1/2/3 scoops €1.80/3.60/4.80; noon-11pm Mon-Thu, 11am-11pm Fri-Sun; ; 49 Volkstheater) Set up by two vegan sisters, Veganista's nondairy ice cream is made with organic, regional ingredients. Each day sees 18 flavours available, with some unusual ones in the mix such as basil, green tea or blueberry-lavender.

TART'A TATA PASTRIES €

Map p244 (07, Lindengasse 35; pastries €1.20-5; 10am-6pm Mon-Sat; Neubaugasse) Exquisite French pastries – rainbows of macarons, glossy eclairs, *babas au rhum* (rum-soaked yeast cakes) and superb *tartes aux fraises* (strawberry tarts) – are laid out like jewels at this patisserie, which also makes flaky, buttery croissants and *pains au chocolat* (chocolate-filled glazed pastries). Pick up treats to take away or dine at its on-site cafe.

KANTINE CAFE €

Map p244 (01-523 82 39; www.mq-kantine.at; 07, Museumsplatz 1; mains €9-13; kitchen 9am-11pm, bar to midnight; ; 49 Volkstheater, Volkstheater, Museumsquartier) In the former stables of the emperor's personal steeds, this upbeat cafe/bar is the most laid-back spot to eat in the MuseumsQuartier. Lit by a disco ball, the vaulted interior has comfy chairs for lounging, surfing and refuelling over a salad, pita wrap or one of 30 cocktails. In summer, tables spill out onto the patio on MuseumsQuartier's main square.

NATURKOST ST JOSEF VEGETARIAN €

Map p244 (01-526 68 18; 07, Mondscheingasse 10; plate small/large €8.30/9.20; 8am-4pm Mon-Fri; ; 49 Siebensterngasse) At canteen-style St Josef, fill a small or large plate from its buffet to dine at the handful of seats downstairs or up on the 1st floor, which centres on a communal table. All-organic ingredients from its neighbouring grocery store at Zollergasse 26 are used in dishes like roasted aubergine stuffed with goat's cheese, or lentil and sweet-potato dahl.

★TIAN BISTRO VEGETARIAN €€

Map p244 (01-890 466 532; www.tian-bistro.com; 07, Schrankgasse 4; mains €9-18; 5.30-10pm Mon, noon-10pm Tue-Fri, 10am-10pm Sat & Sun; ; 49 Siebensterngasse) Colourful tables are set up on the cobbled laneway outside Tian Bistro in summer, while indoors, a glass roof floods the atrium-style, greenery-filled dining room in light. It's the cheaper, more relaxed offspring of Michelin-starred vegetarian restaurant Tian (p83), and serves sensational vegetarian and vegan dishes, such as black-truffle risotto with Piedmont hazelnuts, as well as a weekend brunch.

ULRICH INTERNATIONAL €€

Map p244 (01-961 27 82; www.ulrichwien.at; 07, St-Ulrichs-Platz 1; dishes €6-10.50, mains €12-18; 7.30am-11pm Mon-Fri, 9am-11pm Sat & Sun; ; 49 Volkstheater) A stone's throw from the MuseumsQuartier, this sleek cafe-restaurant always has a buzz, from breakfast (avocado toast, pancakes with seasonal fruit) to light lunches (homemade flatbreads, creative salads) through to mains like pumpkin risotto with *gambas* and pecorino, or wild-boar schnitzel. There's an impressive cocktail and wine list, and a delightful rear cobbled courtyard shaded by umbrellas.

GLACIS BEISL BISTRO €€

Map p244 (01-526 56 60; www.glacisbeisl.at; 07, Breite Gasse 4; mains €8-21.50; kitchen

MQ TICKETS & INFORMATION

If you're planning on visiting several museums, combined tickets are available from the **MQ Point** (01-523 58 81; www.mqw.at; 07, Museumsplatz 1; 10am-7pm; Museumsquartier, Volkstheater).

The **MQ Station Ticket** (€32) includes entry into every museum (Zoom only has a reduction) and a 30% discount on performances in the Tanzquartier Wien.

The **MQ Type Ticket** (€26) gives admission into the Leopold Museum, MUMOK, Kunsthalle and reduced entry into Zoom, plus a 30% discount on the Tanzquartier Wien.

Families will find information on activities for kids at the **WienXtra-Kinderinfo** (Map p244; 01-4000 84 400; www.wienxtra.at/kinderaktiv; 07, Museumsplatz 1; 2-6pm Tue-Fri, 10am-5pm Sat & Sun; ; Museumsquartier), which has knee-high display cases and a small indoor playground.

noon-11pm, bar 11am-2am; ; 49 Volkstheater, UVolkstheater) Hidden downstairs along Breite Strasse in the MuseumsQuartier (follow the signs from MUMOK), Glacis Beisl does an authentic *Krautfleckerl* (cabbage-and-pasta bake), an accomplished Wiener Schnitzel and some other very decent Austrian classics, which you can wash down with Viennese whites and reds. In summer, dine beneath the walnut trees among flowering geraniums in the sprawling courtyard.

KONOBA DALMATIAN €€

Map p244 (01-929 41 11; www.konoba.at; 08, Lerchenfelder Strasse 66-68; mains €9.50-19; 5-10.30pm; 46 Strozzigasse) Few restaurants in the city come close to Konoba's expertise with fish. The Dalmatian chefs know their product inside out and serve some of the freshest catch in town. Zander and *Goldbrasse* (sea bream) are often on the menu, but expect to find a wide array of seasonal dishes, too. The open-plan interior creates a convivial atmosphere.

AMERLINGBEISL AUSTRIAN €€

Map p244 (01-526 16 60; www.amerlingbeisl.at; 07, Stiftgasse 8; mains €8-16; kitchen noon-10pm, bar 11.30am-2am Mon-Fri, 10am-2am Sat & Sun; 49 Siebensterngasse, UVolkstheater) This tucked-away Spittelberg *Beisl* is an enchanting summer choice for its cobbled, lantern-lit courtyard swathed in ivy and vines. The seasonally inspired food hits the mark, too, whether you opt for light dishes like smoked trout salad, or hearty mains such as beef goulash with bread dumplings or crispy schnitzel with cranberry sauce.

VESTIBÜL AUSTRIAN €€€

Map p244 (01-532 49 99; www.vestibuel.at; 01, Universitätsring 2; mains €18-31, 3-/4-course dinner menus €58/72; noon-2.30pm & 6-10.30pm Tue-Fri, 6-10.30pm Sat; D, 1, 71 Rathausplatz/Burgtheater) In the southern wing of the Burgtheater, Vestibül is a showpiece of marble columns and stucco topped off with a glorious sparkling mirrored bar. The menu is a contemporary take on traditional cuisine with a strong regional and seasonal focus; expect such dishes as lobster meat with sauerkraut, or braised veal shoulder with smoked catfish sauce. Reservations are recommended.

DRINKING & NIGHTLIFE

Drinking and nightlife venues, including some fantastic cocktail bars, are scattered throughout this entire neighbourhood. Coffee specialists also abound. Many cafes and restaurants double as bars once food service has stopped for the evening.

★MELETE ART DESIGN COCKTAILS COCKTAIL BAR

Map p244 (www.melete.at; 07, Spittelberggasse 18; 5-10pm Thu & Fri, 3-10pm Sat; ; 49 Volkstheater) Both an art gallery and a hopping bar, Melete ingeniously pairs changing art exhibitions with inventive drinks. Its 'Africa' exhibition, for instance, featured cocktails like Madagascan Sunrise (vanilla-infused rum, hibiscus syrup and mango juice), while 'Art of Light' inspired concoctions such as Solar (yellow Chartreuse, gin, sweet vermouth and yuzu). Artworks exhibited are for sale; check the program online.

★J HORNIG KAFFEEBAR COFFEE

Map p244 (www.jhornig.com; 07, Siebensterngasse 29; 7.30am-7pm Mon-Fri, 9am-7pm Sat & Sun; ; Siebensterngasse) Farm-direct beans roasted on-site at this third-wave coffee specialist are utilised in espresso, pour-over, Aeropress, ice-drip and cold-brew techniques to create a perfect cup, which you can pair with locally baked cakes. The state-of-the-art space has a stainless-steel ceiling, industrial fixtures and designer plywood chairs, and plenty of power sockets to recharge your devices.

ESPRESSO CAFE

Map p244 (www.espresso-wien.at; 07, Burggasse 57; 7.30am-1am Mon-Fri, 10am-1am Sat & Sun; 46 Strozzigasse) Time warping you back to the 1950s with its formica tables, terrazzo floor, red-leather banquettes and vintage bar, this retro cafe is a relaxed spot for a strong shot of Italian espresso, a gourmet breakfast, organic dishes or a slice of homemade cake. Sit on the pavement terrace when sunny.

CAFÉ LEOPOLD BAR

Map p244 (www.cafeleopold.wien; 07, Museumsplatz 1; 9.30am-midnight; ; UMuseumsquartier, Volkstheater) The pick of the MuseumsQuartier bars, Café Leopold sits on top of the Leopold Museum (p110). Its design is sleek, with spacey lighting and

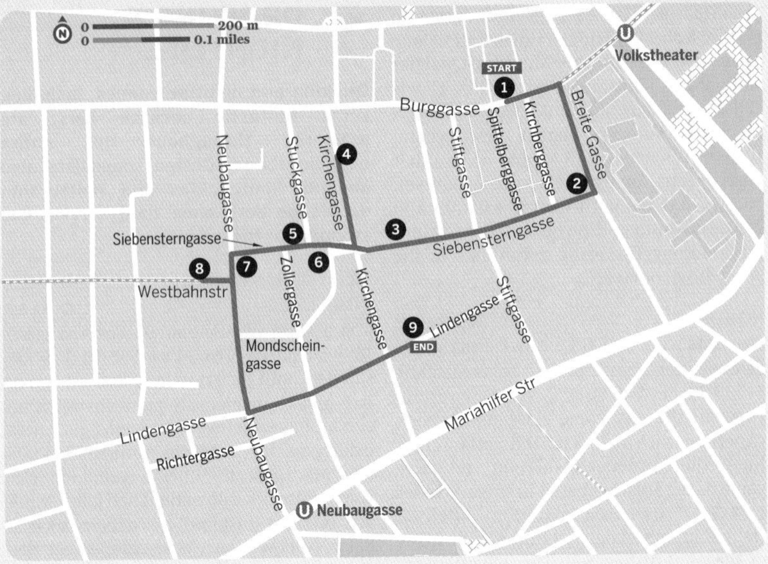

Local Life
Neubau's Design Scene

The ultimate place to tap into Vienna's burgeoning fashion and design scene is the city's happening 7th district, Neubau, a major creative hub where you'll often see artisans at work. This half-day stroll takes you to boutiques showcasing creations by the city's most exciting designers as well as fashion-focused cafes.

1 Coffee & Shopping

Das Möbel (Map p244; www.dasmoebel.at; 07, Burggasse 10; 9am-midnight Mon-Wed, to 1am Thu & Fri, 10am-1am Sat, to 11pm Sun; 49 Volksstheater) is as much of a hip cafe as a shop, serving locally roasted coffee, organic juices and a great breakfast/brunch menu. Meanwhile, it also showcases and sells some of the most original furniture in Vienna.

2 The Workbench

All-white space **Die Werkbank** (Map p244; www.werkbank.cc; 07, Breite Gasse 1; 1-6.30pm Tue-Fri, 11am-5pm Sat; 49 Volkstheater) – 'The Workbench' – operates as a design collective, where some of Vienna's most innovative designers showcase their works. Furniture, lamps, rugs, vases, jewellery, watches, graphic art, bags, even bicycles are among the creations you might find on display.

3 Art Deco & Bauhaus Designs

Stop by **Holzer Galerie** (Map p244; www.galerieholzer.at; 07, Siebensterngasse 32; 10am-noon & 2-6pm Mon-Fri, to 5pm Sat; 49 Siebensterngasse) for high-quality, highly polished furniture, ornaments and lighting mainly from the art deco and Bauhaus periods.

4 Unique Jewellery

Goldsmith Ilga Zemann puts her own imaginative spin on jewellery, from fragile silver leaf necklaces to quirky button rings at the **Schmuckladen** (Map p244; www.schmuckladen.org; 07, Kirchengasse 40; 1-6pm Wed, 11am-6.30pm Thu & Fri, 11am-5pm Sat; 49 Siebensterngasse) workshop.

5 Handcrafted Bags

Understated clutch, shoulder and tote bags, crafted from vegetable-tanned leather by **Ina Kent** (Map p244; www.inakent.com; 07, Siebensterngasse 50; 11am-7pm Mon-Fri, to 6pm Sat; 49 Siebensterngasse), are coveted by locals.

6 Applied Arts

Schauraum (Map p244; 0676 757 67 00; www.schauraum.at; 07, Siebensterngasse 33; by appointment; 49 Siebensterngasse)

Donau, Neubau

zooms in on unusual applied arts. Besides cutting-edge tableware and accessories, you'll find Karin Merkl's clever, versatile clothes made from merino wool or silk.

7 Emerging Talent

Forward-looking boutique **S/GHT** (Map p244; www.sight.at; 07, Neubaugasse 46; ⌚11am-7pm Mon-Fri, to 6pm Sat; 🚊49 Westbahnstrasse/Neubaugasse) promotes emerging Austrian labels along with breakthrough international designers.

8 Experimental Fashion

At **Wiener Konfektion** (Map p244; www.wiener-konfektion.at; 07, Westbahnstrasse 4; ⌚noon-6pm Mon-Fri, to 5pm Sat; 🚊49 Westbahnstrasse/Neubaugasse), all of the women's casualwear pieces are designed and made in Vienna by experimental owner/designer Maria Fürnkranz-Fielhauer. Maria creates T-shirts, skirts, dresses, sweat pants and more using contemporary fabrics and denim and wool blends.

9 Catwalk Trends

Slinky dresses, separates and swimwear by design maven **Elke Freytag** (Map p244; www.elkefreytag.com; 07, Lindengasse 14; ⌚noon-6pm Wed-Fri, 10am-3pm Sat; 🚊49 Siebensterngasse) regularly grace catwalks in Vienna and beyond.

a conservatory overlooking the action on MuseumsQuartier's square, and the atmosphere can feel more club than bar when DJs spin tunes. In chilly months, the outdoor terrace becomes a winter garden.

VREI BAR

Map p244 (☎0677 6200 58 88; www.vrei.at; 07, Lindengasse 53; ⌚4-11pm Thu, to 1am Fri & Sat Jun-Aug, 4-11pm Tue-Thu, to 1am Fri & Sat Sep-May; Ⓤ Zieglergasse) Virtual reality (VR) bar Vrei pairs technology and gaming with thin-crust pizza and beer. Offering free-to-try VR headsets and pay-to-play VR experiences (per 20 minutes €18), there is a wide choice of games to choose from. It also has a flight simulator, racing emulators and retro arcade games.

LE TROQUET BAR

Map p244 (07, Kirchengasse 18; ⌚4pm-2.30am Mon, 11am-2.30am Tue-Sat, 5pm-2am Sun; Ⓤ Neubaugasse) French is lingua franca at Le Troquet, which is styled like a Parisian cafe with a zinc bar. Wines and craft beers are sourced from all over France, and cocktails are retro (Harvey Wallbanger, Cuba Libre). Classic French cafe dishes include *croques monsieur* and *madame* (toasted ham and cheese sandwiches, the latter with a fried egg on top).

DACHBODEN ROOFTOP BAR

Map p244 (www.dachbodenwien.at; 07, Lerchenfelder Strasse 1-3; ⌚3pm-1am; 📶; 🚊46 Auerspergstrasse, Ⓤ Volkstheater) In the 25hours Hotel, Dachboden has stunning views of Vienna's skyline from its beach-bar-style terrace. DJs spin jazz, soul and funk on Wednesday and Friday nights. Inside, wooden crates and mismatched vintage furniture are scattered across the raw-concrete floor beneath chandeliers. Besides Fritz cola and an array of wines, beers, cocktails and speciality teas, there are tapas-style snacks.

DONAU CLUB

Map p244 (www.donautechno.com; 07, Karl-Schweighofer-Gasse 10; ⌚8pm-4am Mon-Thu, to 6am Fri & Sat, to 2am Sun; Ⓤ Museumsquartier) DJs spin techno to a pumped crowd at this underground club with soaring columns, striking digital projections on the walls, and its own on-site *Würstelstand* (sausage stand). It's easily missed – look for the grey metal door. Hours can vary.

SIEBENSTERNBRÄU MICROBREWERY

Map p244 (www.7stern.at; 07, Siebensterngasse 19; ⌚11am-midnight; 📶; 🚊49 Siebensterngasse) Sample some of Vienna's finest microbrews at this lively, no-nonsense brewpub. Besides hoppy lagers and malty ales, there are unusual varieties like chilli or wood-smoked beer. Try them with pretzels or pub grub like schnitzel, goulash and pork knuckles (lunch mains €6.90, dinner mains €7.90 to €18.90). The courtyard garden fills up quickly in the warmer months.

ROTE BAR BAR

Map p244 (www.facebook.com/DieRoteBar; 07, Neustiftgasse 1; ⌚10pm-2am Mon-Fri, to 4am Sat, to 1am Sun; 📶; UVolkstheater) Look for the door to the left of the Volkstheater's main entrance to find the stairs up to this lavish bar with marble, chandeliers and thick red-velvet curtains. It's a gorgeous space for cocktails or by-the-glass wines. Regular events range from performance art sessions to DJ-fuelled Saturday dance nights, tango nights, poetry readings and more.

CAFÉ EUROPA BAR

Map p244 (www.europa-lager.at; 07, Zollergasse 8; ⌚9am-5am; 📶; UNeubaugasse) A long-standing fixture in the 7th district, Europa's series of multicoloured rooms are a chilled hang-out at all hours. During the day, grab a window table for coffee or meal. In the evening, perch at the bar and listen to the DJs spin tunes. Breakfast (including continental, English, vegan and huge house-special 'Europa' options) revives a hungover clientele.

CAFÉ OBEN ROOFTOP BAR

Map p244 (www.oben.at; 07, Urban-Loritz-Platz 2a; ⌚10am-11pm Mon-Fri, 9am-11pm Sat, 10am-3pm Sun; UBurggasse-Stadthalle) *Oben* ('up') on top of the Hauptbücherei Wien (p115), the rooftop terrace here provides a sweeping vista of Vienna. Come for a coffee, organic juice, Viennese wine, Austrian beer, schnapps or cocktails with a view, or a good-value, two-course lunch (€8.20 to €10.60). Sunday brunch (€24.90) is very popular.

WIRR BAR, CLUB

Map p244 (www.wirr.at; 07, Burggasse 70; ⌚8am-2am Sun-Wed, to 4am Thu-Sat; 🚌46 Strozzigasse) On weekends it's often hard to find a seat on the time-worn sofas at this colourful, alternative bar with walls covered in local artists' works. Electro clubbing events take place in the cellar at **Dual** (www.clubdual.at).

☆ ENTERTAINMENT

★BURGTHEATER THEATRE

Map p244 (National Theatre; ☎01-514 44 4140; www.burgtheater.at; 01, Universitätsring 2; seats €7-61, standing room €3.50; ⌚box office 9am-5pm Mon-Fri, closed Jul & Aug; 🚋D, 1, 71 Rathausplatz/Burgtheater) The Burgtheater (p114) is one of the foremost theatres in the German-speaking world, staging some 800 performances a year, from Shakespeare to modern works. The theatre also runs the 500-seater **Akademietheater**, built around 1912.

VOLKSTHEATER THEATRE

Map p244 (☎01-521 11-400; www.volkstheater.at; 07, Arthur-Schnitzler-Platz 1; tickets €9-55; ⌚box office 10am-7.30pm Mon-Sat; UVolkstheater) With a seating capacity close to 1000, the Volkstheater is one of Vienna's largest theatres. Built in 1889, the interior is suitably grand. While most performances are of translated works (anything from Ingmar Bergman to Molière), only German-language shows are staged. Advance bookings are necessary; students can buy unsold tickets for €5 one hour before performances start.

DSCHUNGEL WIEN THEATRE

Map p244 (☎01-522 07 20 20; www.dschungelwien.at; 07, Museumsplatz 1; tickets adult/child from €9/6; ⌚box office 4-6pm Mon-Fri; 👪; UMuseumsquartier, Volkstheater) This theatre for children covers the entire spectrum, from drama and puppetry to music, dance and narrative theatre. There are generally several performances daily in German and occasionally in English; see the website for details. Adults pay children's prices for matinee performances.

VIENNA'S ENGLISH THEATRE THEATRE

Map p244 (☎01-402 12 60-0; www.englishtheatre.at; 08, Josefsgasse 12; tickets €24-47; ⌚box office 10am-7pm Mon-Fri, 5-7pm Sat performance days, closed Jul–mid-Aug; 🚋2 Rathaus, URathaus) Founded in 1963, Vienna's English Theatre is the oldest foreign-language theatre in Vienna (with the occasional show in French or Italian). Productions range from timeless pieces, such as Shakespeare, to contemporary works and comedies. Students receive a 20% discount and are eligible for standby tickets (€10) 15 minutes before showtime.

STADTHALLE SPECTATOR SPORT

(☎01-79 99 979; www.stadthalle.com; 15, Roland-Rainer-Platz 1; UBurggasse-Stadthalle) The

Stadthalle is a major venue for sporting events. Tennis tournaments (including the Austrian Open), horse shows and ice-hockey games are held here, and its swimming pool is a key venue for major aquatic events.

SHOPPING

The MuseumsQuartier and especially Neubau are a hive of creative activity; many Viennese artists and designers have ateliers here.

RUNWAY — FASHION & ACCESSORIES

Map p244 (www.runwayvienna.at; 07, Kirchengasse 48; ⏲11am-12.30pm & 1-6.30pm Tue-Fri, to 6pm Sat; 🚊46 Strozzigasse) Runway is a launching pad for up-and-coming Austrian fashion designers, whose creations sit alongside those of their established compatriots. Framed by arched windows, it showcases the direction of Viennese womenswear through its clothes and accessories.

WIENERKLEID — FASHION & ACCESSORIES

Map p244 (www.wienerkleid.at; 07, Siebensterngasse 20; ⏲12.30-6.30pm Mon-Fri, noon-5pm Sat; 🚊49 Siebensterngasse) 🍃 Doris Bittermann designs and sews seasonal fashion ranges at her Vienna studio that she sells here in her boutique. Her eco-inspired neo-vintage women's wear (dresses, skirts, trousers and tops) mixes organic materials and textures, and incorporates bold colours and prints.

IRENAEUS KRAUS — ART

Map p244 (www.irenaeuskraus.com; 07, Burggasse 28; ⏲11am-7pm Tue-Fri, to 4pm Sat; 🚊49 Siebensterngasse) Gallery-style shop Irenaeus Kraus sells detailed, centuries-old, pedagogical vintage posters covering botany, biology, anatomy, medicine and maps.

WALL — CONCEPT STORE

Map p244 (☎01-524 47 28; www.kaufhauswall.com; 07, Westbahnstrasse 5a; ⏲noon-6pm Tue, Wed, Fri & Sat, to 8pm Thu; 🚊49 Westbahnstrasse/Neubaugasse) Featuring Scandinavian, French and Dutch designs this lifestyle store fills its shelves with clothes, colognes, chunky jewellery, art-design books and plenty more. Wall also offers boutique hairdressing services, tailored to match your new plush leather jacket or ankle boots.

MÜHLBAUER — HATS

Map p244 (www.muehlbauer.at; 07, Neubaugasse 34; ⏲10am-6.30pm Mon-Fri, to 6pm Sat; 🚊49 Westbahnstrasse/Neubaugasse) This large boutique of Austrian milliner **Mühlbauer** (Map p238; www.muehlbauer.at; 01, Seilergasse 10; ⏲10am-6.30pm Mon-Fri, to 6pm Sat; Ⓤ Stephansplatz) uses materials such as felt, alpaca, mohair, rabbit, suede, cashmere, straw, seaweed, fur, merino and moleskin. Every style imaginable is available, including new collections each season. Or you can have a hat custom-made – shipping is available worldwide.

SCHOKOV — CHOCOLATE

Map p244 (www.schokov.com; 07, Siebensterngasse 20; ⏲noon-6.30pm Mon-Fri, 10am-6pm Sat; 🚊49 Siebensterngasse) Thomas Kovazh turned his chocolate-making dream into reality when he opened this sleek gallery-style shop. Today, Schokov sells some of Vienna's best pralines and truffles (over 200 varieties). Chilli, lavender, sea-salt, potato and pepper chocolate – you'll find them all in bar form here. A 1½-hour, 20-chocolate-tasting workshop (English available) costs €29.

ART POINT — FASHION & ACCESSORIES

Map p244 (www.artpoint.eu; 07, Neubaugasse 35; ⏲11am-7pm Mon-Fri, to 5pm Sat; 🚊49 Siebensterngasse, Ⓤ Neubaugasse) This boutique-design platform presents Lena Kvadrat's latest Austrian-Russian collection. Versatility is the hallmark, with pieces often layering fabrics to create unique looks.

SPORTS & ACTIVITIES

WIENER EISTRAUM — ICE SKATING

Map p244 (www.wienereistraum.com; 01, Rathausplatz; adult/child from €8/5.50, preheated skate hire €7.50/5.50; ⏲10am-10pm late Jan-early Mar; 🚊D, 1, 2, 71 Rathausplatz/Burgtheater, Ⓤ Rathaus) In winter, Vienna's Rathausplatz transforms into two connected ice rinks covering a total of 9000 sq metres. It's a magnet for the city's ice skaters, and is complemented by DJs, food stands, special events and *Glühwein* (mulled wine) bars. The skating path zigzags through the nearby park and around the square.

There's a free skating area for beginners and children, open 9am to 4pm Monday to Friday, 8am to 10pm Saturday and Sunday (you still need to pay for skate hire). At 5pm Monday to Friday, eight curling lanes set up.

Alsergrund & the University District

Neighbourhood Top Five

❶ **Sigmund Freud Museum** (p125) Getting in touch with your inner Freudian as you explore the elegant rooms of his former home, with exhibits providing an insight into the life of the father of psychoanalysis.

❷ **Josephinum** (p124) Delving into the anatomical collection of one of Vienna's most weird and wonderful museums.

❸ **Palais Liechtenstein** (p124) Tiptoeing through the palace's baroque apartments and landscaped gardens on a guided tour.

❹ **University Main Building** (p124) Going for an erudite wander through the arcades and courtyards of the 650-year-old university.

❺ **Beethoven Pasqualatihaus** (p124) Conjuring Beethoven's Fourth, Fifth and Seventh Symphonies in the airy apartment in which they were written.

❻ **Schubert Geburtshaus** (p124) Catching a concert in the composer's childhood home with fellow Schubertologists.

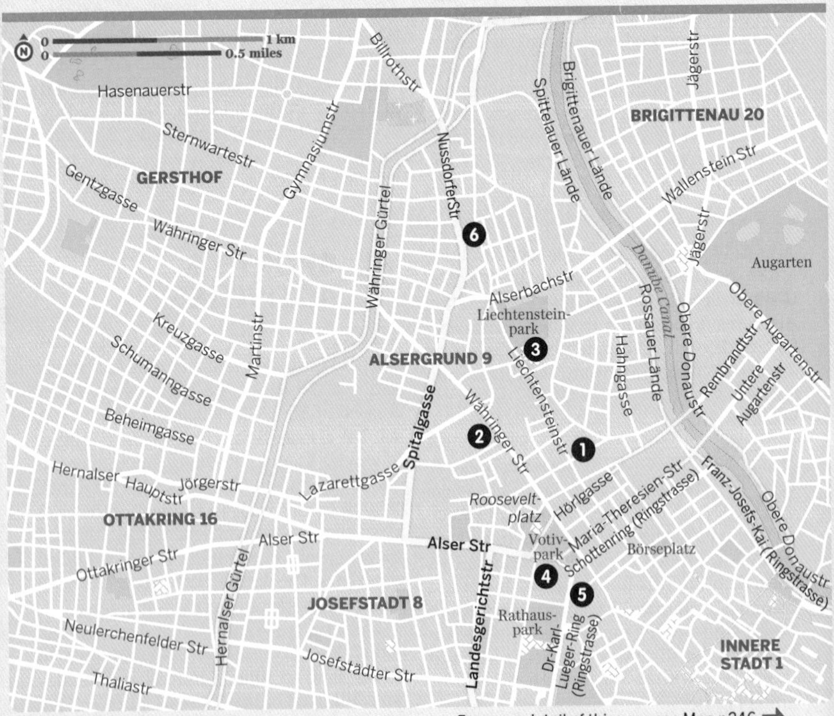

For more detail of this area see Map p246 ➡

Explore Alsergrund & the University District

The cool but far from contrived neighbourhoods of the 8th, 9th and 16th are decidedly local and best experienced at a laid-back Viennese pace. These are streets made for wandering and stopping for well-made coffees, a sneaky *Grüner Veltliner* white wine or quietly smart lunches, rather than ticking off iconic museums or wow-factor vistas. Once you leave the corporate types behind around the Innere Stadt, campus life and its cafes, bars and tiny shops begin in Alsergrund Vorstadt. In Josefstädter Strasse and the little streets running north you'll find a similar mix, or else wander west towards Ottakring for bass-thumping bars and upbeat music haunts hidden under the Gürtel's railway arches.

Local Life

Street Markets Feel Vienna's multiethnic pulse while snacking and strolling around Brunnenmarkt (p126), and find farm-fresh produce at the **Bauernmarkt** (Map p246; 16, Yppenplatz; ⌚8am-1pm Fri & Sat; 🚋44 Yppengasse, Neulerchenfelder Strasse, Ⓤ Josefstädter Strasse) and Bio-Markt Freyung (p132).

Backstreets This is a terrific neighbourhood for getting off the beaten track. Slip down quiet, tree-lined backstreets to find little-known sights like the Museum für Volkskunde (p125).

Cafes Coffee kings POC (p129), studenty Café Stein (p129) and micro-roastery CaffèCouture (p130) all have a loyal local following.

Getting There & Away

U-Bahn The closest stops to the centre for reaching Alsergrund and the university district are Schottentor and Rathaus on the U2 line. The U6 line follows the Gürtel further west; useful stops include Alser Strasse, Josefstädter Strasse and Währinger Strasse/Volksoper.

Tram Schottentor is a handy stop on the Ring. Other tram lines serving this neighbourhood include 44, which runs from Schottentor along Alser Strasse to the Hernalser Gürtel, and 5 and 33, which trundle along Josefstädter Strasse.

Lonely Planet's Top Tip

This neighbourhood throws itself into a festive summer vortex when it plays host to the Summer Stage, with food pavilions and stages strung along Rossauer Lände, on the banks of the Danube Canal (Donaukanal). The mood is incredibly upbeat, and there are regular concerts – some free – reaching from jazz to tango, rock to pop. It's on evenings between 5pm and 1am from May to September (take the U4 to Rossauer Lände). The website has the inside scoop.

Best Places to Eat

- Mamamon (p128)
- La Salvia (p127)
- Stomach (p128)
- La Tavolozza (p128)
- Swing Kitchen (p128)

For reviews, see p128.➡

Best Places to Drink

- Krypt (p129)
- Achtundzwanzig (p129)
- POC Cafe (p129)
- Birdyard (p130)
- Botanical Gardens (p130)
- Weinstube Josefstadt (p130)

For reviews, see p129.➡

Best Shopping

- Brunnenmarkt (p126)
- Staud's (p127)
- Xocolat (p132)

For reviews, see p132.➡

⊙ SIGHTS

The neighbourhoods of the 8th, 9th and 16th are chiefly residential but their collection of scattered, low-key sights can provide a nice counterpoint to the museum-heavy centre. Along with the Sigmund Freud Museum, there's a number of medical-themed museums that sit within the university campus, as well as some famous composers' former apartments and their enchanting (if rather slight) collections.

JOSEPHINUM MUSEUM

Map p246 (www.josephinum.meduniwien.ac.at; 09, Währinger Strasse 25; adult/child €8/free, guided tours €4; ☉4-8pm Wed, 10am-6pm Fri & Sat; ⓜ; ⓤWähringer Strasse/Volksoper) Architecture fans sometimes visit this Enlightenment-era complex for its superb 1785 neoclassical structures alone, although Joseph II's purpose-built medical academy for army surgeons does, in fact, house the city's most unusual museum. The highlight is its large collection of 200-year-old anatomical and obstetric models made of wax: while designed as visual aids for teaching, they were also intended for public viewing and to this day are exhibited in their original display cases, made of rosewood and Venetian glass. There is a guided tour on Fridays at 11am.

PALAIS LIECHTENSTEIN PALACE

Map p246 (☑01-319 57 67-0; www.liechtensteinmuseum.at; 09, Fürstengasse 1; tours €28; ☉guided tours 3pm 1st & 3rd Fri of month; ⓑD Seegasse, ⓤRossauer Lände) Once the architectural muse of Italian landscape painter Canaletto, Palais Liechtenstein is a sublime baroque palace that sits in beautifully landscaped, sculpture-dotted grounds. It also houses the private art collection of Prince Hans-Adam II of Liechtenstein (whose family resided in Vienna until the Nazi *Anschluss* in 1938), with around 200 paintings and 50 sculptures dating from 1500 to 1700. The palace can be visited twice monthly on hour-long guided tours (in German; English-language audio guide available). Book ahead.

UNIVERSITY MAIN BUILDING UNIVERSITY

Map p246 (☑01-427 70, tours 01-427 71 7675; https://events.univie.ac.at; 01, Dr-Karl-Lueger-Ring 1; guided tours adult/child €5/3; ☉7am-10pm Mon-Fri, to 7pm Sat; ⓑD, 1, 71 Schottentor, ⓤSchottentor) FREE Founded in 1365, Vienna's venerable university was the first in the

German-speaking countries. Today it enrols up to 95,000 students. Grand Duke Rudolph IV (1339–65) used Paris' Sorbonne as his inspiration, and it was just as well he wasn't around in 1520 during the Reformation, because in that year his 'Sorbonne' was shoehorned into the Church. There are guided tours in English on Saturdays at 11.30am.

BEETHOVEN PASQUALATIHAUS MUSEUM

Map p246 (www.wienmuseum.at; 01, Mölker Bastei 8; adult/child €5/free; ☉10am-1pm & 2-6pm Tue-Sun; ⓑD, 1, 2 Schottentor, ⓤSchottentor) Beethoven resided on the 4th floor of this house from 1804 to 1814 (he apparently lived in around 80 places in his 35 years in Vienna, but thankfully not all of them are museums). During that time he composed Symphonies 4, 5 and 7 and the opera *Fidelio*, among other works. His two rooms (plus another two from a neighbouring apartment) have been converted into this airy museum, which has a not-too-overwhelming collection of portraits, articles and personal belongings.

SCHUBERT GEBURTSHAUS MUSEUM

Map p246 (www.wienmuseum.at; 09, Nussdorfer Strasse 54; adult/child €5/free; ☉10am-1pm & 2-6pm Tue-Sun; ⓑ37, 38 Canisiusgasse, ⓤWähringer Strasse) The house where Schubert was born in 1797 (in the kitchen) was known at that time as *Zum roten Krebsen* (The Red Crab), but Schubert probably didn't remember much about that – he and his family toddled off to greater things when he was five. Apart from his trademark glasses, the house is rather short on objects. But devoted 'Schubertologists' might like to trek here, especially to catch the occasional concert.

SCHOTTENKIRCHE CHURCH

Map p246 (www.schotten.wien; 01, Freyung; ☉museum 11am-5pm Tue-Sat, church shop 10am-6pm Mon-Fri, to 5pm Sat, closed Mon in high season; ⓤHerrengasse, Schottentor) FREE The Schottenkirche (Church of the Scots), at the northern end of Herrengasse, was founded by Benedictine monks probably originating from Scotia Maior (Ireland); the present facade dates from the 19th century. The interior has a beautifully frescoed ceiling and terracotta-red touches.

KUNSTFORUM GALLERY

Map p246 (www.bankaustria-kunstforum.at; 01, Freyung 8; adult/child €11/6; ☉10am-7pm Sat-Thu, to 9pm Fri; ⓤHerrengasse) The private

Kunstforum museum gets about 300,000 visitors each year, and for good reason – it stages an exciting program of changing exhibitions, usually highlighting crowd-pleasing modernist or big-name contemporary artists. The work of Miquel Barceló, Fernando Botero, Frida Kahlo, Balthus and Martin Kippenberger have all had their turn in recent years.

BETHAUS JEWISH SITE

Map p246 (Alten AKH University; 09, Spitalgasse 2; USchottentor) FREE This tiny Jewish prayer house, replete with an atrium roof, is part of the Alten AKH university campus; it was originally built in 1903 for Jewish patients of the hospital. Destroyed by the Nazis in 1938, it was completely reimagined in postmodernist style in the 1970s, and functions today both as a memorial and as a contemporary art installation. Mostly it's locked, but you can see inside.

VOTIVKIRCHE CHURCH

Map p246 (Votive Church; www.votivkirche.at; 09, Rooseveltplatz; 10am-6pm Tue-Sat, 9am-1pm Sun; D, 1, 71 Schottentor, USchottentor) FREE In 1853 Franz Josef I survived an assassination attempt when a knife-wielding Hungarian failed to find the emperor's neck through his collar. The Votivkirche was commissioned in thanks for his lucky escape; in stepped Heinrich von Ferstel with a twin-towered, mosaic-roofed neo-Gothic construction, completed in 1879. The prize exhibit of the small church museum, closed for refurbishment in 2019 with an uncertain reopening time, is the Antwerp Altar from 1460.

MUSEUM FÜR VOLKSKUNDE MUSEUM

Map p246 (www.volkskundemuseum.at; 08, Laudongasse 15-19; adult/child €8/free; 10am-5pm Tue, Wed & Fri-Sun, to 8pm Thu; 5, 33 Laudongasse, URathaus) Housed in turn-of-the-18th-century **Palais Schönborn**, this folklore museum gives a taste of 18th- and 19th-century rural dwellings, and is stocked with handcrafted sculptures, paintings and furniture from throughout Austria and its neighbouring countries. Many of the pieces have a religious or rural theme, and telltale floral motifs are everywhere. Temporary exhibitions are regularly featured.

WIEN MUSEUM MUSA MUSEUM

Map p246 (www.wienmuseum.at; 01, Felderstrasse 6-8; adult/child €10/free, free 1st Sun of month; 10am-6pm Tue-Sat; URathaus) This

TOP SIGHT
SIGMUND FREUD MUSEUM

The father of modern psychoanalysis spent his most prolific years in this house. He and his family moved there in 1891 and stayed until forced into exile by the Nazis in 1938. Freud's youngest daughter, Anna, helped to transform the apartment into this museum in 1971. A mirror Anna gave to her father and which still hangs in his study is perhaps the most haunting artefact.

Explore the rooms and picture Freud puffing on a cigar as he pondered the unconscious. These include the exquisitely furnished, if a tad claustrophobic, **waiting room**, where the Wednesday Psychological Society first met in 1902; the **consulting room** that once contained Freud's famous couch (now in London); and **Freud's study**. An **audio guide** gives background on exhibits and interview excerpts, including one where Freud talks about psychoanalytic theory.

There are also original editions of books, typescripts and cabinets devoted to Freud's obsessions (travelling, collecting antiquities and, yes, smoking), as well as screenings of black-and-white Edison movies like *An Artist's Dream*. Another room is devoted to Anna Freud, born here in 1895, who became a leading light in the field of child psychoanalysis.

DON'T MISS

- The waiting room
- The consulting room
- Anna Freud's mirror in her father's study

PRACTICALITIES

- Map p246, G4
- www.freud-museum.at
- 09, Berggasse 19
- adult/child €12/4
- 10am-6pm
- 1, D Schlickgasse, USchottentor, Schottenring

exhibition space hosts contemporary art exhibitions, such as retrospectives of major artists. During the renovations of Vienna's history museum, the Wien Museum in Karlsplatz (p92), which are due for completion in 2022, MUSA is also mounting themed temporary exhibitions from the Wien Museum's collections.

SERVITENKIRCHE CHURCH

Map p246 (www.rossau.at; 09, Servitengasse 9; Mass only; U Rossauer Lände) FREE Dominating the Serviten quarter (a small confluence of cobblestone streets lined with bars, restaurants and shops a few blocks from the Ringstrasse), is the 1677 Servitenkirche. It was the only church outside the Innere Stadt (inner city) to survive the second Turkish siege of 1683. Its baroque interior and oval nave were inspired by the Karlskirche, but unfortunately it's only open for Mass (see website for times); outside of this you'll have to make do with peering through iron railings.

The adjoining **monastery** is an oasis of calm, in particular its inner courtyard (entry is through the door on the left).

PALAIS DAUN-KINSKY NOTABLE BUILDING

Map p246 (www.palaisevents.at; 01, Freyung 4; 10am-6pm Mon-Fri; U Herrengasse, Schottentor) Built by Hildebrandt in 1716, Palais Kinsky has a classic baroque facade; its highlight is an elaborate, three-storey stairway off to the left of the first inner courtyard, with elegant banisters graced with statues at every turn. The ceiling fresco is a fanciful creation filled with podgy cherubs, bare-breasted beauties and the occasional strongman. The palace now contains gift shops and upmarket restaurants, and is mainly used for high-end events (concerts, banquets etc).

ROSSAUER KASERNE NOTABLE BUILDING

Map p246 (09, Rossauer Lände 1; D, 1, 71 Börse, U Schottenring) This huge red-brick complex, today housing the police, Defence Department and Vienna's traffic office, was originally built as a barracks after the 1848 revolution. It's a rather fanciful affair, replete with pseudo-medieval turrets and massive entranceways; it was restored after being damaged in bombing during WWII.

PIARISTENKIRCHE CHURCH

Map p246 (www.mariatreu.at; 08, Jodok-Fink-Platz; 8am-6pm; U Rathaus) FREE The Piaristenkirche (Church of the Piarist Order), or Maria Treu Church, is notable for two

Local Life
Stroll from Brunnenmarkt to Yppenplatz

This Saturday-morning stroll dipping into Vienna's 16th district, Ottakring, takes you for a ramble around the city's liveliest and longest street market, Brunnenmarkt. Once an overlooked backwater, this edgy, ethnically diverse neighbourhood is now firmly on the city's hipster radar. Discover its independent boutiques, delis and cafes and get to know the new Vienna.

1 Street Market

Begin Saturday Viennese-style with a mooch around **Brunnenmarkt** (Map p246; 16, Brunnengasse; 6am-6.30pm Mon-Fri, to 5pm Sat; 2 Neulerchenfelder Strasse, U Josefstädter Strasse). Haphazard mountains of fabrics, clothing, fruit and veg, spices and coffee, cheese and meat – this market has the lot. Most stall owners are Turkish or Balkan, and Brunnengasse itself is lined with grocery stores, cafes and bakeries, where you can find authentic *pide* (Turkish pizza), flat bread, halva and baklava.

2 Brunch Break

You could live in Vienna for a year and happily have a new lunchtime favourite in Yppenplatz each Saturday. A long-standing favourite in the area is **Kent** (Map p246; 01-405 91 73; www.kentrestaurant.at; 16, Brunnengasse 67; breakfasts €5-10, mains €8-13.50; 6am-2am; ; U Josefstädter Strasse), a Turkish joint with a pretty tree-shaded garden for summertime snacking.

3 Farm Fresh

The delis and boutiques on tree-dotted Yppenplatz are open most days, but the square is at its bustling best at the Bauernmarkt (p123), when farmers from Vienna's rural fringes sell their fruit, vegetables, meat, honey, preserves, wine and dairy goods. In summer, the cafe crowds spill out onto pavement terraces and the square fills with chatter and street entertainers.

Brunnenmarkt

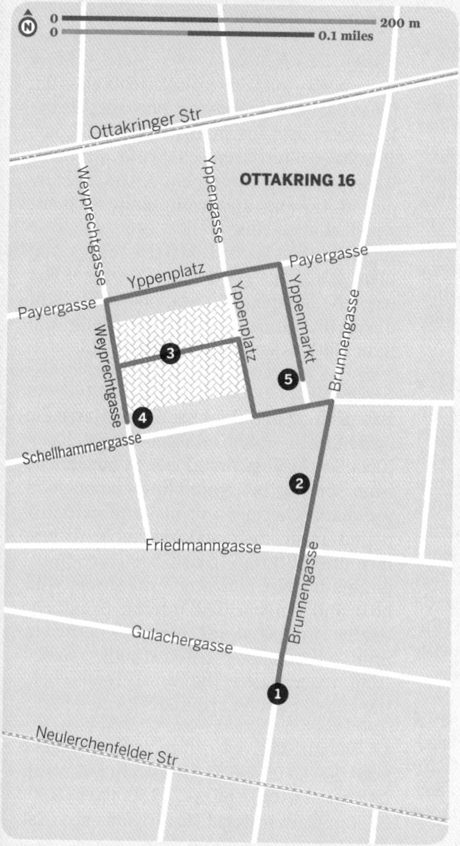

❹ Deli Delight

Deli **La Salvia** (Map p246; ☎01-236 72 27; www.lasalvia.at; 16, Yppenplatz; antipasti plates €7-10, pasta €9-12; ⏱4-10pm Tue-Thu, from 10am Fri, 9am-3pm Sat; 🚊2 Neulerchenfelder Strasse, Ⓤ Josefstädter Strasse) attracts gourmands with its picnic antipasti and stock of brilliant Italian wines, Prosecco, oils and *dolci* (sweets), as well as specialities like wild-boar salami. Taste its wares and revive over a perfectly made cappuccino or Aperol spritz in the bistro-cafe, or stay for lunch.

❺ Design District

Young designers and makers have set up shop on Yppenplatz, with a growing crop of cool boutiques and seasonal pop-ups adding to the market mix. A comparative old-timer, **Staud's** (Map p246; www.stauds.com; 16, Yppenplatz; ⏱8am-12.30pm & 3-6pm Tue-Fri, 8am-1pm Sat; 🚊2 Neulerchenfelder Strasse, Ⓤ Josefstädter Strasse) 🍃 is the go-to place in Vienna for sweet and savoury preserves that make great gifts.

interior features. The stunning **ceiling frescoes**, completed by Franz Anton Maulbertsch in 1753, depict various stories from the Bible, while the **organ** holds the distinction of being used by Anton Bruckner for his entry examination into the music academy.

EATING

With its cultured, cashed-up residents and large student population, this neighbourhood has an eclectic and edgy mix of places to eat. Expect artsy-shabby cafes and taverns serving Viennese staples to sit side by side with places brandishing globally inflected, produce-driven share plates. There's a few budget Asian choices here, as well as a number of very good Thai and Vietnamese midrange places that are great value. But even the more upmarket choices keep prices pleasantly reasonable.

★MAMAMON — THAI €

Map p246 (01-942 31 55; www.mamamonthai-kitchen.com; 08, Albertgasse 15; mains €7.50-10.90; 11.30am-9.30pm Mon-Fri, from noon Sat; U Josefstädter Strasse, Rathaus) Owner Piano, who named her restaurant for her mum Mon, has spiced up Vienna's burgeoning Southeast-Asian food scene with a menu of southern Thai flavours, street-style decor and an indie soundtrack. A young, happy crowd spills out into the courtyard, while single diners pull up a stool at the large communal table or window seats within.

SWING KITCHEN — BURGERS €

Map p246 (www.swingkitchen.com; 08, Josefstädter Strasse 73; burgers €7-10; 11am-10pm; ; U Josefstädter Strasse) Before you yawn when you hear the words 'vegan burger', bear with us – the ones served at Swing have been perfected to a fine, flavoursome, plant-based art. The chef-owners (the Schillingers) care about the environment, too, with non-plastic packaging and fair-trade ingredients going into the likes of the Chicago edgy, a hand-marinated vegan burger with organic ketchup, tomato and pickles.

CAFÉ HUMMEL — CAFE €

Map p246 (www.cafehummel.at; 08, Josefstädterstrasse 66; breakfasts €9-14.50, mains €7.70-17.80; 7am-midnight Mon-Sat, from 8am Sun; ; 2 Albertgasse, U Josefstädter Strasse) Unpretentious Hummel welcomes all comers with a classic *Kaffeehaus* (coffeehouse) vibe. Cakes are baked on the premises, and mains like goulash and schnitzel satisfy. In summer, it's easy to spend hours sitting outside, mulling over the international papers and watching the world go by. Breakfast runs to 11am during the week, and a civilised 2pm on weekends.

SOUPKULTUR — SOUP €

Map p246 (www.soupkultur.at; 01, Wipplingerstrasse 32; soups €2.40-4.90, salads €5-9; 11.30am-3.30pm Mon-Thu, to 3pm Fri; ; D, 1 Wipplingerstrasse, U Schottentor) Organic produce and aromatic spices are blended, sliced and chopped into an assortment of different soups and salads each week, ranging from red-lentil soup to traditional Hungarian goulash, Caesar salad to Thai papaya salad. There's token seating, but count on taking it away via cup or container – a leafy park is just around the corner.

CRÈME DE LA CRÈME — CAFE €

Map p246 (http://cremedelacreme.at; 08, Lange Gasse 76; breakfast & lunch specials €4-10; 9am-6pm Tue-Fri, 10am-5pm Sat & Sun; U Rathaus) Pretty and chic in a minimalist way, with trailing plants, strategically placed flowers and white-painted bentwood chairs, this French cafe-patisserie serves rather special pastries, cakes and tarts. It's also a good choice for breakfast (try the homemade granola) and light dishes like quiche, and organic cheese and ham platters with homemade bread.

STOMACH — AUSTRIAN €€

Map p246 (01-310 20 99; 09, Seegasse 26; mains €15-30; 4pm-midnight Wed-Sat, 10am-10pm Sun; U Rossauer Lände) Stomach has been serving belly-rumblingly good food for years. The menu brims with carefully plated meat, fish and vegetable dishes, including Styrian roast beef, cream-of-pumpkin soup, and, when in season, wild boar and venison. The interior is authentically rural, and the overgrown garden pretty. 'Stomach', interestingly, comes from rearranging the word Tomaschek, the butcher's shop originally located here.

LA TAVOLOZZA — ITALIAN €€

Map p246 (01-406 37 57; www.latavolozza.at; 08, Florianigasse 37; pizza €7-13.50, mains €9.50-23.90; 5pm-midnight Mon-Fri, from noon Sat

& Sun; 2 Lederergasse, U Rathaus) You'll feel part of the *famiglia* at this friendly neighbourhood Italian place, where tightly packed tables are lit by candlelight. The food is superb: crisp bread fresh from a wood oven is followed by generous, well-seasoned portions of grilled fish and meat, washed down with beefy Chianti reds. Seasonal specialities like truffles often star on the menu. Tram to Lederergasse.

GASTHAUS WICKERL AUSTRIAN **€€**

Map p246 (01-317 74 89; www.wickerl.at; 09, Porzellangasse 24a; mains €11.80-21.90; 10.30am-11.30pm Mon-Sat, 11am-11pm Sun; U Rossauer Lände) Wickerl is a beautiful *Beisl* (small tavern) with an all-wood finish and a warm, welcoming vibe. Seasonal fare, such as *Kürbisgulasch* (pumpkin goulash) in autumn, *Marillenknödel* (apricot dumplings) in summer and *Spargel* (asparagus) in spring, are mixed in with the usual Viennese offerings of *Tafelspitz* (prime boiled beef), *Zwiebelrostbraten* (steak with onions) and veal or pork schnitzel.

SCHNATTL INTERNATIONAL **€€€**

Map p246 (01-405 34 00; www.schnattl.com; 08, Lange Gasse 40; mains €19-24, 3-course menus from €42; 11.30am-5pm Mon-Thu, to midnight Fri; ; 2 Rathaus, Josefstädter Strasse, U Rathaus) Despite weekday-only opening hours, Schnattl is a culinary institution in Josefstadt, particularly beloved by thespians and other arty types. The inner courtyard is perfect for summer dining, while bottle-green wood panelling creates a cosy mood inside. The chef plays up seasonal specialities like creamy chestnut soup and meltingly tender organic beef, matured on the bone and served with green-pepper gnocchi.

DRINKING & NIGHTLIFE

Outwardly conservative and often eerily quiet, a number of late-night options, dotted from the Danube (Donau) to the Gürtel. They're joined by a huge selection of pubby taverns (including Vienna's best Irish pub) and a number of both traditional and contemporary wine bars. Coffee can be had two ways here: either traditional, with coffee houses offering the mild, milky Viennese cappuccino called *melange*, or refreshingly 21st-century brews. The latter is represented by a couple of Vienna's best roasters and barista-driven cafes.

★ **POC CAFE** COFFEE

Map p246 (www.facebook.com/pg/poccafe; 08, Schlösselgasse 21; 8am-5pm Mon-Fri; 5, 43, 44 Lange Gasse, U Schottentor) Friendly Robert Gruber is one of Vienna's coffee legends and his infectious passion ripples through this beautifully rambling, lab-like space. POC stands for 'People on Caffeine'; while filter, espresso-style or a summertime iced-cold brew are definitely this place's raison d'etre, it's also known for moreish sweets like killer poppy-seed cake, cheesecake or seasonal fruit tarts.

KRYPT COCKTAIL BAR

Map p246 (www.krypt.bar; 09, cnr Berggasse & Wasagasse; 7pm-1am Wed-Thu, 8pm-3am Sat & Sun; 37, 38, 40, 41, 42 Schwarzspanierstrasse) There's a deliciously secret feel to this blink-and-you'll miss it speakeasy – a cool, underground, brick-vaulted cellar, where the Viennese mingle by candlelight over expertly mixed cocktails.

ACHTUNDZWANZIG WINE BAR

Map p246 (www.achtundzwanzig.at; 08, Schlösselgasse 28; 4pm-1am Mon-Thu, to 2am Fri, 7pm-2am Sat; 1, 43, 44 Lange Gasse, U Schottentor) Austrian wine fans with a rock-and-roll sensibility will feel like they've found heaven at this black-daubed *Vinothek* (wine bar) that vibes casual but takes its wines super seriously. Wines by the glass are all sourced from small producers – many of them are organic or minimal-intervention and friends of the owners – and are well priced at under €4 a glass.

CAFÉ STEIN CAFE

Map p246 (www.cafestein.at; 09, Währinger Strasse 6-8; 8am-1am Mon-Sat, from 9am Sun; ; D, 1, 71 Schottentor, U Schottentor) During the day this multi-level cafe is a popular haunt of students from the nearby university; come evening the clientele metamorphoses into spritz-swilling city workers and DJs bring out their decks. The all-day menu is extensive. In summer there's outside seating, which enjoys pretty views of the Votivkirche. Sister cocktail bar Botanical Gardens (p130) is hidden below.

BIRDYARD COCKTAIL BAR

Map p246 (www.thebirdyard.at; 08, Lange Gasse 74; ⏰5.30pm-2am Tue-Sat; ⓤRathaus) *Wilkommen* (welcome) to one of Vienna's hottest drinking dens, lavishly decked out with trippy exotic murals of tropical birds, flowers and ferns – some of them courtesy of Romanian street artist Saddo. The cocktails are just as weird and wondrous – for instance, Peanut Butter Jelly Time, with Angostura bitters, rum, cranberries and peanut butter.

BOTANICAL GARDENS COCKTAIL BAR

Map p246 (www.botanicalgarden.at; 09, Kolingasse 1; ⏰6pm-2am Tue-Thu, to 3am Fri & Sat; ⓤSchottentor) A subterranean mirror of Cafe Stein's sunny spaces above, Botanical Gardens makes for a cosy, magical retreat once Vienna's weather turns chilly. A dark nautical theme ticks all the cocktail-revival-scene boxes, but with enough local eccentricity to keep things interesting.

However, it's the cocktails (and their makers) that are the star here, with high-quality spirits, fresh juices and an intriguing use of herbs, spices and other botanicals like kaffir, tonka bean and rosemary.

WEINSTUBE JOSEFSTADT WINE BAR

Map p246 (www.facebook.com/WeinstubeJosefstadt; 08, Piaristengasse 27; ⏰4pm-midnight Apr-Dec; ⓤRathaus) Weinstube Josefstadt is one of Vienna's loveliest *Stadtheurigen* (city wine taverns). A leafy green oasis spliced between towering residential blocks, its tables of friendly, well-liquored locals are squeezed in between the trees and shrubs looking onto a pretty, painted *Salettl* (wooden summerhouse). Wine is local and cheap, food is typical, with a buffet-style meat and fritter selection. Cash only.

Note that the location is not well signposted – the only indication of its existence is a metal *Busch'n* (green wreath) hanging from a doorway.

BEAVER BREWING CRAFT BEER

(www.beaverbrewing.at; 09, Liechtensteinstrasse 69; ⏰4pm-midnight Mon-Thu, noon-1am Fri & Sat, noon-10pm Sun; ⓤWien Währinger Strasse) There's an urban beat to this white-walled, postindustrial, American-style microbrewery, which pairs great craft beer, such as Magog (a barrel-aged dark ale) and crisp, hoppy IPAs, with comfort food like pulled-pork nachos, burgers and smoky spare ribs. There are no haughty hipsters here and staff are genuinely eager to please.

TUNNEL BAR

Map p246 (www.tunnel-vienna-live.at; 08, Florianigasse 39; ⏰9am-2am Mon-Sat, to midnight Sun; 📶👶; 🚊2 Lederergasse, ⓤRathaus) This laid-back, endearingly boho cafe attracts students and all comers. By day it's a relaxed spot to grab an ancient wooden table and flick through a communal book or magazine with coffee or opt for lunchtime beers and Latin American snacks. The mood cranks up a notch with (mostly free) gigs at 9pm, from folk to indie, Latin to jazz.

CAFÉ LANDTMANN CAFE

Map p246 (www.landtmann.at; 10, Universitätsring 4; ⏰7.30am-midnight; 📶; 🚊D, 1, 2 Rathausplatz, ⓤRathaus) Freud, Mahler and Marlene Dietrich all had a soft spot for this coffee house, which opened in 1873. Today it attracts politicians and theatre-goers with its elegant interior and close proximity to the Burgtheater, Rathaus and Parliament. The list of traditional coffee specialities is formidable, although at €5 to €9 per cup you need a celebrity income to linger over drinks.

HALBESTADT BAR COCKTAIL BAR

Map p246 (www.halbestadt.at; 09, Stadtbahnbögen 155; ⏰7pm-2am Tue-Thu, to 3am Fri & Sat; ⓤNussdorferstrasse) The impeccable hospitality starts when you can't open the glass door. The host swings it forth, escorts you in and offers to advise you on your order. More than 500 bottles grace the walls of the tiny, atmospheric space under the *Bogen* (railway arch) and mixologists hold court creating enticing cocktails. There's no bookings; it fills up fast.

CAFFÈCOUTURE COFFEE

Map p246 (www.caffecouture.com; Garnisongasse 18; ⏰8.30am-5pm Mon-Fri Oct-Jun, 8.30am-3pm Sep, closed Jul & Aug; 🚊37, 38, 40, 41, 42 Schwarzspanierstrasse, ⓤSchottentor) At the forefront of Vienna's third-wave coffee movement, CaffèCouture is the brainchild of barista Georg Branny. His baby is a La Marzocco Strada EP espresso machine, which he uses to whip up creative coffees in minimalist, art-slung surrounds.

LOFT BAR

Map p246 (www.theloft.at; 07, Lerchenfelder Gürtel 37; ⏰8pm-4am Fri & Sat late Aug–mid-Jun, closed mid-Jun–late Aug; ⓤThaliastrasse) 'Working hard for better parties in Vienna' is the catchphrase of this young Gürtel live wire and you can believe the hype. Most events are free. As well as the regular weekend opening hours, there is plenty of stuff going on in the week too, including some art-house film screenings (Wednesdays) and foosball (table football) tournaments (Thursdays).

SUMMER STAGE BEER GARDEN

Map p246 (☎01-315 52 02; www.summerstage.at; 09, Rossauer Lände; ⏲5pm-1am May-Sep; ⓊSchottenring, Rossauer Lände) This Viennese summer favourite has sprawling, riverside terrace spaces for drinking, with food trucks and a glassed-in area for when the weather turns.

RHIZ BAR

Map p246 (https://rhiz.wien; 08, U-Bahnbogen/Lerchenfelder Gürtel 37; ⏲8pm-4am Mon-Thu, to 5am Fri & Sat; 📶; 🚋2 Josefstädter Strasse, ⓊJosefstädter Strasse) Rhiz' brick arches and glass walls are reminiscent of many bars beneath the U6 line, but its status as a stalwart of the city's electronica scene gives it the edge over the competition. Black-clad boozers and an alternative set cram the interior to hear DJs and live acts year-round, while in summer the large outdoor seating area is overflowing.

★CAFÉ CENTRAL CAFE

Map p246 (www.cafecentral.wien; 01, Herrengasse 14; ⏲7.30am-10pm Mon-Sat, from 10am Sun; 📶; ⓊHerrengasse) Coffee-house legend alert: Trotsky came here to play chess, and turn-of-the-century literary greats like Karl Kraus and Hermann Bahr regularly met here for coffee. Its marble pillars, arched ceilings and chandeliers now mostly play host to tourists, and the queues can be tedious, but once in it's a deliciously storied setting for a *melange* and slices of chocolate-truffle *Altenbergtorte*.

OTTAKRINGER BRAUEREI BREWERY

(☎01-491 005 480; www.ottakringerbrauerei.at; 16, Ottakringer Platz 1; ⏲4pm-12.30am Mon-Thu, to 1.30am Fri, 9.30am-1.30am Sat, to 12.30am Sun; 🚋44 Johann-Nepomuk-Berger-Platz, ⓊOttakringer) Dominating one corner of the 16th district, this is the largest of Vienna's city breweries, home to the beloved Ottakringer beer. Dating from 1837, the industrial-sized rooms and interconnecting alleyways are often used for live gigs, pop-up street-food festivals and design markets. Guided brewery tours should be booked in advance.

☆ ENTERTAINMENT

VOLKSOPER OPERA

Map p246 (People's Opera; ☎01-513 15 13; www.volksoper.at; 09, Währinger Strasse 78; ⏲10am-7pm Sep-Jun; ⓊWähringer Strasse) Offering an intimate experience, the Volksoper specialises in operettas, dance performances, musicals and a handful of standard, heavier operas. Standing and impaired-view tickets cost €3 to €10 and, like many venues, there is a plethora of discounts and reduced tickets for sale 30 minutes before performances. The Volksoper closes for July and August.

WUK ARTS CENTRE

Map p246 (Workshop & Culture House; ☎01-40 12 10; www.wuk.at; 09, Währinger Strasse 59; ⏲information 9am-8pm Mon-Fri, 3-8pm Sat & Sun; ⓊWähringer Strasse) Charmingly housed in a vine-trailed building, WUK is many things to many people. It hosts numerous events in its concert hall: midsize international and local rock acts vie with clubbing nights, classical concerts, film evenings, theatre and children's shows. Women's groups, temporary exhibitions and practical skills workshops are also on-site, along with a cafe with a fabulous cobbled courtyard.

VOTIVKINO CINEMA

Map p246 (☎01-317 35 71; www.votivkino.at; 09, Währinger Strasse 12; 👪; ⓊSchottentor) Built in 1912, the Votiv is one of the oldest cinemas in Vienna. It's been extensively updated since then and is now among the best cinemas in the city. Its three screens feature a mix of Hollywood's more quirky ventures and art-house films in their original language.

B72 LIVE MUSIC

Map p246 (www.b72.at; 08, Hernalser Gürtel 72; ⏲8pm-4am Sun-Thu, to 6am Fri & Sat; 🚋44 Hernalser Gürtel, ⓊAlser Strasse) Fringe live acts, alternative beats and album launches are the mainstay of B72's entertainment line-up, which all attract a predictably youthful crowd. Its tall glass walls and arched brick interior are typical of most bars along the Gürtel, as is the happy grunginess. Its name comes from its location, Bogen 72.

MILES SMILES LIVE MUSIC

Map p246 (www.miles-smiles.at; 08, Lange Gasse 51; ⏲8pm-2am Sun-Thu, to 4am Fri & Sat;

U Rathaus) One of two bars in town named after legend Miles Davis, Miles Smiles is for the discerning jazz fan who knows when to clap for the solo. Live acts are irregular but always enthralling, and the atmosphere enthusiastic and energetic.

CAFÉ CARINA
LIVE MUSIC

Map p246 (www.cafe-carina.at; 08, Josefstädter Strasse 84; ⊙6pm-2am Mon-Thu, to 6am Fri & Sat; U Josefstädter Strasse) Small, alternative and pleasantly dingy, Carina is a musicians' (and a drinker's) bar. Local bands perform most nights – only a few feet from a normally enthusiastic audience – and the music is invariably folk, jazz or country.

THEATER IN DER JOSEFSTADT
THEATRE

Map p246 (✆01-427 003 00; www.josefstadt. org; 08, Josefstädter Strasse 26; ⊙box office 10am-performance time Mon-Fri, 1pm-performance time Sat & Sun; ☐2 Stadiongasse, U Rathaus) Theater in der Josefstadt (1788) is a theatre in the Volkstheater mould, with an ornate interior and traditional German productions. One hour before performances, tickets for students and school children are €6; same-day standing-room tickets are also available for €8 at 1pm for afternoon productions, and at 3pm for evening productions.

 SHOPPING

These neighbourhoods have little in the way of shops or shopping strips but play host to the city's most vibrant markets, Brunnenmarkt and the Yppenmarkt, which keeps it laid-back during the week but turns into a ridiculously popular social event on Saturday mornings. A number of low-key and charming _Christkindlmärkte_ (Christmas markets) also take place in the University district.

XOCOLAT
CHOCOLATE

Map p246 (www.xocolat.at; 09, Servitengasse 5; ⊙10am-6pm Mon-Fri, 9am-1pm Sat; U Rossauer Lände) This upmarket _Konditorei_ (cake shop) offers 40-odd varieties of beautifully decorated handmade chocolates, pralines and truffles – some of which qualify as tiny edible works of art. You can also visit the factory where the chocolates are made.

ALTWIENER CHRISTKINDLMARKT AUF DER FREYUNG
MARKET

Map p246 (www.altwiener-markt.at; 10, Dominikanerbastei 8; ⊙11am-9pm Sun-Thu, 11am-10pm Fri & Sat mid-Nov–Dec; U Herrengasse, Schottentor) A small but particularly atmospheric Christmas market in the Freyung passage that specialises in high-quality crafts. There's also a traditional cultural program that includes folk music and choral performances, as well as children's puppet shows and storytelling.

PALAIS FERSTEL
SHOPPING CENTRE

Map p246 (01, Strauchgasse 4; ⊙10am-7pm Mon-Sat; U Herrengasse) With its hexagonal skylight, allegorical sculptures and beautifully lit arcades in Italian Renaissance style, Palais Ferstel hearkens back to a more glamorous age of consumption. Opened in 1860, it sidles up to the ever-grand Café Central (p131) and likewise bears the hallmark of architect Heinrich von Ferstel, the Habsburgs' blue-eyed boy in the mid-19th century.

Today it shelters upmarket delis, jewellers and chocolatiers; pop in for a mosey even if you have no intention of buying.

ALTES AKH CHRISTMAS MARKET
MARKET

Map p246 (www.weihnachtsdorf.at; 09, Alser Strasse Hof 1; ⊙11am-9pm Sun-Thu, to 10pm Fri & Sat mid-Nov–Dec; ☐1, 5, 43, 44 Lange Gasse, U Schottentor) A favourite of students, this small market occupies a corner of the Altes AKH university's largest courtyard. There are farm animals and a horse-drawn sleigh for the kids.

DIE HÖLLEREI
FOOD & DRINKS

Map p246 (www.diehoellerei.at; 08, Florianigasse 13; ⊙11am-6pm Tue-Fri, 10am-12.30pm Sat; U Rathaus) Alexandra Höller is passionate about Austrian produce and stocks a beautiful range of the best. Take home unusual bounty such as apricot-seed or saffron gin, moist almond cake in a jar, or wonderful pasta and jams from over the border in Südtirol. You can also pick up a bottle of bubbly or wine here.

BIO-MARKT FREYUNG
MARKET

Map p246 (www.biobauernmarkt-freyung.at; 01, Freyung; ⊙9am-6pm Fri & Sat; U Herrengasse, Schottentor) ❧ Great for picking up some picnic fixings, this low-key market exclusively sells organic produce from farmers. Find everything from wood-fired-oven bread, fruit, fish and meat to honey, cheese, wine and even pumpkin-seed oil here.

Schloss Belvedere to the Canal

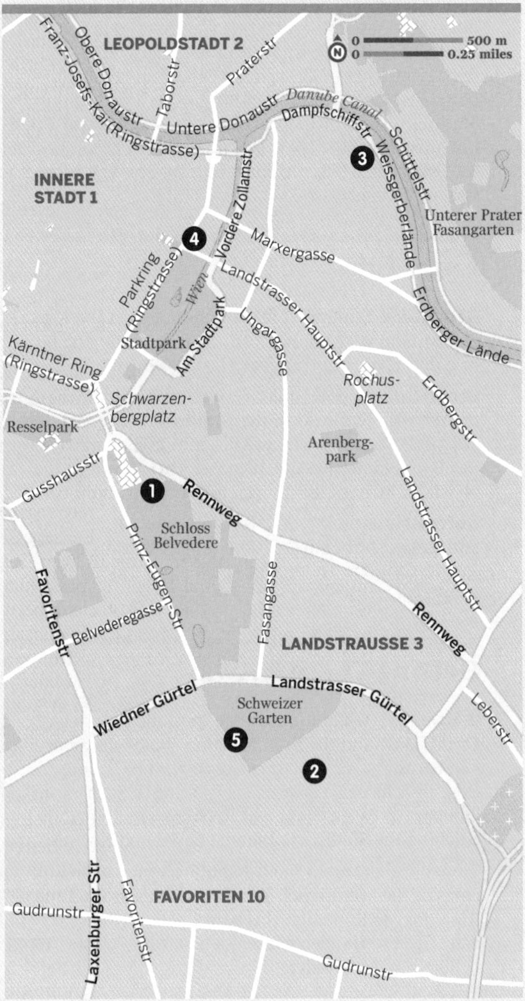

For more detail of this area see Map p252

Neighbourhood Top Five

❶ **Schloss Belvedere** (p135) Drawing breath as you ramble through lavishly frescoed apartments, sculpture-strewn gardens and a gallery home to the ultimate embrace: Klimt's *The Kiss*.

❷ **Heeresgeschichtliches Museum** (p142) Sending shivers down your spine as you venture through the Vienna's war-torn history.

❸ **KunstHausWien** (p144) Being dazzled by Hundertwasser's wonky floors, madcap mosaics and hallucinatory colours.

❹ **Museum für Angewandte Kunst** (p143) Rewinding a century to the dawn of a modernist age at the MAK.

❺ **Belvedere 21** (p138) Zooming in on contemporary art with an Austrian slant at this modernist gallery.

Lonely Planet's Top Tip

Time your visit right and you can save on sight admissions. The Museum für Angewandte Kunst is less than half price from 6pm to 10pm on Tuesday, while the Heeresgeschichtliches Museum won't cost you a cent on the first Sunday of the month.

Best Places to Eat

- Steirereck im Stadtpark (p147)
- Lingenhel (p144)
- Joseph Brot (p146)
- Meierei im Stadtpark (p146)
- Colono (p146)

For reviews, see p144.

Best Places to Drink

- Strandbar Herrmann (p147)
- Café am Heumarkt (p147)
- Salm Bräu (p147)
- Café Zartl (p147)

For reviews, see p147.

Best Entertainment

- Radiokulturhaus (p147)
- Konzerthaus (p147)
- Arnold Schönberg Center (p148)
- Arena Wien (p148)
- Kursalon (p148)

For reviews, see p147.

Explore Schloss Belvedere to the Canal

If you only see one palace in Vienna, make it Schloss Belvedere (p135). What giddy romance is evoked in its sumptuously frescoed baroque halls, replete with Klimt, Schiele and Kokoschka artworks; what stories are conjured wandering its landscaped gardens, which drop like the sudden fall of a theatre curtain to reveal Vienna's skyline. Belvedere is overwhelming in both scale and substance: a day-long marathon of a sight that engrosses from start to finish.

As compelling as Belvedere is, it can be rewarding to explore lesser-known corners of Vienna's third district, Landstrasse, too. Here elegant backstreets lead to art nouveau cafes, low-key market squares and houses bearing the psychedelic imprint of artistic wild child Hundertwasser (p144). The spirits of classical greats linger in parks and cemeteries: from Strauss on a pedestal in the Stadtpark (p134) to Mozart buried at **St Marxer Friedhof** (Cemetery of St Marx; Map p252; www.friedhoefewien.at; 03, Leberstrasse 6-8; ⏲6.30am-8pm Apr-Sep, to 6.30pm Oct-Mar; UZippererstrasse).

Local Life

Canal-Side Summer Embrace summer on the Costa del Danube with your feet in the sand and your bum in a deckchair at Strandbar Herrmann (p147).

Green Spaces Seek quiet respite with a wander in the dappled leafiness of the **Stadtpark** (City Park; Map p252; 2 Weihburggasse, UStadtpark) FREE or the headstone-dotted Zentralfriedhof (p146), where the ghosts of Strauss, Beethoven and Brahms hold court.

Coffee Houses Devote afternoons to coffee, cake and drawn-out conversations at old-world Café Zartl (p147), Café am Heumarkt (p147) and Café Goldegg (p144).

Getting There & Away

U-Bahn The U-Bahn makes the quick hop between Landstrasse and the rest of Vienna. Taubstummengasse and Südtiroler Platz stations, both on the U1 line, are close to Schloss Belvedere. The U3 line to Stubentor, Landstrasse-Wien Mitte and Rochusgasse are handy for reaching the Stadtpark, Danube Canal and Rochusplatz.

Trams Trams trump the U-Bahn for access to some parts of the 3rd district. Tram 2 trundles around the Ring (for MAK, Stadtpark), tram 1 goes to Radetzkyplatz (for the Hundertwasser sights), while trams 71 and D take you to Belvedere.

GABOR KOVACS PHOTOGRAPHY/SHUTTERSTOCK ©

TOP SIGHT
SCHLOSS BELVEDERE & GARDENS

A masterpiece of total art, Belvedere is one of the world's finest baroque palaces. Designed by Johann Lukas von Hildebrandt (1668–1745), it was built as a summer residence for the brilliant military strategist Prince Eugene of Savoy, conqueror of the Turks in 1718. Eugene had grown up around the court of Louis XIV and it shows – this is a chateau to rival Versailles.

Oberes Belvedere

Rising splendidly above the gardens and commanding sweeping views of Vienna's skyline, the **Oberes Belvedere** (Upper Belvedere; Map p252; 03, Prinz-Eugen-Strasse 27; adult/child €16/free, combined ticket with Unteres Belvedere €22/free; ⌚9am-6pm Sat-Thu, to 9pm Fri; 🚋D, 71 Schwarzenbergplatz) is one of Vienna's unmissable sights. Built between 1717 and 1723, its peerless art collection, showcased in rooms replete with marble, frescoes and stucco, attests to the unfathomable wealth and cultured tastes of the Habsburg Empire.

Ground Floor: Medieval & Modern Art

The **Sala Terrena** is a grand prelude to the ground floor, with four colossal Atlas pillars supporting the weight of its delicately stuccoed vault. Spread across four beautifully frescoed rooms, **Medieval Art** leads you through the artistic development of the age, with an exceptional portfolio of Gothic sculpture and altarpieces, many from Austrian abbeys and monasteries. Top billing goes to the Master of Grosslobming's sculptural group, whose fluid, expressive works embodied the figurative ideal; among them is the faceless *St George with Dragon* (1395), with a rather tame-looking dragon at his feet.

DON'T MISS

- The Klimt collection
- Sala Terrena
- The gardens
- The impressionist collection
- Marmorsaal

PRACTICALITIES

- Map p252, B4
- www.belvedere.at
- 03, Prinz-Eugen-Strasse 27
- adult/child Oberes Belvedere €16/free, Unteres Belvedere €14/free, combined ticket €22/free
- ⌚9am-6pm Sat-Thu, to 9pm Fri
- 🚋D, 71 Schwarzenbergplatz, Ⓤ Taubstummengasse, Südtiroler Platz

COMBINED TICKETS

Ordering printable tickets online saves time, but they can't be exchanged or refunded. Several money-saving combined ticket options are available, including one covering the Upper Belvedere and Lower Belvedere (adult/under 19 years €22/free), and one additionally covering Belvedere 21 (adult/under 19 years €25/free). Combined tickets are valid for two weeks after the first visit.

The Nazis seized the property of the wealthy Jewish Bloch-Bauer family following the 1938 *Anschluss* (annexation). Among their substantial collection were five Klimt originals, including the *Portrait of Adele Bloch-Bauer I* (1907). The stolen paintings hung in the Oberes Belvedere until 2006, when a US Supreme Court ruled the Austrian government must return the paintings to their rightful owner, Adele Bloch-Bauer's niece and heir Maria Altmann. The portrait alone fetched US$135 million at auction, at the time the highest price ever paid for a painting, and today hangs in the New York Neue Galerie.

Other heavenly treasures include Joachim's polyptych *Albrechtsaltar* (1435), one of the foremost examples of Gothic realism, and the *Znaim Altar* (1445), a gilded glorification of faith showing the Passion of Christ.

Modern Art & Interwar Period is particularly strong on Austrian expressionism. Attention-grabbers here include Oskar Kokoschka's richly animated portrait of art-nouveau painter *Carl Moll* (1913). Egon Schiele is represented by works both haunting and beguiling, such as *Death and the Maiden* (1915) and his portrait of six-year-old *Herbert Rainer* (1910). Other standouts include Oskar Laske's staggeringly detailed *Ship of Fools* (1923) and Max Oppenheimer's musical masterpiece *The Philharmonic* (1935), with a baton-swinging Gustav Mahler.

First Floor: From Klimt to Baroque

The 1st-floor **Vienna 1880–1914** collection is a holy grail for Klimt fans, with an entire room devoted to erotic golden wonders such as *Judith* (1901), *Salome* (1909), *Adam and Eve* (1917) and *The Kiss* (1908). Works by German symbolist painter Max Klinger (1857–1920), as well as portraits by secessionist Koloman Moser and Norwegian expressionist Edvard Munch, also feature. The centrepiece is the **Marmorsaal**, a chandelier-lit marble, stucco and trompe l'oeil confection, crowned by Carlo Innocenzo Carlone's ceiling fresco (1721–23) celebrating the glorification of Prince Eugene. **Baroque & Early-19th-Century Art** pays tribute to Austrian masters of the age, endowed with highlights such as Johann Michael Rottmayr's lucid *Susanna and the Elders* (1692) and Paul Troger's chiaroscuro *Christ on the Mount of Olives* (1750).

Second Floor: Impressionists & Romantics

In **Neoclassicism, Romanticism & Biedermeier Art**, you'll find outstanding works such as Georg Waldmüller's *Corpus Christi Morning* (1857), a joyous snapshot of impish lads and flower girls bathed in honeyed light. Representative of the neoclassical period are clearer, more emotionally restrained pieces such as Jacques-Louis David's gallant *Napoleon on Great St Bernard Pass* (1801) and François Gérard's portrait *Count Moritz Christian Fries and Family* (1804). The Romantic period is headlined by the wistful, brooding landscapes and seascapes of 19th-century German painter Caspar David Friedrich.

French masters share the limelight with their Austrian and German contemporaries in **Realism & Impressionism**, where you'll feel the artistic pull of Renoir's softly evocative *Woman after the Bath* (1876), Monet's sun-dappled *Garden at Giverny* (1902) and Van Gogh's *Plain at Auvers* (1890), where wheat fields ripple under a billowing sky. Lovis

Corinth's tranquil *Woman Reading Near a Goldfish Tank* (1911) and Max Liebermann's *Hunter in the Dunes* (1913) epitomise the German impressionist style.

Gardens

Belvedere: 'beautiful view'. The reason for this name becomes apparent in the baroque garden linking the upper and lower palaces, which was laid out in around 1700 in classical French style by Dominique Girard, a pupil of André le Nôtre of Versailles fame. Set along a **central axis**, the gently sloping garden commands a broad view of Vienna's skyline, with the Stephansdom and the Hofburg punctuating the horizon.

The three-tiered garden is lined by clipped box hedges and flanked by ornamental parterres. As you stroll to the **Lower Cascade**, with its frolicking water nymphs, look out for Greco-Roman statues of the eight muses and cherubic putti embodying the 12 months of the year. Mythical beasts squirt water across the **Upper Cascade**, which spills down five steps into the basin below. Guarding the approach to the Oberes Belvedere are winged sphinxes, symbols of power and wisdom, which look as though they are about to take flight any minute.

South of the Oberes Belvedere is the **Alpengarten** (Map p252; www.bundesgaerten.at; 03, Prinz-Eugen-Strasse 27; adult/child €3.50/2.50; ⌚10am-6pm late Mar-early Aug; 🚊D, O Quartier Belvedere, Ⓤ Hauptbahnhof), a Japanese-style garden nurturing alpine species, at its fragrant best from spring to summer, when clematis, rhododendrons, roses and peonies are in bloom. North from here is the larger **Botanischer Garten** (Map p252; www.botanik.univie.ac.at; 03, Mechelgasse/Praetoriusgasse; ⌚10am-6pm; 🚊0, 1, 71 Rennweg) FREE, belonging to the Vienna University, with tropical glasshouses and 11,500 botanical species, including Chinese dwarf bamboo and Japanese plum yews.

SCHLOSS BELVEDERE AND GARDENS

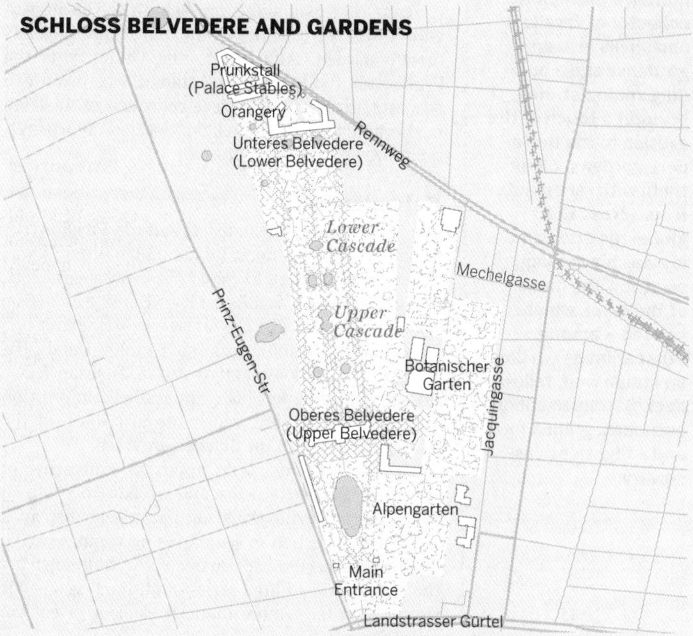

GUIDED TOURS

Audio guides can be hired for €5 at the Upper Belvedere and €4 at the Lower Belvedere, and are available in German, English, French, Italian, Spanish, Japanese and Russian; you'll need to leave ID as a form of deposit. One-hour themed tours shedding light on a specific period or artist cost €4 and are in German. Times and themes vary (see the online calendar), but generally there are tours at 3pm and/or 4pm on weekends, plus 10.30am on Sunday.

Prince Eugene of Savoy was an avid hunter, a passionate collector of fossils and shells, a keen gardener and a budding zoologist. He brought a touch of the exotica to the Belvedere gardens, filling them with rare plants from across the globe. His pride and joy was his menagerie (now the name of the cafe), which housed – among other animals – a lion, an Indian wolf, fallow deer, Sardinian sheep, ostriches, guinea fowl and a flightless cassowary.

Unteres Belvedere

Built between 1712 and 1716, **Unteres Belvedere** (Lower Belvedere; Map p252; 03, Rennweg 6; adult/child €14/free, combined ticket with Oberes Belvedere €22/free; ⌚10am-6pm Sat-Thu, to 9pm Fri; 🚋71 Unteres Belvedere) is a baroque feast of state apartments and ceremonial rooms. Most lavish of all is the red marble **Marmorsaal**, an ode to Prince Eugene's military victories, with stucco trophies, medallions and Martino Altomonte's ceiling fresco showing the glorification of the prince and Apollo surrounded by muses. At eye level are sculptures taken from Georg Raphael Donner's mid-18th-century **fountain** on Neuer Markt. Snake-bearing Providentia (Prudence) rises above four putti grappling with fish, each of which symbolises a tributary of the Danube (Donau).

In the **Groteskensaal**, foliage intertwines with fruit, birds and mythological beasts in the fanciful grotesque style that was all the rage in baroque times. This leads through to the **Marmorgalerie**, a vision of frilly white stucco and marble, encrusted with cherubs and war trophies. The niches originally displayed three classical statues from Herculaneum (now in Dresden), which inspired baroque sculptor Domenico Parodito to create the neoclassical statues you see today. Maria Theresia put her stamp on the palace in the adjacent **Goldkabinett**, a mirrored cabinet dripping in gold.

Temporary exhibitions are held in the **Orangery**, with a walkway gazing grandly over Prince Eugene's private garden. Attached to the Orangery is the **Prunkstall**, the former royal stables, where you can now trot through a 150-piece collection of Austrian medieval art, including religious scenes, altarpieces, sculpture and Gothic triptychs.

Belvedere 21

The modernist, glass-and-steel **Austria Pavilion**, designed by Karl Schwanzer for Expo 58 in Brussels, was reborn as **Belvedere 21** (Map p252; www.belvedere21.at; 03, Arsenalstrasse 1; adult/under 18yr €8/free; ⌚11am-6pm Wed-Sun, to 9pm Fri; 🚋O, 1, 18 Fasangasse, Ⓤ Hauptbahnhof) in 2011, with exhibitions devoted to 20th- and 21st-century art, predominantly with an Austrian focus. Adolf Krischanitz left his clean aesthetic imprint on the open-plan gallery, which sits just south of the Oberes Belvedere in the **Schweizergarten**.

The gallery's dynamic approach embraces an artist-in-residence scheme and a changing rota of contemporary exhibitions. On permanent display is a peerless collection of sculptures by Viennese artist **Fritz Wotruba** (1907–75), many of which deconstruct the human form into a series of abstract, geometric shapes that have more than an element of cubism about them.

OBERES BELVEDERE

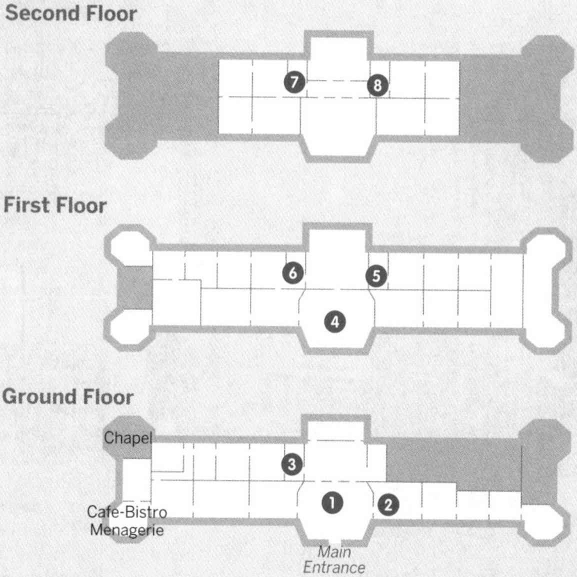

Museum Tour
Oberes Belvedere

LENGTH FOUR HOURS

The Upper Belvedere's scale can be overwhelming. This half-day itinerary will help you pin down the highlights, though bear in mind that paintings are frequently shifted around.

Gaze up to the Atlas pillars supporting the ❶ **Sala Terrena** and turn right into ❷ **Medieval Art**, displayed in frescoed halls. You'll be drawn to the Gothic brilliance of the Master of Grosslobming's sculptures, such as *St George with Dragon* and the softly draped *Kneeling Mary*. Note the soul-stirring *Albrechtsaltar* and the *Znaim Altar* depicting the Passion of Christ. Andreas Lackner created the *Abtenauer Altar* (1518), a gilded trio of bishops that once presided over the high altar of the parish church of Abtenau in Salzburg. Exit and turn left into ❸ **Modern Art & Interwar Period**, with evocative pieces such as Egon Schiele's expressionistic portrait of *Herbert Rainer* and Max Oppenheimer's *The Philharmonic*.

Saunter up the ornately stuccoed Prunkstiege staircase and marvel at the fresco-and-marble opulence of the ❹ **Marmorsaal**. Turn right for ❺ **Vienna 1880–1914**, a peerless repository of fin de siècle and secessionist art. The Klimt collection is second to none, shimmering with golden-period stunners such as *Judith* and *The Kiss*. Across in ❻ **Baroque & Early-19th-Century Art**, look out for light-fantastic works such as Johann Michael Rottmayr's *Susanna and the Elders* and Paul Troger's *Christ on the Mount of Olives*.

On the 2nd floor, turn left into ❼ **Neoclassicism, Romanticism & Biedermeier Art**. Notice neoclassical wonders such as François Gérard's portrait of *Count Moritz Christian Fries and Family*, then move past landscapes and still lifes to the Romantic era. Look out for Caspar David Friedrich's *Rocky Landscape of the Elbe Sandstone Heights*. Georg Waldmüller's mirthful *Corpus Christi Morning* takes pride of place in the Biedermeier collection. Round out with impressionist masterworks in ❽ **Realism & Impressionism**, where exceptional works include Max Liebermann's *Hunter in the Dunes*, Monet's *Woman after the Bath* and Van Gogh's *Plain at Auvers*.

1

Klimt in Vienna

The works of Gustav Klimt (1862–1918) – the shining star of Austria's *Jugendstil* (Art Nouveau) age – are as resonant and alluring today as they were when he sent ripples of scandal through the rigid artistic establishment in fin de siècle Vienna with his exotic, erotic style. For total immersion, your first port of call should be the Schloss Belvedere (p135), which is home to the world's largest Klimt collection.

Judith (1901; Oberes Belvedere)

One of Klimt's seminal artworks, this is an entrancing evocation of the Old Testament heroine Judith, a rich widow who charms and decapitates Holofernes (look for his severed head in the right-hand corner of the canvas). Here Judith is presented as a femme fatale: a pouting, bare-breasted Assyrian goddess with a halo of dark hair and a glimmer of ecstatic desire in her eye. The use of gold-leaf and mosaic-like detail is typical of Klimt's golden period, which was inspired by the Byzantine imagery he saw on his travels to Venice.

The Beethoven Frieze (1902; Secession)

Painted for the 14th Vienna Secessionist exhibition, this monumental frieze is a phantasmagorical depiction of Beethoven's Ninth symphony, anchored in mythological symbolism and the conflict of good and evil. Klimt's golden touch gives a decadent flourish to nymph-like creatures who drift across the walls in flowing white robes and choirs of flower-bearing angels. The trio of gorgons (symbolising sickness, madness and death) and the three women embodying lasciviousness, wantonness and intemperance caused widespread outrage – the latter were considered obscene and pornographic.

BONDROCKETIMAGES/SHUTTERSTOCK ©

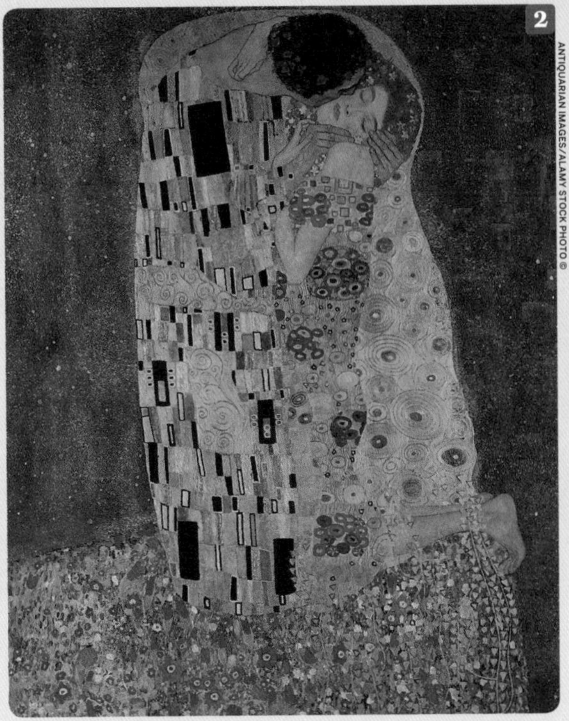

ANTIQUARIAN IMAGES/ALAMY STOCK PHOTO ©

1. Interior of Oberes Belvedere (p135) **2.** *The Kiss*, by Gustav Klimt

The Kiss (1908; Oberes Belvedere)

Klimt believed that all art is erotic, and gazing upon this most sensual of artworks, who can disagree? A couple draped in elaborate robes are shown entwined in an embrace in a flowered meadow. Rumours suggest this to be Klimt and his lifelong lover, Emilie Flöge, a porcelain-skinned, red-headed beauty. With a sinuous waterfall of gold-leaf and elaborate patterning set against a stardust backdrop, the couple appear to transgress the canvas with their dreamlike, rapturous state.

Adam & Eve (1918; Oberes Belvedere)

Klimt was working on this biblical wonder when he suddenly died of a stroke on 6 February 1918. The painting is an ode to the female form Klimt so adored. Adam is less prominent in the background, while in the foreground stands Eve, a celestial vision of radiant skin, voluptuous curves and a cascade of golden hair, with anemones scattered at her feet.

Klimt & the Female Form

Klimt's fascination with women is a common thread in many of his paintings. The artist was most at ease in women's company and lived with his mother and two sisters even at the height of his career. Despite his long-term relationship with the fashion designer Emilie Flöge, Klimt was a philanderer who had countless affairs with his models – in his studio, he apparently wore nothing under his artist's smock – and he fathered around 14 illegitimate children. Though of humble origins, Klimt rapidly climbed the social ladder and was sought out by high-society ladies wishing to have their portrait done.

KIEVVICTOR/SHUTTERSTOCK ©

TOP SIGHT
HEERESGESCHICHTLICHES MUSEUM

More riveting than it sounds, the Heeresgeschichtliches Museum presents a fascinating romp through 400 years of Austro-European military history. In the wake of the 1848 rebellion, Franz Josef I strengthened his defences by ordering the building of the fortress-like Arsenal. This sprawling barracks and munitions depot, completed in 1856, harbours Vienna's oldest public museum.

The museum's whimsical red-brick **arsenal**, with its dome, crenellations, vaulted ceilings, frescos and columns, is a potpourri of Byzantine, Hispano-Moorish and neo-Gothic styles. Spread over two floors, the permanent collection takes a deep breath and plunges headfirst into military history, from the Thirty Years' War (1618–48) to WWII.

On the **ground floor**, the room dedicated to the assassination of Archduke Franz Ferdinand in his car in Sarajevo in 1914 – which triggered a chain of events culminating in the start of WWI – steals the show. Further exhibits home in on WWI and WWII, with excellent displays including Nazi propaganda and Wehrmacht uniforms.

Moving up a level, the **1st floor** races you back to the Thirty Years' War and Peeter Snayers' painting, the Ottoman Wars in the 16th and 17th centuries and the Napoleonic Wars (1789 to 1815). The biggest crowd-puller is a monumental painting showing the 1683 Battle of Vienna.

DON'T MISS

➡ Archduke Franz Ferdinand's car
➡ WWI and WWII halls
➡ Peeter Snayers' Thirty Years' War paintings

PRACTICALITIES

➡ Museum of Military History
➡ Map p252, C7
➡ www.hgm.at
➡ 03, Arsenal
➡ adult/under 19yr €7/free, 1st Sun of month free
➡ 9am-5pm
➡ U Südtiroler Platz

RADIOKAFKA/SHUTTERSTOCK ©

TOP SIGHT
MUSEUM FÜR ANGEWANDTE KUNST

Housed in a stately neo-Renaissance pile on the Ring, Vienna's Museum für Angewandte Kunst (MAK) is a stunning tribute to applied arts and crafts, gathered around an arcaded, skylit courtyard.

On the **ground floor**, exhibition halls are devoted to different styles. One, for instance, is hung with elaborately patterned 16th- and 17th-century Persian, Indian, Turkish and Egyptian carpets, while another spotlights mid-19th-century bentwood **Thonet chairs** – now a Viennese coffeehouse fixture.

In the baroque, rococo and classical collection, the star attraction is the 1740 porcelain room from the **Palais Dubský** in Brno. Italian Renaissance needlepoint lace, jewel-coloured Biedermeier *Steingläser* glasses and Styrian medieval liturgical vestments are other treasures.

The **1st floor** whisks you into Vienna's artistic golden age, from 1890 to 1938. The prized **Wiener Werkstätte** collection, the world's most comprehensive, collates postcards, furniture, fabric patterns, ceramics and distinctive metalwork by modernism pioneers Josef Hoffmann and Koloman Moser and their contemporaries.

The **basement** Study Collection zooms in on materials: glass and ceramics, metal, wood and textiles, with everything from exquisite Japanese lacquerware to unusual furniture (note the red-lips sofa).

DON'T MISS

- Palais Dubský porcelain room
- Thonet chairs
- Wiener Werkstätte collection
- Klimt's sketch for the Palais Stoclet frieze

PRACTICALITIES

- MAK; Museum of Applied Arts
- Map p252, B2
- www.mak.at
- 01, Stubenring 5
- adult/under 19yr €12/free, 6-10pm Tue €5, tours €3.50
- 10am-6pm Wed-Sun, to 10pm Tue, English tours noon Sun
- 2 Stubentor, U Stubentor

SIGHTS

From the wholly absorbing magnificence of Schloss Belvedere and its gardens to the serene greenery of the Stadtpark and the zany, rainbow-bright art of Hundertwasser, this neighbourhood packs in everything from gentle park walks to museums and galleries aplenty. It's spread out, however, so get a day travel card to zip about by public transport.

SCHLOSS BELVEDERE & GARDENS — PALACE

See p135.

HEERESGESCHICHTLICHES MUSEUM — MUSEUM

See p142.

MUSEUM FÜR ANGEWANDTE KUNST — MUSEUM

See p143.

KUNSTHAUSWIEN — MUSEUM

Map p252 (Art House Vienna; www.kunsthauswien.com; 03, Untere Weissgerberstrasse 13; adult/child €12/5; 10am-6pm; 0, 1 Radetzkyplatz) The KunstHausWien, with its bulging ceramics, wonky surfaces, checkerboard facade, technicolor mosaic tilework and rooftop sprouting plants and trees, bears the inimitable hallmark of eccentric Viennese artist and ecowarrior Friedensreich Hundertwasser (1928–2000), who famously called the straight line 'godless'. It is an ode to his playful, boldly creative work, as well as to his green politics.

FÄLSCHERMUSEUM — MUSEUM

Map p252 (Museum of Art Fakes; www.faelschermuseum.com; 03, Löwengasse 28; adult/child €6/3.20; 10am-5pm Tue-Sun; 1 Hetzgasse) Wow, a museum with Schiele, Raphael, Rembrandt and Marc Chagall paintings that nobody knows about? Well, that's because they are all fakes, though spotting the difference is a near impossibility for the untrained eye. The tiny, privately run Fälschermuseum opens a fascinating window on the world of art forgeries. Besides giving background on the who, how, when and what, the museum recounts some incredible stories about master forgers who briefly managed to pull the wool over the experts' eyes.

HUNDERTWASSERHAUS — LANDMARK

Map p252 (03, cnr Löwengasse & Kegelgasse; 1 Hetzgasse) This residential block of flats bears all the wackily creative hallmarks of Hundertwasser, Vienna's radical architect and lover of uneven surfaces, with its curvy lines, crayon-bright colours and mosaic detail.

It's not possible to see inside, but you can cross the road to visit the **Hundertwasser Village** (Map p252; www.hundertwasser-village.com; 03, Kegelgasse 37-39; 9am-6pm; 1 Hetzgasse) FREE, also the handiwork of Hundertwasser.

EATING

Food wise, this neighbourhood has become one to watch in recent years, with a growing crop of exciting new places to eat – from ultrahip delis to gourmet dairies and restaurants with urban edge – especially on and around Landstrasser Hauptstrasse.

CAFÉ GOLDEGG — CAFE €

Map p252 (www.cafegoldegg.at; 04, Argentinierstrasse 49; snacks €3.50-6, mains €10-14; 8am-8pm Mon-Fri, from 9am Sat, 9am-7pm Sun; ; U Südtiroler Platz) Goldegg is a coffee house in the classic Viennese mould, with its green-velvet booths, wood panelling, billiard tables and art nouveau sheen – but with a twist. Staff are refreshingly attentive, and alongside menu stalwarts such as goulash, you'll find lighter dishes like toasted paninis with homemade basil pesto and Ayurvedic vegetable curries.

★LINGENHEL — EUROPEAN €€

Map p252 (01-710 15 66; www.lingenhel.com; 03, Landstrasser Hauptstrasse 74; lunch €10-13, mains €17-26; 8am-10pm Mon-Sat; U Rochusgasse) Lingenhel is an ultraslick deli-shop-bar-restaurant, lodged in a 200-year-old house. Salamis, wines and own-dairy cheeses tempt in the shop, while the pared-back, whitewashed restaurant homes in on season-inflected modern European food. As simple as trout with peas, turnip and orange, and scallop and asparagus risotto, this is food that tastes profoundly of what it ought to.

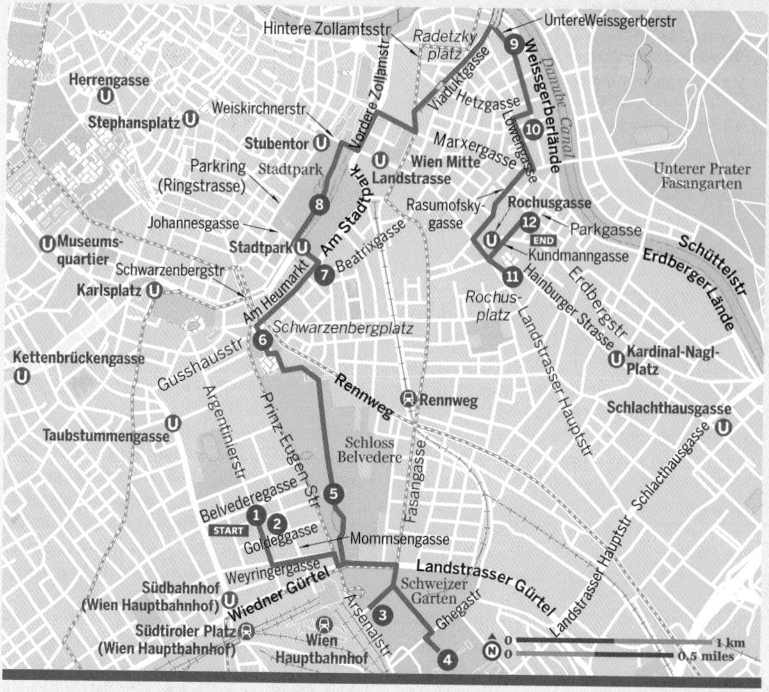

Neighbourhood Walk
Grand Designs in Landstrasse

START SANKT-ELISABETH-PLATZ
END WITTGENSTEINHAUS
LENGTH 8KM; TWO TO FOUR HOURS

Begin by soaking up the neighbourly vibe of ❶ **Sankt-Elisabeth-Platz**, dwarfed by the neo-Gothic Sankt-Elisabeth-Kirche, then nip around the corner to ❷ **Café Goldegg** (p144) for coffee with a dash of art nouveau flair. This old-school coffee house is off the tourist radar so you'll be mingling with locals over strong coffee, strudel or a day special.

Wandering south through the sculpture-dotted Schweizergarten, you'll glimpse the cubical ❸ **Belvedere 21** (p138), the palace's repository for contemporary art. Nearby sits the imposing Arsenal, built in the wake of the 1848 rebellion, which harbours the ❹ **Heeresgeschichtliches Museum** (p142) – a vast repository spelling out Austrian history in artefacts.

Backtrack to the ❺ **Belvedere Gardens** (p137), a swooping ribbon of greenery that threads together the two wings of the baroque palace.You'll emerge at ❻ **Schwarzenbergplatz**, a grand square flanked to the north by a statue of Karl von Schwarzenberg, who led Austrian and Bohemian troops in the Battle of Leipzig (1813).

Rest over a drink in nearby ❼ **Café am Heumarkt** (p147) before tracing the Wien River north through the ❽ **Stadtpark** (p134). Pause for golden snapshots of the memorial commemorating Johann Strauss, king of the waltz. Walk 10 minutes north to spy the chessboard-like facade of ❾ **KunstHausWien** (p144), a mini forest of foliage sprouting from its roof. A five-minute mosey south reveals another of Hundertwasser's creations: the trippy, rainbow-bright ❿ **Hundertwasserhaus** (p144).

Head south to the ⓫ **Rochusmarkt** (Map p252, D3; 03, Landstrasser Hauptstrasse; ⏲6am-7.30pm Mon-Fri, to 5pm Sat; Ⓤ Rochusgasse), where market stalls sell flowers, fruit, meat, cheese, wine and more, then sidle east to the ⓬ **Wittgensteinhaus** at Parkgasse 18. Designed by Paul Engelmann, a talented student of modernist legend Adolf Loos, and the philosopher Ludwig Wittgenstein, this building has strict lines and a stepped design reminiscent of the Bauhaus style. It's now occupied by the Bulgarian embassy.

WORTH A DETOUR

ZENTRALFRIEDHOF

When a Viennese says, *'Er hat den 71er genommen'* ('He took the No 71'), they are, metaphorically speaking, referring to the end of the line: **Zentralfriedhof** (www.friedhoefewien.at; 11, Simmeringer Hauptstrasse 232-244; ⏰7am-8pm, shorter hours in winter; 🚋6, 71 Zentralfriedhof). The cemetery's mammoth scale (2.4 sq km, more than three million resting residents) has made its tram line a euphemism for death. One of Europe's biggest cemeteries, this is where rich and poor, Buddhists and Jews, Catholics and Protestants lie side by side in eternal slumber under ash and maple trees. With leafy avenues and overgrown monuments, it is a remarkably calming place to wander.

The cemetery has three gates: the first leads to the old Jewish graves; the second, the main gate, directs you to the tombs of honour and the **Dr Karl Lueger Kirche**, the cemetery's perkily domed art nouveau church, which bears the hallmark of Austrian architect Max Hegele; and the third is closer to the Protestant and new Jewish graves. The **information centre** and map of the cemetery are at Gate Two.

Just beyond Gate Two are the all-star **Ehrengräber** (Tombs of Honour). Besides the clump of big-name composers such as Beethoven, Brahms, Johann Strauss (father and son), and Schubert, lie Austrian luminaries including artist Hans Makart, sculptor Fritz Wotruba, architect Adolf Loos and 1980s pop icon Falco. Mozart may have a monument here, but he is buried in an unmarked grave in the St Marxer Friedhof (p134).

JOSEPH BROT — BISTRO €€

Map p252 (www.joseph.co.at; 03, Landstrasser Hauptstrasse 4; breakfast €6.90-14.80, lunch mains €10-16.50; ⏰bakery 7.30am-9pm Mon-Fri, 8am-6pm Sat & Sun, bistro 8am-9pm Mon-Fri, to 6pm Sat & Sun; Ⓤ Wien Mitte) Purveyors of Vienna's finest bread, Joseph Brot's bakery, bistro and patisserie is a winner. Besides wonderfully fresh loaves – organic olive-tomato ciabatta and rye-honey-lavender, for instance – it does wholesome breakfasts, speciality teas, healthy smoothies and yummy pastries. Season-driven specials such as sourdough *Spätzle* (noodles) with mountain cheese, lemon shallots and hispi cabbage star on the lunch menu in the stripped-back bistro.

MEIEREI IM STADTPARK — AUSTRIAN €€

Map p252 (☎01-713 31 68; www.steirereck.at; 03, Am Heumarkt 2a; mains €19-22, set breakfasts €21-25; ⏰8am-11pm Mon-Fri, 9am-7pm Sat & Sun; 🖉; Ⓤ Stadtpark) In the green surrounds of Stadtpark, the Meierei is most famous for its goulash served with lemon, capers and creamy dumplings, and its selection of 120 types of cheese. Served until noon, the bountiful breakfast features gastronomic showstoppers such as poached duck egg with forest mushrooms and pumpkin, and corn waffles with warm tomato salad and sheep's cheese.

COLONO — SPANISH €€

Map p252 (☎0660 9362 437; www.colonowien.at; 03, Landstrasser Hauptstrasse 6; tapas & tablas €5-25; ⏰noon-11pm Mon-Sat; Ⓤ U3, U4 Landstrasse) Bringing a dash of Spain to a cool, brick-vaulted, strikingly backlit space on the Landstrasse, Colono is an appetising mix of deli, wine and tapas bar, serving everything from tortilla with truffles to *alubias y almejas* (a hearty bean, clam and vegetable stew) and *tablas* (sharing platters of cured meats, cold cuts and cheeses).

HEUNISCH & ERBEN — AUSTRIAN €€

Map p252 (☎01-286 85 63; www.heunisch.at; 03, Landstrasser Hauptstrasse 17; mains €22-29, 4-/5-course menu €52-62; ⏰3pm-1am Tue-Sat; Ⓤ Landstrasse) This contemporary wine bar and restaurant has carved out a reputation for itself in gastro circles. It's a minimalist, high-ceilinged space, with tall arched windows, bare wood tables and an assemblage of wine crates dangling from the ceiling. The Mediterranean meets Austria in dishes like aubergine with yellow pepper, linseed and stracchino cheese, and tender pork cheeks with root-vegetable mash.

GMOAKELLER — AUSTRIAN €€

Map p252 (☎01-712 53 10; www.gmoakeller.at; 03, Am Heumarkt 25; lunch €8.20, mains €10-18; ⏰11am-midnight Mon-Sat; Ⓤ Stadtpark)

Sizzling and stirring since 1858, this atmospheric cellar is as traditional as it gets, with parquet floors, brick vaults and warm wood panelling. The classic grub – *Zwiebelrostbraten* (onion-topped roast beef) or Carinthian *Kas'nudeln* (cheese noodles) – goes nicely with tangy Austrian wines. Tables spill out onto the pavement in summer.

★STEIRERECK IM STADTPARK GASTRONOMY €€€

Map p252 (☎01-713 31 68; http://steirereck.at; 03, Am Heumarkt 2a; mains €38-58, 6-/7-course menus €149/165; ⏰11.30am-2.30pm & 6.30pm-midnight Mon-Fri; Ⓤ Stadtpark) Heinz Reitbauer is at the culinary helm of this two-starred Michelin restaurant, beautifully lodged in a 20th-century former dairy building in the leafy Stadtpark. His tasting menus are an exuberant feast, fizzing with natural, integral flavours that speak of a chef with exacting standards. Wine pairing is an additional €79/89 (six/seven courses).

DRINKING & NIGHTLIFE

Microbreweries, coffee houses brimming with old-school charm, beach bars by the Danube and cocktail lounges – you'll find the lot in this neighbourhood, though nightlife still remains somewhat low-key in comparison to the 1st district, which it nudges.

STRANDBAR HERRMANN BAR

Map p252 (www.strandbarherrmann.at; 03, Herrmannpark; ⏰10am-2am Apr-early Oct; 📶; 🚋0 Hintere Zollamstrasse, Ⓤ Schwedenplatz) You'd swear you're by the sea at this hopping canal-side beach bar, with beach chairs, sand, DJ beats and hordes of Viennese livin' it up on summer evenings. Cocktail happy hour is from 5pm to 6pm. Cool trivia: it's located on Herrmannpark, named after picture-postcard inventor Emanuel Herrmann (1839–1902).

CAFÉ AM HEUMARKT COFFEE

Map p252 (03, Am Heumarkt 15; ⏰9am-11pm Mon-Fri; Ⓤ Stadtpark) Look for the house number, not the name, as there's no sign at this old-school charmer of a coffee house. Inside it's a 1950s time warp – all shiny parquet, leather banquettes and marble tables. Do as the locals do: grab a newspaper, play billiards and unwind over coffee and no-nonsense Viennese grub.

SALM BRÄU MICROBREWERY

Map p252 (www.salmbraeu.com; 03, Rennweg 8; ⏰11am-midnight; 🚋71 Unteres Belvedere, Ⓤ Karlsplatz) Salm Bräu brews its own *Helles* (pale lager), *Pils* (pilsner), *Märzen* (red-coloured beer with a strong malt taste), *G'mischt* (half *Helles* and half *Dunkel* – dark) and *Weizen* (full-bodied wheat beer, slightly sweet in taste). It is smack next to Schloss Belvedere and hugely popular.

CAFÉ ZARTL COFFEE

Map p252 (03, Rasumofskygasse 7; ⏰7am-10pm; 📶; 🚋1 Rasumofskygasse, Ⓤ Rochusgasse) A withered beauty of a coffee house, Zartl pings you back to when it opened in 1883, with its striped banquettes, cocoon-like warmth and, at times, somnambulant staff. Come for lazy breakfasts, people-watching and coffee with strudel. You'll be mostly among regulars.

ENTERTAINMENT

If it's high culture you're after, without the crowds of the Innere Stadt, you're in the right place. Here you'll find everything from edgy cultural centres to theatres, concert halls and classical-music venues.

★RADIOKULTURHAUS CONCERT VENUE

Map p252 (☎01-501 703 77; http://radiokulturhaus.orf.at; 04, Argentinierstrasse 30a; tickets €19; ⏰box office 4-7pm Mon-Fri; 🚋D Plösslgasse, Ⓤ Taubstummengasse) The line-up swings from classical concerts to jazz quartets and cabaret at the Radiokulturhaus. Housed in several performance venues including the Grosser Sendesaal (home to the Vienna Radio Symphony Orchestra and the Klangtheater, the latter used primarily for radio plays), this is one of Vienna's cultural hotspots.

★KONZERTHAUS CONCERT VENUE

Map p252 (☎01-242 002; www.konzerthaus.at; 03, Lothringerstrasse 20; ⏰box office 9am-7.45pm Mon-Fri, 10am-2pm Sat, plus 45min before performance; 🚋D Gusshausstrasse, Ⓤ Stadtpark) The Konzerthaus is a major venue in classical-music circles, but throughout the

WORTH A DETOUR

THERME WIEN

Rest museum-weary feet or escape the city for a day at **Therme Wien** (☏01-680 09; www.thermewien.at; 11, Kurbadstrasse 14; adult/child 3hr €20/14, full day €27.40/17.50; ⊙9am-10pm Mon-Sat, from 8am Sun; ⛲; ⓤU1 Oberlaa), Austria's largest thermal baths. The water here bubbles at a pleasant 27°C to 36°C and jets, whirlpools, waterfalls and grotto-like pools pummel and swirl you into relaxation. Besides a jigsaw of indoor and outdoor pools, there is an area where kids can splash, dive and rocket down flumes, a sauna complex where grown-ups can detox in herb-scented steam rooms with names like 'morning sun' and 'rainbow', as well as gardens with sun loungers, outdoor massage and games such as volleyball and boules for warm-weather days.

Reaching the spa is now much speedier thanks to the U1 line running to Oberlaa.

year ethnic music, rock, pop or jazz can also be heard in its hallowed halls. Up to three simultaneous performances, in the Grosser Saal, the Mozart Saal and the Schubert Saal, can be staged; this massive complex also features another four concert halls.

ARNOLD SCHÖNBERG CENTER
CLASSICAL MUSIC

Map p252 (☏01-712 18 88; www.schoenberg.at; 03, Schwarzenbergplatz 6; ⊙9am-5pm Mon-Fri; ☐D Schwarzenbergplatz, ⓤStadtpark) This brilliant repository of Arnold Schönberg's archival legacy is a cultural centre and celebration of the Viennese school of the early 20th century, honouring the Viennese-born composer, painter, teacher, theoretician and innovator known for his 12-tone technique. The exhibition hall hosts intimate classical concerts, which in-the-know Viennese flock to.

ARENA WIEN
LIVE MUSIC

(http://arena.wien; 03, Baumgasse 80; tickets around €15; ⓤErdberg, Gasometer) A former slaughterhouse turned music and film venue, Arena is one of Vienna's quirkier places for seeing live acts. Hard rock, rock, metal, reggae and soul (along with cinema) fill its outdoor stage from May to September; in winter bands play in one of its two indoor halls. Regular events include the monthly German–British 1970s New Wave bash 'Iceberg'.

KURSALON
CLASSICAL MUSIC

Map p252 (☏01-512 57 90; www.kursalonwien.at; 01, Johannesgasse 33; tickets €45-99, concert with 3-course dinner €79-133, with 4-course dinner €84-138; ☐2 Weihburggasse, ⓤStadtpark) Fans of Strauss and Mozart will love the performances at Kursalon, which holds daily evening concerts at 8.15pm devoted

to the two masters of music in a splendid, refurbished Renaissance building. Also popular is the concert and dinner package (three- or four-course meal, excluding drinks, at 6pm, followed by the concert) in the equally palatial on-site restaurant.

MARX HALLE
CONCERT VENUE

Map p252 (☏01-888 55 25; https://marxhalle.at; 03, Karl-Farkas-Gasse 19; ☐80A Neu Marz, ☐71 St Marx, ⓤErdbergstrasse) Soaring wrought-iron arches and airy skylights lift the industrial air of this 19th-century market hall, which is now a versatile events space. Expect live gigs, international food festivals and contemporary-art exhibitions across a whopping 22,000 sq metres of heritage-listed architecture by Rudolf Frey.

AKADEMIETHEATER
THEATRE

Map p252 (☏01-514 44 41 40; www.burgtheater.at; 03, Lisztstrasse 1; tickets €3.50-61; ☐4A Akademietheater, ☐D, 71 Schwarzenbergplatz, ⓤStadtpark) Opened in 1922, the 500-seater Akademietheater is the second venue of Vienna's highly esteemed Burgtheater. It stages predominantly contemporary productions.

🏃 SPORTS & ACTIVITIES

WIENER EISLAUFVEREIN
ICE SKATING

Map p252 (www.wev.or.at; 03, Lothringerstrasse 22; adult/child €7.30/6.30, boot hire €6.50; ⊙9am-8pm Sat-Mon, to 9pm Tue-Fri; ☐D Schwarzenbergplatz, ⓤStadtpark) Fancy a twirl? At 6000 sq metres, the Wiener Eislaufverein is the world's largest open-air ice-skating rink. It's close to the Ringstrasse and Stadtpark. Remember to bring mittens and a hat.

Prater & East of the Danube

Neighbourhood Top Five

❶ **Prater** (p151) Enjoying a slice of Viennese park life, with boulevards for strolling, woods for roaming and a funfair. Take a nostalgic twirl above the capital in the *Riesenrad* (ferris wheel), at its twinkling best after dark.

❷ **Johann Strauss Residence** (p153) Waltzing over to where ball chart-topper 'The Blue Danube' was composed.

❸ **Porzellanmuseum im Augarten** (p153) Eyeing banquet-worthy porcelain in the making behind the scenes at the museum.

❹ **Madame Tussauds Vienna** (p153) Meeting Freud, Klimt, Falco and a host of other Austrian waxwork wonders.

❺ **Donauinsel** (p158) Relaxing Viennese-style at a riverside beach or bar in summer.

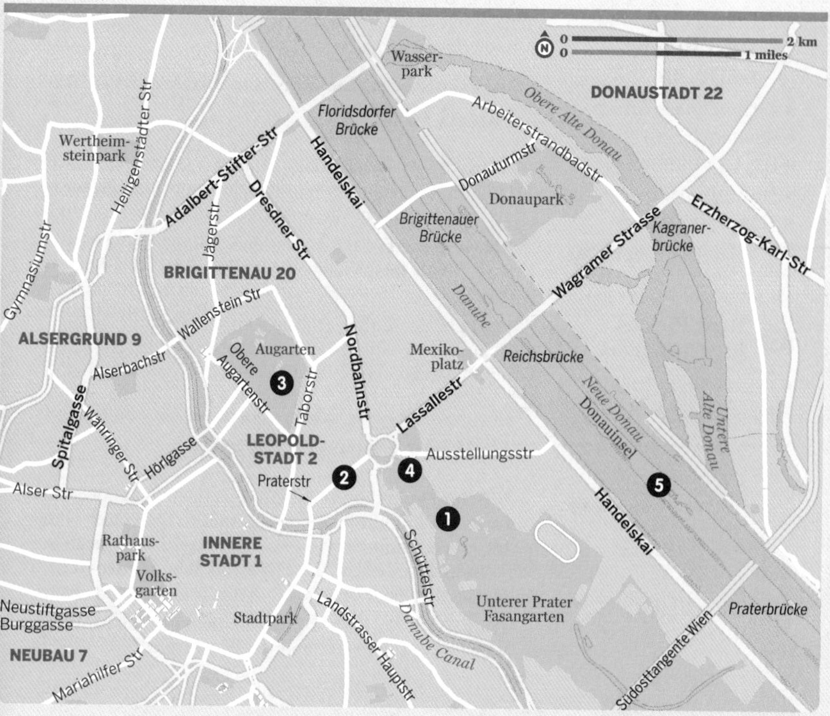

For more detail of this area see Map p250

Lonely Planet's Top Tip

For a truly Viennese experience, visit the 2nd district on a Saturday. Begin with a morning's mooch around the farmers market at Karmelitermarkt, stopping for brunch at one of the deli-cafes, then head southeast for a lazy stroll around the Prater or northwest to the baroque gardens of the Augarten.

Best Places to Eat

- Skopik & Lohn (p155)
- Spelunke (p155)
- Restaurant Mraz & Sohn (p155)
- Wulfisch (p154)
- Harvest (p154)

For reviews, see p154.

Best Places to Drink

- Tel Aviv Beach (p156)
- Sperlhof (p156)
- Das Loft (p156)
- Fluc (p156)
- Tachles (p156)

For reviews, see p155.

Best Places for Children

- Riesenrad (p151)
- Planetarium (p152)
- Alte Donau (p158)
- Donauinsel (p158)

For reviews, see p151.

Explore Prater & East of the Danube

Between the bends of the Danube Canal and the Danube (Donau), Leopoldstadt in Vienna's 2nd district is just a couple of U-Bahn stops from the Innere Stadt, but feels light years away in spirit at times. Here, you can easily tiptoe off the beaten track; not least in the 4.5km ribbon of greenery that is the Prater. The Riesenrad rises above it all, rotating slowly to maximise the skyline views. To the west unfurl the manicured baroque gardens of the Augarten (p153), home to a world-famous porcelain maker.

Leopoldstadt itself is worth more than a cursory glance, with boutiques, delis and cafes continuing to pop up on and around Karmelitermarkt (p156), bringing a dash of gentrification to a once decidedly working-class area. The market, at its vibrant best on a Saturday morning, was previously the centre of a flourishing Jewish quarter, which was all but extinguished during WWII. Yet a glimmer of that legacy is still visible in the district's sprinkling of kosher shops and men wearing wide-brimmed fedoras.

Strung along the banks of the Danube further north is Donaustadt, the 22nd district, whose personality swings between the forests of glass-and-steel skyscrapers in the UNO-City and the serene, deer-dotted woodlands of the Nationalpark Donau-Auen. The long slither of an island called Donauinsel (p158) is a much-loved summertime hang-out of the Viennese for its bars, water-based action and urban beaches.

Local Life

Outdoors Ah, what could be more Viennese than a languid bike ride through the chestnut-filled Prater or a saunter through the Augarten (p153)?

Views Riesenrad not your scene? Join locals to play 'I Spy' with the city's iconic landmarks at Das Loft (p156).

Markets Scoot through the Karmelitermarkt (p156) Viennese-style on a Saturday morn for farm-fresh, organic grub, followed by brunch at a curbside deli.

Getting There & Away

U-Bahn Praterstern (U1 and U2) is the main public-transport link through Leopoldstadt to the Prater, with the U1 continuing on to the Donauinsel. Other handy stops include Nestroyplatz (U1) and Taborstrasse (U2) for the Karmelitermarkt.

Tram Tram No 1 is a useful link between the southern portions of the Prater and the Ringstrasse.

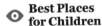

RICHARD NEBESKY/LONELY PLANET ©

TOP SIGHT
PRATER

The Prater describes two distinct areas of parkland, which comprise the city's favourite outdoor playground. First, as you enter, is the Würstelprater, with all the roller-coaster-looping, dodgem-bashing fun of the fair, where the iconic Riesenrad turns. The Unterer Prater is a vast swathe of woodland park, where Habsburgs once went hunting. Today it's perfect for gentle bike rides, walks and warm-day picnics.

Würstelprater

No matter how old you are, you're forever 10 years old with money burning a hole in your pocket at the **Würstelprater** (Prater Vienna; Map p250; www.prater.at; Prater 7; rides €1.50-5; 10am-midnight;). Come summer, this funfair throngs with excitable tots and big kids, gorging on doughnuts and lugging around hoopla-won teddies. The fairground's 250 attractions reach from old-school ghost trains and merry-go-rounds to G-force, human-cannon-like rides.

Several white-knuckle additions to the funfair have cranked up the fear factor, including the **Turbo Boost** that spins at 100km/h; the **Ejection Seat**, a ball that dangles daredevils 90m above the ground; and the **Space Shot**, which shoots thrill-seekers like bullets at up to 80km/h. The 4km **Liliputbahn** (mini railway; Map p250; www.liliputbahn.com; complete circuit adult/child €5/3; mid-Mar–late Oct;) trundles between the Würstelprater and the Ernst-Happel-Stadion.

Riesenrad

Top of every Volksprater wish list is the **Riesenrad** (Ferris wheel; Map p250; www.wienerriesenrad.com; 02, Prater 90; adult/child €12/5; 9am-midnight, shorter hours winter;); at least for anyone of an age to recall Orson Welles' cuckoo-clock speech in British film noir *The Third Man* (1949), set in a shadowy postwar Vienna. This icon also achieved

DON'T MISS

- Riesenrad
- Hauptallee
- Lusthaus
- Planetarium
- Pratermuseum

PRACTICALITIES

- Map p250, D6
- www.wiener-prater.at
- admission free
- U Praterstern

UNTERER PRATER IN SUMMER

While the Unterer Prater can be virtually empty save for the odd horse-drawn carriage and jogger on a monochrome winter's day, warmer weather brings out the Viennese in droves. Hand-holding couples, families, cyclists, in-line skaters, BMX bikers, horse riders and dog walkers all gravitate towards this patch of greenery to stretch their legs and find cool respite under thickets of trees. In mid-April, crowds and runners descend on the park for the Vienna Marathon.

Kids can swing, slide and climb to their hearts' content at the Jesuitenwiese playground, Vienna's biggest, in the Unterer Prater. This meadow is also where friends and families convene to picnic, play beach volleyball or toss a Frisbee.

celluloid fame in the James Bond flick *The Living Daylights,* and *Before Sunrise,* directed by Richard Linklater.

Built in 1897 by Englishman Walter B Basset to celebrate the Golden Jubilee of Emperor Franz Josef I, the Ferris wheel rises to 65m and takes about 20 minutes to rotate its 430-tonne weight one complete circle – giving you ample time to snap some fantastic shots of the city spread out at your feet. It survived bombing in 1945, and has dramatic lighting and a cafe at its base.

Planetarium

The **Planetarium** (Map p250; www.planetarium-wien.at; 02, Oswald-Thomas-Platz 1; adult/child €9/6.50; show times vary), Vienna's extraterrestrial and interstellar viewfinder, is located on the edge of the Würstelprater behind the Riesenrad. Shows change on a regular basis, but usually focus on how the earth fits into the cosmological scheme of things. Shows are in German.

Pratermuseum

Sharing the same building as the Planetarium, this **municipal museum** (Map p250; www.wienmuseum.at; 02, Oswald-Thomas-Platz 1; adult/under 19yr €5/free; 10am-1pm & 2-6pm Tue-Sun) traces the history of the Würstelprater and its woodland neighbour. For all the life and splendour the Prater has seen, unfortunately its museum has only a rather dull mix of photos and stories, mainly from the 19th century. The antique slot machines, some of which are still functioning, are the museum's saving grace.

Unterer Prater

Few places in Vienna can match the Unterer Prater for fresh air, exercise and a burst of seasonal colour. Spread across 60 sq km, central Vienna's biggest park comprises woodlands of poplar and chestnut, meadows and tree-lined boulevards, as well as children's playgrounds, a swimming pool, a golf course and a race track.

Fringed by statuesque chestnut trees that are ablaze with russet and gold in autumn and billowing with delicate white blossom in late spring, the **Hauptallee** avenue is the Unterer Prater's central 4.5km vein, running as straight as a die from the Praterstern to the **Lusthaus**. Originally erected as a 16th-century hunting lodge, the Lusthaus pavilion was rebuilt in 1783 to host imperial festivities and the like. Today, it shelters a chandelier-lit cafe and restaurant.

SIGHTS

Much of the joy of exploring this district is simply wandering its grand parks – the chestnut-lined boulevards of the Prater or the landscaped gardens of the Augarten. The Donauturm provides far-reaching views of Vienna from above, while much water-fuelled action revolves around the Danube when the sun's out.

PRATER PARK

See p151.

PORZELLANMUSEUM IM AUGARTEN MUSEUM

Map p250 (Augarten Porcelain Museum; www.augarten.at; 02, Obere Augartenstrasse 1; adult/child €7/5, incl guided tour €13/11; ⌚10am-6pm Mon-Sat; Ⓤ Taborstrasse) Restored to its former glory and reopened in 2011, this imperial pleasure palace harbours a new museum dedicated to exquisite Augarten porcelain. Founded in 1718, Augarten is the second-oldest porcelain manufacturer in Europe. An engaging chronological spin of the museum takes in lavish rococo creations, boldly coloured Biedermeier pieces, Spanish Riding School equestrian figures and the simpler porcelain fashionable in the 1950s: ceramics may never have got you so fired up!

One-hour tours of the premises are available at 2pm and 3pm on Saturdays, when you can learn about the process of turning white kaolin, feldspar and quartz into delicate creations through the process of moulding, casting, luting, glazing and painting. It's free to get a glimpse of some of Augarten's fabulously detailed creations in the shop, open during the regular opening hours. There is also a nice restaurant facing the adjoining park.

MADAME TUSSAUDS VIENNA MUSEUM

Map p250 (www.madametussauds.com/wien; 02, Riesenradplatz 1; adult/child €24/20; ⌚10am-6pm, to 8pm Jul-Aug; Ⓤ Praterstern) This waxwork wonderland in the Würstelprater is a stage for a host of sculpted celebrities – Nicole Kidman, Michael Jackson and Johnny Depp star among them. Other figures such as Emperor Franz Josef and his beloved Sisi, Klimt, Freud and Falco give the experience a distinctly Austrian edge.

There are hands-on exhibits that let you interact with the wax, from taking an IQ test with Albert Einstein to composing with Mozart and Beethoven. Admission prices are as low as €10 on the website.

JOHANN STRAUSS RESIDENCE MUSEUM

Map p250 (www.wienmuseum.at; 02, Praterstrasse 54; adult/under 19yr €5/free; ⌚10am-1pm & 2-6pm Tue-Sun; Ⓤ Nestroyplatz) Strauss the Younger called Praterstrasse 54 home from 1863 to 1878 and composed *the* waltz, 'The Blue Danube', under its high ceilings. Inside you'll find an above-average collection of Strauss and ballroom memorabilia, including an Amati violin said to have belonged to him and oil paintings from his last apartment, which was destroyed during WWII.

AUGARTEN PARK

(www.kultur.park.augarten.org; 03, Obere Augartenstrasse; ⌚6am-dusk; Ⓤ Taborstrasse) FREE This landscaped park from 1775 is dotted with open meadows and criss-crossed by paths lined with elm, lime, chestnut and maple trees. You can kick a ball in one section, let the kids stage a riot in a playground in another, or visit the porcelain museum. The park contains the city's oldest baroque garden. Among the park's most eye-catching features are the austere *Flaktürme* (flak towers) in its northern and western corners.

WIENER KRIMINALMUSEUM MUSEUM

Map p250 (www.kriminalmuseum.at; 02, Grosse Sperlgasse 24; adult/child €6/3; ⌚10am-5pm Wed-Sun; Ⓤ Taborstrasse) The Vienna Crime Museum is a gruesome chapter in the Viennese obsession with death. It takes a tabloid-style look at crimes and criminals in Austria and dwells on murders in the last 100 years or so with particularly grisly relish; there are skulls of earlier criminals, and even an 18th-century head pickled in a jar.

DONAUTURM TOWER

Map p250 (www.donauturm.at; 22, Donauturmstrasse 4; adult/child €14.50/9.90, combined ticket incl Riesenrad €21.20/11.90; ⌚10am-midnight; Ⓤ Kaisermühlen Vienna International Centre) At 252m, the Danube Tower in Donaupark is Vienna's tallest structure. Its revolving restaurant at 170m, one of several spots to eat within the tower, allows fantastic panoramic views of the city and beyond – the food tends to be tried and trusted Viennese favourites.

WORTH A DETOUR

INTO THE WOODS: THE WIENERWALD

If you really want to get into the great outdoors, scamper across to the Wienerwald. The Austrian capital's rural escape vault, this 45km swathe of forested hills, fringing the capital from the northwest to the southeast, was immortalised in 'Tales from the Vienna Woods,' the concert waltz by Johann Strauss Junior in 1868.

These woods are made for walking and the city-council website (www.wien.gv.at/english/leisure/hiking/paths.html) details 11 walks, a couple of which take you into the forest. You'll need about three hours to complete the 7.2km trail No 4, which threads up to the **Jubiläumswarte**. Rising above the Wienerwald's green canopy, this lookout tower offers sweeping views from the uppermost platform that take in most of Vienna and reach as far as the 2076m hump of Schneeberg. The climb to the top is exhilarating. Grab some picnic supplies, jump on tram 49 to Bahnhofstrasse, and walk in the direction of the tram to Rosentalgasse, then follow the signs. From the Jubiläumswarte, the trail is mainly through suburbs, so it's nicer to return the way you came.

A slightly longer alternative is trail No 1, an 11km loop, which starts in Nussdorf (take tram D from the Ring) and climbs **Kahlenberg** (484m), a vine-streaked hill commanding fine city views. On your return to Nussdorf you can undo all that exercise by imbibing at a *Heuriger* (wine tavern). You can spare yourself the leg work by taking the Nussdorf–Kahlenberg 38A bus in one or both directions.

Another way of exploring the Wienerwald on your own is on one of the 46 marked mountain-bike trails. These are signposted and graded according to difficulty. The website www.wienerwald.info lists and maps the routes.

EATING

Two interesting parts of the neighbourhood to check out for eating are the Karmelitermarkt and Volkertplatz, just west of Nordbahnstrasse.

★SUPERSENSE — CAFE €

Map p250 (https://the.supersense.com; 02, Praterstrasse 70; 2-course lunch €10, breakfast €3.80-9.20; ⌚9.30am-7pm Tue-Fri, 10am-5pm Sat; UPraterstern) Housed in an ornate Italianate mansion dating to 1898, this retro-grand cafe brings a breath of cool air to the Prater area. The cafe at the front, which rolls out locally roasted coffee, great breakfasts and day specials, gives way to a store that trades in everything from vinyl to cult Polaroid cameras, calligraphy sets and hand-bound notebooks.

WULFISCH — SEAFOOD €

Map p250 (☎01-946 18 75; www.wulfisch.at; 02, Haidgasse 5; tapas €4.50-12; ⌚11am-8pm Mon-Fri, 10am-6pm Sat; UTaborstrasse) With zebra-striped awning and pavement decking outside and a small minimalist space inside, Wulfisch prides itself on its fishy tapas, smoked and cured, with fresh crab and oyster dishes, rollmops, North Sea shrimps and smoked salmon. The 'special' with a bit of everything will set you back €12.

HARVEST — VEGAN €

Map p250 (☎0676 492 77 90; www.harvest-bistrot.at; 02, Karmeliterplatz 1; mains €4.50-11, brunch €16.60, lunch €8.80; ⌚2pm-midnight Mon-Fri, from 10am Sat & Sun; 🖉; 🚋2 Karmeliterplatz, UNestroyplatz) A bubble of bohemian warmth, Harvest swears by seasonality in its superhealthy vegetarian and vegan dishes, swinging from lentil, pear, walnut and smoked tofu salad to coconutty vegetable curries. Candles, soft lamplight and mismatched vintage furniture set the scene, and there's a terrace for summer dining. Alt Wien roasted coffee, homemade cakes and weekend brunches round out the picture.

CAKE TREE — CAFE €

Map p250 (www.facebook.com/thecaketreewien; 02, Wolfgang-Schmälzl-Gasse 14; cakes & snacks €4-10; ⌚10am-6pm Tue-Sun; 👪; UPraterstern) This light and airy white-walled space should be high on your list come *Kaffee und Kuchen* (coffee and cake) time. The cakes are rather glorious – whether you plump for mango cheesecake, a warm, cream-topped scone or the chocolate Guinness cake that's a testimony to the

Irish founder. Or go for brunch options like French toast made with homemade brioche.

SCHANK ZUM REICHSAPFEL AUSTRIAN €

Map p250 (☎01-212 25 79; http://zumreichsapfel.at; 02, Karmeliterplatz 3; mains €6.90-15.80; ⏲4pm-midnight Tue-Sat; 🚋2 Karmeliterplatz, UNestroyplatz) This is a delightfully warm, wooden *Heuriger* (wine tavern) in the traditional mould, with dark-wood panelling, a tiled oven and a jovial crowd of locals digging into platters of rustic bread, speck, ham, sausage and salami, and sipping Austrian wines. More substantial mains hailing from Carinthia are of the *Schopfbratl* (pork roast) with dumplings, goulash and *Kasnudeln* (cheese noodles) ilk.

VEGANISTA ICE CREAM €

Map p250 (www.veganista.at; 02, Taborstrasse 15; ice-cream scoops around €2; ⏲noon-11pm Mon-Thu, from 11am Fri-Sun; 🖉; UTaborstrasse) Vegan ice cream has become quite a thing in Vienna, and Veganista was there from the start. Here the 100% natural ice cream and sorbet is whipped up from plant-based milks and organic fruits, and there are options using sweet alternatives to refined sugar, too.

★SKOPIK & LOHN EUROPEAN €€

Map p250 (☎01-219 89 77; www.skopikundlohn.at; 02, Leopoldsgasse 17; mains €11-29; ⏲6pm-1am Tue-Sat; UTaborstrasse) The spidery web of scrawl that creeps across the ceiling at Skopik & Lohn gives an avant-garde edge to an otherwise French-style brasserie – all wainscoting, globe lights, cheek-by-jowl tables and white-jacketed waiters. The menu is modern European, with a Mediterranean slant, delivering spot-on dishes like slow-braised lamb with mint-pea purée, almonds and polenta, and pasta with summer truffle and monkfish.

SPELUNKE FUSION €€

Map p250 (☎01-212 41 51; https://spelunke.at; 02, Taborstrasse 1; mains €14.50-29; ⏲11am-2am Mon-Thu, to 4am Fri & Sat, to midnight Sun; USchwedenplatz) Green-leather banquettes, a wall of vinyl, subtle backlighting and a graffiti mural that references street art lining the Danube Canal make Spelunke a novel choice for a night out. The cool canal-side haunt triumphs in food, too, with dishes from octopus with capers, olives and chorizo butter to truffled turnip salad with miso, and osso bucco with root vegetables.

ROLLERCOASTER RESTAURANT INTERNATIONAL €€

Map p250 (☎0660 244 38 23; www.rollercoaster.rest; 02, Riesenradplatz 6/1; mains €8-12.50; ⏲noon-10pm Mon-Thu, from 11.30am Fri & Sat; ❄📶; UPraterstern) Flashing fluro lights, rattling roller-coaster tracks and thumping dance music welcome you into Vienna's unique Rollercoaster Restaurant. Appropriately nestled in the heart of Prater Park, here you can experience 'Gastronomy 4.0' where robots mix your cocktails and roboticised roller coasters deliver them in strapped-down glass jars. The roller-coaster tracks snake throughout the restaurant to your communal tables for next-generation food service.

SPEZEREI ITALIAN €€

Map p250 (☎0699 1720 0071; www.spezerei.at; 02, Karmeliterplatz 2; antipasti €7.50-15, lunch special €9, pasta €15-17; ⏲5-11pm Mon-Fri; 🖉; 🚋2 Karmeliterplatz, UTaborstrasse) Wine bottles line the walls of this intimate and friendly *Vinothek* (wine bar). Top-quality wines are matched with an array of antipasti and freshly made pasta, such as homemade *fusilli* (spiral-shaped pasta) filled with vanilla-mozzarella or tomato-chilli sauce. The pavement terrace bubbles with life in summer.

RESTAURANT MRAZ & SOHN INTERNATIONAL €€€

Map p250 (☎01-330 45 94; www.mraz-sohn.at; 20, Wallenstein Strasse 59; 9-course menu €144; ⏲7pm-midnight Mon-Fri; 🚋5 Rauscherstrasse, UJägerstrasse) Mraz & Sohn is not only a snappy name, it really is a family-owned-and-run restaurant. The highly esteemed chef de cuisine, Markus Mraz, is the creative force behind the two Michelin stars and other accolades awarded for dishes that shine with creative flair and taste profoundly of their main ingredients – be it succulent Wagyu beef or octopus.

DRINKING & NIGHTLIFE

From new-wave cafes with an alternative edge to electro clubs, high-rise bars with grandstand city views and beach bars on the costa del Danube, this neighbourhood packs in some cracking

KARMELITERMARKT FOR FOODIES

Set in an architecturally picturesque square, the **Karmelitermarkt** (Map p250; 02, Karmelitermarkt; 6am-7.30pm Mon-Fri, to 5pm Sat; 2 Karmeliterplatz, U Taborstrasse) reflects the ethnic diversity of its neighbourhood; you're sure to see Hasidic Jews on bikes shopping for kosher goods here. On Saturday the square features a *Bauernmarkt* (farmers market), where locals set up stalls brimming with seasonal goods from fruit and veg to cheese, freshly baked bread, speciality salamis and organic herbs. The Viennese fill their bags here in the morning before doing brunch or lunch in one of the deli-cafes, many with outdoor seating. Take their lead and rest your shop-weary feet at one of these favourites:

Kaas am Markt (Map p250; www.karmeliter.at; 02, Karmelitermarkt 33-36; light meals & mains €5-10; 9am-6pm Tue-Fri, 8am-2pm Sat; ; 2 Karmeliterplatz, U Taborstrasse) Deli-restaurant making the most of farm-fresh and organic produce. Sells picnic goodies like cheeses, salamis, preserves and apricot liqueur.

Zimmer 37 (Map p250; www.zimmer37.at; 02, Karmelitermarkt 37-39; 2-course lunch €9-10; 10.30am-7.30pm Tue-Fri, 8.30am-2pm Sat; ; 2 Karmeliterplatz, U Taborstrasse) Cosy, oft-candlelit cafe rustling up wholesome lunches like white-bean chilli and homemade pasta.

Tewa (Map p250; 0676 847 74 12 10; http://tewa-karmelitermarkt.at; 02, Karmelitermarkt 25-31; breakfast €5.50-11.50, meals €5.50-13.50; 7am-11pm Mon-Sat; 2 Karmeliterplatz, U Taborstrasse) Great bagels, wraps, salads and breakfasts. The terrace is packed when the sun's out.

nightlife. Naturally, some of the pop-ups down by the river are summer only.

★SPERLHOF — COFFEE

Map p250 (02, Grosse Sperlgasse 41; 4pm-1.30am; ; U Taborstrasse) Every Viennese coffee house ought to be just like the wood-panelled, poster-plastered, fantastically eccentric Sperlhof, which opened in 1923. It still attracts a motley crowd of coffee sippers, daydreamers, billiard and ping-pong players, and chess whizzes today. If you're looking for a novel, check out the selection of second-hand books, many of which are propped up on the outside windowsills.

★DAS LOFT — BAR

Map p250 (www.dasloftwien.at; 02, Praterstrasse 1; noon-2am Mon-Sat, from 12:30pm Sun; 2 Gredlerstrasse, U Schwedenplatz) Wow, what a view! Take the lift to Das Loft on the Sofitel's 18th floor to reduce Vienna to toy-town scale. From this slinky, glass-walled lounge, you can pick out landmarks such as the Stephansdom and the Hofburg over a tonka-bean sour or a mojito. By night, the backlit ceiling swirls with an impressionist painter's palette of colours.

Prices are also sky-high. There is a restaurant here too.

TEL AVIV BEACH — BAR

Map p250 (https://neni.at/restaurants/tel-aviv-beach-bar; 02, Obere Donaustrasse 65; noon-midnight Apr-Oct; U Schottenring) Providing land-locked Austria's capital with a dash of Mediterranean beach life, Tel Aviv started as a pop-up but is now a permanent summer fixture. When the sun's out, it's a fine spot to dig your toes into sand, listen to DJs spin mellow tunes and enjoy a cocktail with oriental-themed food.

FLUC — CLUB

Map p250 (www.fluc.at; 02, Praterstern 5; 6pm-4am; U Praterstern) Located on the wrong side of the tracks (Praterstern can be rough around the edges at times) and housed in a blue-painted converted pedestrian passage, Fluc is the closest Vienna's nightlife scene comes to anarchy – without the fear of physical violence.

TACHLES — BAR

Map p250 (www.cafe-tachles.at; 02, Karmeliterplatz 1; 4pm-1am Mon-Thu, to 2am Fri & Sat, to midnight Sun; ; 2 Karmeliterplatz, U Taborstrasse) Smack on the main square in up-and-coming Leopoldstadt, this bohemian cafe-bar attracts an intellectual and laid-back crowd of locals in relaxed, wood-panelled surrounds. Small bites with a

Slavic slant – pierogi (Polish dumplings), for instance – are on offer and it hosts occasional live music and readings.

CAFE ANSARI CAFE

Map p250 (☎01-276 51 02; www.cafeansari.at; 02, Praterstrasse 15; 2-course lunch €10.80, mains €12.50-26; ⏰8am-11pm Mon-Sat, 9am-3pm Sun; Ⓤ Nestroyplatz) Wood floors, turquoise tiles and cosy niches create a stylishly contemporary look at this cafe, with pavement seating on Praterstrasse. The menu has a pinch of the Orient and Georgia, taking you through from creative breakfasts to antipasti and mains like sweet potato–papaya cakes with chilli dip, and braised lamb with pumpkin, plums and creamy polenta. A 2-course lunch €10.80 while evening mains range from €12.50 to €26.

BALTHASAR CAFE

Map p250 (☎0664 381 68 55; http://balthasar.at; 02, Praterstrasse 38; ⏰7.30am-7pm Mon-Fri, 9am-5pm Sat; Ⓤ Nestroyplatz) With pops of bold colour and lampshades that look like deflated golden helium balloons, this quirky cafe brews some of Vienna's best coffee – including a feisty espresso. The pastries, baguettes and brownies are good, too. With its industrial-chic decor, it's popular with hipsters and caffeine-craving freelancers catching up on emails. Cash only.

PAIM ESPRESSO BAR COFFEE

Map p250 (https://paim-espressobar.business.site; 02, Kleine Pfarrgasse 3/1; ⏰9am-10pm Mon-Thu, to 11pm Fri, to 11.30pm Sat, 10am-7pm Sun; Ⓤ Taborstrasse) On the radar of Viennese coffee fanatics, Paim has a boho vibe and a shabby-chic look and feel. Besides the knockout espresso, the tiny cafe does fresh juice, turmeric lattes and light bites from stuffed vine leaves to chocolate cake.

☆ ENTERTAINMENT

★MUTH CONCERT VENUE

Map p250 (☎01-347 80 80; www.muth.at; 02, Obere Augartenstrasse 1e; Vienna Boys' Choir Fri performance €39-89; ⏰box office 4-6pm Mon-Fri & 1hr before performance; Ⓤ Taborstrasse) This striking baroque-meets-contemporary concert hall is the home of the Wiener Sängerknaben (Vienna Boys' Choir), who previously only performed at the Hofburg. Besides Friday-afternoon choral sessions at 5pm with the angelic-voiced lads, the venue stages a top-drawer roster of dance, drama, opera, classical, rock and jazz performances.

The acoustics are second to none in the 400-seat auditorium and there's a cafe where you can grab a drink before or after a show.

KINO WIE NOCH NIE CINEMA

Map p250 (www.kinowienochnie.at; 02, Augarten; adult/student tickets €8.50/7; Ⓤ Taborstrasse) Every summer the Augarten plays host to this two-month open-air cinema, which screens a mixed bag of art-house, world, cult and classic films.

SHOPPING

Individualism trumps conformity in this slightly offbeat neighbourhood. Shops are spread out, but it's well worth a wander along Taborstrasse and Praterstrasse for edgy design, fashion and retro styles. Or you can join the Viennese at local farmers markets.

TIEMPO BOOKS

Map p250 (http://tiempo.at; 02, Taborstrasse 17a; ⏰10am-7pm Mon-Fri, to 6pm Sat; 🚊2 Karmeliterplatz, Ⓤ Taborstrasse) Travel journals, art books, Vienna-related books, calendars and postcards line the shelves at this self-defined *Genussbuchhandlung* (pleasure bookstore). You can sip a coffee while you browse.

SONG FASHION & ACCESSORIES

Map p250 (www.song.at; 02, Praterstrasse 11-13; ⏰10am-7pm Tue-Fri, to 6pm Sat; 🚊2 Marienbrücke, Ⓤ Schwedenplatz) A holy grail for style seekers, this industrial-minimalist gallery and boutique hosts rotating exhibitions of modern art and is a showcase for designer furnishings, jewellery, accessories and fashion from the revered likes of Dries van Noten, Comme des Garçons and Paul Harnden.

STILWERK WIEN DESIGN

Map p250 (www.stilwerk.de/wien; 02, Praterstrasse 1; ⏰10am-7pm Mon-Fri, to 6pm Sat; 🚊2 Marienbrücke, Ⓤ Schwedenplatz) Plug into Vienna's contemporary-design scene at this cluster of concept and interior stores in the glass-clad Design Tower.

CHRISTA NAGY STRICKDESIGN FASHION & ACCESSORIES

Map p250 (www.nagy-strickdesign.wien; 02, Krummbaumgasse 2-4; ⏲11am-1pm & 2-6pm Tue-Fri, 11am-1pm Sat; UTaborstrasse) The stripy cotton and viscose knitwear here is both classic and up-to-the-minute, with flattering shapes and vivid colours, and designs for hot and cold weather. There are also linen pants and skirts in a refreshing range of bright colours and casual styles.

VORGARTENMARKT MARKET

Map p250 (02, Ennsgasse; ⏲6am-9pm Tue-Fri, to 6pm Sat; UVorgartenstrasse) Sandwiched between the Danube Canal and the Danube River, this organic market trades in everything from fruit and veg to meat, fish, bread and flowers.

HANNOVERMARKT MARKET

Map p250 (20, Hannovergasse; ⏲6am-9pm Mon-Fri, to 6pm Sat; UJägerstrasse) The stalls are heaped with fresh regional produce and Asian foods at this local market.

VOLKERTMARKT MARKET

Map p250 (02, Volkertplatz; ⏲6am-9pm Mon-Fri, to 6pm Sat; UPraterstern) This little farmers market is a good pit stop for bagging some local produce.

SPORTS & ACTIVITIES

★DONAUINSEL OUTDOORS

Map p250 (Danube Island; UDonauinsel) The svelte Danube Island stretches some 21.5km from opposite Klosterneuburg in the north to the Nationalpark Donau-Auen in the south and splits the Danube in two, creating a separate arm known as the Neue Donau (New Danube). Created in 1970, it is Vienna's aquatic playground, with sections of beach (don't expect much sand) for swimming, boating and a little waterskiing.

ALTE DONAU WATER SPORTS

Map p250 (22, Untere Alte Donau; UAlte Donau) The Alte Donau (Old Danube), a landlocked arm of the river, is separated from the Neue Donau by a sliver of land. It carried the main flow of the river until 1875. Now the 160-hectare water expanse is a favourite of Viennese sailing and boating enthusiasts, and also attracts swimmers, walkers, fisherfolk and, in winter (if it's cold enough), ice skaters.

SAILING SCHOOL HOFBAUER BOATING

Map p250 (☎01-204 34 35; www.hofbauer.at; 22, An der Oberen Alten Donau 191; ⏲Apr-Oct; UAlte Donau) Hofbauer rents sailing boats (€19 per hour) and electric boats (€20 per hour) on the eastern bank of the Alte Donau and can provide lessons (in English) for those wishing to learn or brush up on their skills. Pedal boats (€16 per hour) and surfboards/stand-up paddle boards (€18) are also available for hire.

STRANDBAD ALTE DONAU SWIMMING

Map p250 (22, Arbeiterstrandbadstrasse 91; adult/child €5.90/3.20; ⏲9am-8pm Mon-Fri, from 8am Sat & Sun mid-May–mid-Sep; UAlte Donau) This bathing area makes great use of the Alte Donau during the summer months. It's a favourite of Viennese locals and gets crowded at weekends during summer. Facilities include a restaurant, a beach-volleyball court, a playing field, slides and plenty of tree shade.

COPA CAGRANA RAD UND SKATERVERLEIH CYCLING

Map p250 (☎01-263 52 42; www.fahrradverleih.at; 22, Am Damm 1; per hour/half-/full day from €5/15/25; ⏲9am-6pm Mar-Oct, to 9pm May-Aug; UKaisermühlen Vienna International Centre) All manner of bikes are on offer here – city, mountain, trekking, e-bikes, kids' and more. Also has tandems (€12/60 per hour/day), rickshaws (€15/75 per hour/day) and in-line skates (€6/30 per hour/day).

STRANDBAD GÄNSEHÄUFEL SWIMMING

Map p250 (www.gaensehaeufel.at; 22, Moissigasse 21; adult/child €5.90/3.20; ⏲9am-8pm Mon-Fri, 8am-8pm Sat & Sun May–mid-Sep; UKaisermühlen Vienna International Centre) Gänsehäufel occupies half an island in the Alte Donau. It does get crowded in summer, but there's normally enough space to escape the mob. There's a swimming pool and FKK (read: nudist) area. The playground, slides, splash areas and minigolf keep kids amused for hours. Besides swimming, Gänsehäufel offers activities like tennis, volleyball and a climbing zone.

Schloss Schönbrunn & Around

Neighbourhood Top Five

❶ **Schloss Schönbrunn** (p161) Wandering the gloriously over-the-top baroque state apartments and lazing in the fountain-dotted gardens of Vienna's paean to the giddy, gilded late-Habsburg era.

❷ **Klimt Villa** (p165) Diving into the sensual, colour-charged imagination of Klimt at this reproduction of his last studio, in a 1920s villa built on the site of the original property.

❸ **Hermesvilla** (p166) Wandering in Empress Elisabeth's footsteps at this 19th-century mansion romantically nestled in woodland.

❹ **Kirche am Steinhof** (p168) Being amazed by the *Jugendstil* (Art Nouveau) grace of this gold-topped church, Otto Wagner's magnum opus.

❺ **Orangery** (p168) Enjoying the rousing melodies of Strauss and Mozart in Schönbrunn's former imperial greenhouse.

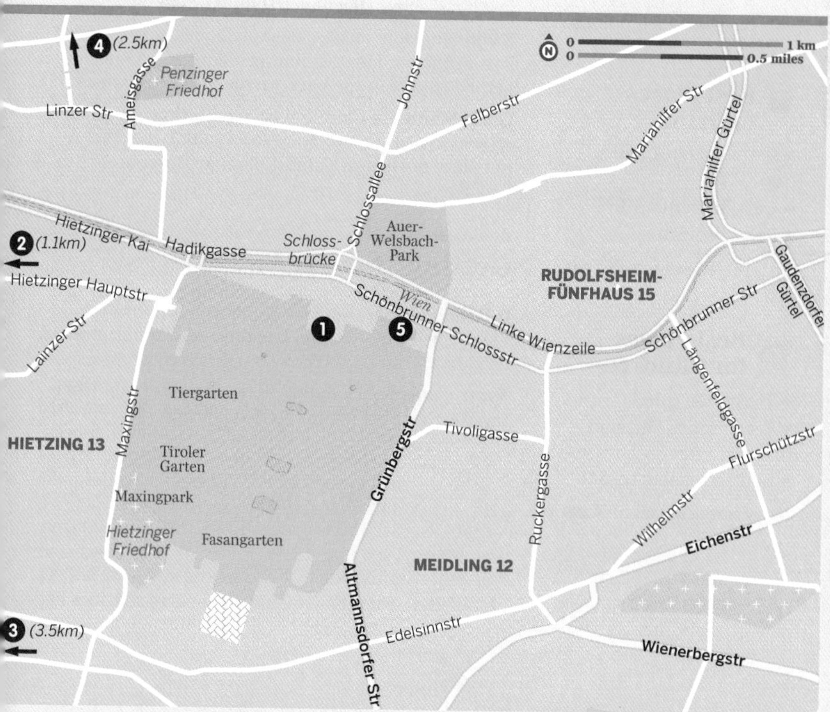

For more detail of this area see Map p254

Lonely Planet's Top Tip

Due to the popularity of the palace, tickets are stamped with a departure time, and there may be a time lag before you're allowed to set off in summer, so buy your ticket straight away and explore the gardens while you wait. Or skip to the front of the queue by buying your ticket in advance online (www.schoenbrunn.at). Simply print the ticket or show it on your phone to be scanned when you enter.

Best Places to Eat

- Landkind (p166)
- Plachutta Hietzing (p166)
- Maxing Stüberl (p167)
- Brandauers Schlossbräu (p166)

For reviews, see p166.

Best Places to Drink

- GOTA Coffee Experts (p167)
- Café Gloriette (p167)
- Reigen (p168)

For reviews, see p167.

Best Places for Children

- Tiergarten (p164)
- Technisches Museum (p165)
- Kindermuseum (p164)

For reviews, see p164.

Explore Schloss Schönbrunn & Around

Few sights in Vienna enthral like Schloss Schönbrunn. The vision of its imposing baroque facade, glowing like warm butter on a sunny afternoon, is not one you are likely to forget in a hurry. You can almost picture the Habsburgs swanning around the fragrant rose beds and mythological fountains in the French-style formal gardens, which provide a harmonious backdrop for the baroque palace, a Unesco World Heritage site.

The palace and gardens' size means the site is best tackled in either a morning or afternoon, or better still over a day. We recommend stops for refreshment within the grounds itself or in one of Hietzing's gently upmarket eating and drinking options. The Klimt Villa (p165) can also be visited with an additional hour or so.

Local Life

Hang-outs Sip microbrews in the tree-shaded courtyard of wonderfully traditional Brandauers Schlossbräu (p166). Or cross the neighbourhood to GOTA Coffee Experts (p167) for standout coffee.

Shopping Give the crowds the slip and window-shop in Altgasse and Hietzinger Hauptstrasse.

Swimming Join locals splashing about or swimming laps in the outdoor swimming complex, Schönbrunnerbad (p168), in the park surrounding the palace.

Quiet Moments Calm the pace with time for quiet reflection at Hietzinger Friedhof (p165), the final resting place of Gustav Klimt, Koloman Moser and Otto Wagner.

Getting There & Away

U-Bahn Schönbrunn is well connected to central Vienna, with the U4 line stopping at Schönbrunn and Hietzing.

Tram Trams 10, 52 and 60 make the short hop from the Westbahnhof station to Schönbrunn.

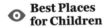

TOP SIGHT
SCHLOSS SCHÖNBRUNN

The Habsburg empire is revealed in all its frescoed, gilded, chandelier-lit glory in the wondrously ornate apartments of Schloss Schönbrunn, which are among Europe's best-preserved baroque interiors. Stories about the first public performance of wunderkind Mozart or Empress Elisabeth's extreme beauty and fitness regimes bring Austrian history to life as you explore the 40 rooms open to the public.

State Apartments

The Imperial Tour (using a free audio guide or app) begins at the frescoed **Blue Staircase**, which makes a regal ascent to the palace's upper level. First up are the 19th-century apartments of Emperor Franz Joseph I and his beloved wife Elisabeth, a beauty praised for her tiny waist and cascading tresses. You then visit lavishly stuccoed, chandelier-lit apartments such as the **Billiard Room**, where army officials would pot a few balls while waiting to attend an audience, and Franz Joseph's **study**, where the emperor worked tirelessly from 5am. The iron bedstead and washstand for morning ablutions in his bedroom reveal his devout, highly disciplined nature.

Empress Elisabeth, or 'Sisi' as she is fondly nicknamed, whiled away many an hour penning poetry in the ruby-red **Stairs Cabinet**, and brushing up on various European languages while her ankle-length locks were tended in the privacy of her **dressing room**. Blue-and-white silk wall hangings adorn the **imperial bedroom** that Franz and Sisi sometimes shared. The neorococo **Empress' Salon** features portraits of some of Maria Theresia's 16 children, including Marie Antoinette in hunting garb, poignantly oblivious to her fate at the French guillotine in 1793.

DON'T MISS

- State Apartments
- Neptunbrunnen
- Gloriette
- Wagenburg

PRACTICALITIES

- Map p254, C3
- ☎01-811 13-0
- www.schoenbrunn.at
- 13, Schönbrunner Schlossstrasse 47
- adult/child Imperial Tour €16/11.50, Grand Tour €20/13, Grand Tour with guide €24/15
- 8am-6.30pm Jul & Aug, to 5.30pm Apr-Jun, Sep & Oct, to 5pm Nov-Mar
- U Schönbrunn, Hietzing

Laid with leaded crystal and fragile porcelain, the table in the **Marie Antoinette Room** is where Franz Joseph used to dig into hearty meals of goulash and schnitzel (health-conscious Sisi preferred beef broth and strawberries out of view).

More portraits of Maria Theresia's brood fill the **Children's Room** and the **Balcony Room**, graced with works by court painter Martin van Meytens. Keep an eye out for the one of ill-fated daughter **Maria Elisabeth**, considered a rare beauty before she contracted smallpox. The disease left her so disfigured that all hope of finding a husband vanished, and she entered convent life.

In the exquisite white-and-gold **Mirror Room**, a six-year-old Mozart performed for a rapturous Maria Theresia in 1762. Fairest of all is the 40m-long **Great Gallery**, where the Habsburgs threw balls and banquets, a frothy vision of stucco, mirrors and gilt chandeliers, topped with a fresco by Italian artist Gregorio Guglielmi showing the glorification of Maria Theresia's reign. Decor aside, this was where the historic meeting between John F Kennedy and Soviet leader Nikita Khrushchev took place in 1961.

Wandering through the porcelain-crammed **Chinese Cabinets** brings you to the equestrian fanfare of the **Carousel Room** and the **Hall of Ceremonies**, with five monumental paintings showing the marriage of Joseph, heir to the throne, to Isabella of Parma in 1760. Mozart, only four at the time of the wedding, was added as an afterthought by the artist, who took several years to complete the picture, by which time the virtuoso was a rising star.

If you have a Grand Tour ticket, you can continue through to the palace's **east wing**. Franz Stephan's apartments begin in the sublime **Blue Chinese Salon**, where the intricate floral wall paintings are done on Chinese rice paper. The jewel-box pietra dura tables, inlaid with semiprecious stones, are stellar examples of Florentine craftsmanship. The negotiations that led to the collapse of the Austro-Hungarian Empire in 1918 were held here. A century before, Napoleon chose Schönbrunn as his HQ when he occupied Vienna in 1805 and 1809, and the **Napoleon Room** was where he may have dreamed about which country to conquer next. Look for the portrait of his only legitimate son, Napoleon II, Duke of Reichstadt, shown as a cherubic lad in the park at Schloss Laxenburg.

Passing through the exquisite rosewood **Millions Room**, the **Gobelin Salon**, filled with Flemish tapestries, and the **Red Salon** brimming with Habsburg portraits, you reach Maria Theresia's **bedroom**, with a throne-like four-poster bed covered in red velvet and gold embroidery. This is where Franz

PALMENHAUS

Londoners may think they're experiencing déjà vu on sighting the **Palmen House** (Palm House; Map p254; 13, Maxingstrasse 13b; adult/child incl Wüstenhaus €6/4.50; ⏰9.30am-6pm May-Sep, to 5pm Oct-Apr; Ⓤ Hietzing). This was built in 1882 by Franz Segenschmid as a replica of the one in London's Kew Gardens. Inside is a veritable jungle of tropical plants from around the world.

The small Wüstenhaus (Desert House; Map p254; ☎01-877 92 94-500; www.zoovienna.at; 13, Maxingstrasse 13b; adult/child €6/4.50; ⏰9am-6pm May-Sep, to 5pm Oct-Apr; Ⓤ Hietzing) near the Palmenhaus makes good use of the once-disused Sonnenuhrhaus (Sundial House) to recreate arid desert scenes. Its four sections – Africa, the Middle East, the Americas and Madagascar – are home to rare cacti and live desert animals, such as the naked mole rat from East Africa.

Joseph was born in 1830. Gilt-framed portraits of the Habsburgs hang on the red-damask walls of Archduke Franz Karl's **study**, and the tour concludes in the **Hunting Room**, with paintings noting Schönbrunn's origins as a hunting lodge.

Schloss Schönbrunn Gardens

The beautifully tended formal **gardens** (Map p254; ⏲6.30am-dusk) FREE of the palace are appealing whatever the season: a symphony of colour in the summer and a wash of greys and browns in winter. Opened to the public by Joseph II in 1779, the grounds contain a number of attractions in the tree-lined avenues that were arranged according to a grid and star-shaped system between 1750 and 1755. Between 1772 and 1780 Johann Ferdinand Hetzendorf added some of the final touches to the park under the instructions of Joseph II: fake **Roman ruins** in 1778; the **Neptunbrunnen** (Neptune Fountain; ⏲10am-4pm mid-Apr–Sep), an equally empire-boosting Greek-mythology-themed folly in 1781; and the crowning glory, the **Gloriette** (adult/child €4.50/3.20; ⏲9am-7pm Jul & Aug, to 6pm Apr-Jun & Sep, to 5pm Oct-early Nov), in 1775. The view from the Gloriette is, as the name suggests, glorious.

The palace gained its name from the **Schöner Brunnen** (⏲10am-4pm mid-Apr–Sep). The original fountain now pours through the stone pitcher of a nymph near the Roman ruins. The garden's 630m-long **Irrgarten** (Maze; adult/child €6/3.50, combination ticket with Kindermuseum €12/8, with Kindermusum & Tiergarten €28/16; ⏲9am-6pm mid-Mar–early Nov; 👪) is a classic hedge design based on the original maze that occupied its place from 1720 to 1892; adjoining this is the **Labyrinth**, a playground with games, climbing equipment and a giant mirror kaleidoscope.

East of the palace is the **Kronprinzengarten**, a replica of the baroque garden that occupied the space around 1750.

SCHLOSS SCHÖNBRUNN AND GARDENS

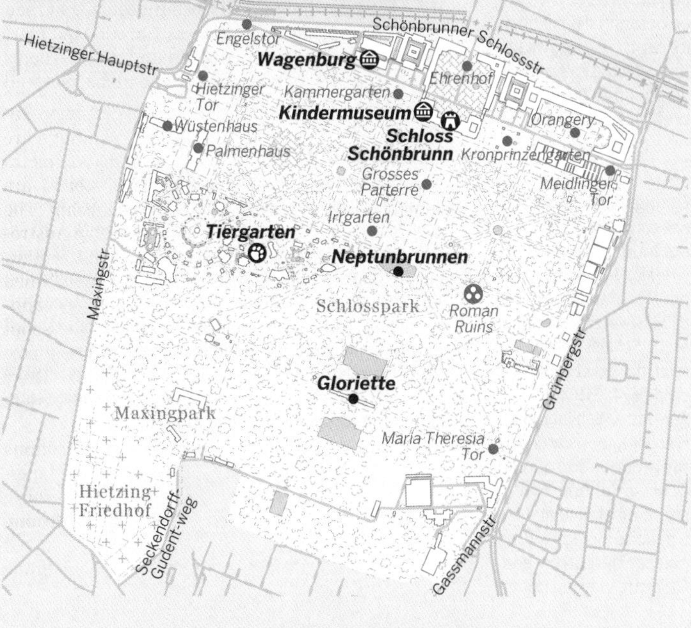

SCHÖNBRUNN ZOO

Established in 1752 as a menagerie by Franz Stephan, the Schönbrunn **Tiergarten** (Map p254; www.zoovienna.at; 13, Maxingstrasse 13b; adult/child €20/10, combination ticket with Irrgarten & Kindermuseum €28/16; 9am-6.30pm Apr-Sep, to 5.30pm Mar & Oct, to 5pm Feb, to 4.30pm Nov-Jan; 56A, 56B, 58A Tiroler Gasse, Hietzing) is the world's oldest continually operating zoo. Among its 8500 resident animals are giant pandas, polar bears, giraffes and Siberian tigers. Feeding times are staggered throughout the day – check maps to find out who's dining when. The zoo is laid out like a bicycle wheel, with pathways as spokes and an octagonal pavilion at its centre. The pavilion dates from 1759 and was used as the imperial breakfast room.

During the summer season, a little 50 minute tourist 'train' (on wheels), the Schönbrunner Panoramabahn (Map p254; www.zoovienna.at; 13, Schloss Schönbrunn; day ticket adult/child €8/4; 10am-5pm Apr-Oct; Schönbrunn, Hietzing), loops around the grounds surrounding Schloss Schönbrunn, stopping at nine attractions including the palace, Tiergarten, and Gloriette viewing point.

Interior of Schloss Schönbrunn

Kindermuseum

Schönbrunn's **Kindermuseum** (Children's Museum; www.kaiserkinder.at; adult/child €9.50/7.50, combination ticket with Irrgarten €12/8, with Irrgarten & Tiergarten €28/16; 10am-5pm;) does what it knows best: imperialism. Activities and displays help kids discover the day-to-day life of the Habsburg court, and then dress up in princely or princessly outfits and start ordering the serfs (parents) around. Other rooms devoted to toys, natural science and archaeology all help to keep them entertained.

Wagenburg

The **Wagenburg** (Imperial Coach Collection; Map p254; www.kaiserliche-wagenburg.at; 13, Schloss Schönbrunn; adult/child €9.50/free; 9am-5pm mid-Mar–Nov, 10am-4pm Dec–mid-Mar) is *Pimp My Ride,* imperial-style. On display is a vast array of carriages, including Emperor Franz Stephan's coronation carriage, with its ornate gold plating, Venetian glass panes and painted cherubs. The whole thing weighs an astonishing 4000kg. Also look for the dainty child's carriage built for Napoleon's son, with eagle-wing-shaped mudguards and bee motifs.

SIGHTS

Most visitors come to Hietzing for one of Vienna's biggest drawcards, the Unesco World Heritage site Schloss Schönbrunn and its collection of associated museums and its extensive Imperial gardens. Beyond the palace apartments itself, these include a science museum, a small zoo and a quaint museum of Imperial coaches. Schloss Schönbrunn's gardens contain a number of notable monuments, a maze, viewing platforms and baroque follies such as imitation Roman ruins, and anywhere else would be an attraction in itself. The Klimt Villa and the Hermesvilla (p166), a gift for Empress Elisabeth from Franz Joseph I, are among the area's lesser-known treasures, but both tell significant Viennese stories.

SCHLOSS SCHÖNBRUNN — PALACE

See p161.

KLIMT VILLA — MUSEUM

(www.klimtvilla.at; 13, Feldmühlgasse 11; adult/child €10/5; ⏲10am-6pm Tue-Sun; 🚊10 Verbindungsbahn) The Klimt Villa immerses you in the sensual world of Vienna's most famous Secessionist. The 1920s neo-baroque villa was built on the site of the original rustic studio, the artist's last, where he worked from 1911 to 1918. His reconstructed studio features carefully reproduced furnishings and carpets. Regular exhibitions take place here.

TECHNISCHES MUSEUM — MUSEUM

Map p254 (☎01-899 98-0; www.technischesmuseum.at; 14, Mariahilfer Strasse 212; adult/child €14/free; ⏲9am-6pm Mon-Fri, 10am-6pm Sat & Sun; 👪; 🚊10, 46, 49, 52, 60 Winckelmannstrasse) Opened in 1918, the Technical Museum is dedicated to science, technology and engineering. There are loads of gadgets for you to conduct experiments, but the most interesting aspect is its historical collection. There's a 1950 Mercedes Silver Arrow, a 1923 Model T Ford and penny-farthing bicycles, to name a few.

Its musical-instrument collection focuses mainly on keyboard instruments. The permanent exhibition is complemented by temporary ones; anyone with an engineering bent will love it, as will two- to six-year-olds, for the well-thought-out Das Mini section.

HIETZINGER FRIEDHOF — CEMETERY

Map p254 (www.friedhoefewien.at; 13, Maxingstrasse 15; ⏲7am-dusk Mar-Oct, 8am-5pm Nov-Feb; 🚌56A, 56B, 58A Montecuccoliplatz, Ⓤ Hietzing) **FREE** Aficionados of Vienna's Secessionist movement will want to make the pilgrimage to the Hietzinger cemetery to pay homage to some of its greatest members. Gustav Klimt, Koloman Moser and Otto Wagner are all buried here. Others buried in the cemetery include composer Alban Berg.

TICKETS FOR SCHLOSS SCHÖNBRUNN

The best way to get a ticket is to buy it in advance online. Print the ticket yourself or show it on your phone to be scanned on entry.

An **Imperial Tour** ticket (adult/child €16/11.50) includes an audio-guided (or app-guided) tour of 22 rooms. A **Grand Tour** ticket (audio-guided adult/child €20/13, with guide €24/15) includes all rooms in the Imperial Tour and the additional 18 rooms of the palace that can be visited. The palace's Grand Tour accompanied by an English-speaking guide departs at 11am and 3pm daily year-round.

If you plan to see several sights at Schönbrunn, it's worth purchasing a combination ticket.

From April to October, the summer-season **Classic Pass** (adult/child €26.50/16.50) is valid for an audio-guided Grand Tour of Schloss Schönbrunn (including all 40 rooms open to the public) and visits to the Kronprinzengarten (Crown Prince Garden), Irrgarten (maze) and Labyrinth, and Gloriette with its panoramic viewing terrace. A Classic Pass that includes a guided Grand Tour per adult/child costs €30.50/18.50.

The summer-season **Classic Pass Plus** adds in the Tiergarten (zoo). With an audio-guided Grand Tour per adult/child it costs €40/23, with a guided Grand Tour it costs €44/25.

Year-round, the Sisi Ticket (p68) covering key Hofburg sites includes Schloss Schönbrunn.

WORTH A DETOUR

LAINZER TIERGARTEN

Covering 25 sq km, the **Lainzer Tiergarten** (www.lainzer-tiergarten.at; 13, Hermesstrasse; 8am-dusk; 55A Lainzer Tor) is the largest (and wildest) of Vienna's city parks. The *Tiergarten* (zoo) refers to the abundant wild boar, deer, woodpeckers and squirrels that freely inhabit the densely forested park, and the famous Lipizzaner horses that summer here. Opened by Emperor Ferdinand I in 1561, the park was once the hunting ground of Habsburg royalty. Today it offers extensive walking possibilities through lush woodlands of beech and oak, as well as attractions including the six-storey **Hubertus-Warte**, a viewing platform on top of Kaltbründlberg that's 508m above sea level.

On the eastern edge of the park sits the stately **Hermesvilla** (01-804 13 24; www.wienmuseum.at; 13, Lainzer Tiergarten; adult/child €7/free; 10am-6pm Tue-Sun mid-Mar–Oct; 55A Lainzer Tor, 62 Hermesstrasse), commissioned by Franz Joseph I and presented to his wife as a gift. It is named after the white marble statue of Hermes, which guards the garden in front of the palace. Built by Karl von Hasenauer between 1882 and 1886, with Klimt and Hans Makart on board as interior decorators, it's extremely plush – it's more a mansion than simply a 'villa'. Empress Elisabeth's bedroom is totally over the top, with the walls and ceiling covered in motifs from Shakespeare's *A Midsummer Night's Dream*. A visit also takes in the room where Elisabeth, or 'Sisi', used to exercise vigorously in order to keep her famous 40cm (16in) waist.

EATING

With a population of discerning locals, the streets surrounding the Schloss turn up some good options for every taste, from ultratraditional produce-driven dining rooms to bright, supermodern cafes serving international favourites.

WALDEMAR — CAFE €

Map p254 (0664 361 61 27; www.waldemar-tagesbar.at; 13, Altgasse 6; dishes €6-11.50; 8am-8pm Mon-Fri, 9am-3pm Sat & Sun; ; Hietzing) Stylish and airy, with polished concrete floors and art and photography on the white-painted walls, this breakfast-to-aperitif spot is contemporary in both menu and look. Breakfast includes baguettes and jam, and a dedicated 'müsli & co' menu. At lunch, pop in for a bowl of curry or dhal.

CAFÉ RESIDENZ — AUSTRIAN €

Map p254 (01-24 10 03 00; www.cafe-residenz.at; 13, Kavaliers 52; dishes €6-9.50, mains €9-23; cafe 9am-8pm; ; Schönbrunn) On the grounds of Schloss Schönbrunn (p161), Café Residenz serves sweet and savoury strudels, and classic Viennese cakes. The basement hosts **strudel show** cookery demonstrations – held on the hour between 11am and 4pm and at a cost of €6, or €11.50 with a coffee and strudel. Take a two-hour **strudel-making class** at 6pm for €75. Shows and classes are in English.

★LANDKIND — MARKET €€

Map p254 (www.landkind.wien; 15, Schwendermarkt, Stand 16; dishes €5-14.50; 9am-9pm Wed-Fri, to 3pm Sat; ; 5, 9, 18, 49, 52, 60 Rustengasse) Part organic market stall, part cafe and local hang-out, Landkind sources produce from small-scale sustainable farmers. Browse its shelves for fruits, vegetables, cheeses, jams, wines, gins and cakes, or squeeze into the tiny space to dine on soups, strudels, salads and sharing platters.

PLACHUTTA HIETZING — AUSTRIAN €€

Map p254 (01-877 70 87-0; www.plachutta-hietzing.at; 13, Auhofstrasse 1; mains €18.50-25; 11.30am-2.30pm & 6-10.30pm Mon-Fri, 11.30am-10.30pm Sat & Sun; ; Hietzing) Emperor Franz Joseph I declared *Tafelspitz* (boiled beef) his favourite meal, and this restaurant serves 10 varieties, made from organic, pasture-reared Austrian beef, in gleaming copper saucepans. Schnitzel, pan-roasted calf's liver, and trout with bread dumplings with mushroom sauce are all excellent, too.

Its handful of other restaurants in Vienna include one near Stephansdom (p83).

BRANDAUERS SCHLOSSBRÄU — AUSTRIAN €€

Map p254 (01-879 59 70; www.bierig.at; 13, Am Platz 5; mains €10.50-25; 10am-midnight; ; Hietzing) This microbrewery rolls out hoppy house brews, speciality beers and above-average pub fare. Spare ribs feature alongside goulash and schnitzel as well as vegetarian options including salads and cheese-laden dumplings. The buffet lunch is €9.90.

MAXING STÜBERL AUSTRIAN €€

Map p254 (www.maxingstuberl.at; 13, Maxingstrasse 7; mains €9-18.50; ⌚5pm-midnight Mon-Fri, 1pm-midnight Sat & Sun; ⓤHietzing) Johann Strauss' one-time favourite, this restaurant serves produce from the owner's home region of Pielachtal, Lower Austria. Start with boiled beef aspic with onions and pumpkin-seed oil; continue with fried blood sausage with sauerkraut and roasted potatoes or chicken cooked on an iron griddle; and finish with curd dumplings and stewed berries.

DA FERDINANDO ITALIAN €€

Map p254 (☎01-877 80 36; www.daferdinando.at; 13, Hietzinger Hauptstrasse 26; mains €10.50-25; ⌚11am-11pm; 📶🌶; ⓤHietzing) Top-quality Italian dishes at this restaurant span wood-fired pizzas and homemade pastas (including vegetarian varieties) to mains such as veal in lemon-and-brandy sauce or grilled sea bass with roast tomato and fennel. Desserts include a coffee-laced tiramisu. Dine in the classic front room, in the contemporary back dining room or in the flower-filled courtyard.

DAS EDUARD CAFE €€

Map p254 (☎01-892 29 78; www.das-eduard.jimdo.com; 15, Sparkassplatz 1; mains €9-23; ⌚4-10pm Mon, 8.30am-10pm Tue-Fri, 9.30am-10pm Sat & Sun; 📶; 🚌12A, 57A Stiegergasse) All-rounder Das Eduard is a buzzing spot for breakfast (until 11am), oversized caffe lattes and homemade cakes, plus more substantial dishes from schnitzel to burgers, bagels, wraps, salads and steaks. Come summer, the tree-shaded terrace hums with the clink of white-wine spritzers and refreshing *Radlers* (beer and lemonade) as the sun sets.

HOLLEREI VEGETARIAN €€

Map p254 (☎01-892 33 56; www.hollerei.at; 15, Hollergasse 9; mains €8-17; ⌚11am-10.30pm Mon-Fri, 9am-10.30pm Sat, 9am-2.30pm Sun; 🌶; ⓤMeidling Hauptstrasse) Whether you go for quinoa with sweet potato and date-and-nut pesto, homemade spinach gnocchi with sun-dried tomatoes, or wild garlic dumplings with mushroom sauce, the food at this all-vegetarian bistro has a welcome freshness. On weekdays, the two-course lunch menu costs €10.90. Cash only.

QUELL AUSTRIAN €€

Map p254 (☎01-893 24 07; www.gasthausquell.at; 15, Reindorfgasse 19; mains €8-15; ⌚11am-10.45pm Mon-Fri; 🚊5, 9, 18, 49, 52, 60 Kranzgasse) The wood-panelled interior of this traditional *Beisl* (small tavern) looks as if it's been untouched for years and the archaic wooden chandeliers and ceramic stoves wouldn't be out of place in a folklore museum. The menu is thoroughly Viennese, with goulash, pork cutlets and schnitzel featuring prominently.

DRINKING & NIGHTLIFE

You'll have no trouble finding a decent glass of wine in the area, with lots of pretty wine shops and bars to choose from. Once the palace closes, it becomes a very local scene. There are also a handful of clubs.

★**GOTA COFFEE EXPERTS** COFFEE

Map p254 (www.facebook.com/gotacoffeevienna; 15, Mariahilfer Strasse 192; ⌚7am-6pm Mon-Fri, 8am-4pm Sat, 7am-4pm Sun; 📶; 🚊5, 9, 18, 49, 52, 60 Rustengasse) 🍃 A multiple title holder of Austrian Barista of the year, GOTA is worth a cross-town trip for its third-wave coffee creations made from carefully sourced fair-trade beans. The small, simple cafe has a chatty, welcoming and unhurried atmosphere.

Breakfast includes vegan and vegetarian options; many of its cakes are vegan, too.

CAFÉ GLORIETTE COFFEE

Map p254 (www.gloriette-cafe.at; 13, Gloriette, Schloss Schönbrunn; ⌚9am-dusk; ⓤSchönbrunn, Hietzing) Café Gloriette occupies the neoclassical Gloriette, high on a hill behind Schloss Schönbrunn, built for the pleasure of Maria Theresia in 1775. With sweeping views of the Schloss, its gardens and the districts to the north, Gloriette has arguably one of the best vistas in all of Vienna. It's a welcome pit stop after the short climb up the hill.

U4 CLUB

Map p254 (www.u4.at; 12, Schönbrunner Strasse 222; ⌚10pm-6am Tue-Sat; ⓤMeidling Hauptstrasse) U4 was the birthplace of techno clubbing in Vienna, and its longevity is a testament to its ability to roll with the times. It still draws a young crowd thanks to regular student nights, '90s nights (Wednesdays), and thumping

WORTH A DETOUR

KIRCHE AM STEINHOF

Perched on the crest of the Baumgartner Höhe, **Kirche am Steinhof** (www.erzdioezese-wien.at; 14, Baumgartner Höhe 1; tour €8; ⌚4-5pm Sat, noon-4pm Sun, tours 3pm Sat, 4pm Sun; 🚌48A Otto-Wagner-Spital), built from 1904 to 1907, is Otto Wagner's crowning glory. It's a steepish walk up to the church, nestled in the grounds of the Psychiatric Hospital of the City of Vienna and commanding fine views of the city.

Koloman Moser chipped in with the mosaic windows, and the roof is topped by a copper-covered dome that earned the nickname *Limoniberg* (Lemon Mountain) from its original golden colour. It's a bold statement in an asylum that has other *Jugendstil* (Art Nouveau) buildings, and it could only be pushed through by Wagner because the grounds were far from the public gaze. The church interior can only be visited by guided tour (in German).

house, hip-hop and R&B (Thursdays), rock (Fridays), and themed nights and events on Saturdays.

ENTERTAINMENT

ORANGERY CONCERT VENUE

Map p254 (☎01-812 50 04; www.imagevienna.com; 13, Schloss Schönbrunn; tickets €42-126; Ⓤ Schönbrunn) Schönbrunn's lovely former imperial greenhouse is the location for year-round Mozart and Strauss concerts. Performances last around two hours and begin at 8.30pm daily, with a separate schedule during the Christmas season.

MARIONETTEN THEATER PUPPET THEATRE

Map p254 (☎01-817 32 47; www.marionettentheater.at; 13, Schloss Schönbrunn; tickets adult €11-39, child €9-25; ⌚Mon, Wed & Fri-Sun; 👪; Ⓤ Schönbrunn) This small theatre in Schloss Schönbrunn (p161) puts on marionette performances of much-loved productions such as *The Magic Flute* and *Aladdin,* with longer performances for adults and shorter ones for families that delight kids.

REIGEN LIVE MUSIC

Map p254 (☎01-894 00 94; www.reigen.at; 14, Hadikgasse 62; ⌚6pm-2am Sun-Thu, to 4am Fri & Sat, closed late May–mid-Jun; Ⓤ Hietzing) Enjoy a drink in front of Reigen's tiny stage, which is the setting for jazz, blues, Latin and world music in a simple space housing changing art and photography exhibits.

SHOPPING

This is an enjoyable destination for a shopping stroll with ultralocal shops selling everything from wine to gluten-free cakes to guitars. It's also the place to come for one of Vienna's most atmospheric Christmas markets.

DIE SCHWALBE FASHION & ACCESSORIES

Map p254 (☎01-952 98 40; www.die-schwalbe.at; 15, Reindorfgasse 38; ⌚noon-6.30pm Mon, 10.30am-6.30pm Tue & Wed, 10.30am-7pm Thu & Fri, 10am-5pm Sat; 🚋52, 60 Rustengasse) 'Eco-urban steetwear' here spans hoodies and pullovers to T-shirts, jackets, shorts and pants, plus accessories such as beanies, caps and scarves from small-scale labels. There's an in-house piercing lounge.

1130WEIN FOOD & DRINKS

Map p254 (www.1130wein.at; 13, Lainzerstrasse 1; ⌚10am-7pm Mon-Fri, to 3pm Sat; Ⓤ Hietzing) This *Vinothek* (wine shop) does tastings with the delightful Robert Sponer-Triulzi, who stocks a huge range of interesting, top-quality (though not always expensive) wines from all over Austria. He'll challenge you and make sure you come away with a drop you'll love. There are chilled whites if you're picnicking.

SPORTS & ACTIVITIES

SCHÖNBRUNNERBAD SWIMMING

Map p254 (☎01-817 53 53; www.schoenbrunnerbad.at; 13, Schloss Schönbrunn Schlosspark; adult/child half-day ticket €11/8, evening ticket €8/7; ⌚8.30am-10pm Jun–mid-Aug, to 8pm mid-Aug–early Sep, to 7pm Apr, May & early Sep-early Oct; 👪; Ⓤ Schönbrunn) The Schlosspark surrounding the palace shelters this outdoor swimming complex that has an Olympic-size (50m) pool for laps, and a 25m recreation pool to splash about in, with a separated shallow area for kids. Also here are several saunas, a cafe with a terrace, and a beach-volleyball court.

Day Trips from Vienna

Two-Day Trip to Salzburg p170

Crowned by its hilltop fortress (Mozart's birthplace and the backdrop for the evergreen musical *The Sound of Music)* has a fairy-tale charm.

Krems an der Danau p179

Gateway to the Wachau, quaint Krems centres on its historic core by the Danube (Donau) and makes an ideal starting point for a loop through the beautiful Danube Valley.

Melk & Around p182

Easily reached from the Austrian capital, Stift Melk and nearby Shallaburg castle are an unmissable architectural duo.

Two-Day Trip to Salzburg

Explore

Visiting Salzburg from Vienna is doable in two days, but consider tagging on a third day to explore at a more leisurely pace. High on your itinerary for day one should be the Unesco-listed baroque Altstadt (old town), which is burrowed below steep hills, with the main trophy sights clustering on the left bank of the Salzach River. You can walk everywhere in this compact, largely pedestrianised city.

On your second day, whizz up to the medieval clifftop fortress, Festung Hohensalzburg, for sublime city and mountain views, or take a spin around the galleries and Mozart museums. With an extra day, you could take a tour of locations featured in *The Sound of Music*. Base yourself centrally to see Salzburg beautifully illuminated at night. Classical-music performances and beer gardens are the big draws after dark.

The Best...

➜ **Sight** Altstadt (old town)

➜ **Place to Eat** Magazin (p175)

➜ **Place to Drink** Augustiner Bräustübl (p176)

Top Tip

The **Salzburg Card** (1-/2-/3-day card €29/38/44) gets you entry to all of the major sights and attractions and unlimited use of public transport (including cable cars).

Getting There & Away

Car The A1/E60 motorway links Vienna to Salzburg; it's (approximately a three-hour drive).

Train Frequent trains link Vienna with Salzburg (€55.60, 2½ to three hours). Österreiche Bundesbahn (ÖBB; www.oebb.at) is the main operator. Trains depart from the Wien Hauptbahnhof, with some services also stopping at Wien Meidling. Westbahn (www.westbahn.at) also runs intercity services to/from Salzburg.

Getting Around

Bicycle Salzburg is one of Austria's most bike-friendly cities. It has an extensive network of scenic cycling trails heading off in all directions, including along the banks of the Salzach River. See www.movelo.com for a list of places renting out electric bikes (e-bikes). **A'Velo** (☎0676-435 59 50; Willibald-Hauthaler-Strasse 10; bicycle rental half-day/full day/week €14/20/75, e-bike €20/33/144; ⏱9.30am-6pm Mon-Fri, 9am-12.30pm Sat) provides bike and e-bike rental.

Bus Bus drivers sell single (€2.70), 24-hour (€6) and weekly tickets (€16.40). Single tickets bought in advance from machines are slightly cheaper. Kids under six travel for free, while all other children pay half-price. Information and timetables are available at www.salzburg-verkehr.at.

Need to Know

Area Code ☎0662

Location 296km west of Vienna

Main Tourist Office (☎0662-88 98 70; www.salzburg.info; Mozartplatz 5; ⏱9am-6pm daily, to 7pm Jul/Aug)

SIGHTS

RESIDENZPLATZ — SQUARE

Map p172 With its horse-drawn carriages, palace and street entertainers, this stately baroque square is the Salzburg of a thousand postcards. Its centrepiece is the **Residenzbrunnen** (Map p172), an enormous marble fountain. The plaza is the late 16th-century vision of Prince-Archbishop Wolf Dietrich, who, inspired by Rome, enlisted Italian architect Vincenzo Scamozzi to design it.

★RESIDENZ — PALACE

Map p172 (www.domquartier.at; Residenzplatz 1; DomQuartier ticket adult/child €13/5; ⏱10am-5pm Wed-Mon Sep-Jun, to 6pm daily Jul & Aug) The crowning glory of Salzburg's DomQuartier, the Residenz is where the prince-archbishops held court until Salzburg became part of the Habsburg Empire in the 19th century. An audio-guide tour takes in the exuberant **state rooms**, lavishly adorned with tapestries, stucco and frescos by Johann Michael Rottmayr. The 3rd floor is given over to the **Residenzgalerie**, where the focus is on Flemish and Dutch masters. Must-sees include Rubens' *Allegory on Emperor Charles V* and Rembrandt's chiaroscuro *Old Woman Praying*.

Nowhere is the pomp and circumstance of Salzburg more tangible than at this regal palace. A man of grand designs, Wolf Dietrich von Raitenau, the prince-archbishop of Salzburg from 1587 to 1612, gave the go-ahead to build this baroque palace on the site of an 11th-century bishop's residence.

DOM — CATHEDRAL

Map p172 (Cathedral; ☎0662-804 77 950; www.salzburger-dom.at; Domplatz; guided tours €5; ⏲8am-7pm Mon-Sat, from 1pm Sun May-Sep, shorter hours Oct-Apr) Gracefully crowned by a bulbous copper dome and twin spires, the Dom stands out as a masterpiece of baroque art. Bronze portals symbolising faith, hope and charity lead into the cathedral. In the nave, both the intricate stucco and Arsenio Mascagni's ceiling frescos recounting the Passion of Christ guide the eye to the polychrome dome.

Italian architect Santino Solari redesigned the cathedral during the Thirty Years' War and it was consecrated in 1628. Its origins date to an earlier cathedral founded by Bishop Virgil in 767.

For more on the history, take one of the guided tours (though in German only), offered 2pm Monday to Friday in July and August.

ERZABTEI ST PETER — MONASTERY

Map p172 (St Peter's Abbey; www.stift-stpeter.at; Sankt-Peter-Bezirk 1-2; catacombs adult/child €2/1.50; ⏲church 8am-noon & 2.30-6.30pm, cemetery 6.30am-7pm, catacombs 10am-12.30pm & 1-6pm) A Frankish missionary named Rupert founded this abbey-church and monastery in around 700, making it the oldest in the German-speaking world. Though a vaulted Romanesque portal remains, today's church is overwhelmingly baroque, with rococo stucco, statues – including one of archangel Michael shoving a crucifix through the throat of a goaty demon – and striking altar paintings by Martin Johann Schmidt.

Take a stroll around the **cemetery**, where the graves are miniature works of art with intricate stonework and filigree wrought-iron crosses. Composer Michael Haydn (1737–1806), opera singer Richard Mayr (1877–1935) and renowned Salzburg confectioner Paul Fürst (1856–1941) lie buried here; the last is watched over by skull-bearing cherubs.

The cemetery is home to the **catacombs** – cave-like chapels and crypts hewn out of the Mönchsberg cliff face.

★FESTUNG HOHENSALZBURG — FORT

Map p172 (www.salzburg-burgen.at; Mönchsberg 34; adult/child/family €10/5.70/22.20, incl funicular €12.90/7.40/28.60; ⏲9.30am-5pm Oct-Apr, 9am-7pm May-Sep) Salzburg's most visible icon is this mighty, 900-year-old clifftop fortress, one of the biggest and best preserved in Europe. It's easy to spend half a day up here, roaming the ramparts for far-reaching views over the city's spires, the Salzach River and the mountains. The fortress is a steep 15-minute walk from the centre or a speedy ride up in the glass **Festungsbahn funicular** (Map p172; Festungsgasse 4; one way/return adult €6.90/8.60, child €3.70/4.70; ⏲9am-8.30pm May-Sep, to 5pm Oct-Apr).

The fortress began life as a humble bailey, built in 1077 by Gebhard von Helffenstein at a time when the Holy Roman Empire was at loggerheads with the papacy. The present structure, however, owes its grandeur to spendthrift Leonard von Keutschach, prince-archbishop of Salzburg from 1495 to 1519 and the city's last feudal ruler.

Highlights of a visit include the **Golden Hall** – where lavish banquets were once held – with a gold-studded ceiling imitating a starry night sky. Your ticket also gets you into the **Marionette Museum**, where skeleton-in-a-box Prince-Archbishop Wolf Dietrich steals the (puppet) show, and the **Fortress Museum**, which showcases a 1612 model of Salzburg, as well as medieval instruments, armour and some pretty gruesome torture devices.

The Golden Hall is the backdrop for year-round **Festungskonzerte** (fortress concerts), which often focus on Mozart's works. See www.salzburghighlights.at for times and prices.

MOZART'S GEBURTSHAUS — MUSEUM

Map p172 (Mozart's Birthplace; www.mozarteum.at; Getreidegasse 9; adult/child €11/3.50; ⏲9am-5.30pm Sep-Jun, 8.30am-7pm Jul & Aug) Wolfgang Amadeus Mozart, Salzburg's most famous son, was born in this bright-yellow townhouse in 1756, and spent the first 17 years of his life here. Today's museum harbours a collection of instruments, documents and portraits. Highlights include the mini-violin he played as a toddler, plus a lock of his hair and buttons from his jacket.

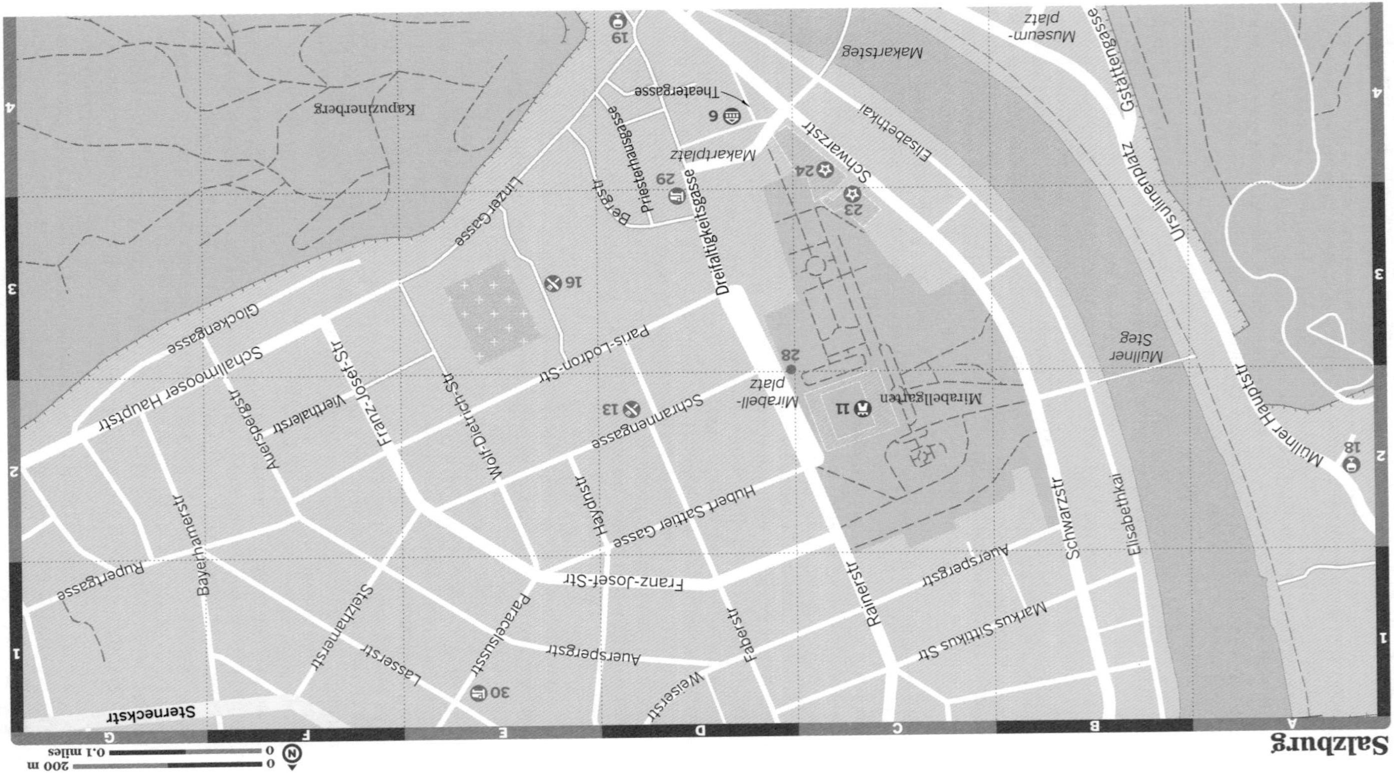
Salzburg
0 200 m
0 0.1 miles
Sterneckstr
Rupertgasse
Bayerhamerstr
Auerspergstr
Schallmooser Hauptstr
Glockengasse
Vierthalerstr
Stelzhamerstr
Franz-Josef-Str
Lasserstr
Wolf-Dietrich-Str
Kapuzinerberg
Linzer Gasse
Paracelsusstr
Paris-Lodron-Str
Haydnstr
Schrannengasse
Hubert Sattler Gasse
Weiserstr
Faberstr
Dreifaltigkeitsgasse
Bergstr
Priesterhausgasse
Theatergasse
Makartplatz
Mirabell-
platz
Mirabellgarten
Rainerstr
Schwarzstr
Elisabethkai
Makartsteg
Markus-Sittikus Str
Müllner Steg
Museum-
platz
Gstättengasse
Ursulinenplatz
Müllner Hauptstr
6
11
13
16
18
19
23
24
28
29
30

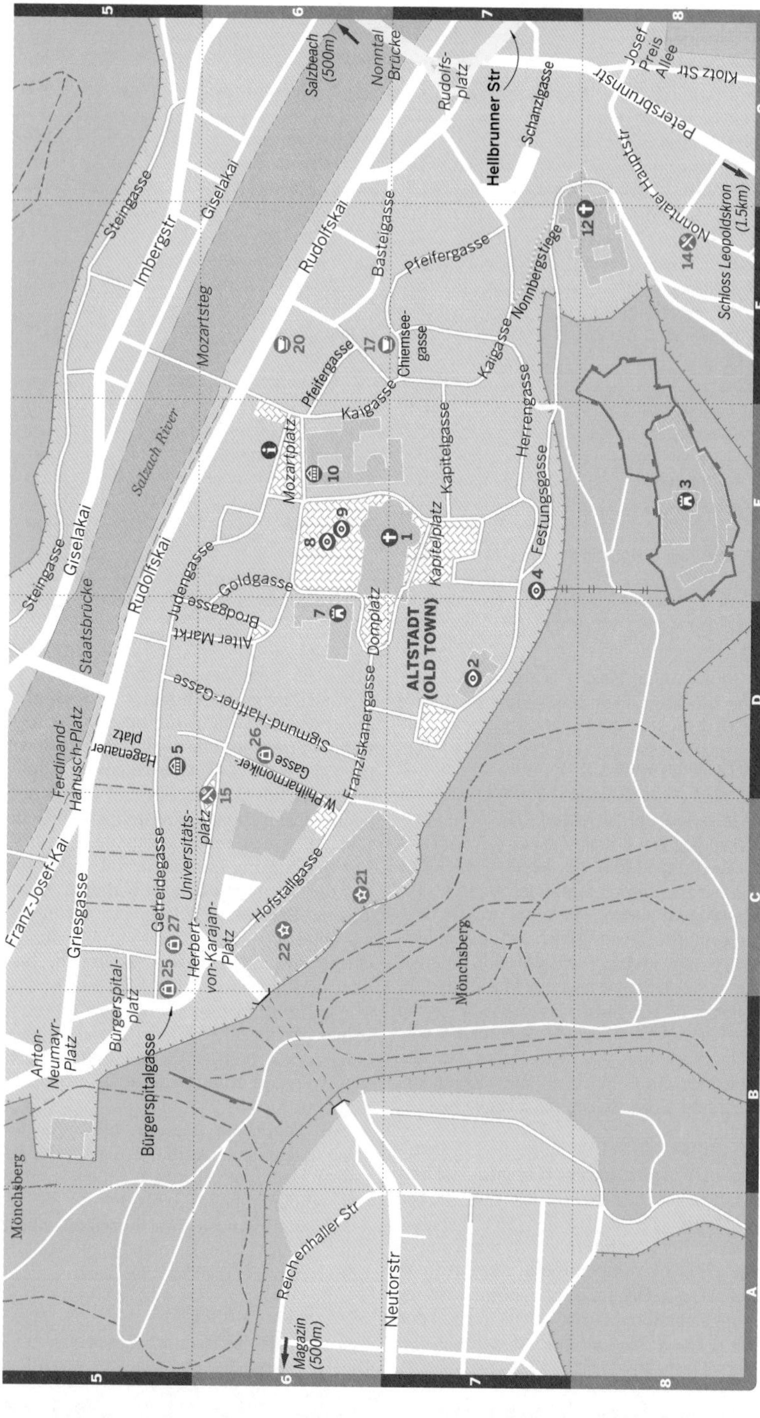
Salzbeach (500m)
Nonntal Brücke
Rudolfs-platz
Hellbrunner Str
Schanzlgasse
Josef Preis Allee
Klotz Str
Petersbrunnstr
Nonntaler Hauptstr
Schloss Leopoldskron (1.5km)
Steingasse
Imbergstr
Giselakai
Mozartsteg
Salzach River
Rudolfskai
Basteigasse
Pfeifergasse
Chiemsee-gasse
Kaigasse
Nonnbergstiege
Kapitelgasse
Herrengasse
Festungsgasse
Mozartplatz
Kapitelplatz
Judengasse
Goldgasse
Brodgasse
Alter Markt
Domplatz
ALTSTADT (OLD TOWN)
Staatsbrücke
Sigmund-Haffner-Gasse
Franziskanergasse
Ferdinand-Hanusch-Platz
Hagenauer platz
W Philharmoniker-Gasse
Universitäts-platz
Franz-Josef-Kai
Griesgasse
Getreidegasse
Herbert-von-Karajan-Platz
Hofstallgasse
Mönchsberg
Anton-Neumayr-Platz
Bürgerspital-platz
Bürgerspitalgasse
Reichenhaller Str
Neutorstr
Magazin (500m)

Salzburg

In one room, Mozart is shown as a holy babe beneath a neon-blue halo – we'll leave you to draw your own analogies.

MOZART-WOHNHAUS MUSEUM

Map p172 (Mozart's Residence; www.mozarteum.at; Makartplatz 8; adult/child €11/3.50; ⌚9am-5.30pm Sep-Jun, 8.30am-7pm Jul & Aug) Tired of the cramped living conditions on Getreidegasse, the Mozart family moved in 1773 to this roomier abode, where the prolific Wolfgang composed works such as the *Shepherd King* (K208) and *Idomeneo* (K366). Emanuel Schikaneder, a close friend of Mozart and the librettist of *The Magic Flute*, was a regular guest here. An audio guide accompanies your visit, serenading you with opera excerpts. Alongside family portraits and documents, you'll find Mozart's original fortepiano.

SALZBURG MUSEUM MUSEUM

Map p172 (www.salzburgmuseum.at; Mozartplatz 1; adult/child €9/3; ⌚9am-5pm Tue-Sun; 👪) Housed in the baroque Neue Residenz palace, this flagship museum takes you on a fascinating romp through Salzburg past and present. Ornate rooms showcase everything from Roman excavations to royal portraits. There are free **guided tours** at 6pm every Thursday.

A visit starts beneath the courtyard in the strikingly illuminated **Kunsthalle**, presenting rotating exhibitions of art. Upstairs, prince-archbishops glower down from the walls at **Mythos Salzburg**, which celebrates the city as a source of artistic and poetic inspiration. Showstoppers include Carl Spitzweg's renowned painting *Sonntagsspaziergang* (Sunday Stroll; 1841), the portrait-lined **prince-archbishop's room** and the **Ständesaal** (Sovereign Chamber), an opulent vision of polychrome stucco curling around frescos depicting the history of Rome according to Titus Livius. The early 16th-century Milleflori tapestry, Prince-Archbishop Wolf Dietrich's gold-embroidered pontifical shoe, and Flemish tapestries are among the other attention-grabbers.

The **Panorama Passage** also provides some insight into Salzburg's past, with its Roman walls, potter's kiln and models of the city at different points in history.

Salzburg's famous 35-bell **carillon**, which chimes daily at 7am, 11am and 6pm, is on the western flank of the Neue Residenz

SCHLOSS MIRABELL PALACE

Map p172 (Mirabellplatz 4; ⌚Schloss Mirabell 8am-6pm, Marble Hall 8am-4pm Mon, Wed & Thu,

1-4pm Tue & Fri, gardens 6am-dusk) FREE Prince-Archbishop Wolf Dietrich built this splendid palace in 1606 to impress his beloved mistress, Salome Alt. It must have done the trick because she went on to bear the archbishop some 15 children (sources disagree on the exact number – poor Wolf was presumably too distracted by spiritual matters to keep count). Johann Lukas von Hildebrandt, of Schloss Belvedere fame, remodelled the palace in baroque style in 1721. The lavish interior, replete with stucco, marble and frescos, is free to visit.

The **Marmorsaal** (Marble Hall) provides a sublime backdrop for evening chamber concerts (p177).

The flowery parterres, rose gardens and leafy arbours are less crowded first thing in the morning and early evening. The lithe *Tänzerin* (dancer) sculpture is a great spot to photograph the gardens with the fortress as a backdrop. *The Sound of Music* fans will of course recognise the Pegasus statue, the steps and the gnomes of the Zwerglgarten (Dwarf Garden), where the mini von Trapps practised their 'Do-Re-Mi'.

STIFT NONNBERG CONVENT

Map p172 (Nonnberg Convent; Nonnberggasse 2; ⌚6.45am-dusk) FREE A short climb up the Nonnbergstiege staircase from Kaigasse or along Festungsgasse brings you to this Benedictine convent, founded 1300 years ago and made famous as the nunnery in *The Sound of Music*. You can visit the beautiful rib-vaulted **church**, but the rest of the convent is off limits. Take €0.50 to switch on the light that illuminates the beautiful **Romanesque frescos**.

UNTERSBERG MOUNTAIN

(www.untersbergbahn.at; cable car up/down/return €16/15/25, free with Salzburg Card; ⌚cable car 8.30am-5.30pm Jul-Sep, shorter hours Oct & mid-Dec–Jun, closed Nov–mid-Dec) Rising above Salzburg and straddling the German border is the rugged 1853m peak of Untersberg. Spectacular views of the city, the Rositten Valley and the Tyrolean, Salzburg and Bavarian alpine ranges unfold from the summit. The mountain is a magnet for local skiers in winter, and hikers, climbers and paragliders in summer. From the cable car's top station, short, easy trails lead to nearby viewpoints at **Geiereck** (1805m) and **Salzburg Hochthron** (1853m), while others take you deeper into the Alps.

A cable car runs every half-hour to the peak. To reach the cable-car valley station, take bus 25 from Salzburg's Hauptbahnhof or Mirabellplatz to St Leonhard and the valley station.

EATING

BISTRO DE MÁRQUEZ INTERNATIONAL €

Map p172 (☎0680-236 96 64; www.bistrodemarquez.at; Schrannengasse 6; small plates €2.50-5.90, day special €6.90; ⌚11.30am-2pm & 3-7pm Tue-Fri, 11.30am-8pm Sat) Piedad brings a little piece of her native Colombia to the table at this sweet, cosy bistro, where she cooks soul food including *arepas* (filled maize crêpes) to dip in salsas, and *pandebono* (Colombian cheese bread). It's all delicious, affordable and served with a smile.

GRÜNMARKT MARKET €

Map p172 (Green Market; Universitätsplatz; ⌚7am-7pm Mon-Fri, 6am-3pm Sat) A one-stop picnic shop on one of Salzburg's grandest squares, for regional cheese, ham, fruit, bread and gigantic pretzels.

LUDWIG BURGERS €

Map p172 (☎0662-87 25 00; www.ludwig-burger.at; Linzer Gasse 39; burgers €7.60-13.80; ⌚11am-10pm Tue-Fri, 9am-10pm Sat & Sun; ✎) Gourmet burger joints are all the rage in Austria and this hip restaurant fits the bill nicely, with its burgers made from organic, regional ingredients, which go well with hand-cut fries and homemade lemonade and shakes. It also rustles up superfood salads and vegan nut-mushroom-herb burgers. An open kitchen is the centrepiece of the slick, monochrome interior.

MAGAZIN GASTRONOMY €€

(☎0662-84 15 84; www.magazin.co.at; Augustinergasse 13a; 2-course lunch €18, mains €18-29; ⌚noon-2pm & 6-10pm Tue-Sat) In a courtyard below Mönchsberg's sheer rock wall, Magazin shelters a deli, wine store and restaurant. The menus fizz with seasonal flavours – dishes such as scallops with white wine and coriander, and veal cheeks with wild broccoli, are matched with wines from the 850-bottle cellar, and served alfresco or in the industrial-chic, cave-like interior.

GREEN GARDEN VEGETARIAN €€

Map p172 (☎0662-84 12 01; www.thegreengarden.at; Nonntaler Hauptstrasse 16; mains

DIY SOUND OF MUSIC TOUR

Do a Julie Andrews and sing as you stroll on a self-guided tour of *The Sound of Music* film locations. Let's start at the very beginning:

The Hills Are Alive Cut! Make that *proper* mountains. The opening scenes were filmed around the jewel-coloured Salzkammergut lakes. Maria makes her twirling entrance on alpine pastures just across the border in Bavaria.

A Problem Like Maria Nuns waltzing on their way to mass at Benedictine Stift Nonnberg (p175) is fiction, but it's fact that the real Maria von Trapp intended to become a nun here before romance struck.

Have Confidence Residenzplatz (p170) is where Maria belts out 'I Have Confidence' and playfully splashes the spouting horses of the Residenzbrunnen fountain.

So Long, Farewell The grand rococo palace of **Schloss Leopoldskron** (www.schloss-leopoldskron.com; Leopoldskronstrasse 56-58), a 15-minute walk from Festung Hohensalzburg, is where the lake scene was filmed. Its Venetian Room was the blueprint for the Trapps' lavish ballroom, where the children bid their farewells.

Do-Re-Mi The Pegasus fountain, the steps with fortress views, the gnomes...the Mirabellgarten at Schloss Mirabell (p175) might inspire a rendition of 'Do-Re-Mi' – especially if there's a drop of golden sun.

Sixteen Going on Seventeen The loved-up pavilion of the century hides out in **Hellbrunn Park** (www.hellbrunn.at; Fürstenweg 37; adult/child/family €12.50/5.50/26.50, gardens free; 9am-9pm Jul & Aug, to 5.30pm May, Jun & Sep, to 4.30pm Apr & Oct;), where you can act out those 'Oh, Liesl'/'Oh, Rolf' fantasies.

Edelweiss & Adieu The **Felsenreitschule** (Summer Riding School; Map p172; Hofstallgasse 1) is the dramatic backdrop for the Salzburg Festival in the movie, where the Trapp Family Singers win the audience over with 'Edelweiss' and give the Nazis the slip with 'So Long, Farewell'.

Climb Every Mountain To Switzerland, that is. Or content yourself with alpine views from Untersberg (p175), which appears briefly at the end of the movie when the family flees the country.

€10.90-15.50; noon-3pm & 5.30-10pm Tue-Fri, 9am-2pm & 5.30-10pm Sat, 9am-2pm Sun;) The Green Garden is a breath of fresh air for vegetarians and vegans. Locavore is the word at this bright, modern cottage-style restaurant, pairing dishes such as summer rolls, truffle tortellini and vegan burgers with organic wines in a totally relaxed setting. It also rustles up tasty Buddha bowls, and weekend brunches (€25) are invariably popular.

DRINKING & NIGHTLIFE

★**AUGUSTINER BRÄUSTÜBL** BREWERY

Map p172 (www.augustinerbier.at; Augustinergasse 4-6; 3-11pm Mon-Fri, 2.30-11pm Sat & Sun) Who says monks can't enjoy themselves? Since 1621, this cheery, monastery-run brewery has served potent home brews in beer steins, in the vaulted hall and beneath the chestnut trees of the 1000-seat beer garden. Get your tankard filled at the foyer pump and visit the snack stands for hearty, beer-swigging grub including *Stelzen* (ham hock), pork belly and giant pretzels.

★**KAFFEE ALCHEMIE** CAFE

Map p172 (www.kaffee-alchemie.at; Rudolfskai 38; 7.30am-6pm Mon-Fri, 10am-6pm Sat & Sun) Making coffee really is rocket science at this vintage-cool cafe by the river, which spotlights high-quality, fair-trade, single-origin beans. Talented baristas make spot-on espressos (on a Marzocco GB5, in case you're wondering), cappuccinos and speciality coffees, which go nicely with the selection of cakes and brownies. Not a coffee fan? Try the supersmooth coffee-leaf tea.

DARWIN'S COCKTAIL BAR

Map p172 (www.darwins-salzburg.at; Steingasse 1; ⏰9am-midnight Sun-Thu, to 2am Fri & Sat) Darwin might well have been partial to an expertly mixed cocktail or two at this glam vaulted bar, while dreaming up his theory of evolution or pondering the origin of the species. The great man himself is portrayed as an ape-man alongside other doodles of globes and quotes. The bar makes a mean espresso martini.

220 GRAD CAFE

Map p172 (www.220grad.com; Chiemseegasse 5; ⏰9am-7pm Tue-Fri, to 6pm Sat; 📶) In a tucked-away corner of the Altstadt, this retro-cool cafe is up there with the best for its freshly roasted coffee, breakfasts and decked terrace (always rammed in summer). Its name alludes to the perfect temperature for roasting beans, and the skilled baristas make a terrific single-origin espresso and house blends, which pair with cakes including sweet potato with lime cream.

ENTERTAINMENT

★SALZBURGER MARIONETTENTHEATER PUPPET THEATRE

Map p172 (☎0662-87 24 06; www.marionetten.at; Schwarzstrasse 24; tickets €28-152; 👪) The red curtain goes up on a miniature stage at this marionette theatre, a lavish stucco, cherub and chandelier-lit affair founded in 1913. The repertoire star is *The Sound of Music,* with a life-sized Mother Superior and a marionette-packed finale. Other enchanting productions include Mozart's *The Magic Flute* and Tchaikovsky's *The Nutcracker*. All have multilingual surtitles.

The theatre is a Unesco World Heritage site, proclaimed in 2017.

SCHLOSSKONZERTE CLASSICAL MUSIC

Map p172 (www.schlosskonzerte-salzburg.at; tickets adult €34-40, child €15; ⏰concerts 8pm) A fantasy of coloured marble, stucco and frescos, the baroque Marmorsaal (Marble Hall) at Schloss Mirabell (p175) is the exquisite setting for these chamber-music concerts. Internationally renowned soloists and ensembles perform works by Mozart and other well-known composers such as Haydn and Chopin. Tickets are available on the 1st floor of the palace from 3pm to 8pm.

MOZARTEUM CLASSICAL MUSIC

Map p172 (☎0662-87 31 54; www.mozarteum.at; Schwarzstrasse 26; ⏰box office 10am-3pm Mon-Fri) Opened in 1880 and revered for its supreme acoustics, the Mozarteum highlights the life and works of Mozart through chamber music (October to June), concerts and opera. The annual highlight is **Mozart Week** in January.

GROSSES FESTSPIELHAUS THEATRE

Map p172 (☎0662-804 50; Hofstallgasse 1) Designed by architect Clemens Holzmeister in 1956 and built into the sheer sides of the Mönchsberg, the cavernous Grosses Festspielhaus stages the majority of performances during the Salzburg Festival and can accommodate 2179 theatregoers.

SHOPPING

★FÜRST CHOCOLATE

Map p172 (www.original-mozartkugel.com; Getreidegasse 47; ⏰10am-6.30pm Mon-Sat, noon-5pm Sun) Pistachio, nougat and dark-chocolate dreams, the *Mozartkugeln* (Mozart balls) here are still handmade to Paul Fürst's original 1890 recipe. Other specialities include cube-shaped *Bach Würfel* – coffee, nut and marzipan truffles dedicated to yet another great composer.

SALZBURG SALZ GIFTS & SOUVENIRS

Map p172 (Wiener-Philharmoniker-Gasse 6; ⏰10am-6pm Mon-Sat) Pure salt from Salzburgerland and the Himalayas, herbal salts and rock-salt tea lights are among the high-sodium wonders here.

SPIRITUOSEN SPORER WINE

Map p172 (Getreidegasse 39; ⏰9.30am-7pm Mon-Fri, 8.30am-5pm Sat) In Getreidegasse's narrowest house, family-run Sporer has been intoxicating local folk with Austrian wines, herbal liqueurs and famous *Vogelbeer* (rowan berry) schnapps since 1903.

SPORTS & ACTIVITIES

FRÄULEIN MARIA'S BICYCLE TOURS CYCLING

Map p172 (www.mariasbicycletours.com; Mirabellplatz 4; adult/child €35/15; ⏰9.30am Apr-Oct, plus 4.30pm Jun-Aug) Belt out *The Sound of Music*

DRIVING & CYCLING TOUR OF THE DANUBE VALLEY

Starting and ending in Krems, this 150km tour should take a full day.

From the Krems-Stein roundabout in **Krems an der Donau** take the B3 southwest towards Spitz. About 3km from Krems-Stein you approach the small settlement of **Unterloiben**, where you can see the Franzosendenkmal (French Monument), erected in 1805 to celebrate the victory of Austrian and Russian troops here over Napoleon. Shortly afterwards the lovely town of **Dürnstein**, 6km from Krems, comes into view with its blue-towered Chorherrenstift backed by Kuenringerburg, the castle where Richard the Lionheart was imprisoned in 1192.

The valley is punctuated by picturesque terraced vineyards as you enter the heart of the Wachau. In **Weissenkirchen**, 12km from Krems, you'll find a fortified parish church on the hilltop. The Wachau Museum here houses work by artists of the Danube school.

A couple of kilometres on, just after Wösendorf, you find the church of **St Michael**, in a hamlet with 13 houses. If the kids are with you, now's the time to ask them to count the terracotta hares on the roof of the church (seven, in case they're not reading this!).

Some 17km from Krems, the pretty town of **Spitz** swings into view, surrounded by vineyards and lined with quiet, cobblestone streets. Some good trails lead across hills and to *Heurigen* (wine taverns) here (start from the church).

Turn right at Spitz onto the B217 (Ottenschläger Strasse). The terraced hill on your right is **1000-Eimer-Berg**, so-named for its reputed ability to yield 1000 buckets of wine each season. On your left, above the valley opening, is the castle ruin **Burgruine Hinterhaus**. Continue along the B217 to the mill wheel and turn right towards **Burg Oberranna** (Ⓟ), 6km west of Spitz in Mühldorf. Surrounded by woods, this castle and hotel overlooking the valley is furnished with period pieces and has a refreshing old-world feel.

From here, backtrack down to the B3 and continue the circuit. The valley opens up and on the left, across the Danube, you glimpse the ruins of Burg Aggstein.

Willendorf, located 21km from Krems, is where the 25,000-year-old Venus of Willendorf was discovered. It is today housed in the Naturhistorisches Museum in Vienna. Continuing along the B3, the majestic Stift Melk rises up across the river. There's some decent swimming in the backwaters here if you're game to dip into the Danube.

At Klein Pöchlarn, a sign indicates a turn-off on Artstettner Strasse (L7255): follow it for 5km to **Artstetten**, famous for its many onion domes and castle. From here, the minor road L7257 winds 6.5km through a green landscape to **Maria Taferl** where the baroque church Pfarr-und Wallfahrtskirche Maria Taferl rises above the Danube Valley.

Head 6km down towards the B3. Turn left at the B3 towards Krems and follow the ramp veering off to the left and across the river at the Klein Pöchlarn bridge. Follow the road straight ahead to the B1 (Austria's longest road) and turn left towards Melk.

This first section along the south bank is uninteresting, but it soon improves. Unless the weather isn't playing along, across the river you can make out Artstetten in the distance, and shortly must-see Stift Melk (p183) will rise up ahead, its celebrated monastery emerging in golden shimmering splendour.

From Stift Melk, a 7km detour leads south to the splendid Renaissance castle of Schloss Schallaburg (p183). To reach the castle from the abbey in Melk, follow the signs to the *Bahnhof* (train station) and Lindestrasse east, turn right into Hummelstrasse/Kirschengraben (L5340) and follow the signs to the castle.

Backtrack to the B33. Be careful to stay on the south side of the river. When you reach the corner of Abt-Karl-Strasse and Bahnhofstrasse, go right and right again at the river. Follow the B1 for 4km to **Schloss Schönbühel**, a 12th-century castle standing high on a rock some 5km northeast of Melk. Continue along this lovely stretch of the B33 in the direction of Krems. About 10km from Schloss Schönbühel the ruins of **Burg Aggstein** (www.ruineaggstein.at; Aggsbach Dorf; adult/child €6.90/4.90; ⏲9am-6pm Apr-Oct) swing into view. This 12th-century hilltop castle was built by the Kuenringer family and now offers a grand vista of the Danube.

About 27km from Melk some pretty cliffs rise up above the road. From Mautern it's a detour of about 6km toStift Göttweig (p181), another bombastic monastery. From here, make your way back to Krems.

faves as you pedal along on one of these jolly 3½-hour bike tours, taking in locations from the film, including Schloss Mirabell (p175), Stift Nonnberg (p175), Schloss Leopoldskron (p176) and Hellbrunn. Advance bookings (tickets are available online) are highly recommended.

SALZBEACH BEACH

(Volksgarten; ⌚9am-10pm May-Sep) Salzburg's urban beach – complete with sand, potted palms and *Strandkörbe* (wicker-basket chairs) – sprouts up in the Volksgarten each summer. Besides lounging, there's a volleyball court plus open-air events over the course of the summer, from free musical gigs to cinema nights.

SLEEPING

★HAUS BALLWEIN GUESTHOUSE €

(☎0662-82 40 29; www.haus-ballwein.at; Moosstrasse 69a; s €55-65, d €72-88, tr €85-90, q €90-100; P 📶) With its bright, pine-filled rooms, mountain views and garden, this place is big on charm. The largest, quietest rooms face the back and have balconies and kitchenettes. It's a 10-minute trundle from the Altstadt; take bus 21 to Gsengerweg. Breakfast is a wholesome spread of fresh rolls, eggs, fruit, muesli and cold cuts. Bring cash as credit cards are not accepted.

YOHO SALZBURG HOSTEL €

Map p172 (☎0662-87 96 49; www.yoho.at; Paracelsusstrasse 9; dm €23-34, d €70-88; @📶) Free wi-fi, secure lockers, comfy bunks, plenty of cheap beer and good-value schnitzels – what more could a backpacker ask for? Except, perhaps, a merry singalong with *The Sound of Music* screened daily (yes, *every* day). The friendly crew can arrange tours, adventure sports such as rafting and canyoning, and bike hire (€10 per day).

★VILLA TRAPP HOTEL €€

(☎0662-63 08 60; www.villa-trapp.com; Traunstrasse 34; s €76-135, d €90-280, ste €165-563; P 📶) Marianne and Christopher have transformed the original von Trapp family home into a beautiful guesthouse. The 19th-century villa is elegant, if not *quite* as palatial as in the movie, with tasteful wood-floored rooms and a balustrade for sweeping down à la Baroness Schräder.

GÄSTEHAUS IM PRIESTERSEMINAR GUESTHOUSE €€

Map p172 (☎0662-877 495 10; www.gaestehaus-priesterseminar-salzburg.at; Dreifaltigkeitsgasse 14; s €67-87, d €120-134) The peace is heavenly at this one-time seminary tucked behind the Dreifältigkeitskirche. Its parquet-floored rooms have received a total makeover, but the place still brims with old-world charm thanks to its marble staircase, antique furnishings and fountain-dotted courtyard. It's still something of a secret, though, so whisper about it quietly...

Krems an der Donau

Explore

Krems, as it's more commonly known, is the prettiest of the larger towns on the Danube and marks the beginning of the Wachau. Enjoyable eating and drinking, an atmospheric historical centre, rivers of top-quality wine from local vineyards and a couple of excellent museums attract visitors in summer but the rest of the year it's considerably quieter. Stop by churches and museums, strolling the banks of the Danube and sampling the local tipples as you go.

Krems comprises three parts: Krems to the east, the small settlement of Stein (formerly a separate town) to the west, and the connecting suburb of Und. Hence the local witticism: *Krems und Stein sind drei Städte* (Krems and Stein are three towns). A day is ample time to explore the trio.

The Best...

- **Sight** Landesgalerie NÖ (p180)
- **Place to Eat** Zum Kaiser von Österreich (p182)
- **Place to Drink** Weinstein (182)

Top Tip

The 1.6km-long Kunstmeile (Art Mile) stretches from the Minoritenkirche to the Dominikanerkirche. There are eight attractions visitors can access; a single combi ticket (€18) covers them all.

Getting There & Away

Car From Vienna take the A22 north towards Stockerau, then take the S5 west to Krems. The journey takes about an hour.

Train Frequent daily trains connect the Wien Hauptbahnhof with Krems (€18.40, 70 minutes) and Tulln (€10.30, 39 minutes).

Need to Know

Area Code ☎02732

Location 76km northwest of Vienna

Tourist Office (☎02732-82 676; www.krems.info; Utzstrasse 1; ⏲9am-6pm Mon-Fri, 11am-6pm Sat, 11am-4pm Sun; shorter hours in winter)

SIGHTS

★LANDESGALERIE NÖ GALLERY

Map p181 (☎02732-908 010; www.landesgalerie-noe.at; Museumsplatz 1; adult/child €10/3.50; ⏲10am-6pm Tue-Sun) From one side it looks like a squashed cube, from the other as though it's about to topple over – welcome to the latest addition to Krems' Kunstmeile: a bold, 21st-century statement in grey aluminium tiles that looms over the newly created Museumsplatz like an alien spacecraft. It's a more than apt setting for the ever-changing exhibitions of edgy modern art and contemporary installations inside, and gives focus to the 'Art Mile' that had been missing up until it opened in 2019.

★FORUM FROHNER GALLERY

Map p181 (Kunstmeile; ☎02732-908 010; www.forum-frohner.at; Minoritenplatz 4; adult/child €5/4; ⏲11am-7pm Tue-Sun) Part of Krems' Kunsthalle network, this contemporary white cube is named after the artist Adolf Frohner and is housed in the former Minorite monastery. It has an impressive calendar of conceptual work, both international and Austrian.

KUNSTHALLE KREMS GALLERY

Map p181 (www.kunsthalle.at; Museumsplatz 5; adult/child €10/3.50; ⏲10am-6pm Tue-Sun) One of the main attractions on Krems' Kunstmeile, the Kunsthalle has a program of changing exhibitions. These might be mid-19th-century landscapes or hard-core conceptual works, but are always well curated.

PIARISTENKIRCHE CHURCH

Map p181 (Frauenbergplatz; ⏲dawn-dusk) Reached by a covered stairway (Piaristenstiege) from Pfarrplatz, Krems' most impressive church has a wonderful webbed Gothic ceiling and huge, austerely plain windows. It's most atmospheric after dark when you can best imagine the spectacle of the massive baroque altar for the 18th-century parishioners.

KARIKATURMUSEUM MUSEUM

Map p181 (☎02732-908-010; www.karikaturmuseum.at; Museumsplatz 3; adult/child €10/3.50; ⏲10am-6pm) Austria's sole caricature museum occupies a suitably tongue-in-cheek chunk of purpose-built architecture, its spiky facade tearing the blue Austrian sky. Changing exhibitions and a large permanent collection of caricatures of prominent Austrian and international figures make for a fun diversion if the other art in the Kunstmeile gets too heavy.

MUSEUM KREMS MUSEUM

Map p181 (www.museumkrems.at; Körnermarkt 14; admission €7.50; ⏲10am-6pm daily mid-Apr–Oct; P) Housed in a former Dominican monastery, the town's museum has collections of religious and modern art, including works by Kremser Schmidt, who painted the frescos in Pfarrkirche St Veit (p180), as well as winemaking artefacts and a section on the famous Krems mustard.

PFARRKIRCHE ST VEIT CHURCH

Map p181 (Pfarrplatz 5; ⏲dawn-dusk) Known as the 'Cathedral of the Wachau', the large baroque parish church boasts colourful frescos by Martin Johann Schmidt, an 18th-century local artist who was also known as Kremser Schmidt. The baroque building is the work of Cipriano Biasino, who worked on several churches in the Wachau, including the abbey church at Stift Göttweig. The cool single nave has many examples of trompe-l'œ lending it 3D features it doesn't have, and is peppered with gilt cherubs and laurel wreathes.

STIFT GÖTTWEIG MONASTERY

(Göttweig Abbey; ☎02732-855 81-0; www.stiftgoettweig.at; Furth bei Göttweig; adult/child €8.50/5; ⏲10am-6pm Apr-Oct) Founded in 1083, the abbey was devastated by fire in the early 18th century and so sports an impressive baroque interior. It's still a working monastery today. Aside from the sublime

Krems an der Donau

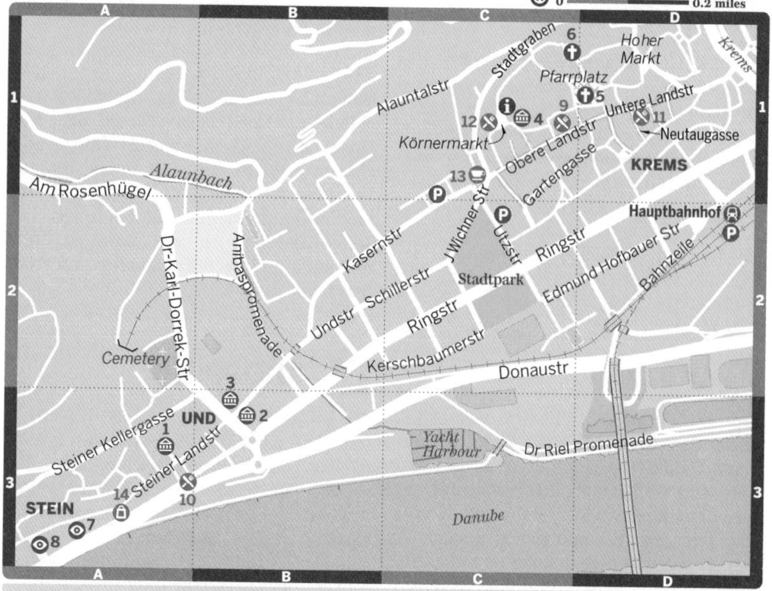

Krems an der Donau

Sights p180

1 Forum Frohner A3
2 Karikaturmuseum B3
3 Kunsthalle Krems B3
Landesgalerie NÖ .... (see 2)
4 Museum Krems C1
5 Pfarrkirche St Veit D1
6 Piaristenkirche C1
7 Rathausplatz A3
8 Schürerplatz A3

Eating p181

9 MOYOme C1
10 Salzstadl A3
11 Schwarze Kuchl D1
12 Zum Kaiser von Österreich C1

Drinking & Nightlife p182

13 Stadtcafe Ulrich C1
Weinstein .... (see 14)

Shopping p182

14 Volkskultur A3

view back across the Danube Valley from its garden terrace and restaurant, the abbey's highlights include the Imperial Staircase with a heavenly ceiling fresco painted by Paul Troger in 1739, and the over-the-top baroque interior of the Stiftskirche, which has a Kremser Schmidt work in the crypt.

Fully guided tours take in the abbey's Imperial Wing, church and summer vestry; shorter tours explore either the Imperial Wing or the church and vestry.

The best way to reach Göttweig is by train from Krems (10 minutes, hourly), though it's a steep walk uphill from the village station.

EATING

SCHWARZE KUCHL AUSTRIAN €

Map p181 (www.schwarze-kuchl.at; Untere Landstrasse 8; mains €4-15; 9am-7.30pm Mon-Fri, to 6pm Sat) For some good, filling local food, a 9am beer or a salady lunch, head to this Krems institution on the main drag through town where you can enjoy veal goulash, apricot-filled pancakes and Waldviertel potato-and-beef hotpot *(Gröstl)* while warming your toes on the huge tiled oven. Spills out among the shoppers on busy days.

WALKING KREMS

A walk through the cobblestone streets of Krems and Stein is one of the delights of a visit. Some of the most atmospheric parts to explore are on and behind **Schürerplatz** (Map p181) and **Rathausplatz** (Map p181) in Stein (don't miss these two wonderful squares), dominated by the baroque Mazzettihaus and the 18th-century Steiner Rathaus respectively; here you could be forgiven for thinking you had stumbled upon an isolated Adriatic village.

SALZSTADL AUSTRIAN €

Map p181 (☑02732-703 12; www.salzstadl.at; Steiner Donaulände 32; mains €5-15; ⊘11am-3pm & 6-11pm; 🛜) Housed in an old salt store, this well-established restaurant has been banging down local favourites such as pike-perch, goulash and grilled chicken for over 20 years. It also doubles as a theatre/ music venue with live jazz and other genres taking to the stage at least once a month. Check the website for the programme.

★ZUM KAISER VON
ÖSTERREICH AUSTRIAN €€€

Map p181 (☑0800 400 171 052; www.kaiser-von-oesterreich.at; Körnermarkt 9; menus €42.50-72.50, cover €4.60; ⊘6-11pm Tue-Sat) The 'Emperor of Austria' is one of Krems' most well-loved upmarket restaurants. Interiors recall a hunting lodge with menus built around the region's bounty of game, from deer to pheasant to rabbit. Other hyperlocal ingredients like Wachau apples and apricots, wild herbs and mushrooms, Waldviertel fish and Weinviertel pumpkins are also used in the finely crafted, imaginative dishes.

Book in advance want to get a table here.

DRINKING & NIGHTLIFE

WEINSTEIN WINE BAR

Map p181 (☑0664 1300 331; www.weinstein.at; Steiner Donaulände 56; ⊘from 5pm Mon-Sat) A Danube-facing, columned wine bar that stocks a comprehensive lineup of local wines by the glass. The kitchen turns out good drinking food, say carpaccio in summer or a house burger in winter.

STADTCAFE ULRICH CAFE

Map p181 (☑02732-820 94; Südtirolerplatz 7; ⊘7am-11pm Mon-Thu, to midnight Sat, 9am-11pm Sun; 🛜) Krems' busiest cafe is this elegantly high-ceilinged, open-all-hours Viennese job next to the Steinertor (the medieval gateway into the old town). The coffee and strudel here makes a great breakfast and there's a small terrace out front.

 ## SHOPPING

VOLKSKULTUR GIFTS & SOUVENIRS

Map p181 (☑02732-850 15 15; www.volkskultureuropa.org; Haus der Regionen, Steiner Donaulände 56; ⊘10am-noon & 1-6pm Mon-Sat) A wonderfully kitsch- and junk-free showcase of quality Austrian craftsmanship, spanning traditional clothing, fabrics, scarves, jewellery and kitchenware. Look out for the iconic Reiss enamelware with folk patterns, apricot specialities and glass paintings.

Melk & Around

Explore

With its blockbuster abbey-fortress perched above the valley, Melk is a high point of any visit to the Danube Valley. Separated from the river by a stretch of woodland, this pretty town makes for an easy and rewarding day trip from Vienna. Combine a visit with nearby Renaissance-era Schloss Schallaburg, 6km south of town, and you have yourself a day packed with architectural interest.

Melk is one of the most popular destinations in Austria so you certainly won't be alone on its cobbled streets. It's also one of the few places in the Wachau that has a pulse in winter, making it a year-round option.

The Best...

➡ **Sight** Stift Melk

➡ **Place to Eat** Zur Post

➡ **Exhibitions** Schloss Schallaburg

Top Tip

Boats operated by **Brandner** (☎07433-25 90 21; www.brandner.at; Ufer 15, Wallsee) leave from the canal by Pionierstrasse, 400m north of the abbey, for Krems and Spitz.

Getting There & Away

Car The A1/E60 motorway runs all the way west from Vienna to Melk. It's about a 90-minute journey.

Train Trains run from Vienna's Hauptbahnhof and Westbahnhof (€18.40, 50 minutes, twice hourly) to Melk; some require a change in St Pölten.

Need to Know

Area Code ☎02752

Location 87km west of Vienna

Tourist Office (☎02752-511 60; www.stadt-melk.at; Kremser Strasse 5; ⏰9.30am-6pm Mon-sat, to 4pm Sun Apr-Oct, 9am-5pm Mon-Thu, to 2.30pm Fri Nov-Mar)

SIGHTS

★STIFT MELK ABBEY

(Benedictine Abbey of Melk; www.stiftmelk.at; Abt Berthold Dietmayr Strasse 1; adult/child €12.50/6.50, with guided tour €14.50/8.50; ⏰9am-5.30pm, tours 10am-4pm Apr-Oct) Of the many abbeys in Austria, Stift Melk is the most famous. Possibly Lower Austria's finest, the monastery church dominates the complex with its twin spires and high octagonal dome. The interior is baroque gone barmy, with a riot of chubby cherubs, barley sugar twirls and polished faux marble. The theatrical high-altar scene, depicting St Peter and St Paul (the church's two patron saints), is by Peter Widerin. Johann Michael Rottmayr created most of the ceiling paintings, including those in the dome.

Historically, Melk was of great importance to the Romans and later to the Babenbergs, who built a castle here. In 1089, the Babenberg margrave Leopold II donated the castle to Benedictine monks, who converted it into a fortified abbey. Fire destroyed the original edifice, which was completely baroque-ified between 1702 and 1738 according to plans by Jakob Prandtauer and his disciple, Josef Munggenast. It's claimed nine million bricks were used to create the 500 rooms, most of the complex is taken up by a school, monks' quarters and offices.

Besides the monastery church, highlights include the **Bibliothek** (Library) and the **Marmorsaal** (Marble Hall); both have amazing trompe-l'œ-painted tiers on the curved ceiling (by Paul Troger) to give the illusion of greater height. Eleven of the imperial rooms, where dignitaries (including Napoleon) stayed, are now used as a somewhat overcooked concept museum.

Take a spin around the **Nordbastei** (north bastion) where you'll discover some quirky temporary exhibitions, a viewing terrace and the Stift's gift shop.

English tours run at 10.55am and 2.55pm as well as 2pm May to September.

SCHLOSS SCHALLABURG PALACE

(☎02754-6317; www.schallaburg.at; Schallaburg 1; adult/child €11/3.50; ⏰9am-5pm Mon-Fri, to 6pm Sat & Sun mid-Mar–Oct) This palace is famous not only for its stunning architecture but also for the innovative exhibitions it houses, along with its lovely gardens. A wonderful curio are the 400 terracotta sculptures, completed between 1572 and 1573, the largest of which support the upper-storey arches of the palace. The excellently curated yearly shows are thematically conceived, and can cover anything from world handicrafts to The Beatles.

Combined tickets with Stift Melk cost €21. To reach Schallaburg, take the shuttle bus (€2.30) that leaves Melk train station at 9.30am, 10.30am, 12.30pm and 2.45pm.

EATING

ZUR POST AUSTRIAN €€

(☎02752-523 45; Linzer Strasse 1; mains €14-20; ⏰11.30am-10pm, closed Sun evening & Mon; 📶🌿) This traditional and understated restaurant is in the hotel of the same name on Melk's main drag. *Tafelspitz*, Wiener schnitzel, local venison and organic lamb grace the menu, which also features vegetarian options.

Sleeping

Vienna's lodgings cover it all, from luxury establishments where chandeliers, antique furniture and original 19th-century oil paintings abound and cutting-edge, statement-making design hotels to inexpensive youth hostels. In between are homey, often family-run Pensionen (guesthouses), many traditional, and less ostentatious hotels, plus a smart range of apartments.

Reservations & Cancellations

It's wise to book ahead at all times. In the winter and autumn low and shoulder seasons (except for Christmas and New Year) a day or two is usually sufficient for most places, but for the best value, especially in the centre, a few weeks ahead is advisable. From around Easter to September you will need to book at least several weeks in advance, and some places in the centre are booked out a month or longer ahead. Confirmed reservations in writing are binding, and cancellations within several days of expected arrival often involve a fee or full payment.

Hotels & Pensionen

Two stars Expect functional rooms starting around €50/90 a single/double close to the centre. It's often better to stay in a hostel.

Three stars Most hotels and *Pensionen* are in this category. You can count on paying about €70/130 for a single/double, less in winter or when booking online. Rooms should be clean, with a decent buffet breakfast, wi-fi, minibar, flat-screen TV and pleasant showers. Some have bathtubs.

Four & five stars Rooms in four-star hotels are generally larger than three-star rooms and should have sound insulation and contemporary or quality furnishing; some have wellness facilities. Five-star hotels have premium wellness facilities.

Hostels & Student Residences

Vienna has a smattering of *Jugendherbergen* (youth hostels), both private and hostels affiliated with Hostelling International (HI). In the former, no membership is required.

Apartment Rentals

The advantage of an apartment is that you have a kitchen and can save on food costs. Most central apartments cost from around €120 per night.

The following websites are useful:

Apartment.at (www.apartment.at) A broad selection from a group of owners.

waytostay (www.waytostay.com/vienna-apartments) Apartments in all price categories.

Chez Cliche (www.chezcliche.com) Five stylish apartments, decorated with a mish-mash of design pieces and flea-market finds. They're scattered across the city, from the Innere Stadt's backstreets to student-hub Alsergrund.

Useful Websites

Lonely Planet (lonelyplanet.com/austria/vienna/hotels) Recommendations and bookings.

Hostelling International (www.hihostels.com) Global youth-hostel organisation.

Tourist Info Wien (www.wien.info/en/hotels) Vienna's tourist office.

Lonely Planet's Top Choices

Grand Ferdinand Hotel (p187) Dorms through to luxury suites with private champagne bars and Maseratis to rent.

Magdas (p190) Funky boutique hotel near the Prater run by refugees.

Grätzlhotel (p190) Slick, architect-designed boutique hotel/suites in formerly abandoned shops.

my MOjO vie (p188) Hostel with upbeat style.

DO & CO (p188) Sexiest hotel in the centre.

Hotel Imperial (p188) Favourite for European royalty.

Sans Souci Wien (p189) Original designer furniture, pop art and a brilliant location opposite the MuseumsQuartier.

Best by Budget

€

Hotel am Brillantengrund (p189) Set around a sociable courtyard.

my MOjO vie (p188) Hostel with bright flair.

Wombat's City Hostel Naschmarkt (p188) Directly overlooking the Naschmarkt, so you can put its self-catering kitchen to use.

€€

Hotel Kunsthof (p190) A crossover between a gallery and a hotel.

Boutiquehotel Stadthalle (p189) Cosy and eco-aware.

Mooons (p190) High-tech design hotel with a great rooftop terrace.

Hotel Capricorno (p187) Shimmering interiors and canal-side balconies.

€€€

Hotel Sacher (p187) Olde-worlde glamour and the city's most famous coffee house on the premises.

Best Classic Viennese Pensionen

Hotel Drei Kronen (p188) Old-fashioned flair in *Jugendstil* (Art Nouveau) pension.

Angel's Place (p190) Heaven in the shape of a wine cellar–turned-guesthouse.

Spiess & Spiess (p189) Elegant pension run by a hospitable family.

Best Design Hotels

Hotel Rathaus Wein & Design (p189) An oenologist's delight: minimalist-chic rooms themed by wine and vine.

Altstadt (p189) Razor-sharp design and original art bring this historic property bang up to date.

Magdas (p190) Retro-cool near the Prater.

Grätzlhotel (p190) By some of Vienna's top architects.

Ruby Sofie (p190) Inside a grand former concert hall.

Best Hostels

my MOjO vie (p188) Closest thing to a designer hostel, with everything from netbooks to musical instruments.

Grand Ferdinand Hotel (p187) Not only sumptuous rooms and suites but mahogany bunk beds too.

Wombat's City Hostel Naschmarkt (p188) Sociable facilities at this modern hostel include a lively bar.

NEED TO KNOW

Price Ranges

The following price ranges refer to a double with private bathroom.

€	less than €80
€€	€80–€200
€€€	over €200

Breakfast

Generally not included in the rate at higher-end hotels. An increasing number of midrange hotels don't automatically include it. Heading to a coffee house or cafe can be a better-value, more atmospheric option.

Parking

Very few establishments have their own parking on-site, though many have deals with parking garages nearby. Expect to pay between €22 and €55 for 24 hours.

Tipping

Only bell hops and room service in luxury hotels (€1 or €2).

Wi-Fi

Almost always free, fast and reliable.

Where to Stay

NEIGHBOURHOOD	FOR	AGAINST
The Hofburg & Around	Central, close to the Hofburg, some accommodation close to MuseumsQuartier.	High prices. Less opportunity to interact with locals than some other neighbourhoods.
Stephansdom & the Historic Centre	Quintessential Viennese architecture. Close to key sights, bars and restaurants, great shopping. Easy access to the entire city.	More expensive. Very popular. Green spaces only on fringes.
Karlsplatz & Around Naschmarkt	Proximity to Naschmarkt. Good bars and restaurants. Excellent transport connections. Less expensive.	More travel time is needed to get to sights from outlying areas.
The Museum District & Neubau	Great local neighbourhood, especially closer to the Ringstrasse. Near museums, the Hofburg, bars and restaurants.	Relatively low hotel density. Dependence on trams in some parts.
Alsergrund & the University District	Student atmosphere near the campuses. Creative cafes and boutiques. Good nightlife options. Handful of good, inexpensive hotels.	Transport to other districts often indirect unless near the Ringstrasse.
Schloss Belvedere to the Canal	Quiet and close to the palace.	Few sights except Belvedere itself. Limited restaurants and bars.
Prater & East of the Danube	Increasingly hip, gentrifying areas, especially Leopoldstadt. Good transport to centre and to the Prater. Great markets. Lots of outdoor activities.	Limited sights except the Prater.
Schloss Schönbrunn & Around	Some parts are close to Schönbrunn, others to the lively Brunnenmarkt eating and drinking area.	Light on sights except for Schönbrunn. Some sections along the Gürtel are seedy.

The Hofburg & Around

AVIANO PENSION €€

Map p238 (01-512 83 30; www.avianoboutiquehotel.com; 01, Marco-d'Aviano-Gasse 1; s/d/ste from €89/119/135; ; UStephansplatz) Aviano offers a supercentral position, high standards and all-round value for money. Rooms feature high ceilings and whitewashed antique furnishings; corner rooms have a charming alcove and bay window. Breakfast (€12) is served in a bright, sunny room and on a small balcony overlooking the courtyard in summer. Extra beds (per person €30 to €39) make it a good family option.

PERTSCHY PALAIS HOTEL HOTEL €€

Map p238 (01-534 49-9; www.pertschy.com; 01, Habsburgergasse 5; s/d/f from €142/157/233; ; UHerrengasse, Stephansplatz) The baroque, 18th-century-built Palais Cavriani's quiet yet central location, just off the Graben, is hard to beat. Staff are exceedingly friendly, and children are warmly welcomed (toys for toddlers and high chairs for tots are available). Decorated in creams, royal reds and golds, its 55 spacious, antique-furnished rooms have parquet floors. Family rooms have period fireplaces (alas, not in use).

★**HOTEL SACHER** HISTORIC HOTEL €€€

Map p238 (01-514 561 555; www.sacher.com; 01, Philharmonikerstrasse 4; d/ste from €417/767; ; D, 1, 2, 71 Kärntner Ring/Oper, UKarlsplatz) Stepping into Hotel Sacher is like turning back the clocks 100 years. The lobby's dark-wood panelling, original oil paintings, deep-red shades and heavy gold chandelier are reminiscent of a fin-de-siècle bordello. The smallest rooms are surprisingly large and suites are truly palatial. Extras include a taste of the cafe's (p70) famous *Sacher Torte* on arrival.

RADISSON BLU STYLE HOTEL DESIGN HOTEL €€€

Map p238 (01-227 800; www.radissonblu.com/stylehotel-vienna; 01, Herrengasse 12; d/ste from €189/302; P; UHerrengasse) Although part of a global chain, this glamorous 78-room hotel is a contender for the title of 'most fashionable hotel address' in Vienna, with overtones of *Jugendstil* and art deco in its snazzy contemporary decor, and amenities including in-room Nespresso machines. There's a sauna and a gym. Breakfast costs €25 per person.

Stephansdom & the Historic Centre

★**GRAND FERDINAND HOTEL** DESIGN HOTEL €€

Map p236 (01-918 80; www.grandferdinand.com; 01, Schubertring 10-12; dm/d/ste from €30/176/470; ; 2, 71 Schwarzenbergplatz) An enormous taxidermied horse stands in the reception area of this ultrahip hotel. The Grand Ferdinand is shaking up Vienna's accommodation scene by offering parquet-floored eight-bed dorms with mahogany bunks alongside richly coloured designer rooms with chaise longues and chandeliered suites with private champagne bars. Breakfast (€29) is served on the panoramic rooftop terrace, adjacent to the heated, open-air infinity pool.

HOTEL CAPRICORNO HOTEL €€

Map p236 (01-533 31 04-0; www.schick-hotels.com/hotel-capricorno; 01, Schwedenplatz 3-4; s/d from €124/148; P; 1, 2 Schwedenplatz, USchwedenplatz) Set behind an unpromising mid-20th-century facade, Hotel Capricorno has been stunningly made over in lustrous velveteens in zesty lime, orange, lemon and aubergine shades. Most of its 42 rooms have balconies (front rooms overlook the Danube Canal; rear rooms are quieter). It's 600m northeast from Stephansdom (around a 10-minute stroll).

RUBY LISSI BOUTIQUE HOTEL €€

Map p236 (01-205 55 18-0; www.ruby-hotels.com; 01, Fleischmarkt 19; d from €119; @; 1, 2 Schwedenplatz, USchwedenplatz) Guitars are available for loan at this rocking hotel, which has in-room Marshall amps (and soundproofing!). The hotel's own radio station plays in the bar and can be streamed on in-room tablets. Rooms have vintage and designer furniture; bathrooms are open-plan but can be screened by curtains. Breakfast (€16) is organic; bike hire per day costs €10.

HOTEL AUSTRIA HOTEL €€

Map p236 (01-515 23; www.hotelaustria-wien.at; 01, Fleischmarkt 20; s/d/tr/q from €88/120/174/192; @; 1, 2 Schwedenplatz, UStephansplatz, Schwedenplatz) This elegant 46-room hotel offers some of the best value in the Innere Stadt (inner city). Cosy rooms come with minibars and kettles for tea and coffee. Cheaper singles (from

€71) and doubles (from €103) have private showers but share toilets. Bike hire costs €8 per day. The 2nd-floor terrace stays open until 10pm. Cots and babysitting services are available.

HOTEL KÄRNTNER HOF HOTEL €€

Map p236 (01-512 19 23; www.karntnerhof.com; 01, Grashofgasse 4; s/d/tr/ste from €88/126/188/239; P @ ; U Stephansplatz) Renovations have restored the 41-room Hotel Kärntner Hof to its art-nouveau-era glory with *Jugendstil* colours (grey and sage), English wallpapers and Italian fabrics while retaining the original oak floors, period paintings lining the walls and the wood- and frosted-glass-panelled lift to the roof terrace.

★DO & CO DESIGN HOTEL €€€

Map p236 (01-241 88; www.docohotel.com; 01, Stephansplatz 12; d/ste from €248/706; ; U Stephansplatz) Up-close views of Stephansdom extend from higher-priced rooms at this swanky hotel, and all 43 rooms and suites come with state-of-the-art entertainment systems and multicountry power sockets. Some have in-room Jacuzzis, but be aware that bathrooms (not toilets) have transparent glass walls. Cathedral views also unfold from the 6th-floor bar and 7th-floor rooftop restaurant and terrace.

Karlsplatz & Around Naschmarkt

WOMBAT'S CITY HOSTEL NASCHMARKT HOSTEL €

Map p240 (01-897 23 36; www.wombats-hostels.com; 04, Rechte Wienzeile 35; dm/s/d from €22/65/86.50; @ ; U Kettenbrückengasse) Bright and modern, Wombat's City Hostel Naschmarkt directly overlooks Vienna's biggest market, and is within easy walking distance of the city's main sights. Well-lit, airy dorms and private rooms come with en suite bathrooms and free lockers; great facilities include a self-catering kitchen, laundry and a lively bar. The all-you-can-eat breakfast costs €4.90. Its original Vienna hostel is near Westbahnhof.

DAS TYROL DESIGN HOTEL €€

Map p240 (01-587 54 15; www.das-tyrol.at; 06, Mariahilfer Strasse 15; d/studios from €175/215; P ; U Museumsquartier) Design is the watchword at Das Tyrol. Done out in taupes, creams and golds, the spacious rooms feature bold original artworks, marble bathrooms and amenities including Nespresso machines. Corner rooms have small balconies overlooking Mariahilfer Strasse. The gold-tiled spa has a sauna and a 'light therapy' shower where you can watch fish swim in the aquarium.

HOTEL DREI KRONEN PENSION €€

Map p240 (01-587 32 89; www.hotel3kronen.at; 04, Schleifmühlegasse 25; s/d/tr/q from €85/109/179/209; ; U Kettenbrückengasse) Within footsteps of the Naschmarkt (p94) (some rooms overlook it), this family-owned abode is a delight. Elegant touches – shiny marble, polished brass and a spiral staircase – are distinctly Viennese, but nonetheless a casual feel prevails. Rooms are slick and modern, with the occasional pop of colour.

★HOTEL IMPERIAL HISTORIC HOTEL €€€

Map p240 (01-501 100; www.marriott.com; 01, Kärntner Ring 16; d/ste from €364/470; @ ; D, 1, 71 Karlsplatz, U Karlsplatz) This rambling former palace, with all the marble and majesty of the Habsburg era, has service as polished as its crystal. Suites are filled with 19th-century paintings and genuine antique furniture (and come with butler service), while 4th- and 5th-floor rooms in Biedermeier style are far cosier and may come with a balcony. A lavish breakfast buffet costs €41.

The Museum District & Neubau

★MY MOJO VIE HOSTEL €

Map p244 (0676 551 11 55; www.mymojovie.at; 07, Kaiserstrasse 77; dm €25, d/tr/q with private bathroom €80/100/120, s/d/tr/q with shared bathroom €44/60/80/100; @ ; 5 Burggasse/Kaiserstrasse, U Burggasse-Stadthalle) An old-fashioned cage lift rattles up to these design-focused backpacker digs. Everything you could wish for is here – well-equipped dorms with two power points per bed, a self-catering kitchen, tablets for surfing, guidebooks for browsing and musical instruments for your own jam session. There's no air-con but fans are available in summer.

HOTEL AM BRILLANTENGRUND HOTEL €

Map p244 (☎01-523 36 62; www.brillantengrund.com; 07, Bandgasse 4; s/d/tr/q from €59/69/89/109; @; 49 Westbahnstrasse/Zieglergasse) In a lemon-yellow building set around a courtyard strewn with potted palms, this community linchpin works with local artists and hosts regular exhibitions, along with DJs, live music and other events such as pop-up markets and shops. Parquet-floored rooms are simple but decorated in '50s to '70s themes with vintage furniture, local artworks, and retro wallpapers and light fittings.

★ **BOUTIQUEHOTEL STADTHALLE** HOTEL €€

Map p244 (☎01-982 42 72; www.hotelstadthalle.at; 15, Hackengasse 20; s/d/f from €78/128/181; P; 9/49 Beingasse) Achieving a zero-energy balance, this hotel makes the most of solar power, rainwater collection and LED lighting and has a roof planted with fragrant lavender. Vivid shades of purple, pink and peach enliven the 79 vintage-meets-modern rooms. They're split over two buildings divided by an ivy-draped courtyard where organic breakfasts (including honey from its rooftop hives) are served in fine weather.

HOTEL RATHAUS WEIN & DESIGN BOUTIQUE HOTEL €€

Map p244 (☎01-400 11 22; www.hotel-rathaus-wien.at; 08, Lange Gasse 13; d/tr/f from €116/134/279; ; 2 Rathaus, U Rathaus) Each of the 39 open-plan, minimalist-chic rooms at this boutique hotel is dedicated to an Austrian winemaker and the minibars are stocked with premium wines from the growers themselves. With clever backlighting, rooms reveal a razor-sharp eye for design, especially the opalescent ones with hybrid beds and bathtubs. Some rooms overlook the inner courtyard space.

ALTSTADT PENSION €€

Map p244 (☎01-522 66 66; www.altstadt.at; 07, Kirchengasse 41; s/d/ste from €134/175/240; ; 46 Strozzigasse) Otto Ernst Wiesenthal has poured his passion and impeccable taste into creating one of Vienna's most outstanding guesthouses, here in Spittelberg. Design elements by Vitra and Philippe Starck merge seamlessly with original art from luminaries including Andy Warhol and Markus Prachensky. The 49 individually decorated rooms have high ceilings, plenty of space and natural light.

SANS SOUCI WIEN DESIGN HOTEL €€€

Map p244 (☎01-522 25 20; www.sanssouci-wien.com; 07, Burggasse 2; d/ste from €260/350; ; 49 Volkstheater) Directly opposite the Volkstheater (p120) and MuseumsQuartier (p110), this stunning 19th-century property has original designer furniture by Arne Jacobsen and Philippe Starck and pop art by Roy Lichtenstein, Steve Kaufman and Allen Jones in its 63 rooms and public areas. Top-flight amenities include a champagne bar pouring 60 varieties of bubbly, gourmet restaurant, basement spa, indoor lap pool, and a rooftop sundeck.

Alsergrund & the University District

HOTEL HARMONIE HOTEL €€

Map p246 (☎01-317 66 04; www.harmonie-vienna.at; 09, Harmoniegasse 5-7; s €153-228, d €173-243, ste €218-258; @; U Rosauer Lande) Lodged in an original Otto Wagner building, this family-run, eco-conscious hotel is a cut above most hotels in Alsergrund. The bright, allergy-friendly rooms are jazzed up by the dynamic paintings of artist Luis Casanova Sorolla. There's also a fitness room and a library lounge area. Prosecco and honey from a Viennese beekeeper appear at breakfast, which emphasises regional and organic produce.

Schloss Belvedere to the Canal

SPIESS & SPIESS PENSION €€

Map p252 (☎01-714 85 05; www.spiess-vienna.at; 03, Hainburger Strasse 19; d €125-230; ; U Rochusgasse) The Spiess family goes out of its way to make you welcome at this elegant pension occupying a late 19th-century house. The spacious, contemporary, crisp white rooms have been designed with care and utmost taste; the pricier ones come with fireplaces and balconies. The region-driven breakfast is an organic smorgasbord of fresh fruit salad, bacon and eggs, cereals and pastries.

MOOONS BOUTIQUE HOTEL €€

Map p252 (☎01-962 26; www.mooons.com; 04, Wiedner Gürtel 16; d €89-150; 📶; UHauptbahnhof) Boutique-chic Mooons brings a dash of contemporary cool to the neighbourhood surrounding Schloss Belvedere. A striking black facade dotted with circular windows gives way to a sexy, monochrome, gold-kissed interior that's very millennial glam. Rooms are minimalist, with smart TV, rain showers and a 'virtual concierge', and there's a fitness room and roof terrace with far-reaching city views.

RUBY SOFIE BOUTIQUE HOTEL €€

Map p252 (☎01-20 57 71 20; www.ruby-hotels.com; 03, Marxergasse 17; d €103-205; P📶; UWien Mitte) 'Lean luxury' is the ethos of this slick boutique hotel occupying the Sofiensäle, a grand former concert hall. Interiors are minimal-stylish, the vibe laid-back, and the pared-down rooms with oak floors have vintage furnishings, docking stations, in-room tablets and rain showers. There's also a library, a bar that loans out a guitar, a yoga terrace and bike rental (€10 per day).

Prater & East of the Danube

★MAGDAS BOUTIQUE HOTEL €€

Map p250 (☎01-720 02 88; www.magdas-hotel.at; 02, Laufbergergasse 2; d €70-150; UPraterstern) How clever: the Magdas is a hotel making a difference as the staff who welcome guests are refugees. The former retirement home turned modestly priced boutique hotel is sustainable on all levels. The rooms are retro cool, with one-of-a-kind donated artworks, knitted lampshades courtesy of nimble-fingered volunteers, and upcycling. The pick have balconies overlooking the Prater, just around the corner.

★GRÄTZLHOTEL BOUTIQUE HOTEL €€

Map p250 (☎01-208 39 04; www.graetzlhotel.com; 02, Grosse Sperlgasse 6; d excl breakfast €93-125; UTaborstrasse) Where electricians, lamp makers and bakers once plied a trade, the Grätzlhotel has injected new life into Leopoldstadt with ultracool interiors courtesy of some of Vienna's top architects. Just around the corner from Karmelitermarkt, the suites are minimalist and streamlined, with vintage lights and homey touches – kitchens with Nespresso makers, retro radios and Viennese Saint Charles Apotheke toiletries.

HOTEL KUNSTHOF BOUTIQUE HOTEL €€

Map p250 (☎01-214 31 78; www.hotelkunsthof.at; 02, Mühlfeldgasse 13; d €75-95, incl breakfast €85-105; @📶🐾; UPraterstern) Modern art and striking light installations breathe new life into the historic shell of Hotel Kunsthof, which rightly bills itself as a crossover between a gallery and a hotel. Spruced up with Italian designer furniture, rooms swing stylistically between traditional and contemporary. There's a pleasing vine-trailed courtyard, an honesty lobby bar, and breakfast features Viennese coffee, ham and fresh breads.

Schloss Schönbrunn & Around

ANGEL'S PLACE GUESTHOUSE €

Map p254 (☎0660 773 05 35; www.angelsplacevienna.com; 15, Weiglgasse 1; d/apt from €55/133; 📶; USchönbrunn) A wine cellar has been converted into this cute guesthouse a 650m stroll northeast of Schloss Schönbrunn's gates. Its basement rooms are cosy, with wood floors, whitewashed walls and original brick vaulting, and guests can use a shared kitchen. The ground-floor, four-person apartment comes with its own kitchen and a private entrance.

SPRINGER SCHLÖSSL HOTEL €€

Map p254 (☎01-813 39 29 35; www.springer-schloessl.at; 12, Tivoligasse 73; s/d from €85/110; P📶; 🚌9A Tivoligasse, USchönbrunn) Set in leafy parkland roamed by squirrels, this modern hotel 500m southeast of the palace gates has 38 spick-and-span rooms (two of which are wheelchair accessible), an in-house bar, and free on-site parking with two electric charge points. The grounds also shelter an 1887-built *Schlössl* (mansion) and an 18th-century half-timbered former stable, both of which are now used as conference rooms.

Understand Vienna

Vienna Today

In 2019 Vienna topped the Mercer Quality of Living Survey for the 10th consecutive year, based on its economic and sociocultural environment, health, pollution levels, public services and transportation. Despite national political ripples, the capital is becoming even more liveable thanks to expanding infrastructure and a commitment to becoming a 'smart city' integrating technological advancements with a green focus. And tourism – at an all-time high – is being enhanced by socially minded initiatives.

Best on Film

The Third Man (1949) Graham Greene's classic film noir set in postwar Vienna.

Amadeus (1984) Oscar-sweeping account of a fictionalised murder attempt on Mozart by a rival composer.

Before Sunrise (1995) Follows star-crossed lovers Jesse (Ethan Hawke) and Céline (Julie Delpy) over one night in Vienna.

Letter from an Unknown Woman (1948) Unrequited love set in Vienna, underscoring the fragility of the human psyche.

Best in Print

The Piano Teacher (Elfriede Jelinek; 1983) By the Nobel Prize–winning author, about a repressed pianist and a sadomasochistic relationship.

The Road into the Open (Arthur Schnitzler; 1908) The story of an affair, with insights into Viennese society and culture in the early 20th century.

The World of Yesterday (Stefan Zweig; 1943) An autobiography of Zweig's life up to WWII, describing many well-known Viennese figures.

City of Ghosts (Shawn Kobb; 2015) Fast-paced thriller set in current-day Vienna following an American student caught up in a crime ring.

Local Politics

Vienna is a city-state, meaning the mayor doubles as the head of a state government. The capital has been governed by the Sozialdemokratischen Partei Österreichs (Social Democratic Party of Austria; SPÖ) and headed by an SPÖ mayor uninterrupted since 1945.

The SPÖ has also won an outright majority in state elections all but twice since 1945: in 1996, and again in the 2010 election, when the right-wing populist Freiheitliche Partei Österreichs (Freedom Party of Austria; FPÖ) took 25% of the vote. The SPÖ wooed voters on its good record, longer-term infrastructure and quality of life, winning again in 2015 with 49% of the vote.

Today, under Bürgermeister and Landeshauptmann (mayor and governor) Michael Ludwig, the SPÖ governs Vienna in coalition with the Greens party, which picked up 10% of the 2015 vote. The next state elections will be held in 2020.

National Issues

If recent headlines are indicative, there is a growing nationalist discontent simmering below Austria's surface. Indeed, the rise of the far right has echoes of a disturbing past that many Austrians would rather leave well behind them.

Until the collapse of the coalition government in May 2019, the right-wing populist Freedom Party (FPÖ) were going strong. More worrying perhaps is the Identitarian Movement Austria (IBÖ), whose alt-right leader, Martin Sellner, once admitted to having been involved with a neo-Nazi group. He was condemned by the former Austrian chancellor, Sebastian Kurz, for his Islamophobic, anti-multiculturalism beliefs. Acutely aware of the threat to liberal democracy, Austrian president Alexander Van der Bellen has warned young people not to be 'taken in' by far-right and neo-fascist ideologies.

Chancellor Kurz, hailed as a political wunderkind when he gained power in 2017 as the EU's youngest head of government, was ousted in May 2019. Kurz lost a vote of confidence after his FPÖ coalition partner Heinz-Christian Strache was embroiled in a scandal after video captured on hidden camera showed Strache attempting to trade political favours for state contracts on Ibiza. Strache was forced to resign, prompting Kurz to terminate the coalition and call snap elections.

Brigitte Bierlein, head of the constitutional court, stepped in as Austria's first female chancellor, helming an interim government. The September 2019 snap election saw Kurz' ÖVP garner 37.5% of the vote, with new coalition talks ongoing at the time of writing.

In other national news, Austria legalised same-sex marriage in 2019, following long-term campaigning by human-rights groups.

Going Green

The goal of Vienna's ruling SPÖ party is to ensure optimal quality of life by minimising resource consumption. Strategies include reducing CO^2 emissions to zero, and for 100% of Vienna's gross energy consumption to originate from renewable sources such as solar and wind-turbine power. The target date for both is 2050, by which date diesel and petrol cars will be banned; a 15% reduction of motorised traffic is planned by 2030.

To this end, the U-Bahn is expanding: construction is underway on the extension of the existing underground line U2 from Vienna's Rathaus (City Hall) station to Wienerberg in the south, and the new U5 line from the Rathaus to Elterleinplatz in the northwest. Both are due for completion in 2024.

Green spaces are planned to remain at over 50% of urban space within the city.

Meaningful Tourism

Vienna's tourism star continues to rise, hitting a record high of 16.5 million bednights in 2018, thanks in part to a raft of new flights. Crowd-pulling events such as the centennial of the modernist era in 2018 and the 150th anniversary of the Staatsoper in 2019 have helped bolster these figures.

Despite this, travel here is increasingly meaningful thanks to a growing crop of social tourism enterprises. These include the likes of Magdas (p190), a boutique guesthouse run by refugees; Vollpension (p94), a retro-cool cafe where retirees bake cakes to bolster their pensions; and Shades (shades-tours.com), insightful city tours run by the city's homeless.

Unhashtag Vienna (www.unhashtag.vienna.info) encourages travellers to set their smartphones aside and stop seeing the city through the lens of social media, instead encouraging a deeper exploration of the city. A follow-up campaign, Unrating Vienna (www.unrating.wien.info), aims to counter online rating obsessions, asking visitors 'who decides what you like?'

if Vienna were 100 people

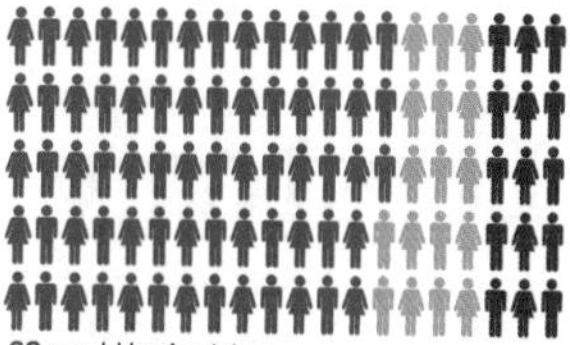

68 would be Austrian
17 would be other European
15 would be other

belief systems

(% of population)

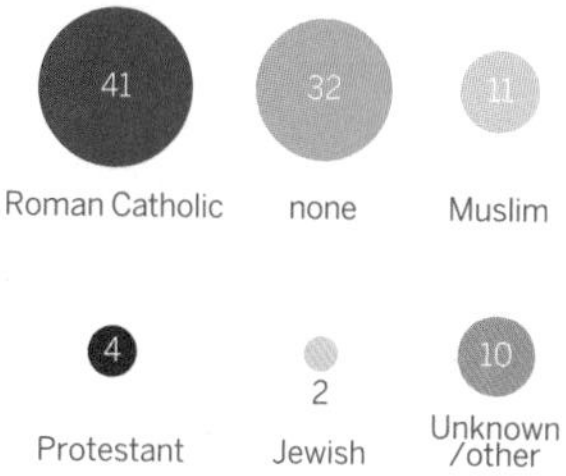

population per sq km

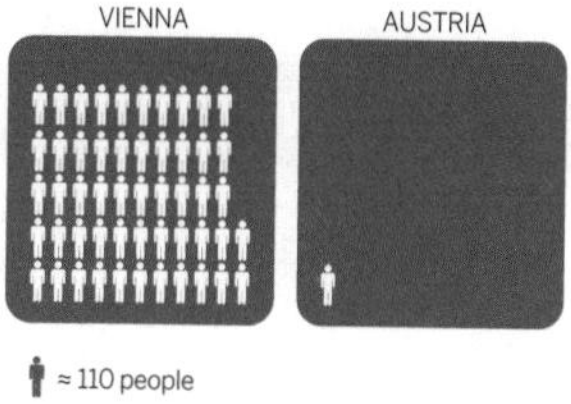

History

A key Roman outpost, then the hub of the Holy Roman Empire and the last bastion of the Occident against Ottoman Turks, Vienna experienced a creative explosion of high culture from the 18th century. Wars, the abolition of the monarchy, uprising and Austro-fascism followed before the city reemerged in the mid-20th century as the capital of a modern Austrian state.

Early Vienna

The early history of Vienna dates back to the Palaeolithic age, around 35,000 years ago, evidence of which is the 25,000-year-old statuette called 'the Venus of Willendorf', which is today exhibited in the Naturhistorisches Museum.

Situated at a natural crossing of the Danube (Donau), it was probably an important trading post for the Celts when the Romans arrived around 15 BC. The Romans established Carnuntum as a provincial capital of Pannonia in AD 8, and around the same time created Vindobona, a second military camp that was located in what today is Vienna's Innere Stadt (inner city). A civil town flourished in the 3rd and 4th centuries, and around this time a visiting Roman Emperor, Probus, introduced vineyards to the hills of the Wienerwald (Vienna Woods). During this early period, Vindobona developed into a town of around 15,000 inhabitants and was important for trade and communication within the Roman Empire. Today, you can find remnants of this Roman town on Hoher Markt and Michaelerplatz.

The Holy Roman Empire grew out of the Frankish Reich, which was seen as the successor to the Roman Empire. It began life in 962 and finally collapsed in 1806, when Kaiser Franz II abdicated. Except for the period 1291–98, the Habsburgs ruled the empire from 1273.

The Babenberg Dynasty

In the year 976 a Bavarian Ostmark (Bavarian Eastern March) was established along the Danube River, and this gradually expanded to the north and east, lending greater importance to Vienna. The Eastern March was ruled by the Babenbergs, a wealthy Bavarian dynasty that held onto power until 1248. During their reign, the Babenbergs expanded their sphere of influence to include modern-day Lower Austria and

TIMELINE

AD 8

Vindobona, the forerunner of Vienna's Innere Stadt, becomes part of the Roman province of Pannonia.

5th century

The Roman Empire collapses and the Romans are beaten back from Vindobona by invading Goth and Vandal tribes.

1137

Vienna is first documented as a city in the Treaty of Mautern, negotiated between the Babenbergs and the Bishops of Passau.

Vienna, Styria and much of Upper Austria. In 1156, under the Babenberg monarch Heinrich II 'Jasmirogott', the Eastern March was elevated to a duchy (ie with its own duke and special rights) and Vienna became the capital. In 1221, two decades before the Babenberg dynasty died out, Vienna was granted its charter, achieving the status of a city.

Habsburg Vienna: Late Middle Ages & Renaissance

The Babenbergs moved their residence to Vienna in the mid-12th century, setting the stage for Vienna to grow considerably. By the late 12th century it had become a significant trading capital, with links to Central and Western European capitals, Kiev (Ukraine) in the east and Venice in the south.

In 1273 Rudolf von Habsburg was elected king of the Romans (Rudolf I), ruling over the Holy Roman Empire and beginning the era of the Habsburgs. The dynasty would retain power until the 20th century.

In the 14th century, Vienna struggled under a string of natural disasters that made everyday life more difficult for many residents: first a plague of locusts in 1338; then the Black Death in 1349, which wiped out one-third of the city's population; followed by a devastating fire. Despite these setbacks, the centuries following the rise of the Habsburg dynasty gave Vienna a new scope of power. This was due in no small part to clever politicking on the part of monarchs – and even cleverer marriage alliances that catapulted this family of rulers to new heights.

In 1453 Friedrich III was elected Holy Roman Emperor; in 1469 he persuaded the pope to raise Vienna to a bishopric. Friedrich's ambition knew few bounds – his motto *'Austria est imperator orbi universo'* (AEIOU) made clear his view that the whole world was Austria's empire.

On the whole, the Habsburgs proved to be more adept at marriage than waging war. Maximilian I, the son of Friedrich III, acquired Burgundy through a clever marriage, while his son Philip the Handsome acquired Spain (and its overseas territories). The marriages of Maximilian's grandchildren brought the crowns of Bohemia and Hungary. This prompted the proverb, adapted from Ovid: 'Let others make war; you, fortunate Austria, marry!'

A ruler on the cusp of the Middle Ages and the Renaissance, Maximilian encouraged the teaching of humanism in Vienna's university and also founded the Vienna Boys' Choir.

Vienna of the 9th century consisted of a handful of Slavic and Avar tribal settlements, with the former Roman military road running through, and Roman ruins, which served the Carolingian rulers as a basis for constructing a small fortress.

When Richard the Lionheart was captured and held to ransom in 1192 while passing through Austria on his return from one of the Crusades, part of the ransom paid for his release was used to build a mint, which funded a new city wall on today's Ringstrasse.

1155–56

Vienna becomes a residence of the Babenbergs; a new fortress is built on Am Hof and Babenberg's Margavate is elevated to Duchy.

1221

Vienna is granted its charter, achieving the status of a city.

1273–82

Otakar II hands the throne to a little-known count from Habichtsburg (read: Habsburg); Rudolf I of Habsburg resides in Vienna and the Habsburg dynasty begins.

1420

Habsburg ruler Albrecht V issues a pogrom, expelling Vienna's Jewish population; many are blackmailed, imprisoned or murdered.

THE TURKS & VIENNA

The first of the Ottoman Empire's two great sieges of Vienna, in 1529, was undertaken by Suleiman the Magnificent, but the 18-day endeavour was not sufficient to break the resolve of the city. The Turkish sultan subsequently died at the Battle of Szigetvár in 1566, but his death was kept secret for several days in an attempt to preserve the morale of the army. This subterfuge worked – for a while. Messengers were led into the presence of the embalmed body, which was placed in a seated position on the throne, and unknowingly relayed their news to the corpse. The lack of the slightest acknowledgement of his minions by the sultan was interpreted as regal impassiveness.

At the head of the Turkish siege of 1683 was the general Kara Mustapha. Amid the 25,000 tents of the Ottoman army that surrounded Vienna he installed his 1500 concubines. These were guarded by 700 African eunuchs. Their luxurious quarters may have been set up in haste, but were still overtly opulent, with gushing fountains and regal baths.

Again, it was all to no avail. Mustapha failed to put garrisons on the Kahlenberg and was surprised by a quick attack from a German/Polish army rounded up by Leopold I, who had fled the city on news of the approaching Ottomans. Mustapha was pursued from the battlefield and defeated once again, at Gran. At Belgrade he was met by the emissary of the sultan. The price of failure was death, and Mustapha meekly accepted his fate. When the Austrian imperial army conquered Belgrade in 1718, Mustapha's head was dug up and brought back to Vienna in triumph.

Everyday Life

Everyday life in Vienna in the late Middle Ages and early Renaissance was far removed from the pomp and circumstance of its Habsburg rulers. Hoher Markt was not only the city's most important marketplace, it doubled as a site for Vienna's many public executions, undertaken for political as well as criminal activities; being beheaded or quartered was the usual method. At other sites around the city, convicted criminals were executed by being drowned in the Danube or burned alive.

The first stone houses were erected around 1250, and the first mention of a public bath in Vienna dates to 1300. Fire and flooding were usual, and three earthquakes struck the city between 1267 and 1356.

Vienna's rapid growth led to the establishment of mendicant orders to feed the poor. These orders began arriving in Vienna in the mid-13th century, establishing monasteries and churches inside the city walls, such as the Minoritenkloster (Minoritenkirche), the Dominikanerkloster (later replaced by today's church) and an Augustine monastery that was later replaced by another in the Hofburg. These monasteries also cared for travellers and pilgrims.

1453

Friedrich III is elected Holy Roman Emperor. 16 years later he persuades the pope to raise Vienna to a bishopric.

1520–30s

The Protestant Reformation spreads rapidly within Austria, and is embraced by the nobility. Ferdinand I defends the catholic church.

1529

The first Turkish siege of Vienna takes place – but the Turks mysteriously retreat, leaving the city. Vienna survives and fortification of the city walls begins.

1670

The second expulsion of Jews is ordered by Leopold I; the financial strength of Vienna is severely weakened and Jews are soon invited back to the city.

In comparison with other European cities, Vienna was one of the most stable, largely thanks to privileges (*Ratswahlprivileg*, or the city council election privilege) introduced in 1396 that saw the city council divided up equally among patricians, merchants and tradesmen, creating a balance of interests.

Turks & Religious Troubles

The 16th and 17th centuries – a time in Vienna's history that included the high Renaissance and early baroque periods – were marked by Turkish attempts to take the capital; the Reformation and Thirty Years' War; a deadly plague; and, ultimately, an end to the Ottoman threat, paving the way for high baroque.

The era began badly when Karl V became Holy Roman Emperor and left the Austrian territories in the hands of his younger brother, Ferdinand I, a Spaniard by birth who didn't even speak German. An unpopular ruler, he soon had to deal with attacks from the Ottoman Turks who, having overrun the Balkans and Hungary, were on Vienna's doorstep by 1529. The city managed to defend itself under the leadership of Count Salm, but the 18-day siege highlighted glaring holes in Vienna's defences. Ferdinand moved his court to Vienna in 1533 (having spent most of his time elsewhere before then) and fortified the city's walls to include bastions, *ravelins* (star-shaped reinforcements of the outer wall) and ramparts, as well as a perimeter ditch, all of which are now followed by today's Ringstrasse. He rebuilt the Hofburg in the 1550s, adding the Schweizer Tor (Swiss Gate) you see today, with his own royal titles engraved on it.

Vienna built its first city wall around 1200 (funded by the ransom paid for the captured King Richard the Lionheart). Its main gates today live on as names along the city's Ringstrasse (Ring Road): Stubentor, Kärntner Tor, Schottentor and Rotenturmtor.

From 1517, the year Martin Luther called for church reforms, the Reformation quickly spread to Austria. The nobility embraced it, and four of every five burghers became practising Protestants. After the Turkish siege of 1529, however, Ferdinand began purging Vienna of Protestantism. He invited the Jesuits to the city, one step in the Europe-wide Counter-Reformation that ultimately led to the Thirty Years' War (1618–48).

Towards the end of the 17th century Vienna suffered terribly. The expulsion of the Jews left its finances in a sorry state, and in 1679 the bubonic plague killed between 75,000 and 150,000. (The baroque Pestsäule was built shortly afterwards as a reminder of the epidemic.) In 1683, the city was once again besieged by the Turks. Vienna rebuffed this attack, however, and the removal of the Turkish threat helped lead the city to a new golden age.

1683

The Turks are repulsed at the gates of Vienna for the second time; Europe is free of the Ottoman threat and Vienna begins to reestablish itself as the Habsburgs' permanent residence.

1740–90

The age of reform, influenced by the ideas of the Enlightenment, kicks into gear under the guidance of Empress Maria Theresia and her son Joseph II.

1805 & 1809

Napoleon occupies Vienna twice and removes the Holy Roman Emperor crown from the head of Franz II, who reinvents himself as Kaiser Franz I.

1815–48

The Metternich system, aimed at shoring up the monarchies of Austria, Russia and Prussia, ultimately begins the 19th-century middle-class revolution.

The Golden Age of an Imperial City

After the Turks were beaten back from the gates of Vienna for the last time in 1683 and peace was restored, the path was clear for Vienna to experience a golden age of baroque culture and architecture throughout the 18th century. During the reign of Karl VI, from 1711 to 1740, baroque architectural endeavours such as Schloss Belvedere, the Karlskirche and the Peterskirche transformed Vienna into a venerable imperial capital.

By 1740 the Habsburg dynasty had failed to deliver a male heir, and Maria Theresia ascended the throne (the first and only female Habsburg to ever rule). She took up residence in Schloss Schönbrunn, which she enlarged from its original dimensions (which dated from 1700), gave a rococo style, and had painted in her favourite colour (the distinctive 'Schönbrunn yellow'). Although her rule was marred by wars – she was challenged by Prussia, whose star was on the rise, and by others who questioned the Pragmatic Sanction that gave her the right to the throne – Maria Theresia is widely regarded as the greatest of the Habsburg rulers. During her 40-year reign, Austria began to take on the forms of a modern state.

Vienna and the Jews, 1867–1938 by Steven Beller describes the role of Vienna's Jews in Viennese cultural and intellectual life.

The talented joined the wealthy and the great who frequented the opulent Schönbrunn palace during the reigns of Maria Theresia and the reform-minded Joseph II. A six-year-old Wolfgang Amadeus Mozart and his 10-year-old sister, Nannerl, performed in the palace's Spiegelsaal in 1762, while Joseph Haydn and other composers worked in the palace theatre. In the latter half of the 18th century (and beginning of the 19th) Vienna witnessed a blossoming musical scene never found in Europe before or since. During this time, Christoph Willibald Gluck, Haydn, Mozart, Ludwig van Beethoven and Franz Schubert all lived and worked in Vienna, producing some of their most memorable music.

Vienna in the Biedermeier Period

Napoleon swept across Europe in the early 19th century, triggering the end of the anachronistic Holy Roman Empire and the Kaiser who ruled it. The Habsburg Kaiser, Franz II, reinvented himself in 1804 as Franz I, Austria's first emperor, and formally dissolved the Holy Roman Empire two years later, following Napoleon's victory over Russian and Austrian troops in the Battle of Austerlitz (1805). Vienna was occupied twice by Napoleon (1805 and 1809), and the cost of war caused the economy to spiral into bankruptcy, from which Vienna took years to recover.

Following the defeat of Napoleon at the Battle of Waterloo in 1815, the European powers pieced together a post-Napoleonic Europe in

1857

City walls are demolished to make way for the creation of the monumental architecture today found along the Ringstrasse.

1866–67

Austria suffers defeat at the hands of Prussia (paving the way for a unified Germany without Austria) and is forced to create the dual Austro-Hungarian monarchy.

1873

Vienna hosts the World Fair, with the motto 'Culture and Education'; the events is marred by a cholera outbreak and the crash of the Vienna stock market.

1910–14

Vienna's population breaks the two million barrier, the largest is has ever been. The rise is mainly due to high immigration numbers, the majority of whom are Czechs.

the Congress of Vienna. The Congress was dominated by the skilful Austrian foreign minister, Klemens von Metternich. The period between the Congress of Vienna and 1848 – the year a middle-class revolution took hold of Europe – is known as the Biedermeier period. During this period Franz I and von Metternich presided over a period of repression that saw the middle classes retreat into private life to cultivate domestic music and a distinctive style of interior architecture, clothing and literature, known as Biedermeier from the word *bieder,* meaning 'staid' or 'stuffy'.

The lower classes suffered immensely, however: the Industrial Revolution created substandard working conditions, disease sometimes reached epidemic levels, and Vienna's water supply was completely inadequate.

THE JEWS OF VIENNA

Historically, Vienna has had an ambivalent relationship with its Jewish population, who first settled in the city in 1194. By 1400 they numbered about 800, mostly living in the Jewish quarter centred on a synagogue on Judenplatz.

In 1420 the Habsburg ruler Albrecht V issued a pogrom against the Jews, who later drifted back into the city and prospered until the arrival of bigoted Leopold I and his even more bigoted wife, Margarita Teresa, who blamed her miscarriages on Jews. In 1670, Jews were expelled from the city and their synagogue destroyed, but this weakened the financial strength of Vienna, and the Jewish community was invited back.

The following centuries saw Jews thrive under relatively benign conditions and in the 19th century they were given equal civil rights and prospered in the fields of art and music. The darkest chapter in Vienna's Jewish history began on 12 March 1938 when the Nazis occupied Austria; with them came persecution and curtailment of Jewish civil rights. Businesses were confiscated (including some of Vienna's better-known coffee houses) and Jews were banned from public places; they were obliged to wear a Star of David and go by the names of 'Sara' and 'Israel'. Violence exploded on the night of 9 November 1938 with the November Pogrom, when synagogues and prayer houses were burned and 6500 Jews were arrested. Of the 180,000 Jews living in Vienna before the *Anschluss* (annexation), more than 100,000 managed to emigrate before the borders were closed in May 1939; another 65,000 died in ghettos or concentration camps. Only 6000 survived to see the liberation by Allied troops in 1945.

Most survivors left afterwards. Today the city's Jewish population is approximately 7000 people, including many who immigrated from Eastern Europe and Russia. The English-language website Jewish News from Austria (www.jewishnews.at) is an excellent resource on contemporary Jewish life in Vienna.

1914–18

WWI rumbles through Europe, and Vienna experiences a shortage of food and clothes. War-induced inflation destroys the savings of many middle-class Viennese.

1918

The Austrian Republic is declared on the steps of Vienna's Parlament (parliament); white and red are chosen as the colours of the nation's flag.

1919

The Treaty of St Germain is signed; the Social Democrats take control of the Vienna City Council, marking the beginning of a period known as Rotes Wien (Red Vienna).

1938

Hitler invades Austria in the *Anschluss* (annexation) to Germany; he is greeted by 200,000 Viennese at Heldenplatz. Austria is officially wiped off the map of Europe.

Vienna in the Late 19th & Early 20th Centuries

The repressive mood of the Biedermeier period in first half of the 19th century in Vienna culminated in reaction and revolution among the middle classes, with calls for reform and, especially, freedom of expression. In March 1848 the war minister was hanged from a lamppost. Von Metternich, who had been decisive in shaping the repressive Biedermeier period, fled to Britain and Emperor Ferdinand I abdicated, to be replaced by the 18-year-old Franz Josef I.

This liberal interlude was brief, however, and the army reimposed an absolute monarchy. In 1857 Franz Josef instigated the massive Ringstrasse developments around the Innere Stadt. In 1854 he married Elisabeth of Bavaria, affectionately nicknamed 'Sisi' by her subjects. The couple lived together in the Kaiserappartements of the Hofburg, which today house the Sisi Museum.

When Napoleon occupied Vienna he established his headquarters in Schloss Schönbrunn, sleeping in what's known today as the Napoleonzimmer (Napoleon Room). In 1810 he married the daughter of Franz I, Marie Louise. A few years later, he demolished part of Vienna's city walls, creating space for Burggarten and Volksgarten.

In the latter half of the 19th century and going into the 20th century, Vienna enjoyed a phase of rapid development. Massive improvements were made to infrastructure – trams were electrified, gasworks built and fledgling health and social policies instigated. Universal male suffrage was introduced in Austro-Hungarian lands in 1906 (women achieved suffrage in 1919 following the demise of the Habsburg dynasty). The city hosted the World Fair in 1873. Culturally, the period was one of Vienna's richest; these years produced Sigmund Freud, Gustav Klimt, Oskar Kokoschka, Gustav Mahler, Johannes Brahms, Egon Schiele, Johann Strauss, as well as Otto Wagner, the most influential architect in fin de siècle Vienna and whose legacy is found throughout the city today.

Vienna: Capital of a Modern Republic

Vienna enjoyed enormous growth in the early 20th century, with its population reaching an all-time peak of over two million in 1910–14. However, the cataclysm of WWI (1914–18) led to a 'Red Vienna' period in the 1920s, during which left- and right-wing political forces clashed on Vienna's streets.

The 1938 *Anschluss* (annexation) by Adolf Hitler saw Vienna and the Austrian Republic as a whole become part of Hitler's Third Reich. Following WWII (1939–45), it was liberated by the Soviet Union and occupied by the Allied powers, before the proclamation of Austria as a neutral, independent country in 1955.

Most of these events are associated with one or more iconic features of the capital. Vienna's neo-Gothic Rathaus is closely tied to the Social Democrats, who, following the collapse and abdication of the Habsburg

1938–39

In the Pogromnacht (Pogrom Night) of November 1938, Jewish businesses and homes are plundered and destroyed; 120,000 Jews leave Vienna over the next six months.

1945

WWII ends and a provisional government is established in Austria; Vienna is divided into four occupied quarters: American, British, Soviet Union and French.

1955

Austria regains its sovereignty as the Austrian State Treaty is signed at the Schloss Belvedere; over half a million Austrians take to the streets of the capital in celebration.

1972–88

The Donauinsel (Danube Island) is created to protect the city against flooding. Today it serves as one of the city's recreation areas, with parks, river beaches, trails and forest.

RED VIENNA

In the 1920s, Vienna was a model of social democratic municipal government, the most successful Europe has ever witnessed. The period is known as Rotes Wien (Red Vienna).

The fall of the Habsburg Empire left a huge gap in the governing of Vienna. By popular demand the Social Democratic Workers' Party (SDAP) soon filled it, winning a resounding victory in the municipal elections in 1919. Over the next 14 years they embarked on an impressive series of social policies and municipal programs, particularly covering communal housing and health, aimed at improving the plight of the working class. Their greatest achievement was to tackle the severe housing problem Vienna faced after the war by creating massive housing complexes across the city. The plan was simple: provide apartments with running water, toilets and natural daylight, and housing estates with parkland and recreational areas. This policy not only gained admiration from within Austria but also won praise throughout Europe. Many of these colossal estates can still be seen in the city; the most celebrated, the Karl-Marx-Hof, was designed by Karl Ehn and originally contained an astounding 1600 apartments. Even so, Karl-Marx-Hof is by no means the biggest – Sandleitenhof in Ottakring and Friedrich-Engels-Hof in Brigittenau are both larger.

monarchy in 1918, gained an absolute majority in all free elections from 1919 to 1996. The Palace of Justice, which was set on fire in 1927 by left-wing demonstrators following the controversial acquittal of members of the Frontkämpfervereinigung (a right-wing paramilitary group) on charges of assassination, perhaps best symbolises the political struggle of the era. This struggle culminated in several days of civil war in 1934. Hitler, who had departed Vienna many years before as a failed and disgruntled artist, returned to the city in triumph and held a huge rally at Heldenplatz (in the Hofburg) on 15 March 1938 in front of 200,000 ecstatic Viennese. A Holocaust memorial on Judenplatz is dedicated to the Jews who suffered under Nazism.

The Austrians: A Thousand Year Odyssey by Gordon Brook-Shepherd is a highly readable take on Austrian history.

In March 1945, the Soviet Union liberated Vienna, today celebrated by the Russian Heroes' Monument on Schwarzenbergplatz, while Vienna's UNO-City, hosting the United Nations Office, best symbolises the city's post-WWII neutrality and evolution into a modern nation.

1980

A third UN headquarters opens in Vienna as the headquarters for the International Atomic Energy Agency, the Office on Drugs & Crime, and other functions.

1986

Vienna ceases to be the capital of the surrounding *Bundesländ* of Niederösterreich (Lower Austria), replaced by Sankt Pölten.

1995

After resounding support from its populace and a referendum where 60% voted 'Yes' to joining, Austria enters the EU.

2019

Vienna tops the Mercer Quality of Living Survey – judged on factors such as the economic and sociocultural environment, health, pollution levels, public services and transportation – for the 10th consecutive year.

City of Music

With Mozart, Beethoven, Strauss and Schubert among its historical repertoire, Vienna is the world capital of opera and classical music. The rich musical legacy that flows through the city is evident everywhere, from buskers hammering out tunes on the streets to formal performances in one of the capital's renowned venues. Music also takes centre stage during festivals held throughout the year.

Habsburg Musical Tradition

The Habsburgs began acting as patrons to court musicians as far back as the 13th century, and by the 18th and 19th centuries they had created a centre for music that was unrivalled in the world. Many of the Habsburgs themselves were accomplished musicians. Leopold I (1640–1705) played violin; his granddaughter Maria Theresia (1717–80) played a respectable double bass; and her son Joseph II (1741–90) was a deft hand at the harpsichord.

Above: Staatsoper (p90)

Hofmusik

Hofmusik (music of the royal court) had its beginnings in the Middle Ages when it developed as a form of music to accompany church Masses. From around 1300 a tradition of choirs with multiple voice parts established itself in Austria. The Habsburgs adopted this tradition and, with the collapse of the Habsburg monarchy, the Austrian state took over the *Hofkapelle* (imperial chapel), which today includes members of Vienna's Philharmonic Orchestra, the Vienna State Opera and, above all, the young boys who traditionally provided the 'female' voice parts, the Wiener Sängerknaben – aka the Vienna Boys' Choir (p46). This tradition lives on with Sunday performances of the Vienna Boys' Choir in the Burgkapelle (p61) inside the Hofburg, and other venues.

COMPOSERS AT A GLANCE

Vienna and music go hand in hand. The following is a selection of composers who either came from Vienna or lived and worked in the capital.

Christoph Willibald Gluck (1714–87) Major works include *Orfeo* (1762) and *Alceste* (1767).

Wolfgang Amadeus Mozart (1756–91) Wrote some 626 pieces; among the greatest are *The Marriage of Figaro* (1786), *Don Giovanni* (1787), *Cosí fan Tutte* (1790) and *The Magic Flute* (1791). The Requiem Mass, apocryphally written for his own death, remains one of the most powerful works in the classical canon. Listen to Piano Concerto Nos 20 and 21, which comprise some of the best elements of Mozart: drama, comedy, intimacy and a whole heap of ingenuity in one easy-to-appreciate package.

Joseph Haydn (1732–1809) Wrote 108 symphonies, 68 string quartets, 47 piano sonatas and about 20 operas. His greatest works include Symphony No 102 in B-flat Major, the oratorios *The Creation* (1798) and *The Seasons* (1801), and six Masses written for Miklós II.

Ludwig van Beethoven (1770–1827) Studied briefly with Mozart in Vienna in 1787; he returned in late 1792. Beethoven produced a lot of chamber music up to the age of 32, when he became almost totally deaf and, ironically, began writing some of his best works, including the Symphony No 9 in D Minor, Symphony No 5 and his late string quartets.

Franz Schubert (1797–1828) Born and bred in Vienna, Schubert was a prolific composer whose best-known works are his last symphony (the Great C Major Symphony), his Mass in E-flat and the Unfinished Symphony.

The Strausses & the Waltz The early masters of the genre were Johann Strauss the Elder (1804–49) and Josef Lanner (1801–43). Johann Strauss the Younger (1825–99) composed over 400 waltzes, including Vienna's unofficial anthem, 'The Blue Danube' (1867) and 'Tales from the Vienna Woods' (1868).

Anton Bruckner (1824–96) Works include Symphony No 9, Symphony No 8 in C Minor and Mass in D Minor.

Johannes Brahms (1833–97) At the age of 29, Brahms moved to Vienna, where many of his works were performed by the Vienna Philharmonic. Best works include *Ein Deutsches Requiem*, his Violin Concerto and Symphony Nos 1 to 4.

Gustav Mahler (1860–1911) Known mainly for his nine symphonies; best works include *Das Lied von der Erde* (The Song of the Earth) and Symphony Nos 1, 5 and 9.

Second Vienna School Arnold Schönberg (1874–1951) founded the Second Vienna School of Music and developed theories on the 12-tone technique. His *Pieces for the Piano* Op 11 (1909) goes completely beyond the bounds of tonality. Viennese-born Alban Berg (1885–1935) and Anton Webern (1883–1945) also explored the 12-tone technique. At the first public performance of Berg's composition *Altenberg-Lieder*, the concert had to be cut short due to the audience's outraged reaction.

Baroque Music

The first dedicated theatre for opera north of the Alps was built in Innsbruck in 1650, but opera was also playing a role in Vienna's cultural scene as early as the 1620s, capturing the hearts of the Habsburg rulers through its paraphernalia of excess – elaborate costumes and stage props, and performers who sang, danced and acted great dramas on stage.

Today the baroque era of music is most audible in performances of the works of two German masters of baroque church music, Johann Sebastian Bach (1685–1750) and Georg Friedrich Händel (1695–1759), performed in many of the churches around town.

Musical Masterpieces

Fifth Symphony in C Minor – Beethoven

Cradle Song, Op 49, No 4 – Brahms

The Creation – Haydn

The Magic Flute – Mozart

Vienna's Philharmonic

An unmissable Viennese musical experience is a visit to the Vienna Philharmonic (www.wienerphilharmoniker.at), which performs mainly in the Grosser Saal of the Musikverein (p100). The Philharmonic has the privilege of choosing its conductors, whose ranks have included the likes of Gustav Mahler, Richard Strauss and Felix Weingartner. The instruments used by the Philharmonic generally follow pre-19th-century design and more accurately reflect the music that Mozart and Beethoven wrote.

Vienna Classic

Wiener Klassik (Vienna Classic) dates back to the mid- and late 18th century and saw Vienna at the centre of a revolution that today defines the way we perceive classical music. Music moved away from the churches and royal courts into the salons and theatres of upper-middle-class society. The period is associated with great composers such as Wolfgang Amadeus Mozart (1756–91), Joseph Haydn (1732–1809), Ludwig van Beethoven (1770–1827) and Franz Schubert (1797–1828) – which later gave way to a new wave of classical composers in the 19th century, such as Franz Liszt (1811–86), Johannes Brahms (1833–97) and Anton Bruckner (1824–96).

The Klangforum Wien (www.klangforum.at), an ensemble of 24 artists from 10 countries, is a unique collaboration between conductors and composers, who perform at various venues. See the website for current performances.

Contemporary Sounds

Vienna's impact on international jazz, rock or pop music is minimal, but it does have an interesting scene. Falco (1957–98), a household name for 1980s teenagers, reached the world stage with his hit 'Rock Me Amadeus', inspired by the 1984 film *Amadeus*.

Artists such as Kruder & Dorfmeister, Patrick Pulsinger and Erdem Tunakan have proved a powerful source for new electronic music. The city's scene has experienced a revival, with old and new artists once again creating waves in the electronic genre. Tosca, a side project of Richard Dorfmeister, is well regarded; DJ Glow is known for his electro beats; the Vienna Scientists produce tidy house compilations; the Sofa Surfers' dub-hop tracks are often dark but well received; and the likes of Makossa & Megablast, Ill.Skillz, Camo & Krooked and mind.in.a.box are going from strength to strength.

Visual Arts & Architecture

Vienna is one of the world's most fascinating capitals when it comes to the visual arts and architecture. The Habsburg monarchs fostered and patronised the arts in grand style, leaving a rich legacy of fine historic paintings, sculptures and buildings. Complemented today by modern and contemporary works, they're visible at every turn when you walk through the city's streets.

Baroque & Rococo

Unwittingly, the Ottomans helped form much of Vienna's architectural make-up as seen today. The second Turkish siege was the major catalyst for architectural change; with the defeat of the old enemy (achieved with extensive help from German and Polish armies), the Habsburgs were freed from the threat of war from the east. Money and energy previously spent on defence was poured into urban redevelopment, resulting in a frenzy of building in the baroque period in the 17th and early 18th centuries.

Learning from the Italian model, Johann Bernhard Fischer von Erlach (1656–1723) developed a national style called Austrian baroque. This mirrored the exuberant ornamentation of Italian baroque with a few local quirks, such as coupling dynamic combinations of colour with undulating silhouettes. Johann Lukas von Hildebrandt (1668–1745), the other famous architect of the baroque era, was responsible for a number of buildings in the city centre.

Rococo, an elegant style incorporating pale colours and an exuberance of gold and silver, was all the rage in the 18th century. It was a great favourite with Maria Theresia, and Austrian rococo is sometimes referred to as late-baroque Theresien style.

Fresco painting in Austria dates back to the 11th century; the oldest secular murals in the capital, from 1398, are the Neidhart-Fresken. The dizzying heights of fresco painting, however, were reached during the baroque period, when Johann Michael Rottmayr (1654–1730), Daniel Gran (1694–1757) and Paul Troger (1698–1762) were active in Vienna and across the country.

Rottmayr was Austria's foremost baroque painter. He spent his early years as a court painter to the Habsburgs in Salzburg before moving to Vienna in 1696, where he became the favoured painter of the architect Fischer von Erlach. He worked on many of Fischer von Erlach's projects and is often compared to the Flemish painter Peter Paul Rubens, bringing together Italian and Flemish influences.

Like Rottmayr, the fresco painter Gran studied in Italy, but his style reined in most of the extravagant elements found in Rottmayr's work and offered a foretaste of neoclassicism – best illustrated in a magnificent ceiling fresco in the Nationalbibliothek.

Medieval & Earlier Architecture

Michaelerplatz (Roman ruins)

Hoher Markt (Roman ruins)

Ruprechtskirche (Romanesque)

Stephansdom (Gothic)

Maria am Gestade (Gothic)

Michaelerkirche (Gothic)

Museum Judenplatz (Jewry)

Dom- & Diözesanmuseum (religious art)

What to See

It's hard to turn a corner in the Innere Stadt without running into a baroque wall. Much of the Hofburg is a baroque showpiece; In der Burg square is surrounded on all sides by baroque wings, but its triumph is the Nationalbibilothek by Fischer von Erlach, whose Prunksaal (grand hall) was painted by Gran and is arguably one of the finest baroque interiors in Austria.

Herrengasse, running north from the Hofburg's Michaelertor, is lined with baroque splendour, including Palais Kinsky at No 4. The Peterskirche is the handiwork of Hildebrandt, with frescos by Rottmayr, but its dark interior and oval nave is topped by Karlskirche, another of Erlach's designs with Rottmayr frescoes – this time with Byzantine touches. The highly esteemed Schloss Belvedere is also a Hildebrandt creation, which includes a large collection of masters from the baroque period, featuring works by Rottmayr, Troger, Franz Anton Maulbertsch (1724–96) and others.

Nicolas Pacassi is responsible for the masterful rococo styling at Schloss Schönbrunn, but the former royal residence is upstaged by its graceful baroque gardens.

The Habsburgs were generous patrons of the arts, and their unrivalled collection of baroque paintings from across Europe is displayed at the Kunsthistorishes Museum Vienna.

Sculpture's greatest period in Vienna was during the baroque years – the Providentia Fountain by George Raphael Donner, and Balthasar Permoser's statue *Apotheosis of Prince Eugene* in the Unteres Belvedere are striking examples. The magnificent 1692 Pestsäule was designed by Erlach.

Johann Michael Rottmayr's frescos adorn the Karlskirche (where a lift/elevator ascends 70m into the cupola for a close-up view), the Peterskirche and, outside town, Stift Melk in the Danube Valley. A ceiling fresco he painted in Schloss Schönbrunn was lost during work on the palace in the 1740s.

Neoclassical, Biedermeier & the Ringstrasse

From the 18th century (but culminating in the 19th), Viennese architects – like those all over Europe – turned to a host of neoclassical architectural styles.

The end of the Napoleonic wars and the ensuing celebration at the Congress of Vienna in 1815 ushered in the Biedermeier period (named after a satirical middle-class figure in a Munich paper). Viennese artists produced some extraordinary furniture during this period, often with clean lines and minimal fuss. Ferdinand Georg Waldmüller (1793–1865), whose evocative, idealised peasant scenes are captivating, is the period's best-known artist.

In the mid-19th century, Franz Josef I called for the fortifications to be demolished and replaced with a ring road lined with magnificent imperial buildings. Demolition of the old city walls began in 1857, and glorious buildings were created by architects such as Heinrich von Ferstel, Theophil von Hansen, Gottfried Semper, Karl von Hasenauer, Friedrich von Schmidt and Eduard van der Nüll. Some of the earlier buildings are Rundbogenstil (round-arched style, similar to neo-Roman) in style, but the typical design for the Ringstrasse is High Renaissance. This features rusticated lower storeys and columns and pilasters on the upper floors. Some of the more interesting ones stray from this standard, however; Greek Revival, neo-Gothic, neo-baroque and neo-rococo all play a part in the boulevard's architectural make-up.

What to See

The Hofmobiliendepot has an extensive collection of Biedermeier furniture, and more can be seen in the Museum für Angewandte Kunst

(MAK). Ferdinand Georg Waldmüller's Biedermeier paintings hang in the Oberes Belvedere and one of the few uniformly Biedermeier houses is the Geymüllerschlössel.

Taking a tram ride around the Ringstrasse provides a quick lesson in neoclassicism. High Renaissance can be seen in von Hansen's Palais Epstein, Gottfried Semper's Naturhistorisches Museum and von Hasenauer's Kunsthistorisches Museum Vienna.

Von Hansen also designed the Ring's Parlament, one of the last major Greek Revival works built in Europe. Von Ferstel's Votivkirche is a classic example of neo-Gothic, but the showiest building on the Ring, with its dripping spires and spun-sugar facades, is von Schmidt's unmissable Rathaus in Flemish-Gothic. The most notable neo-baroque example is van der Nüll's Staatsoper, though it's also worth having a look at Semper's Burgtheater.

While Franz Josef was emperor he had a new wing, the Neue Burg, added to the Hofburg. Gottfried Semper (1803–79) was instrumental in the planning of the Neue Burg and its museums, and the architect, von Hasenauer, stuck very closely to a traditional baroque look, though there are some 19th-century touches – a certain heavy bulkiness to the wing – that reveal it is actually neo-baroque.

The Fin de Siècle Years

- *Klimt – Beethoven Frieze; The Kiss*
- *Loos – Loos Haus*
- *Schiele – Anything in the Leopold Museum*
- *Wagner – Kirche am Steinhof; Postsparkasse*

Jugendstil & the Secession

Vienna's branch of the Europe-wide art nouveau movement, known as *Jugendstil* (Youthful Style), had its genesis from within the Akademie der Bildenden Künste (Academy of Fine Arts). The academy was a strong supporter of neoclassicism and wasn't interested in supporting any artists who wanted to branch out, so in 1897 a group of rebels, including Gustav Klimt (1862–1918), seceded. Architects such as Otto Wagner (1841–1918), Joseph Maria Olbrich (1867–1908) and Josef Hoffman (1870–1956) followed.

By the second decade of the 20th century, Wagner and others were moving towards a uniquely Viennese style, called Secession, which stripped away some of the more decorative aspects of *Jugendstil*. Olbrich designed the Secession Hall, the showpiece of the Secession, which was used to display other graphic and design works produced by the movement. The building is a physical representation of the movement's ideals, functionality and modernism, though it retains some striking decorative touches, such as the giant 'golden cabbage' on the roof.

Hoffman, who was inspired by the British Arts and Crafts movement led by William Morris, and also by the stunning art nouveau work of Glaswegian designer Charles Rennie Mackintosh, ultimately abandoned the flowing forms and bright colours of *Jugendstil* in 1901, becoming one of the earliest exponents of the Secession style. His greatest artistic influence in Vienna was in setting up the Wiener Werkstätte design studio in 1903, which included Klimt and Koloman Moser (1868–1918); they set out to break down the high-art/low-art distinction and bring *Jugendstil* into middle-class homes. In 1932 the Wiener Werkstätte closed, unable to compete with the cheap, mass-produced items being churned out by other companies.

Must-See Buildings

- *Stephansdom*
- *Schloss Belvedere*
- *Hofburg*
- *Schloss Schönbrunn*
- *Rathaus*

No one embraced the sensualism of *Jugendstil* and Secessionism more than Klimt. Perhaps Vienna's most famous artist, Klimt was traditionally trained at the Akademie der Bildenden Künste but soon left to pursue his own colourful and distinctive, nonnaturalistic style.

A contemporary of Klimt's, Egon Schiele (1890–1918) is considered to be one of the most notable early existentialists and expressionists. His gritty, confrontational paintings and works on paper created a huge stir in the early 20th century. Alongside his sketches, he also produced many self-portraits and a few large, breathtaking painted canvases. The other major exponent of Viennese expressionism was playwright, poet and painter Oskar Kokoschka (1886–1980), whose sometimes turbulent works show his interest in psychoanalytic imagery and baroque-era religious symbolism.

The last notable Secessionist – and the one most violently opposed to ornamentation – was Czech-born, Vienna-based designer Adolf Loos (1870–1933). Up until 1909, Loos mainly designed interiors, but in the ensuing years he developed a passion for reinforced concrete and began designing houses with no external ornamentation. The result was a collection of incredibly flat, planar buildings with square windows that offended the royal elite no end. They are, however, key works in the history of modern architecture.

What to See

As well as 35 of Vienna's metro stations, Otto Wagner's works include the Stadtbahn Pavillons at Karlsplatz, and the Kirche am Steinhof, in the grounds of a psychiatric hospital.

Klimt protégé Egon Schiele attracted controversy: in 1911 he moved to Bohemia with his 17-year-old model and lover 'Wally' Neuzil but was driven out by offended locals. In 1912 he was detained for three weeks and later found guilty of corrupting minors with his erotic drawings and paintings.

A prolific painter, Klimt's works hang in many galleries around Vienna. His earlier, classical mural work can be viewed in the Kunsthistorisches Museum Vienna, while his later murals, in his own distinctive style, grace the walls of Secession, where you will find his famous *Beethoven Frieze,* and MAK. An impressive number of his earlier sketches are housed in the Leopold Museum, while his fully fledged paintings can also be seen in the Leopold and Oberes Belvedere.

The largest collection of Schiele works in the world belongs to the Leopold Museum. More of his exceptional talent is on display at the Albertina and Oberes Belvedere; Kokoschka can also be seen at the Oberes Belvedere and Leopold.

One of the most accessible designs of Loos' is the dim but glowing Loos American Bar, a place of heavy ceilings and boxy booths. Also worth a look are his public toilets on Graben. The Loos Haus is his most celebrated work. Pieces by the Wiener Werkstätte are on display at the MAK and can be bought from Woka and Altmann & Kühne.

Modern Architecture

WWI not only brought an end to the Habsburg Empire, but also the heady fin de siècle years. Vienna's Social Democrat leaders set about a program of radical social reforms, earning the city the moniker 'Red Vienna'; one of their central themes was housing for the working class, best illustrated by Karl-Marx-Hof. Not everyone was pleased with the results – some of Vienna's leading architects, Adolf Loos included, criticised the government for failing to produce a unified aesthetic vision.

Since the late 1980s a handful of multicoloured, haphazard-looking structures have appeared in Vienna; these buildings were given a unique design treatment by maverick artist Friedensreich Hundertwasser (1928–2000). Hundertwasser felt that 'the straight line is Godless' and faithfully adhered to this principle in all his building projects, proclaiming that his uneven floors 'become a symphony, a melody for the feet, and bring back natural vibrations to man'. Although he complained that his more radical building projects were quashed by the authorities, he still transformed a number of council buildings with his unique style.

OTTO WAGNER

Otto Wagner (1841–1918) was one of the most influential Viennese architects at the end of the 19th century (also known as the fin de siècle). He was trained in the classical tradition, and became a professor at the Akademie der Bildenden Künste. His early work was in keeping with his education, and he was responsible for some neo-Renaissance buildings along the Ringstrasse. But as the 20th century dawned he developed an art nouveau style, with flowing lines and decorative motifs. Wagner left the academy to join the looser, more creative Secession movement in 1899 and attracted public criticism in the process – one of the reasons his creative designs for Vienna's Historical Museum were never adopted. In the 20th century, Wagner began to strip away the more decorative aspects of his designs, concentrating instead on presenting the functional features of buildings in a creative way.

The most accessible of Wagner's works are his metro stations, scattered along the network. The metro project, which lasted from 1894 to 1901, included 35 stations as well as bridges and viaducts. All of them feature green-painted iron, some neoclassical touches (such as columns) and curvy, all-capitals fin de siècle typefaces. The earlier stations, such as Hütteldorf-Hacking, show the cleaner lines of neoclassicism, while Karlsplatz, built in 1898, is a curvy, exuberant work of Secessionist gilding and luminous glass.

What to See

The municipality buildings of Red Vienna are scattered throughout the city. The most famous is Karl-Marx-Hof. Hundertwasserhaus attracts tourists by the busload, as does the nearby KunstHausWien, but Hundertwasser's coup d'état is the Fernwärme incinerator; opened in 1992, it's the most non-industrial-looking heating plant you'll ever see.

Of the 21st-century architectural pieces, the MuseumsQuartier impresses the most, with its integration of the historic and the post-modern into the city's most popular space. On a 109-hectare site near Südtyroler Platz, Vienna's 2015-opened *Hauptbahnhof* is as large as the Josefstadt district and goes beyond its functional role as a station to form a city district in itself for 30,000 people, with some 5000 apartments, a large park, offices, schools and a kindergarten.

Hans Hollein (1934–2014) was one of Vienna's more influential architects since the 1960s. Works include Retti candle shop (Kohlmarkt 8–10); two jewellery stores designed for Schullin (Graben 26), which have been described as 'architectural Fabergés'; and Haas Haus, whose 'peeling' facade seems to reveal the curtain wall of glass below.

Contemporary Arts

Vienna has a thriving contemporary arts scene with a strong emphasis on confrontation, pushing boundaries and exploring new media – incorporating the artist into the art has a rich history in this city. Standing in stark contrast to the more self-consciously daring movements such as Actionism, Vienna's extensive Neue Wilde group emphasises traditional techniques and media.

One of Vienna's best-known contemporary artists, Arnulf Rainer (b 1929) worked in the 1950s with automatic painting (letting his hand draw without trying to control it). He later delved into Actionism, foot-painting, painting with chimpanzees and the creation of death masks.

Sculptor and photographer Erwin Wurm (b 1954) creates humorous large-scale works subverting everyday objects, such as bent yachts, flat cars and inverted houses.

Eva Schlegel (b 1960) works in a number of media, exploring how associations are triggered by images. Some of her most powerful work has been photos of natural phenomena or candid street shots printed onto a chalky canvas then overlaid with layers of oil paint and lacquer.

Martina Steckholzer (b 1974) utilises video footage to produce paintings with distorted illusions of shape and tone.

Vienna in Print & on Film

Despite Vienna's renowned quality of life, Viennese writing and cinema is often bowed down by the weight of personal and national histories. Living under an autocratic empire, dealing with the end of the empire, the guilt of *Anschluss* (annexation), the horror of Nazism, the emotional legacy of WWII, neo-Nazism, misanthropy, religious upbringing, and a real or imagined bleakness of life are all enduringly popular themes.

Literature

The best place to get an overview of Vienna's – and Austria's – literary past and present is at the 2015-opened Literaturmuseum (p77).

Top Books

The Play of the Eyes (Elias Canetti; 1985)

The Radetzky March (Joseph Roth; 1932)

The Third Man (Graham Greene; 1950)

Across (Peter Handke; 1986)

Measuring the World (Daniel Kehlmann; 2005)

Nineteenth to mid-20th Century

Austria's literary tradition really took off around the end of the 19th century. Karl Kraus (1874–1936) was one of the period's major figures; his apocalyptic drama *Die Letzten Tage der Menschheit* (The Last Days of Mankind) employed a combination of reports, interviews and press extracts to tell its tale.

Peter Altenberg (1859–1919) was a drug addict, an alcoholic, a fan of young girls and a poet who depicted the bohemian lifestyle of Vienna. Whenever asked where he lived, he reputedly always gave the address of Café Central, where his papier-mâché figure still adorns the room today. Two of his collected works are *Evocations of Love* (1960) and *Telegrams of the Soul: Selected Prose of Peter Altenberg* (2005).

Robert Musil (1880–1942) was one of the most important 20th-century writers, but he achieved international recognition only after his death, when his major literary achievement about belle époque Vienna, *Der Mann ohne Eigenschaften* (The Man Without Qualities), was – at seven volumes – still unfinished.

Stefan Zweig (1881–1942), another of the greatest writers in German, was born in Vienna. In his autobiography, *The World of Yesterday* (Die Welt von Gestern; 1942–3), he vividly describes the Vienna of the early 20th century. A poet, playwright, translator, paranoiac and pacifist, Zweig believed Nazism had been conceived specifically with him in mind; when he became convinced in 1942 that Hitler would take over the world, he killed himself in exile in Brazil.

Arthur Schnitzler (1862–1931), a friend of Sigmund Freud, was a prominent Jewish writer in Vienna's fin de siècle years. His play *Reigen* (Hands Around), set in 1900 against a Viennese backdrop, was described by Hitler as 'Jewish filth'; it gained considerable fame in the English-speaking world as Max Ophul's film *La Ronde*.

Joseph Roth (1894–1939), who was primarily a journalist, wrote about the concerns of Jews in exile and of Austrians uncertain of their identity at the end of the empire. His book *What I Saw: Reports from Berlin* is part of an upsurge of interest in this fascinating writer; his most famous works,

Radetzky March and *The Emperor's Tomb,* are both gripping tales set in the declining Austro-Hungarian Empire.

Modern & Contemporary

Dutch-born Thomas Bernhard (1931–89) grew up and lived in Austria. He was obsessed with disintegration and death, and in later works like *Holzfällen: Eine Erregung* (Cutting Timber: An Irritation) turned to controversial attacks against social conventions and institutions. His novels are seamless (no chapters or paragraphs, few full stops) but surprisingly readable.

Peter Handke's (b 1942) postmodern, abstract output encompasses innovative and introspective prose works and stylistic plays. His book *The Goalie's Anxiety at the Penalty Kick* (1970) brought him acclaim; a film based on the book was directed by Wim Wenders. Handke's essay on the Balkan wars of the 1990s, *A Journey to the Rivers: Justice for Serbia* (1997), took an unpopular stance on Serbia and further cemented his reputation for controversy.

The provocative novelist Elfriede Jelinek (b 1946), winner of the Nobel Prize for Literature in 2004, dispenses with direct speech, indulges in strange flights of fancy and takes a very dim view of humanity. Her works are hoften disturbingly pornographic, and either loved or hated by critics. Jelinek's *Women as Lovers* (1994) and *The Piano Teacher* (1983) are two of her most acclaimed works. Her controversial *Greed* (2000) focuses on gender and the relationships between men and women.

Wolf Haas (b 1960) is well known for his dark-humoured crime novels featuring Detective Simon Brenner. Three have been made into films, including the Vienna-set *Komm, süsser Tod* (Come, Sweet Death; 1998); the film was released in 2000.

The most successful of Vienna's contemporary writers is arguably Daniel Kehlmann (b 1975), who achieved widespread acclaim with his *Measuring the World* (2005), based on the lives of Alexander von Humboldt and Carl Friedrich Gauss. A 2012 film was directed by the German director and actor Detlev Buck. Kehlmann's follow-ups have included *You Should Have Left* (2018), about a screenwriter and his family's ill-fated trip to the Alps; it was turned into a 2019 film starring Kevin Bacon.

Many Viennese authors are also playwrights – perhaps the Viennese fondness for the avant-garde encourages the crossing of artistic boundaries. Schnitzler, Bernhard, Jelinek and Handke have all had their plays performed at the premier playhouse in Austria, Vienna's Burgtheater.

Theatre

The roots of theatre in Vienna date back to religious liturgies and passion plays of the mid- and late Middle Ages. Baroque operas staged from the late 16th century were influenced by Italian styles, and under Habsburg monarchs such as Ferdinand III and Karl VI, baroque theatre of the royal court rose to its zenith. In 1741 Maria Theresia had a hall used for playing the tennis-like game *jeu de paume* converted into the original Burgtheater on Michaelerplatz. This later moved to the Ringstrasse into the premises of today's Burgtheater.

Important figures in the modern era of Austrian theatre were the playwright Franz Grillparzer (1791–1872), Johann Nestroy (1801–62) and Ferdinand Raimund (1790–1836), the latter whose works include *Der Alpenkönig und der Menschenfeind* (The King of the Alps and the Misanthrope).

Cinema

The Austrian film industry is lively and productive, turning out Cannes Film Festival–sweepers like Michael Haneke, whose *The Piano Teacher* (2001, based on the novel by Jelinek), *Funny Games* (2008), *The White Ribbon* (2009) and *Amour* (2012) have all picked up prizes at Cannes. *Amour* also won the Academy Award for Best Foreign Film.

Government arts funding keeps the film industry thriving, as does the Viennese passion for a trip to the *Kino* (cinema). Home-grown films are showcased at the Metro Kinokulturhaus (p86), opened in 2015 and part of the national film archive. Local, independent films are as well attended as blockbusters by Graz native, Arnie Schwarzenegger. The annual Viennale Film Festival (p46) draws experimental and fringe films from all over Europe, while art-house cinemas such as the gorgeous *Jugendstil* **Breitenseer Lichtspiele** (☎01-982 21 73; www.bsl-wien.at; 14, Breitenseer Strasse 21; tickets adult/child €9/7.50; ⓤHütteldorfer Strasse) keep the Viennese proud of their rich cinematic history.

That history has turned out several big Hollywood names. Director Fritz Lang made the legendary *Metropolis* (1926), the story of a society enslaved by technology, and *The Last Will of Dr Mabuse* (1932), during which an incarcerated madman spouts Nazi doctrine. Billy Wilder, writer and director of massive hits like *Some Like it Hot, The Apartment* and *Sunset Boulevard,* was Viennese, though he moved to the US early in his career. Hedy Lamarr – Hollywood glamour girl and inventor of submarine guidance systems (and technology still used in wi-fi and GPS) – was also born in Vienna. Klaus Maria Brandauer, star of *Out of Africa* and *Mephisto,* is another native. Vienna itself has been the star of movies such as *The Third Man* (1949), *The Night Porter* (1974), *Amadeus* (1984) and *Before Sunrise* (1995).

Vienna's oldest theatres that still exist include the Burgtheater, founded in 1741; the two *Vorstädte* theatres, Theater in der Josefstadt (1788) and Theater an der Wien (1801); and the Volkstheater (1889).

Documentary-maker Ulrich Seidl has made *Jesus, You Know* (2003), following six Viennese Catholics as they visit their church for prayer, and *Animal Love* (1995), an investigation of Viennese suburbanites who have abandoned human company for that of pets. Lately he has branched into features with *Dog Days* (2001). Director Jessica Hausner's films include *Lovely Rita* (2001), about a suburban girl who kills her parents in cold blood, and *Lourdes* (2009), centring on an atheistic woman with multiple sclerosis who makes a pilgrimage to Lourdes. Hausner's *Little Joe* (2019), about genetic modification, was an award winner at Cannes.

THE THIRD MAN

Sir Alexander Korda asked English author Graham Greene to write a film about the four-power occupation of postwar Vienna. Greene flew to Vienna in 1948 and searched with increasing desperation for inspiration. Nothing came to mind until, with his departure imminent, Greene had lunch with a British intelligence officer who told him about the underground police who patrolled the huge network of sewers beneath the city, and the black-market trade in penicillin. Greene put the two ideas together and created his story.

Shot in Vienna in the same year, the film perfectly captures the atmosphere of postwar Vienna using an excellent play of shadow and light. The plot is simple but gripping: Holly Martins, an out-of-work writer played by Joseph Cotton, travels to Vienna at the request of his old schoolmate Harry Lime (played superbly by Orson Welles), only to find him dead under mysterious circumstances. Doubts over the death drag Martins into the black-market penicillin racket and the path of the multinational forces controlling Vienna. Accompanying the first-rate script, camera work and acting is a mesmerising soundtrack. After filming one night, director Carol Reed was dining at a *Heuriger* (wine tavern) and fell under the spell of Anton Karas' zither playing. Although Karas could neither read nor write music, Reed flew him to London to record the soundtrack. His bouncing, staggering 'Harry Lime Theme' dominated the film, became a chart hit and earned Karas a fortune.

The Third Man was an instant success, and has aged with grace and style. It won first prize at Cannes in 1949 and the Academy Award for Best Cinematography (Black-and-White) in 1951, and was selected by the British Film Institute as 'favourite British film of the 20th century' in 1999. For years, the Burg Kino (p100) has screened the film on a weekly basis.

The film's popularity has spawned the Third Man Museum (p92). True aficionados may want to take the English-language Third Man Tour (p28), covering the main locations used in the film, or 3.MannTour (p28) of Vienna's 19th-century former sewers as clips from the black-and-white film are projected on the walls.

Survival Guide

Transport

ARRIVING IN VIENNA

Air

Vienna is well connected by air to most major European cities, as well as several destinations in Asia, the United States and the Middle East.

Vienna International Airport

Located 19km southwest of the city centre, **Vienna International Airport** (VIE; ☎01-700 722 233; www.viennaairport.com; 📶) operates services worldwide. Facilities include restaurants and bars, banks and ATMs, money-exchange counters, supermarkets, a post office, car-hire agencies and two left-luggage counters open 5.30am to 11pm (per 24 hours €4 to €8; maximum six-month storage).

BUS

Vienna Airport Lines (☎517 17; www.viennaairportlines.at) has three services connecting different parts of Vienna with the airport. The most central is the **Vienna Airport Lines bus stop** (Map p236; 01, Morzinplatz) at Morzinplatz/Schwedenplatz (bus 1185; one way/return €8/13, 20 minutes), running via the Wien-Mitte train station.

TAXI

A taxi to/from the airport costs between €25 and €50. The yellow **Taxi 40100** (☎01-401 00; www.taxi40100.at) in the arrivals hall (near the bookshop) has a fixed airport rate of €36. **C&K Airport Service** (☎01-444 44; www.cundk.at) has rates starting at €33.

An Uber (www.uber.com) between the airport and city centre costs around €21 to €29.

TRAIN

The **City Airport Train** (CAT; www.cityairporttrain.com; single/return €11/19; 🚋1 Landstrasse-Wien Mitte, Ⓤ Landstrasse) departs from Vienna International Airport every 30 minutes from 6.09am to 11.39pm, and from Wien-Mitte train station every 30 minutes from 5.37am to 11.07pm. Journey time is 16 minutes.

The S7 suburban train (€4.20, 37 minutes) does the same journey to/from the airport. It runs from 5.18am to 12.18am from the airport to Wien-Mitte, and from 4.19am to 11.49pm from Wien-Mitte to the airport.

Bratislava Airport (Letisko)

Bratislava, Slovakia's capital, is only 60km east of Vienna, and **Bratislava Airport** (BTS; ☎02-3303 3353; www.bts.aero; Ivanská cesta), serving Bratislava, makes a feasible alternative to flying into Austria.

BUS

Slovaklines (www.slovaklines.sk) in conjunction with Eurolines (www.eurolines.com) runs buses between Bratislava Airport and Vienna International Airport and on to Südtiroler Platz at Vienna's *Hauptbahnhof* (one way/return €10/20, 90 minutes, hourly or better).

Buses leave outside the Bratislava Airport arrival hall between 8.30am and 9.35pm daily, and from Südtiroler Platz at Vienna's *Hauptbahnhof* between 8.30am and 9.35pm daily.

FlixBus (www.flixbus.com) runs services from both Bratislava Airport and Bratislava's city centre to central Vienna; fares start from €7.

You can also take bus 61 to the centre of Bratislava (€3.10) and pick up a frequent train (€16, one hour; up to two per hour) from Bratislava train station to Vienna.

Boat

The Danube is a traffic-free access route for arrivals and departures from Vienna. Eastern Europe is the main destination; **Twin City Liner** (Map p236; ☎01-904 88 80; www.twincityliner.com; 01, Schiffstation, Schwedenplatz; one-way adult €30-35; 🚋1, 2 Schwedenplatz, Ⓤ Schweden-

CLIMATE CHANGE & TRAVEL

Every form of transport that relies on carbon-based fuel generates CO_2, the main cause of human-induced climate change. Modern travel is dependent on aeroplanes, which might use less fuel per kilometre per person than most cars but travel much greater distances. The altitude at which aircraft emit gases (including CO_2) and particles also contributes to their climate change impact. Many websites offer 'carbon calculators' that allow people to estimate the carbon emissions generated by their journey and, for those who wish to do so, to offset the impact of the greenhouse gases emitted with contributions to portfolios of climate-friendly initiatives throughout the world. Lonely Planet offsets the carbon footprint of all staff and author travel.

platz) connects Vienna with Bratislava in 1½ hours.

Slovakian ferry company **LOD** (Map p250; ☎in Slovakia 421 2 529 32 226; www.lod.sk; Vienna departure point 02, Schiffstation Reichsbrücke, Handelskai 265; one way/return €24/39; ⏲late Apr-early Oct; Ⓤ Vorgartenstrasse) runs hydrofoils between Bratislava and Vienna (1½ hours) five to seven days per week from late April to early October. The season can vary depending on weather conditions.

Bus

Eurolines (www.eurolines.eu) Has bus routes connecting Austria with the rest of Europe. Its main terminal is at the U3 U-Bahn station Erdberg but some buses stop at Südtiroler Platz by Vienna's *Hauptbahnhof*.

FlixBus (www.flixbus.com) Serves destinations across Europe. Buses use the terminal at the U3 U-Bahn station Erdberg.

Car & Motorcycle

Bordering eight countries (Czech Republic, Hungary, Germany, Slovakia, Slovenia, Italy, Switzerland and Liechtenstein), Austria is easily reached by road. If you're bringing your own vehicle, you'll need a Motorway Vignette (toll sticker). For 10 days/two months it costs €9.20/26.80 per car, €5.30/13.40 per motorcycle. Buy it at petrol stations in neighbouring countries before entering Austria. More information is available at www.austria.info.

Train

Austria's train network is a dense web reaching the country's far-flung corners and beyond. The system is fast, efficient, frequent and well used. Österreiche Bundesbahn (ÖBB; www.oebb.at) is the main operator, and has information offices at all of Vienna's main train stations. Tickets can be purchased online, at ticket offices or from train-station ticket machines. Long-distance train tickets can be purchased onboard but incur a €3 service charge. Tickets for local, regional and intercity trains must be purchased before boarding.

International trains include a growing network of overnight trains; see www.night-trains.com.

The website www.seat61.com has up-to-date rail information.

Wien Hauptbahnhof

Vienna's main train station, the Wien Hauptbahnhof, 3km south of Stephansdom, handles all international trains as well as trains from all of Austria's provincial capitals, and many local and regional trains. Topped by a diamond-shaped translucent glass-and-steel roof, the 2015-opened station has over 50 shops, bars and restaurants, parking for 600 cars, three bike garages, e-bike charging points and two **Citybike Wien** (Vienna City Bike; www.citybikewien.at; per 1/2/3hr free/€1/2, per hour thereafter €4) bike-share-scheme rental stations.

S-Bahn S1, S2 and S3 connect Wien Hauptbahnhof with Wien Meidling, Wien-Mitte and Praterstern.

U-Bahn U1 serves Karlsplatz and Stephansplatz.

Tram 0 to Praterstern, 18 to Westbahnhof and Burggasse/Stadthalle. Tram D connects Hauptbahnhof-Ost with the Ringstrasse.

Bus 13A runs through Vienna's *Vorstädte* (inner suburbs) Margareten, Mariahilf, Neubau and Josefstadt, all between the Ringstrasse and the Gürtel.

Wien Meidling

All western and southwestern regional trains, including services to Graz, stop at Wien Meidling before continuing to the *Hauptbahnhof.*

S-Bahn S1, S2 and S3 connect Wien Meidling with the *Hauptbahnhof,* Wien-Mitte and Praterstern.

U-Bahn U6 (Wien Meidling/Philadelphiabrücke) serves the Westbahnhof and the Gürtel stations.

Wien Westbahnhof

Primarily a commuter station serving Vienna's outer suburbs, Westbahnhof is also the terminus for the Westbahn (www.westbahn.at) intercity service to/from Salzburg via Linz.

U-Bahn U6 runs along the Gürtel, U3 to Stephansplatz via Herrengasse.

GETTING AROUND

Vienna's comprehensive and unified public-transport network is one of the most efficient in Europe. Flat-fare tickets are valid for trains, trams, buses, the underground (U-Bahn) and the S-Bahn regional trains. Services are frequent and you rarely have to wait more than 10 minutes.

Transport maps are posted in all U-Bahn stations and at many bus and tram stops. Free maps are available from **Wiener Linien** (☎01-790 91 00; www.wienerlinien.at), located in U-Bahn stations. The Karlsplatz, Stephansplatz and Westbahnhof information offices are open 6.30am to 6.30pm Monday to Friday and 8.30am to 4pm Saturday and Sunday. Those at Schottentor, Praterstern, Floridsdorf, Philadelphiabrücke and Erdberg are closed at weekends.

Bicycle

Vienna is a fabulous place to get around by bike. Bicycles can be carried free of charge on carriages marked with a bike symbol on the S-Bahn and U-Bahn from 9am to 3pm and after 6.30pm Monday to Friday, after 9am Saturday and all day Sunday. It's not possible to take bikes on trams or buses. The city also runs the **Citybike Wien** (Vienna City Bike; www.citybikewien.at; per 1/2/3hr free/€1/2, per hour thereafter €4) shared-bike program, with bike stands scattered throughout the city.

Bus

Bus connections can be useful for outlying parts of town or for travellers with limited physical mobility.

Regular Buses

Most lines run from 5am to midnight, with fewer (sometimes nonexistent) services on weekends.

13A Runs north–south through the Vorstädte between Hauptbahnhof and Alser Strasse.

2A Connects Schwarzenbergplatz, Stephansplatz, Schwedenplatz and Michaelerplatz.

3A Connects Börsenplatz and Schottentor with Stephansplatz and Stubentor.

Night Buses

Nightline routes cover much of the city and run every half-hour from 12.30am to 5am. Note that on early Saturday and Sunday mornings (ie after midnight Friday and Saturday) the U-Bahn runs all night. Schwedenplatz, Schottentor and Kärntner Ring/Oper are stopping points for many night bus services; look for buses and bus stops marked with an 'N'. All transport tickets are valid for Nightline services.

N25 Runs around the Ringstrasse then via Schwedenplatz and Leopoldstadt to Kagraner Platz and beyond on weekdays.

Car & Motorcycle

Driving

You may consider hiring a car to see some of the outer sights but in Vienna itself it's best to stick with the excellent public-transport system.

Hire

All the big car-hire names have desks in the *Hauptbahnhof* and Vienna International Airport; some also have branches in the city.

Megadrive (☎05-010 541 20; www.megadrive.at; 03, Erdbergstrasse 202; ⏰7am-7pm Mon-Fri, 8am-2pm Sat, 8am-1pm Sun; Ⓤ Erdberg) An inexpensive Austrian car-hire company.

Train

Vienna's network of S-Bahn and U-Bahn trains is efficient and inexpensive.

TICKETS & PASSES

Tickets and passes for Wiener Linien services (U-Bahn, trams and buses) can be purchased at U-Bahn stations and on trams and buses, in a *Tabakladen* (*Trafik;* tobacco kiosk), as well as from a few staffed ticket offices.

Single ticket *(Einzelfahrschein;* €2.40) Good for one journey, with line changes; costs €2.60 if purchased on trams and buses (correct change required).

24-/48-/72-hour tickets (€8/14.10/17.10) Require validation.

Eight-day ticket *(8-Tage-Klimakarte;* €40.80) Valid for eight days, not necessarily consecutive; validate the card as and when you need it.

Weekly ticket *(Wochenkarte;* €17.10) Valid Monday to Sunday only (ie tickets purchased on a Friday are still only valid to the Sunday).

U-Bahn

The U-Bahn (underground rail) is a quick, efficient and inexpensive way of getting around the city. There are five lines: U1 to U4 and U6 (there is currently no U5; construction started in 2018 and is scheduled for completion in 2023). Stations have lifts as well as escalators. Platforms have timetable information and signs showing the exits and nearby facilities. The U-Bahn runs from 5am to midnight Monday to Thursday and continuously from Friday through to Sunday night.

U-Bahn and tram services get you close to most sights, especially in the centre and fringing *Vorstadt* areas (ie between the Ringstrasse and Gürtel).

S-Bahn

S-Bahn trains, designated by a number preceded by an 'S', operate 10 lines from train stations and service the suburbs or satellite towns. Trains run from 4.30am to 1.10am. If you're travelling outside of Vienna, and outside of the ticket zone, you'll probably have to purchase an extension on your standard Vienna transport ticket or buy a ticket from a machine at the station; check on maps posted in train stations.

Tram

There's something romantic about travelling by tram, even though they're slower than the U-Bahn. Vienna's tram network is extensive, with 29 lines, and it's the perfect way to view the city on the cheap. Trams are either numbered or lettered (eg 1, 2, D) and cover the city centre and some suburbs. Services run from 5.15am to 11.45pm.

Taxi

Taxis are reliable and relatively cheap by Western European standards. City journeys are metered; the minimum charge is roughly €3.80 from 6am to 11pm Monday to Saturday and €4.30 any other time, plus a per-kilometre fee of €1.42. A telephone reservation costs an additional €2.80. A tip of 10% is expected. Taxis are easily found at train stations and taxi stands all over the city. To order one, contact **Taxi 40100** (☎01-401 00; www.taxi40100.at) or **60160 Taxi** (☎01-601 60; www.taxi1718.at). These accept common credit and debit cards (check before hopping in, though). Uber (www.uber.com) operates in Vienna.

Directory A–Z

Accessible Travel

Vienna is becoming increasingly accessible. Ramps are common (though by no means ubiquitous). Most U-Bahn stations have wheelchair lifts. All U-Bahn stations have guiding strips for the blind. All buses have ramps (the driver will assist) and tilt technology, and the vast majority of the trams have low-floor access allowing entry in a wheelchair. Traffic lights 'bleep' to indicate when pedestrians can safely cross the road.

Tourist Info Wien (p221) can give advice and information. Its detailed booklet *Accessible Vienna*, in German or English, provides information on hotels and restaurants with disabled access, plus addresses of hospitals, medical-equipment shops, parking places, toilets and much more. It's available for download at www.wien.info/en/travel-info/accessible-vienna.

Download Lonely Planet's free Accessible Travel guide from http://lptravel.to/AccessibleTravel.

Discount Cards

Vienna Card (*Die Wien-Karte;* 24/48/72 hours €17/25/29) Unlimited travel on the public-transport system (including night buses) and hundreds of discounts at selected museums, cafes, *Heurigen* (wine taverns), restaurants and shops across the city, and on guided tours and the City Airport Train (CAT). The discount usually amounts to 5% to 25% off the normal price. It can be purchased online or at Tourist Info Wien (p221), the city's main tourist office, the **Airport Information Office** (www.wien.info; Vienna International Airport; ⏰7am-10pm) and many concierge desks at the top hotels.

PRACTICALITIES

Newspapers & Magazines Newspapers remain very popular in Vienna and English-language papers are widely available. Many coffee houses have a good selection of daily UK newspapers.

Weights & Measures Austria uses the metric system.

Electricity

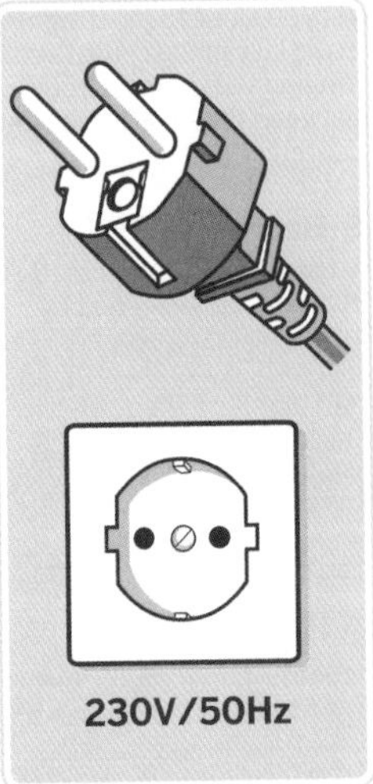

Emergency

In case of emergency, the general number for ambulance, fire and police is 112.

Ambulance *(Rettung)*	☎ 144
Fire *(Feuerwehr)*	☎ 122
Police *(Polizei)*	☎ 133

Insurance

Comprehensive travel insurance to cover theft, loss and

medical problems is highly recommended.

Worldwide travel insurance is available at www.lonelyplanet.com/travel-insurance. You can buy, extend and claim online anytime – even if you're already on the road.

Internet Access

Virtually all hostels and hotels in Vienna offer free wi-fi, called WLAN (pronounced vee-lan) in German. Many cafes, coffee houses and bars also offer free wi-fi; check locations at www.freewave.at/en/hotspots.

The city has more than 400 free hotspots, which are mapped on www.wien.gv.at/stadtplan. Search for 'wien.at Public WLAN', accept the terms of use and connect.

Alternatively, if your phone is unlocked, you can purchase a pre-paid SIM card with a data allowance from phone shops, kiosks and *Tabakladen* (tobacconists). You'll need your passport or ID card to register it.

LGBT+ Travellers

Vienna is increasingly open towards gay and lesbian couples (more so than the rest of Austria), and the country has legalised civil same-sex partnerships and marriages as of 2019. A sign of the capital's openness is its traffic lights, which have male-male and female-female pairings (with love hearts in between) on its pedestrian walk signals, in addition to male-female couplings.

Hang-Outs

Mariahilf (6th district) and Margareten (5th district), fanning out around the Naschmarkt, have a higher than average concentration of gay and lesbian bars.

Festivals & Events

The headlining event on the gay and lesbian calendar is the **Regenbogen Parade** (Rainbow Parade; www.viennapride.at/regenbogenparade; ⏲mid-Jun).

Information

Vienna's main point for gay and lesbian information, **Die Villa** (Map p240; ☎01-586 81 50; www.dievilla.at; 06, Linke Wienzeile 102; ⏲5-8pm Mon, Wed & Fri; ⓤPilgramgasse), has advice and information on what's on offer in the city. The tourist office website www.wien.info/en/vienna-for/gay-lesbian has extensive information on the scene.

Other resources:

Gay Agent (www.gayagent.com/vienna)

Gay Guide (www.gayguide.me)

Gayboy (www.gayboy.at)

Gaynet (www.gaynet.at)

Vienna Pride (www.viennapride.at)

Wiener Antidiskriminierungsstelle (www.queer.wien.at) Also has information for transgender locals and visitors.

Medical Services

Vienna's main hospital, **Allgemeines Krankenhaus** (☎01-40 40 00; www.akhwien.at; 09, Währinger Gürtel 18-20; ⓤMichelbeuern-AKH), better known as AKH, has a 24-hour Accident & Emergency department.

Nachtapotheken (night pharmacies) rotate; check www.nachtapotheke.wien for locations and opening times.

Money

ATMs are widely available. Credit cards are not always accepted in budget hotels or budget to midrange restaurants. Bars and cafes usually only accept cash.

ATMs

Bankomats (ATMs), which accept credit cards and debit cards such as Maestro, are never very far away in Vienna – just look for a neon sign with two green and blue stripes sticking out from a bank facade. *Bankomats* can also be found in the main train stations and at the airport.

Changing Money

It's cheaper to use debit cards in ATMs than changing money.

Banks are the best places to exchange cash, but it pays to shop around as exchange rates and commission charges can vary a little between them. Typically, there's a charge of about 3% on currency exchange, with a minimum charge, so it's best to exchange larger amounts at one time.

There are plenty of exchange offices in the Innere Stadt (inner city), particularly around Stephansplatz and on Kärntner Strasse. Commission charges are around the same here as at banks, but quite often their exchange rates are uncompetitive.

Credit Cards

Visa, EuroCard and MasterCard are more widely accepted than American Express and Diners Club, although a surprising number of shops and restaurants refuse to accept any credit cards at all. Boutiques, high-end shops and restaurants will usually accept cards, though, and the same applies for hotels. Train tickets can be usually bought by credit card in main stations, but not all non-European cards will work – ask your bank for advice before you leave.

Currency

Austria's currency is the euro, which is divided into 100 cents. There are coins for one, two, five, 10, 20 and 50 cents, and €1 and €2. Notes come in denominations of €5, €10, €20, €50, €100, €200 and €500.

Tipping

Restaurants and cafes Tips are generally expected; round up smaller bills (to the nearest €0.50 or euro) when buying coffee or beer, and add 5% to 10% to the bill for full meals. Tip at the time of payment as one lump sum with the bill.

Taxis Drivers will expect around 10% extra.

Hotel porters and cloakroom attendants Tip a euro or two.

Opening Hours

Many restaurants, bars, entertainment venues and smaller shops shut in July/August.

Pubs and clubs Hours vary; generally pubs from 11am or 4pm (or 5pm), to between midnight and 4am (those serving food open earlier); clubs approximately 10pm to around 4am Thursday to Saturday.

Restaurants Generally 11am to 2pm and 6pm to 10pm or 11pm.

Shops Usually 9am to 6.30pm Monday to Friday (many to 9pm Thursday, some Friday) and until 5pm Saturday. All close Sunday.

Supermarkets Normally 8am to 8pm Monday to Friday, to 6pm Saturday. All close Sunday.

Post

Austria's postal service (www.post.at) is reliable and easy to use. Post offices are commonplace, as are bright-yellow postboxes. Stamps can be bought at post office counters or machines. The **Main Post Office** (Map p236; www.post.at; 01, Fleischmarkt 19; ⏲7am-10pm Mon-Fri, 9am-10pm Sat & Sun; 🚋1, 2 Schwedenplatz, Ⓤ Schwedenplatz) has extended opening hours.

Public Holidays

The only establishments remaining open on holidays are bars, cafes and restaurants. Museums are usually open except for New Year's Day, Christmas Day and sometimes May Day. The big school break is July and August; most families go away during this time, so you'll find the city is quieter, but the downside is that a high percentage of restaurants and entertainment venues close.

New Year's Day (Neujahr) 1 January

Epiphany (Heilige Drei Könige) 6 January

Easter Monday (Ostermontag) March or April

Labour Day (Tag der Arbeit) 1 May

Ascension Day (Christi Himmelfahrt) Sixth Thursday after Easter

Whit Monday (Pfingstmontag) Sixth Monday after Easter

Corpus Christi (Fronleichnam) Second Thursday after Pentecost

Assumption (Maria Himmelfahrt) 15 August

National Day (Nationalfeiertag) 26 October

All Saints' Day (Allerheiligen) 1 November

Immaculate Conception (Mariä Empfängnis) 8 December

Christmas Eve (Heiligabend) 24 December; everything closed afternoon

Christmas Day (Christfest) 25 December

St Stephen's Day (Stephanitag) 26 December

Safe Travel

Vienna is a very safe city and in general women and men will have no trouble walking around at night.

- Karlsplatz station and Gumpendorfer Strasse can be boisterous late in the evening.
- The Prater and Praterstern can get a little dodgy at night. Ausstellungsstrasse is best avoided due to sex workers and kerb-crawlers.
- The Gürtel has a sprinkling of red-light clubs: north of Westbahnhof along the Neubaugürtel has a high concentration (with fewer around Thaliastrasse), and directly south to Gumpendorfer Strasse can be seedy.
- S-Bahn and tram stops along Margareten and Wiedner Gürtel can be edgy.

Taxes & Refunds

Austria has a *Mehrwertsteuer* (MWST; value-added tax) of 20% on most items. It's always included in the price but listed separately on a formal receipt. Visitors from outside the EU can claim back around 13% for individual purchases over €75.01 when departing the EU; see www.globalblue.com for instructions. Vienna International Airport has refund desks; otherwise submit the paperwork by post.

Telephone

Country code Austria's country code is ☎0043.

Area code Vienna's area code is ☎01. When calling from overseas drop the zero in the Vienna code.

Mobile Phones

You can use your mobile phone (*Handy* in German) in Austria provided it is GSM and tri-band or quad-band. Check with your service provider about using your phone in Austria.

Prepaid SIM cards Phone shops, kiosks and *Tabakladen* sell prepaid SIM cards for phone calls and data. To use one, your phone needs to be unlocked.

Data roaming Make sure the data-transfer capability is deactivated while you are roaming. Austria has lots of wi-fi hotspots which can be used for surfing on smartphones with wi-fi capability.

Time

Austria is on Central European time, one hour ahead of GMT/UTC. Clocks go forward one hour on the last Saturday night in March and back again on the last Saturday night in October. In 2019 the European Parliament voted to scrap daylight saving time. Although the law had yet to be finalised at the time of writing, the practice is expected to end in 2021.

Note that in German *halb* is used to indicate the half-hour before the hour, hence *halb acht* (half-eight) means 7.30, not 8.30.

Toilets

➡ Large shopping centres have facilities that are free to use.

➡ Facilities at U-Bahn stations and public places marked by a 'WC' sign usually incur a small charge (around €0.50).

➡ Museums reliably have good, clean facilities.

➡ At cafes and bars, facilities are only for paying customers; ask first or consider investing in a coffee.

Tourist Information

Tourist Info Wien (Map p238; ☎01-245 55; www.wien.info; 01, Albertinaplatz; ⏲9am-7pm; wi-fi; tram D, 1, 2, 71 Kärntner Ring/Oper, U Stephansplatz) Vienna's main tourist office, with a ticket agency, hotel booking service, free maps and every brochure under the sun.

WienXtra-Kinderinfo (Map p244; ☎01-4000 84 400; www.wienxtra.at/kinderaktiv; 07, Museumsplatz 1; ⏲2-6pm Tue-Fri, 10am-5pm Sat & Sun; child-friendly; U Museumsquartier) Marketed primarily at children (check out the knee-high display cases), this tourist office has loads of information on activities for kids and a small indoor playground. It's located inside the MuseumsQuartier courtyard, near the Mariahilfer Strasse entrance.

Airport Information Office (www.wien.info; Vienna International Airport; ⏲7am-10pm) Full services, with maps, Vienna Card and walk-in hotel booking. Located in the Vienna International Airport arrival hall.

Jugendinfo (Vienna Youth Information; Map p240; ☎01-4000 84 100; www.wienxtra.at/jugendinfo; 01, Babenbergerstrasse 1; ⏲2.30-6.30pm Mon-Fri; tram D, 1, 2, 71 Burgring, U Museumsquartier) Offers various reduced-priced event tickets for 14 to 26 year olds. Staff can tell you about events around town.

Rathaus Information Office (Map p244; ☎01-502 55; www.wien.gv.at; 01, Rathaus; ⏲7.30am-6pm Mon-Fri; tram D, 1, 2, 71 Rathausplatz/Burgtheater, U Rathaus) Vienna's City Hall provides information on social, cultural and practical matters, and is geared as much to residents as to tourists. There's a useful info-screen.

Visas

Until 2021, visas for stays of up to 90 days are not required for citizens of the EU, the European Economic Area (EEA) and Switzerland, much of Eastern Europe, Israel, USA, Canada, the majority of Central and South American nations, Japan, Malaysia, Singapore, Australia or New Zealand. All other nationalities, including nationals of China, Russia and South Africa, require a visa.

The Federal Ministry for Europe, Integration & Foreign Affairs (www.bmeia.gv.at) website has a list of Austrian embassies where you can apply. For some nationals a biometric passport is required.

Austria is part of the Schengen Agreement, which includes all EU states (minus Britain and Ireland) and a handful of European countries including Switzerland. In general, a visa issued by one Schengen country is good for all the other member countries.

From 2021, non-EU nationals who don't require a visa for entry to the Schengen Area will need prior authorisation to enter under the new European Travel Information and Authorisation System (ETIAS). Travellers can apply online; the cost will be €7 for a three-year, multientry authorisation. Visit www.etias.com for more information.

Language

German is the national language of Austria. It belongs to the West Germanic language family and has around 100 million speakers worldwide.

German is easy for English speakers to pronounce because almost all of its sounds are also found in English. If you read our coloured pronunciation guides as if they were English, you should be understood just fine. Note that kh sounds like the 'ch' in 'Bach' or in the Scottish *loch* (pronounced at the back of the throat), r is also pronounced at the back of the throat, zh is pronounced as the 's' in 'measure', and ü as the 'ee' in 'see' but with rounded lips. The stressed syllables are indicated with italics in our pronunciation guides. The markers 'pol' and 'inf' indicate polite and informal forms.

BASICS

Hello.	*Guten Tag./ Servus.*	*goo*·ten tahk/ *zer*·vus
Goodbye.	*Auf Wiedersehen.*	owf *vee*·der·zay·en
Bye.	*Tschüss./ Tschau.*	chüs/ chow
Yes.	*Ja.*	yah
No.	*Nein.*	nain
Please.	*Bitte.*	*bi*·te
Thank you.	*Danke.*	*dang*·ke
You're welcome.	*Bitte.*	*bi*·te
Excuse me.	*Entschuldigung.*	ent·*shul*·di·gung
Sorry.	*Entschuldigung.*	ent·*shul*·di·gung

WANT MORE?

For in-depth language information and handy phrases, check out Lonely Planet's *German Phrasebook*. You'll find it at **shop.lonelyplanet.com**, or you can buy Lonely Planet's iPhone phrasebooks at the Apple App Store.

How are you?

Wie geht es Ihnen/dir? (pol/inf)	vee gayt es *ee*·nen/deer

Fine. And you?

Danke, gut.	*dang*·ke goot
Und Ihnen/dir? (pol/inf)	unt *ee*·nen/deer

What's your name?

Wie ist Ihr Name? (pol)	vee ist eer *nah*·me
Wie heißt du? (inf)	vee haist doo

My name is ...

Mein Name ist ... (pol)	main *nah*·me ist ...
Ich heiße ... (inf)	ikh *hai*·se ...

Do you speak English?

Sprechen Sie Englisch? (pol)	*shpre*·khen zee *eng*·lish
Sprichst du Englisch? (inf)	shprikhst doo *eng*·lish

I don't understand.

Ich verstehe nicht.	ikh fer·*shtay*·e nikht

ACCOMMODATION

guesthouse	*Pension*	pahng·*zyawn*
hotel	*Hotel*	ho·*tel*
inn	*Gasthof*	*gast*·hawf
youth hostel	*Jugendherberge*	*yoo*·gent·her·ber·ge

Do you have a ... room?	*Haben Sie ein ...?*	*hah*·ben zee ain ...
double	*Doppelzimmer*	*do*·pel·tsi·mer
single	*Einzelzimmer*	*ain*·tsel·tsi·mer

How much is it per ...?	*Wie viel kostet es pro ...?*	vee feel *kos*·tet es praw ...
night	*Nacht*	nakht
person	*Person*	per·*zawn*

Is breakfast included?

Ist das Frühstück inklusive?	ist das *frü*·shtük in·kloo·*zee*·ve

DIRECTIONS

Where's ...?
Wo ist ...? — vaw ist ...

What's the address?
Wie ist die Adresse? — vee ist dee a·*dre*·se

How far is it?
Wie weit ist es? — vee vait ist es

Can you show me (on the map)?
Können Sie es mir (auf der Karte) zeigen? — *ker*·nen zee es meer (owf dair *kar*·te) *tsai*·gen

How can I get there?
Wie kann ich da hinkommen? — vee kan ikh dah *hin*·ko·men

EATING & DRINKING

I'd like to reserve a table for ...	*Ich möchte einen Tisch für ... reservieren.*	ikh *merkh*·te *ai*·nen tish für ... re·zer·*vee*·ren
(eight) o'clock	*(acht) Uhr*	(akht) oor
(two) people	*(zwei) Personen*	(tsvai) per·*zaw*·nen

I'd like the menu, please.
Ich hätte gern die Speisekarte, bitte. — ikh *he*·te gern dee *shpai*·ze·kar·te *bi*·te

What would you recommend?
Was empfehlen Sie? — vas emp·*fay*·len zee

I'm a vegetarian.
Ich bin Vegetarier/ Vegetarierin. (m/f) — ikh bin ve·ge·*tah*·ri·er/ ve·ge·*tah*·ri·e·rin

That was delicious.
Das hat hervorragend geschmeckt. — das hat her·*fawr*·rah·gent ge·*shmekt*

Cheers!
Prost! — prawst

Please bring the bill.
Bitte bringen Sie die Rechnung. — *bi*·te *bring*·en zee dee *rekh*·nung

Key Words

bar (pub)	*Kneipe*	*knai*·pe
bottle	*Flasche*	*fla*·she
breakfast	*Frühstück*	*frü*·shtük
cold	*kalt*	kalt
cup	*Tasse*	*ta*·se
desserts	*Nachspeisen*	*nahkh*·shpai·zen
dinner	*Abendessen*	*ah*·bent·e·sen
drink list	*Getränkekarte*	ge·*treng*·ke·kar·te
fork	*Gabel*	*gah*·bel
glass	*Glas*	glahs
hot (warm)	*warm*	warm
knife	*Messer*	*me*·ser
lunch	*Mittagessen*	*mi*·tahk·e·sen
market	*Markt*	markt
plate	*Teller*	*te*·ler
restaurant	*Restaurant*	res·to·*rahng*
spoon	*Löffel*	*ler*·fel
with/without	*mit/ohne*	mit/*aw*·ne

NUMBERS

1	*eins*	ains
2	*zwei*	tsvai
3	*drei*	drai
4	*vier*	feer
5	*fünf*	fünf
6	*sechs*	zeks
7	*sieben*	*zee*·ben
8	*acht*	akht
9	*neun*	noyn
10	*zehn*	tsayn
20	*zwanzig*	*tsvan*·tsikh
30	*dreißig*	*drai*·tsikh
40	*vierzig*	*feer*·tsikh
50	*fünfzig*	*fünf*·tsikh
60	*sechzig*	*zekh*·tsikh
70	*siebzig*	*zeep*·tsikh
80	*achtzig*	*akht*·tsikh
90	*neunzig*	*noyn*·tsikh
100	*hundert*	*hun*·dert
1000	*tausend*	*tow*·sent

Meat & Fish

beef	*Rindfleisch*	*rint*·flaish
carp	*Karpfen*	*karp*·fen
fish	*Fisch*	fish
herring	*Hering*	*hay*·ring
lamb	*Lammfleisch*	*lam*·flaish
meat	*Fleisch*	flaish
pork	*Schweinefleisch*	*shvai*·ne·flaish
poultry	*Geflügelfleisch*	ge·*flü*·gel·flaish
salmon	*Lachs*	laks
sausage	*Wurst*	vurst
seafood	*Meeresfrüchte*	*mair*·res·frükh·te
shellfish	*Schaltiere*	*shahl*·tee·re
trout	*Forelle*	fo·*re*·le
veal	*Kalbfleisch*	*kalp*·flaish

Fruit & Vegetables

apple	*Apfel*	*ap*·fel
banana	*Banane*	ba·*nah*·ne
bean	*Bohne*	*baw*·ne
cabbage	*Kraut*	krowt
capsicum	*Paprika*	*pap*·ri·kah
carrot	*Mohrrübe*	*mawr*·rü·be
cucumber	*Gurke*	*gur*·ke
grapes	*Weintrauben*	*vain*·trow·ben
lemon	*Zitrone*	tsi·*traw*·ne
lentil	*Linse*	*lin*·ze
lettuce	*Kopfsalat*	*kopf*·za·laht
mushroom	*Pilz*	pilts
nuts	*Nüsse*	*nü*·se
onion	*Zwiebel*	*tsvee*·bel
orange	*Orange*	o·*rahng*·zhe
pea	*Erbse*	*erp*·se
plum	*Pflaume*	*pflow*·me
potato	*Kartoffel*	kar·*to*·fel
spinach	*Spinat*	shpi·*naht*
strawberry	*Erdbeere*	*ert*·bair·re
tomato	*Tomate*	to·*mah*·te
watermelon	*Wasser-melone*	*va*·ser·me·law·ne

Other

bread	*Brot*	brawt
cheese	*Käse*	*kay*·ze
egg/eggs	*Ei/Eier*	ai/*ai*·er
honey	*Honig*	*haw*·nikh
jam	*Marmelade*	mar·me·*lah*·de
pasta	*Nudeln*	*noo*·deln
pepper	*Pfeffer*	*pfe*·fer
rice	*Reis*	rais
salt	*Salz*	zalts
soup	*Suppe*	*zu*·pe
sugar	*Zucker*	*tsu*·ker

Drinks

beer	*Bier*	beer
coffee	*Kaffee*	*ka*·fay
juice	*Saft*	zaft
milk	*Milch*	milkh
orange juice	*Orangensaft*	o·*rang*·zhen·zaft
red wine	*Rotwein*	*rawt*·vain
tea	*Tee*	tay
water	*Wasser*	*va*·ser
white wine	*Weißwein*	*vais*·vain

EMERGENCIES

Help!	*Hilfe!*	*hil*·fe
Go away!	*Gehen Sie weg!*	*gay*·en zee vek

Call the police!
Rufen Sie die Polizei! — roo·fen zee dee po·li·*tsai*

Call a doctor!
Rufen Sie einen Arzt! — roo·fen zee *ai*·nen artst

Where are the toilets?
Wo ist die Toilette? — vo ist dee to·a·*le*·te

I'm lost.
Ich habe mich verirrt. — ikh *hah*·be mikh fer·*irt*

I'm sick.
Ich bin krank. — ikh bin krangk

I'm allergic to ...
Ich bin allergisch gegen ... — ikh bin a·*lair*·gish *gay*·gen ...

SHOPPING & SERVICES

I'd like to buy ...
Ich möchte ... kaufen. — ikh *merkh*·te ... *kow*·fen

Can I look at it?
Können Sie es mir zeigen? — *ker*·nen zee es meer *tsai*·gen

How much is this?
Wie viel kostet das? — vee feel *kos*·tet das

That's too expensive.
Das ist zu teuer. — das ist tsoo *toy*·er

There's a mistake in the bill.
Da ist ein Fehler in der Rechnung. — dah ist ain *fay*·ler in dair *rekh*·nung

ATM	*Geldautomat*	*gelt*·ow·to·maht
post office	*Postamt*	*post*·amt
tourist office	*Fremden-verkehrsbüro*	*frem*·den·fer·kairs·bü·raw

SIGNS

Ausgang	Exit
Damen	Women
Eingang	Entrance
Geschlossen	Closed
Herren	Men
Offen	Open
Toiletten (WC)	Toilets
Verboten	Prohibited

TIME & DATES

What time is it?
Wie spät ist es? vee shpayt ist es

It's (10) o'clock.
Es ist (zehn) Uhr. es ist (tsayn) oor

At what time?
Um wie viel Uhr? um vee feel oor

At ...
Um ... um ...

morning	*Morgen*	*mor*·gen
afternoon	*Nachmittag*	*nahkh*·mi·tahk
evening	*Abend*	*ah*·bent
yesterday	*gestern*	*ges*·tern
today	*heute*	*hoy*·te
tomorrow	*morgen*	*mor*·gen

Monday	*Montag*	*mawn*·tahk
Tuesday	*Dienstag*	*deens*·tahk
Wednesday	*Mittwoch*	*mit*·vokh
Thursday	*Donnerstag*	*do*·ners·tahk
Friday	*Freitag*	*frai*·tahk
Saturday	*Samstag*	*zams*·tahk
Sunday	*Sonntag*	*zon*·tahk

TRANSPORT

boat	*Boot*	bawt
bus	*Bus*	bus
metro	*U-Bahn*	*oo*·bahn
plane	*Flugzeug*	*flook*·tsoyk
train	*Zug*	tsook

At what time's the ... bus?	*Wann fährt der ... Bus?*	van fairt dair... bus
first	*erste*	*ers*·te
last	*letzte*	*lets*·te
next	*nächste*	*naykhs*·te

A ... to (Linz).	*Eine ... nach (Linz).*	*ai*·ne ... nahkh (lins)
1st-/2nd-class ticket	*Fahrkarte erster/ zweiter Klasse*	*fahr*·kar·te *ers*·ter/ *tsvai*·ter *kla*·se
one-way ticket	*einfache Fahrkarte*	*ain*·fa·khe *fahr*·kar·te
return ticket	*Rückfahrkarte*	*rük*·fahr·kar·te

Does it stop at ...?
Hält es in ...? helt es in ...

What station is this?
Welcher Bahnhof ist das? *vel*·kher *bahn*·hawf ist das

QUESTION WORDS

What?	*Was?*	vas
When?	*Wann?*	van
Where?	*Wo?*	vaw
Who?	*Wer?*	vair
Why?	*Warum?*	va·rum

What's the next stop?
Welches ist der nächste Halt? *vel*·khes ist dair *naykh*·ste halt

I want to get off here.
Ich möchte hier aussteigen. ikh *merkh*·te heer *ows*·shtai·gen

Please tell me when we get to ....
Könnten Sie mir bitte sagen, wann wir in ... ankommen? *kern*·ten zee meer *bi*·te *zah*·gen van veer in ... *an*·ko·men

Please take me to (this address).
Bitte bringen Sie mich zu (dieser Adresse). *bi*·te *bring*·en zee mikh tsoo (*dee*·zer a·*dre*·se)

platform	*Bahnsteig*	*bahn*·shtaik
ticket office	*Fahrkarten-verkauf*	*fahr*·kar·ten·fer·kowf
timetable	*Fahrplan*	*fahr*·plan

I'd like to hire a ...	*Ich möchte ein ... mieten.*	ikh *merkh*·te ain ... *mee*·ten
bicycle	*Fahrrad*	*fahr*·raht
car	*Auto*	*ow*·to

How much is it per ...?	*Wie viel kostet es pro ...?*	vee feel *kos*·tet es praw ...
day	*Tag*	tahk
week	*Woche*	*vo*·khe

bicycle pump	*Fahrradpumpe*	*fahr*·raht·pum·pe
child seat	*Kindersitz*	*kin*·der·zits
helmet	*Helm*	helm
petrol	*Benzin*	ben·*tseen*

Does this road go to ...?
Führt diese Straße nach ...? fürt *dee*·ze *shtrah*·se nahkh ...

Can I park here?
Kann ich hier parken? kan ikh heer *par*·ken

Where's a petrol station?
Wo ist eine Tankstelle? vaw ist *ai*·ne *tangk*·shte·le

I need a mechanic.
Ich brauche einen Mechaniker. ikh *brow*·khe *ai*·nen me·*khah*·ni·ker

Are there cycling paths?
Gibt es Fahrradwege? geept es *fahr*·raht·vay·ge

Behind the Scenes

SEND US YOUR FEEDBACK

We love to hear from travellers – your comments keep us on our toes and help make our books better. Our well-travelled team reads every word on what you loved or loathed about this book. Although we cannot reply individually to your submissions, we always guarantee that your feedback goes straight to the appropriate authors, in time for the next edition. Each person who sends us information is thanked in the next edition – the most useful submissions are rewarded with a selection of digital PDF chapters.

Visit **lonelyplanet.com/contact** to submit your updates and suggestions or to ask for help. Our award-winning website also features inspirational travel stories, news and discussions.

Note: We may edit, reproduce and incorporate your comments in Lonely Planet products such as guidebooks, websites and digital products, so let us know if you don't want your comments reproduced or your name acknowledged. For a copy of our privacy policy visit lonelyplanet.com/privacy.

WRITER THANKS

Catherine Le Nevez

Vielen Dank first and foremost to Julian, as well as all the locals and fellow travellers in Vienna and throughout Austria for insights, information and good times during this update and over the years. Huge thanks, too, to my Vienna co-author Kerry and the Austria team, and to Brana Vladisavljevic, Dan Fahey, and everyone at LP. As ever, *merci encore* to my parents, brother, *belle-sœur*, *neveu* and *nièce*.

Kerry Walker

A big thank you goes out to all the people who I met on my Austria travels, including tourism professionals Bettina Jamy-Stowasser and Helena Hartlauer in Vienna, Martina Trummer in Salzburg, and Peter Unsinn in Innsbruck. Special thanks, too, to Eugene Quinn at Space and Place in Vienna and Maggie Ritson in St Anton for ideas and inspiration.

Marc Di Duca

Huge thanks go to Manuela of Weingut Burg Taggenbrunn and all the staff at various tourist offices around the region, but in particular those in Klagenfurt, Krems and Eisenstadt. Finally, enormous thanks to my wife, Tanya, for holding the fort while I was away researching.

ACKNOWLEDGEMENTS

Climate map data adapted from Peel MC, Finlayson BL & McMahon TA (2007) 'Updated World Map of the Köppen-geiger Claime Classification', Hydrology and Earth System Sciences, 11, 163344. Cover photograph: Kunsthistorisches Museum Vienna, Gonzalo Azumendi/Getty Images ©

THIS BOOK

This 9th edition of Lonely Planet's *Vienna* guidebook was researched and written by Catherine Le Nevez, Kerry Walker and Marc Di Duca. The previous two editions were written by Anthony Haywood, Catherine, Kerry and Donna Wheeler. This guidebook was produced by the following:

Destination Editor Brana Vladisavljevic
Senior Product Editors Daniel Bolger, Sandie Kestell, Genna Patterson
Regional Senior Cartographer Mark Griffiths
Product Editor Fergus O'Shea
Book Designer Jessica Rose
Assisting Editors Nigel Chin, Victoria Harrison,Trent Holden, Jodie Martire, Kristin Odijk, Charlotte Orr
Cover Researcher Meri Blazevski
Thanks to Carolyn Boicos, Gwen Cotter, Jeffrey Dudgeon, Mark Ebery, Amy Lynch, Randy Presant, Angela Tinson

Index

See also separate subindexes for:

- EATING P230
- DRINKING & NIGHTLIFE P230
- ENTERTAINMENT P231
- SHOPPING P231
- SLEEPING P232
- SPORTS & ACTIVITIES P232

Sights 000
Map Pages **000**
Photo Pages **000**

EATING

Sights 000
Map Pages **000**
Photo Pages **000**

DRINKING & NIGHTLIFE

☆ ENTERTAINMENT

SHOPPING

Vienna Maps

Sights

- Beach
- Bird Sanctuary
- Buddhist
- Castle/Palace
- Christian
- Confucian
- Hindu
- Islamic
- Jain
- Jewish
- Monument
- Museum/Gallery/Historic Building
- Ruin
- Shinto
- Sikh
- Taoist
- Winery/Vineyard
- Zoo/Wildlife Sanctuary
- Other Sight

Activities, Courses & Tours

- Bodysurfing
- Diving
- Canoeing/Kayaking
- Course/Tour
- Sento Hot Baths/Onsen
- Skiing
- Snorkelling
- Surfing
- Swimming/Pool
- Walking
- Windsurfing
- Other Activity

Sleeping

- Sleeping
- Camping
- Hut/Shelter

Eating

- Eating

Drinking & Nightlife

- Drinking & Nightlife
- Cafe

Entertainment

- Entertainment

Shopping

- Shopping

Information

- Bank
- Embassy/Consulate
- Hospital/Medical
- Internet
- Police
- Post Office
- Telephone
- Toilet
- Tourist Information
- Other Information

Geographic

- Beach
- Gate
- Hut/Shelter
- Lighthouse
- Lookout
- Mountain/Volcano
- Oasis
- Park
- Pass
- Picnic Area
- Waterfall

Population

- Capital (National)
- Capital (State/Province)
- City/Large Town
- Town/Village

Transport

- Airport
- Border crossing
- Bus
- Cable car/Funicular
- Cycling
- Ferry
- Metro station
- Monorail
- Parking
- Petrol station
- S-Bahn/Subway station
- Taxi
- T-bane/Tunnelbana station
- Train station/Railway
- Tram
- U-Bahn/Underground station
- Other Transport

Routes

- Tollway
- Freeway
- Primary
- Secondary
- Tertiary
- Lane
- Unsealed road
- Road under construction
- Plaza/Mall
- Steps
- Tunnel
- Pedestrian overpass
- Walking Tour
- Walking Tour detour
- Path/Walking Trail

Boundaries

- International
- State/Province
- Disputed
- Regional/Suburb
- Marine Park
- Cliff
- Wall

Hydrography

- River, Creek
- Intermittent River
- Canal
- Water
- Dry/Salt/Intermittent Lake
- Reef

Areas

- Airport/Runway
- Beach/Desert
- Cemetery (Christian)
- Cemetery (Other)
- Glacier
- Mudflat
- Park/Forest
- Sight (Building)
- Sportsground
- Swamp/Mangrove

Note: Not all symbols displayed above appear on the maps in this book

MAP INDEX

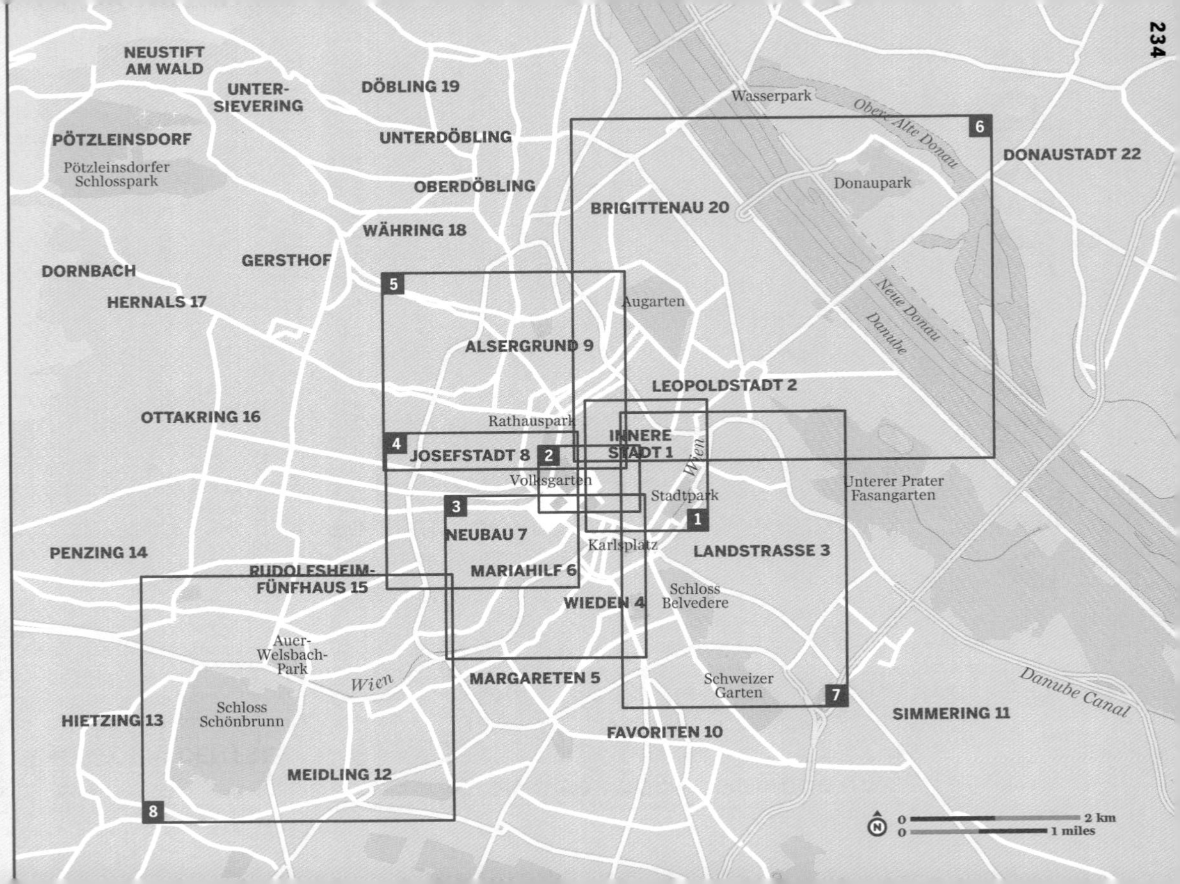

NEUSTIFT AM WALD
UNTER-SIEVERING
DÖBLING 19
PÖTZLEINSDORF
Pötzleinsdorfer Schlosspark
UNTERDÖBLING
OBERDÖBLING
WÄHRING 18
GERSTHOF
DORNBACH
HERNALS 17
BRIGITTENAU 20
Wasserpark
Obere Alte Donau
Donaupark
DONAUSTADT 22
Neue Donau
Danube
Augarten
ALSERGRUND 9
LEOPOLDSTADT 2
OTTAKRING 16
Rathauspark
INNERE STADT 1
JOSEFSTADT 8
Volksgarten
Wien
Stadtpark
Unterer Prater Fasangarten
NEUBAU 7
Karlsplatz
LANDSTRASSE 3
PENZING 14
RUDOLFSHEIM-FÜNFHAUS 15
MARIAHILF 6
WIEDEN 4
Schloss Belvedere
Auer-Welsbach-Park
Wien
MARGARETEN 5
Schweizer Garten
Danube Canal
Schloss Schönbrunn
HIETZING 13
SIMMERING 11
FAVORITEN 10
MEIDLING 12
1
2
3
4
5
6
7
8
N
0
2 km
0
1 miles

STEPHANSDOM & THE HISTORIC CENTRE *Map on p236*

Top Sights (p75)
1 Haus der Musik ... C7
2 Stephansdom ... C5

Sights (p77)
3 Am Hof ... A3
4 Ankeruhr ... D3
Cathedral Pummerin ... (see 2)
Cathedral South Tower ... (see 2)
5 Dokumentationsarchiv des Österreichischen Widerstandes ... C3
6 Dom- & Diözesanmuseum ... D4
7 Dominikanerkirche ... E4
8 Dr-Ignaz-Seipel-Platz ... E4
Fleischmarkt ... (see 10)
9 Franziskanerkirche ... D6
Graben ... (see 21)
10 Griechenkirche zur Heiligen Dreifaltigkeit ... E3
11 Holocaust-Denkmal ... B3
12 Jesuitenkirche ... E4
13 Kirche Am Hof ... B3
14 Literaturmuseum ... C6
15 Maria am Gestade ... B2
Monument to the Victims of Fascism ... (see 16)
16 Morzinplatz ... D2
17 Mozarthaus Vienna ... D5
18 Museum Judenplatz ... B3
19 Neidhart-Fresken ... C3
20 Österreichische Akademie der Wissenschaften ... E4
21 Pestsäule ... B5
22 Peterskirche ... B4
23 Postsparkasse ... F4
24 Römer Museum ... C3
25 Ruprechtskirche ... D3
26 Stadttempel ... D3
Stephansdom Katakomben ... (see 2)
27 Uhren Museum ... B3

Eating (p82)
28 Artner ... D6
29 Beim Czaak ... E4
30 Brezl Gwölb ... B3
31 Café Korb ... C4
32 Figlmüller ... D4
33 Figlmüller ... D4
34 Griechenbeisl ... E3
35 Huth Gastwirtschaft ... D7
36 Konstantin Filippou ... F3
37 Motto am Fluss ... E3
38 Plachutta ... E5
39 Simply Raw Bakery ... B3
40 Tian ... D6
41 Wrenkh ... C4
42 Zanoni & Zanoni ... D4
43 Zum Schwarzen Kameel ... B4

Drinking & Nightlife (p84)
44 1516 Brewing Company ... C7
45 Café Prückel ... F5
46 Diglas ... D5
47 Enrico Panigl ... E4
48 Fenster Café ... E3
49 Kaffee Alt Wien ... D4
50 Kleines Café ... D6
51 Kruger's American Bar ... C7
52 Needle Vinyl Bar ... B3
53 Sky Bar ... C6
54 Vinothek W-Einkehr ... E3
Vis-à-vis ... (see 32)
55 Why Not? ... B2
56 Zwölf Apostelkeller ... D4

Entertainment (p86)
57 Gartenbaukino ... E6
58 Jazzland ... D3
59 Metro Kinokulturhaus ... C6
60 Porgy & Bess ... E6
61 Roncher ... D6

Shopping (p86)
62 Altmann & Kühne ... C5
63 Cuisinarum ... C5
64 Schau Schau ... D4
65 So Austria ... D4
Steffl ... (see 53)
66 Unger und Klein ... C2
67 Vom Fass ... C4
68 Wald & Wiese ... E5
69 Wein & Co ... C4
70 Woka ... D5

Sports & Activities (p87)
71 Badeschiff ... G3
72 DDSG Blue Danube ... E3
73 Hotrod Tour Wien ... D3
74 ÖTK ... E4
75 Ring Tram ... E3
76 Vienna Explorer ... C1
Wrenkh Cookery School ... (see 41)

Sleeping (p187)
77 DO & CO ... C5
78 Grand Ferdinand Hotel ... D8
79 Hotel Austria ... E4
80 Hotel Capricorno ... E3
81 Hotel Kärntner Hof ... D4
82 Ruby Lissi ... E4

STEPHANSDOM & THE HISTORIC CENTRE

Key on p235

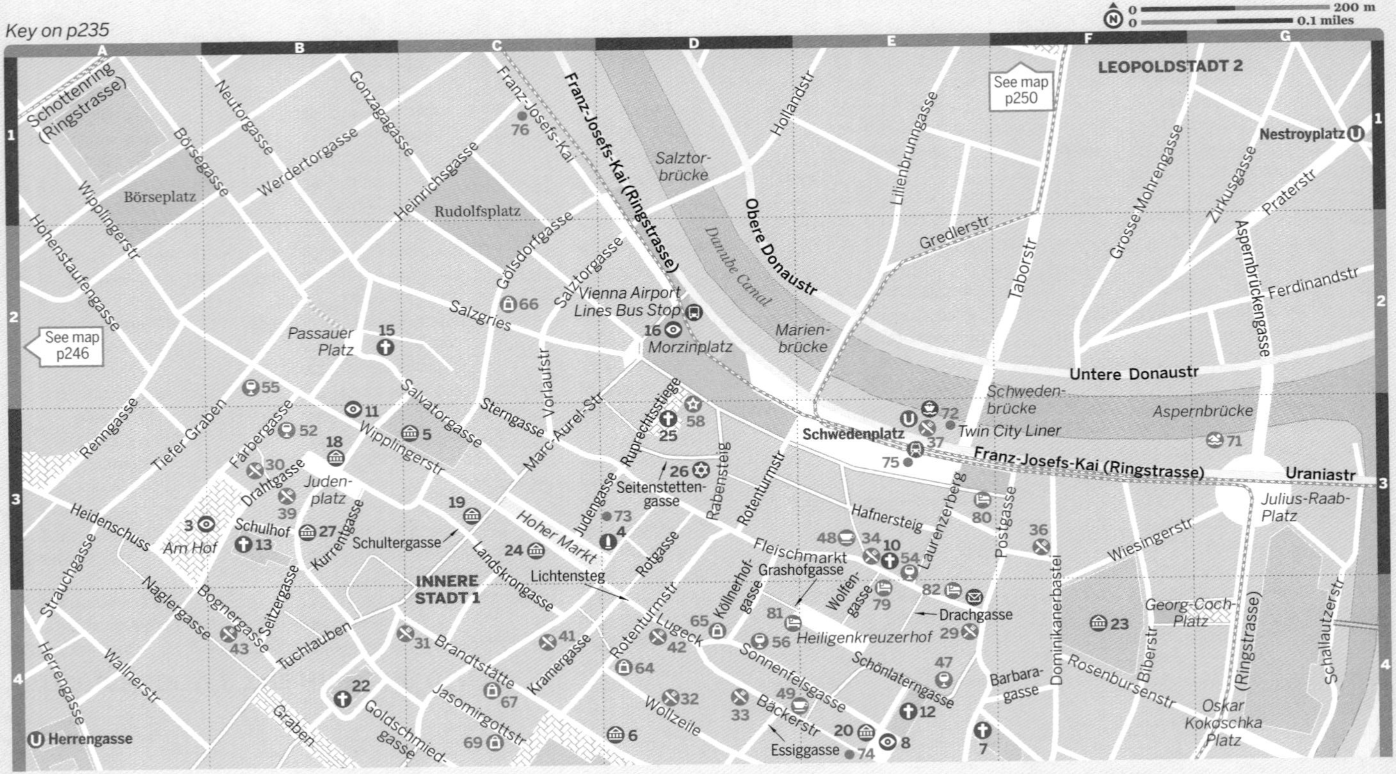

STEPHANSDOM & THE HISTORIC CENTRE

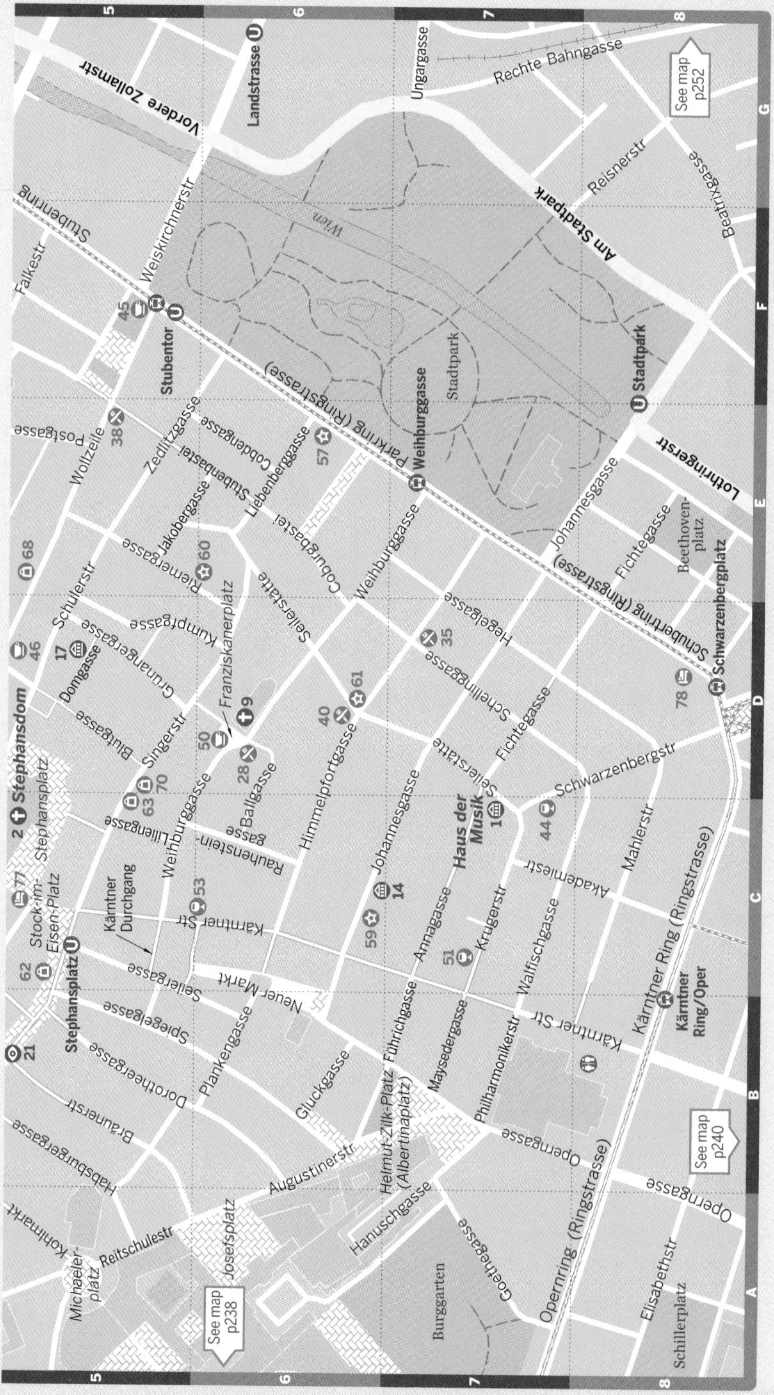

THE HOFBURG & AROUND

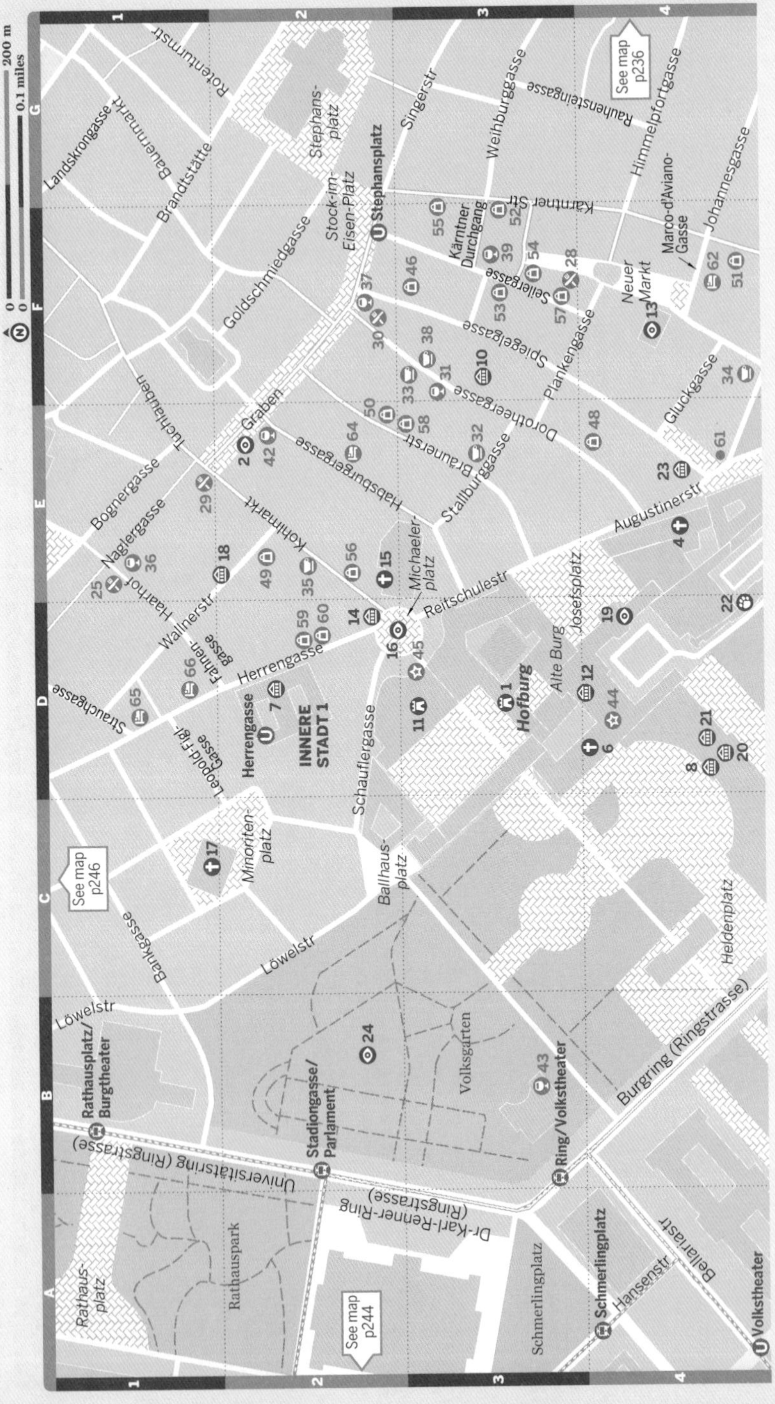

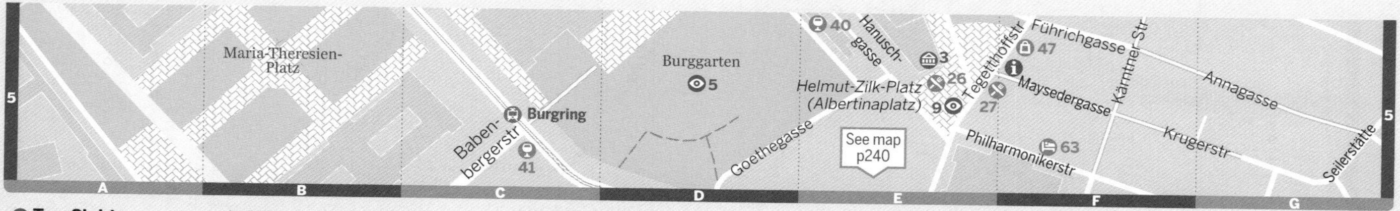

Top Sights **(p60)**
1 Hofburg D3

Sights **(p66)**
2 Adolf Loos' Public Toilets E2
3 Albertina E5
4 Augustinerkirche E4
5 Burggarten D5
6 Burgkapelle D4
Esperantomuseum .... (see 7)
7 Globenmuseum D2
8 Haus der Geschichte Österreich D4
9 Helmut-Zilk-Platz E5
10 Jüdisches Museum F3
11 Kaiserappartements D3
12 Kaiserliche Schatzkammer D4
13 Kapuzinergruft F4
Kapuzinerkirche .... (see 13)
14 Loos Haus D2
Mahnmal Gegen Krieg und Faschismus .... (see 9)
15 Michaelerkirche E2
16 Michaelerplatz Roman Ruins D2
17 Minoritenkirche C1
18 Museum der Illusionen E2
19 Nationalbibliothek Prunksaal D4
20 Neue Burg Museums D4
21 Papyrusmuseum D4
22 Schmetterlinghaus D4
Silberkammer .... (see 11)
Sisi Museum .... (see 11)
23 TheaterMuseum E4
24 Volksgarten B2

Eating **(p68)**
25 Bierhof E1
26 Bitzinger Würstelstand am Albertinaplatz E5
27 Café Mozart E5
28 Le Bol F3
29 Meinl's Restaurant E1
Restaurant Herrlich .... (see 66)
30 Trześniewski F2

Drinking & Nightlife **(p69)**
31 Blue Mustard F3
32 Café Bräunerhof E3
33 Café Leopold Hawelka F3
Café Sacher .... (see 63)
34 Café Tirolerhof F4
35 Demel E2
36 Esterházykeller E1
37 Fledermaus F2
38 Kaffee Rösterei Hawelka F3
39 Loos American Bar F3
Meinl's Weinbar .... (see 29)
40 Palmenhaus E5
41 Passage C5
42 Villon E2
43 Volksgarten ClubDiskothek B3

Entertainment **(p71)**
Burgkapelle Vienna Boys' Choir Tickets .... (see 6)
44 Hofburg Concert Halls D4
Österreichisches Filmmuseum .... (see 3)
45 Spanish Riding School D3

Shopping **(p71)**
46 Augarten Wien F3
47 Bonbons Anzinger F5
48 Dorotheum E4
49 Freytag & Berndt E2
50 Gmundner E2
51 J&L Lobmeyr Vienna F4
Julius Meinl am Graben .... (see 29)
52 Lanz F3
53 Mühlbauer F3
54 Oberlaa F3
55 Österreichische Werkstätten F3
56 Rozet und Fischmeister E2
57 Schella Kann F3
58 Steiff E3
59 United Nude D2
60 Zuckerlwerkstatt D2

Sports & Activities
61 Redbus City Tours E4

Sleeping **(p187)**
62 Aviano F4
63 Hotel Sacher F5
64 Pertschy Palais Hotel E2
65 Radisson Blu Style Hotel D1
66 Steigenberger Hotel Herrenhof D1

Key on p242

KARLSPLATZ & AROUND NASCHMARKT

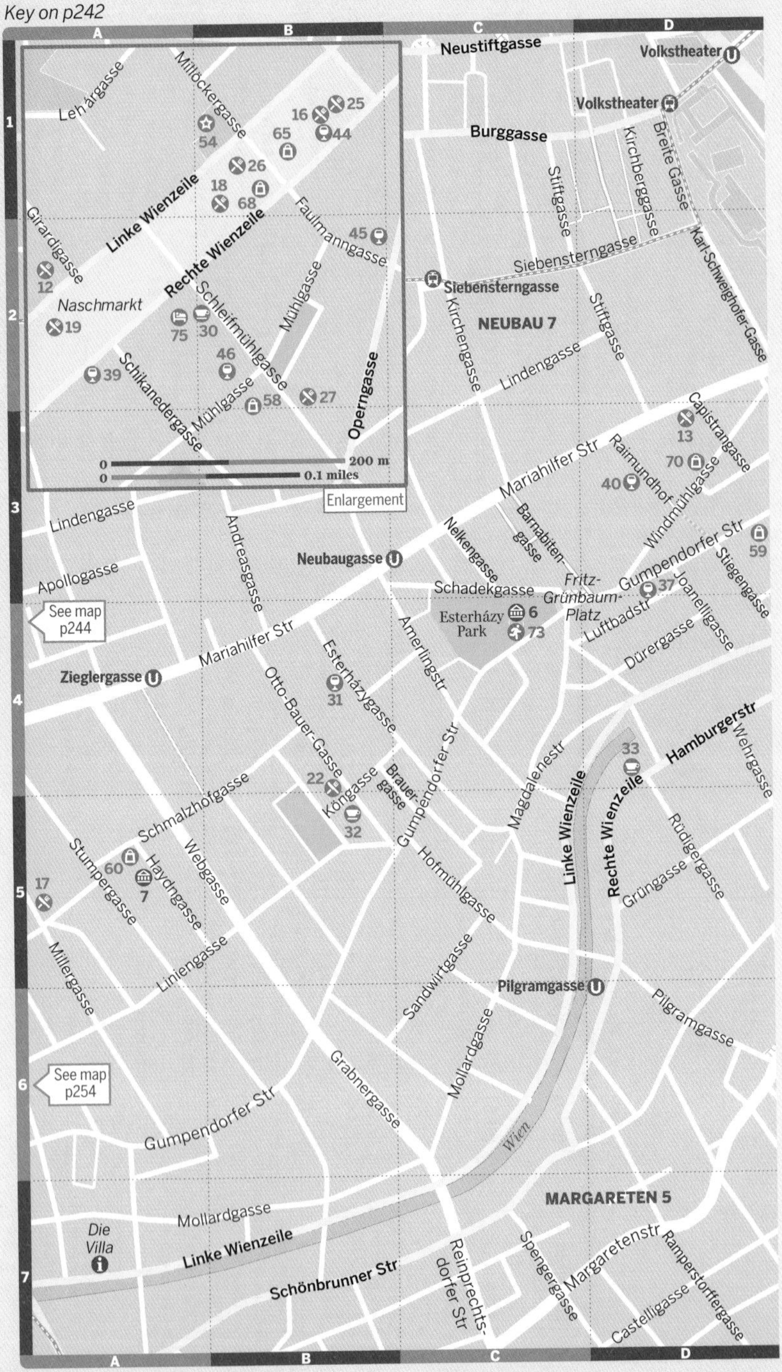

Neustiftgasse
Volkstheater
Volkstheater
Burggasse
Stiftgasse
Kirchberggasse
Breite Gasse
Siebensterngasse
Siebensterngasse
Karl-Schweighofer-Gasse
NEUBAU 7
Kirchengasse
Stiftgasse
Lindengasse
Capistrangasse
Mariahilfer Str
Raimundhof
Windmühlgasse
Barnabitengasse
Nelkengasse
Neubaugasse
Gumpendorfer Str
Stiegengasse
Schadekgasse
Fritz-Grünbaum-Platz
Esterházy Park
Luftbadstr
Joanelligasse
Dürergasse
Lindengasse
Apollogasse
See map p244
Andreasgasse
Mariahilfer Str
Zieglergasse
Esterházygasse
Amerlingstr
Otto-Bauer-Gasse
Gumpendorfer Str
Magdalenestr
Hamburgerstr
Wehrgasse
Linke Wienzeile
Rechte Wienzeile
Köngasse
Brauergasse
Schmalzhofgasse
Stumpergasse
Haydngasse
Webgasse
Hofmühlgasse
Rüdigergasse
Grüngasse
Millergasse
Liniengasse
Sandwirtgasse
Pilgramgasse
Pilgramgasse
Mollardgasse
See map p254
Grabnergasse
Gumpendorfer Str
Wien
MARGARETEN 5
Mollardgasse
Die Villa
Linke Wienzeile
Reinprechtsdorfer Str
Spengergasse
Margaretenstr
Ramperstorffergasse
Schönbrunner Str
Castelligasse
Lehárgasse
Millöckergasse
Linke Wienzeile
Rechte Wienzeile
Faulmanngasse
Girardigasse
Naschmarkt
Schleifmühlgasse
Mühlgasse
Schikanedergasse
Mühlgasse
Operngasse
0 200 m
0 0.1 miles
Enlargement

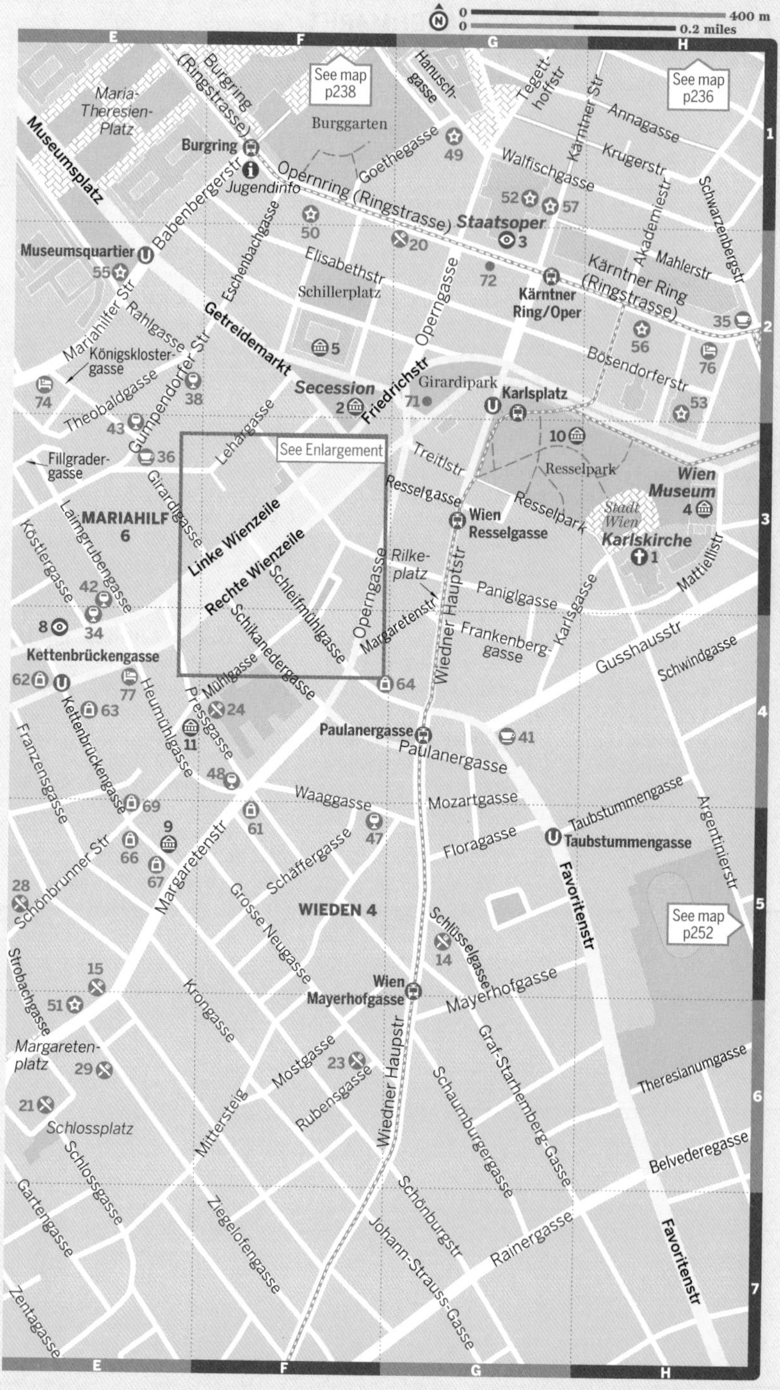
KARLSPLATAZ & AROUND NASHMARKT
0
400 m
0
0.2 miles
See map p238
See map p236
See map p252
See Enlargement
Maria-Theresien-Platz
Museumsplatz
Burgring (Ringstrasse)
Burgring
Burggarten
Jugendinfo
Opernring (Ringstrasse)
Goethegasse
Hanusch-gasse
Tegett-hoffstr
Kärntner Str
Annagasse
Krugerstr
Walfischgasse
Akademiestr
Schwarzenbergstr
Mahlerstr
Staatsoper
Kärntner Ring (Ringstrasse)
Kärntner Ring/Oper
Museumsquartier
Babenbergerstr
Eschenbachgasse
Elisabethstr
Schillerplatz
Getreidemarkt
Operngasse
Mariahilfer Str
Rahlgasse
Königsklostergasse
Gumpendorfer Str
Theobaldgasse
Secession
Friedrichstr
Girardipark
Karlsplatz
Bösendorferstr
Lehargasse
Fillgradergasse
Treitlstr
Resselpark
Wien Museum
Resselgasse
Wien Resselgasse
Stadt Wien
Karlskirche
MARIAHILF 6
Girardigasse
Linke Wienzeile
Rechte Wienzeile
Schleifmühlgasse
Rilke-platz
Paniglgasse
Mattiellistr
Karlsgasse
Köstlergasse
Laimgrubengasse
Schikanedergasse
Margaretenstr
Wiedner Hauptstr
Frankenberg-gasse
Gusshausstr
Schwindgasse
Kettenbrückengasse
Mühlgasse
Heumühlgasse
Pressgasse
Paulanergasse
Franzensgasse
Kettenbrückengasse
Waaggasse
Mozartgasse
Taubstummengasse
Argentinierstr
Floragasse
Schönbrunner Str
Schäffergasse
Favoritenstr
Grosse Neugasse
WIEDEN 4
Schlüsselgasse
Strobachgasse
Krongasse
Wien Mayerhofgasse
Mayerhofgasse
Margaretenplatz
Graf-Starhemberg-Gasse
Mostgasse
Rubensgasse
Schaumburgergasse
Theresianumgasse
Mittersteig
Schlossplatz
Schlossgasse
Belvederegasse
Schönburgstr
Gartengasse
Ziegelofengasse
Rainergasse
Johann-Strauss-Gasse
Zentagasse

KARLSPLATZ & AROUND NASCHMARKT *Map on p240*

MUSEUM DISTRICT & NEUBAU *Map on p244*

Key on p243

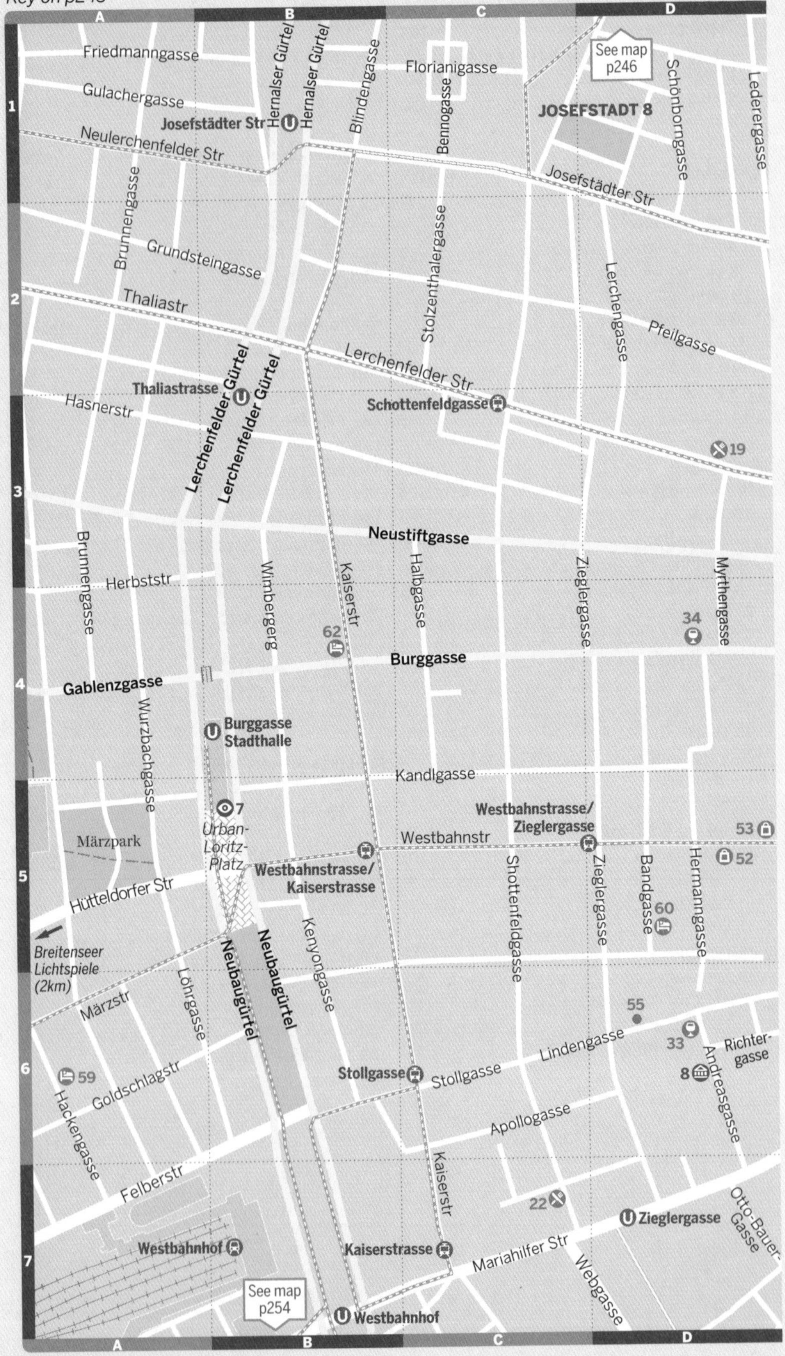
A
B
C
D
1
2
3
4
5
6
7
See map p246
See map p254
JOSEFSTADT 8
Friedmanngasse
Gulachergasse
Josefstädter Str
Hernalser Gürtel
Hernalser Gürtel
Blindengasse
Florianigasse
Bennogasse
Schönborngasse
Lederergasse
Neulerchenfelder Str
Josefstädter Str
Brunnengasse
Grundsteingasse
Stolzenthalergasse
Lerchengasse
Pfeilgasse
Thaliastr
Lerchenfelder Str
Thaliastrasse
Lerchenfelder Gürtel
Lerchenfelder Gürtel
Hasnerstr
Schottenfeldgasse
19
Neustiftgasse
Brunnengasse
Herbststr
Wimberggasse
Kaiserstr
Halbgasse
Zieglergasse
Myrthengasse
34
62
Burggasse
Gablenzgasse
Wurzbachgasse
Burggasse Stadthalle
Kandlgasse
7
Urban-Loritz-Platz
Westbahnstrasse/ Zieglergasse
Märzpark
Westbahnstr
53
52
Westbahnstrasse/ Kaiserstrasse
Shottenfeldgasse
Zieglergasse
Bandgasse
Hermanngasse
60
Hütteldorfer Str
Breitenseer Lichtspiele (2km)
Neubaugürtel
Neubaugürtel
Kenyongasse
Märzstr
Löhrgasse
55
33
Richter-gasse
Lindengasse
59
Goldschlagstr
Stollgasse
Stollgasse
8
Andreasgasse
Hackengasse
Apollogasse
Felberstr
Kaiserstr
22
Zieglergasse
Otto-Bauer-Gasse
Westbahnhof
Kaiserstrasse
Mariahilfer Str
Webgasse
Westbahnhof

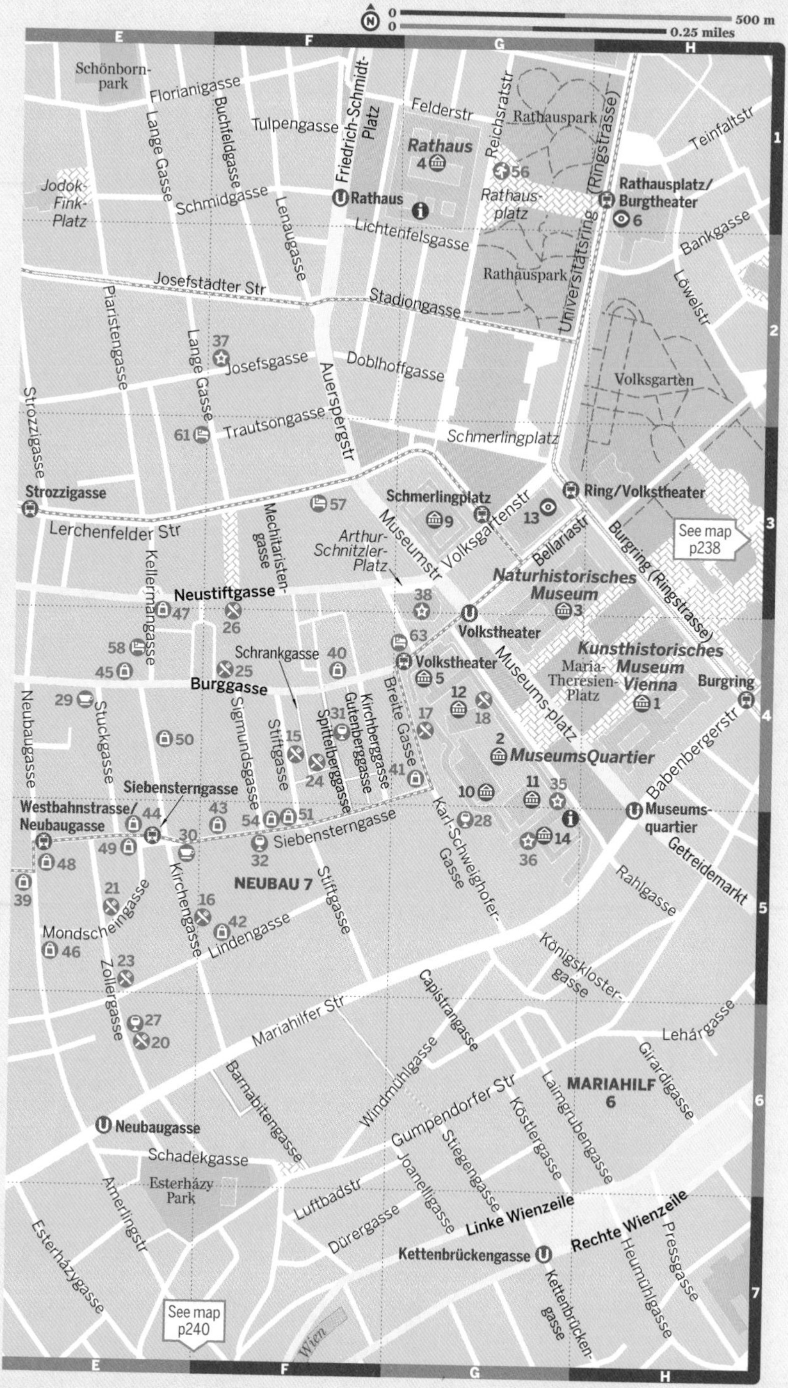
0 500 m
0 0.25 miles
E
F
G
H
1
2
3
4
5
6
7
Schönborn-park
Florianigasse
Buchfeldgasse
Lange Gasse
Tulpengasse
Friedrich-Schmidt-Platz
Felderstr
Reichsratsstr
Rathauspark
Teinfaltstr
Rathaus
4
56
Jodok-Fink-Platz
Schmidgasse
Lenaugasse
Rathaus
Rathausplatz
Rathausplatz/ Burgtheater
6
Lichtenfelsgasse
Universitätsring (Ringstrasse)
Bankgasse
Rathauspark
Löwelstr
Josefstädter Str
Stadiongasse
Piaristengasse
Lange Gasse
37
Josefsgasse
Doblhoffgasse
Auerspergstr
Volksgarten
Strozzigasse
Trautsongasse
61
Schmerlingplatz
Strozzigasse
57
Schmerlingplatz
9
Ring/Volkstheater
13
Volksgartenstr
Lerchenfelder Str
Mechitaristen-gasse
Museumstr
Arthur-Schnitzler-Platz
Bellariastr
Burgring (Ringstrasse)
See map p238
Kellermanngasse
Neustiftgasse
47
26
Naturhistorisches Museum
38
3
Volkstheater
63
58
Schrankgasse
40
Kunsthistorisches Museum Vienna
45
25
Volkstheater
Museums-platz
Maria-Theresien-Platz
Burggasse
5
Burgring
29
Neubaugasse
Stuckgasse
Sigmundsgasse
12
18
1
31
Kirchberggasse
Gutenberggasse
Spittelberggasse
17
Breite Gasse
50
15
Stiftgasse
2
MuseumsQuartier
24
Babenbergerstr
41
Siebensterngasse
10
11
35
Westbahnstrasse/ Neubaugasse
44
43
54
51
Karl-Schweighofer-Gasse
Museums-quartier
28
Siebensterngasse
14
49
30
32
36
48
Getreidemarkt
39
Kirchengasse
NEUBAU 7
Stiftgasse
Rahlgasse
21
16
Mondscheingasse
42
Lindengasse
46
Königsklostergasse
23
Zollergasse
Capistrangasse
Mariahilfer Str
27
20
Lehárgasse
Windmühlgasse
Girardigasse
Barnabitengasse
MARIAHILF 6
Laimgrubengasse
Köstlergasse
Gumpendorfer Str
Neubaugasse
Stiegengasse
Schadekgasse
Esterházy Park
Amerlingstr
Joanelligasse
Luftbadstr
Linke Wienzeile
Dürergasse
Rechte Wienzeile
Pressgasse
Heumühlgasse
Kettenbrückengasse
Esterházygasse
Kettenbrücken-gasse
See map p240
Wien

Key on p248

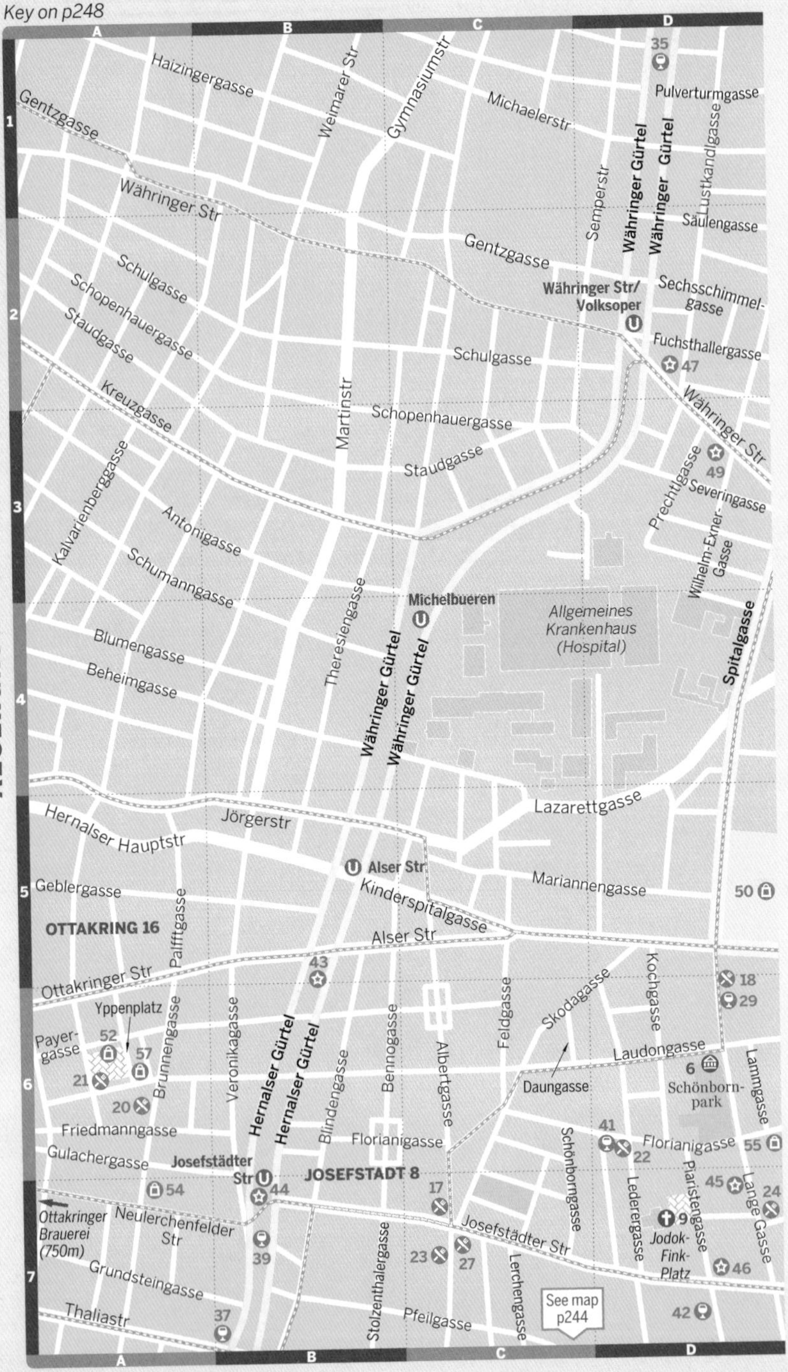
A
B
C
D
1
2
3
4
5
6
7
Haizingergasse
Gentzgasse
Weimarer Str
Gymnasiumstr
Michaelerstr
Pulverturmgasse
35
Währinger Str
Semperstr
Währinger Gürtel
Währinger Gürtel
Lustkandlgasse
Säulengasse
Gentzgasse
Schulgasse
Schopenhauergasse
Staudgasse
Währinger Str/
Volksoper
Sechsschimmel-
gasse
Fuchsthallergasse
47
Schulgasse
Kreuzgasse
Martinstr
Schopenhauergasse
Währinger Str
49
Staudgasse
Prechtlgasse
Severingasse
Kalvarienberggasse
Antonigasse
Schumanngasse
Wilhelm-Exner-
Gasse
Michelbueren
Allgemeines
Krankenhaus
(Hospital)
Theresiengasse
Spitalgasse
Blumengasse
Beheimgasse
Währinger Gürtel
Währinger Gürtel
Lazarettgasse
Hernalser Hauptstr
Jörgerstr
Alser Str
Mariannengasse
Geblergasse
Kinderspitalgasse
50
OTTAKRING 16
Palffgasse
Alser Str
Ottakringer Str
43
Kochgasse
18
29
Yppenplatz
Skodagasse
Feldgasse
Payer-
gasse
52
57
Brunnengasse
Veronikagasse
Hernalser Gürtel
Hernalser Gürtel
Bennogasse
Albertgasse
Laudongasse
Lammgasse
21
6
Daungasse
Schönborn-
park
20
Blindengasse
Friedmanngasse
Florianigasse
41
Florianigasse
55
Gulachergasse
Josefstädter
Str
22
Schönborngasse
JOSEFSTADT 8
Piaristengasse
45
24
54
44
17
Ledergasse
Lange Gasse
Ottakringer
Brauerei
(750m)
Neulerchenfelder
Str
9
Josefstädter Str
Jodok-
Fink-
Platz
39
23
27
Stolzenthalergasse
46
Grundsteingasse
Lerchengasse
See map
p244
Thaliastr
37
Pfeilgasse
42

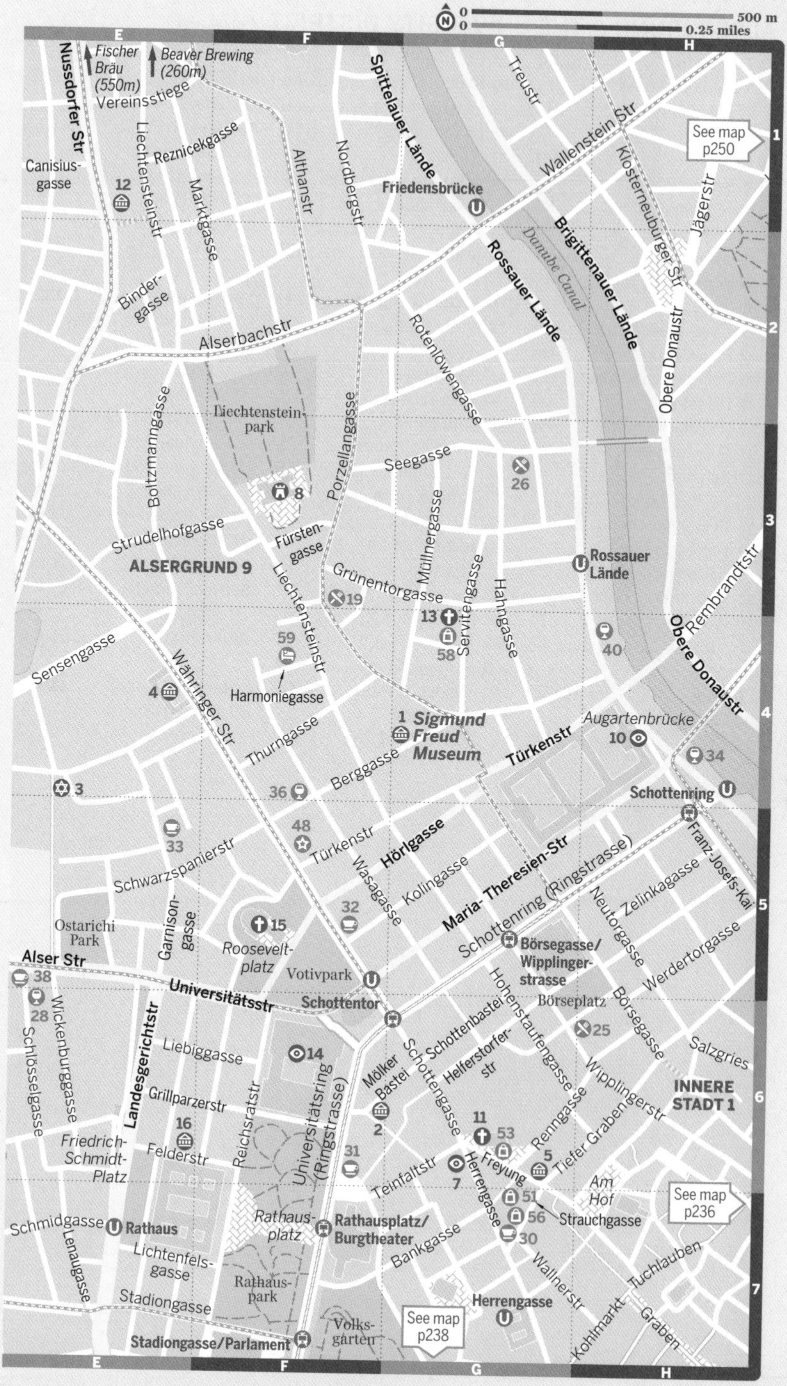
0 500 m
0 0.25 miles
E
F
G
H
1
2
3
4
5
6
7
Fischer Bräu (550m)
Beaver Brewing (260m)
Nussdorfer Str
Vereinsstiege
Liechtensteinstr
Reznicekgasse
Canisius-gasse
12
Marktgasse
Althanstr
Nordbergstr
Spittelauer Lände
Friedensbrücke
Treustr
Wallenstein Str
See map p250
Klosterneuburger Str
Jägerstr
Danube Canal
Brigittenauer Lände
Rossauer Lände
Binder-gasse
Alserbachstr
Rotenlöwengasse
Obere Donaustr
Boltzmanngasse
Liechtenstein-park
Porzellangasse
Seegasse
26
8
Müllnergasse
Strudelhofgasse
Fürsten-gasse
ALSERGRUND 9
Grünentorgasse
Servitengasse
Hahngasse
Rossauer Lände
19
13
58
59
40
Rembrandtstr
Obere Donaustr
Sensengasse
Währinger Str
Liechtensteinstr
Harmoniegasse
4
1 Sigmund Freud Museum
Augartenbrücke
10
Thurngasse
Türkenstr
34
3
Berggasse
36
Schottenring
48
33
Türkenstr
Hörlgasse
Maria-Theresien-Str
Schottenring (Ringstrasse)
Franz-Josefs-Kai
Schwarzspanierstr
Wasagasse
Kolingasse
Neutorgasse
Zelinkagasse
32
Garnison-gasse
Ostarichi Park
15
Roosevelt-platz
Börsegasse/ Wipplinger-strasse
Werdertorgasse
Alser Str
38
28
Votivpark
Universitätsstr
Schottentor
Börseplatz
Börsegasse
Hohenstaufengasse
Schottenbastei
25
Salzgries
Wickenburggasse
Schlösselgasse
Landesgerichtstr
Liebiggasse
14
Mölker Bastei
Schottengasse
Helferstorfer-str
Wipplingerstr
INNERE STADT 1
Grillparzerstr
Reichsratstr
Universitätsring (Ringstrasse)
2
11
53
Renngasse
Friedrich-Schmidt-Platz
16
Felderstr
31
Teinfaltstr
7
Herrengasse
Freyung
5
Tiefer Graben
Am Hof
See map p236
51
56
Strauchgasse
Schmidgasse
Rathaus
Lenaugasse
Rathaus-platz
Rathausplatz/ Burgtheater
30
Lichtenfels-gasse
Bankgasse
Wallnerstr
Tuchlauben
Rathaus-park
Stadiongasse
Herrengasse
Kohlmarkt
Graben
See map p238
Stadiongasse/Parlament
Volks-garten

ALSERGRUND & THE UNIVERSITY DISTRICT *Map on p246*

Top Sights (p125)

1 Sigmund Freud Museum G4

Sights (p124)

2 Beethoven Pasqualatihaus F6
3 Bethaus E4
4 Josephinum E4
5 Kunstforum G6
6 Museum für Volkskunde D6
7 Palais Daun-Kinsky G6
8 Palais Liechtenstein F3
9 Piaristenkirche D7
10 Rossauer Kaserne H4
11 Schottenkirche G6
12 Schubert Geburtshaus E1
13 Servitenkirche G4
14 University Main Building F6
15 Votivkirche F5
16 Wien Museum MUSA E6

Eating (p128)

17 Café Hummel C7
18 Crème de la Crème D6
19 Gasthaus Wickerl F3
20 Kent A6
21 La Salvia A6
22 La Tavolozza D6
23 Mamamon C7
24 Schnattl D7
25 Soupkultur H6
26 Stomach G3
27 Swing Kitchen C7

Drinking & Nightlife (p129)

28 Achtundzwanzig E6
29 Birdyard D6
Botanical Gardens .... (see 32)
30 Café Central G7
31 Café Landtmann F6
32 Café Stein F5
33 CafféCouture E5
34 Flex H4
35 Halbestadt Bar D1
36 Krypt F4
37 Loft B7
38 POC Cafe E5
39 Rhiz B7
40 Summer Stage H4
41 Tunnel D6
42 Weinstube Josefstadt D7

Entertainment (p131)

43 B72 .... B5
44 Café Carina B7
45 Miles Smiles D7
46 Theater in der Josefstadt D7
47 Volksoper D2
48 Votivkino F5
49 WUK D3

Shopping (p132)

50 Altes AKH Christmas Market D5
51 Altwiener Christkindlmarkt auf der Freyung G7
52 Bauernmarkt Yppenplatz A6
53 Bio-Markt Freyung G6
54 Brunnenmarkt A7
55 Die Höllerei D6
56 Palais Ferstel G7
57 Staud's A6
58 Xocolat G4

Sleeping (p189)

59 Hotel Harmonie F4

PRATER & EAST OF THE DANUBE *Map on p250*

Key on p249

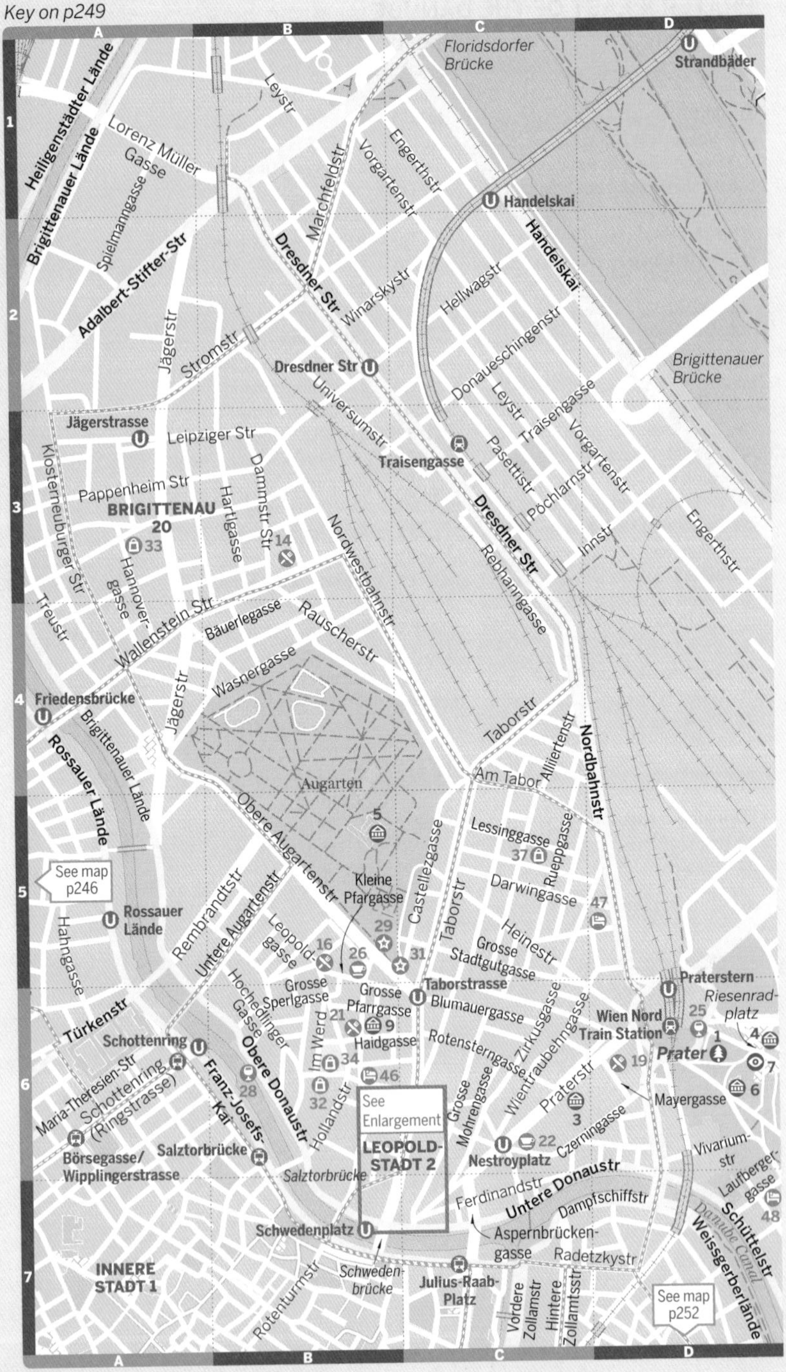
A
B
C
D
1
2
3
4
5
6
7
Floridsdorfer Brücke
Strandbäder
Heiligenstädter Lände
Brigittenauer Lände
Lorenz Müller Gasse
Leystr
Marchfeldstr
Vorgartenstr
Engerthstr
Handelskai
Spielmanngasse
Adalbert-Stifter-Str
Dresdner Str
Winarskystr
Hellwagstr
Jägerstr
Stromstr
Dresdner Str
Universumstr
Donaueschingenstr
Brigittenauer Brücke
Leystr
Traisengasse
Jägerstrasse
Leipziger Str
Traisengasse
Pasettistr
Vorgartenstr
Klosterneuburger Str
Pappenheim Str
Dammstr
Pöchlarnstr
BRIGITTENAU 20
Hartlgasse
Nordwestbahnstr
Dresdner Str
Engerthstr
33
Str
14
Rebhanngasse
Innstr
Hannover-gasse
Treustr
Wallenstein Str
Bäuerlegasse
Rauscherstr
Wasnergasse
Friedensbrücke
Jägerstr
Taborstr
Alliiertenstr
Brigittenauer Lände
Nordbahnstr
Rossauer Lände
Augarten
Am Tabor
Obere Augartenstr
5
Lessinggasse
Rueppgasse
Castellezgasse
37
See map p246
Kleine Pfargasse
Darwingasse
Rembrandtstr
Untere Augartenstr
Taborstr
47
Rossauer Lände
Heinestr
Hahngasse
Leopold-gasse
29
Grosse Stadtgutgasse
16
26
31
Grosse Sperlgasse
Grosse Pfarrgasse
Taborstrasse
Praterstern
Riesenrad-platz
Hochedlinger Gasse
Blumauergasse
21
9
Wien Nord Train Station
25
Türkenstr
Schottenring
Haidgasse
Rotensterngasse
Zirkusgasse
Wintraubengasse
1
4
Obere Donaustr
Im Werd
34
Prater
7
Franz-Josefs-Kai
Praterstr
19
Schottenring (Ringstrasse)
28
46
Maria-Theresien-Str
Hollandstr
32
Grosse Mohrengasse
See Enlargement
3
Mayergasse
6
LEOPOLD-STADT 2
Czerningasse
Vivarium-str
Börsegasse/ Wipplingerstrasse
Salztorbrücke
22
Nestroyplatz
Laufberger-gasse
Salztorbrücke
Untere Donaustr
Ferdinandstr
Dampfschiffstr
48
Schüttelstr
Schwedenplatz
Aspernbrücken-gasse
Danube Canal
Radetzkystr
Weissgerberlände
INNERE STADT 1
Schweden-brücke
Julius-Raab-Platz
Rotenturmstr
Vordere Zollamstr
Hintere Zollamtsstr
See map p252

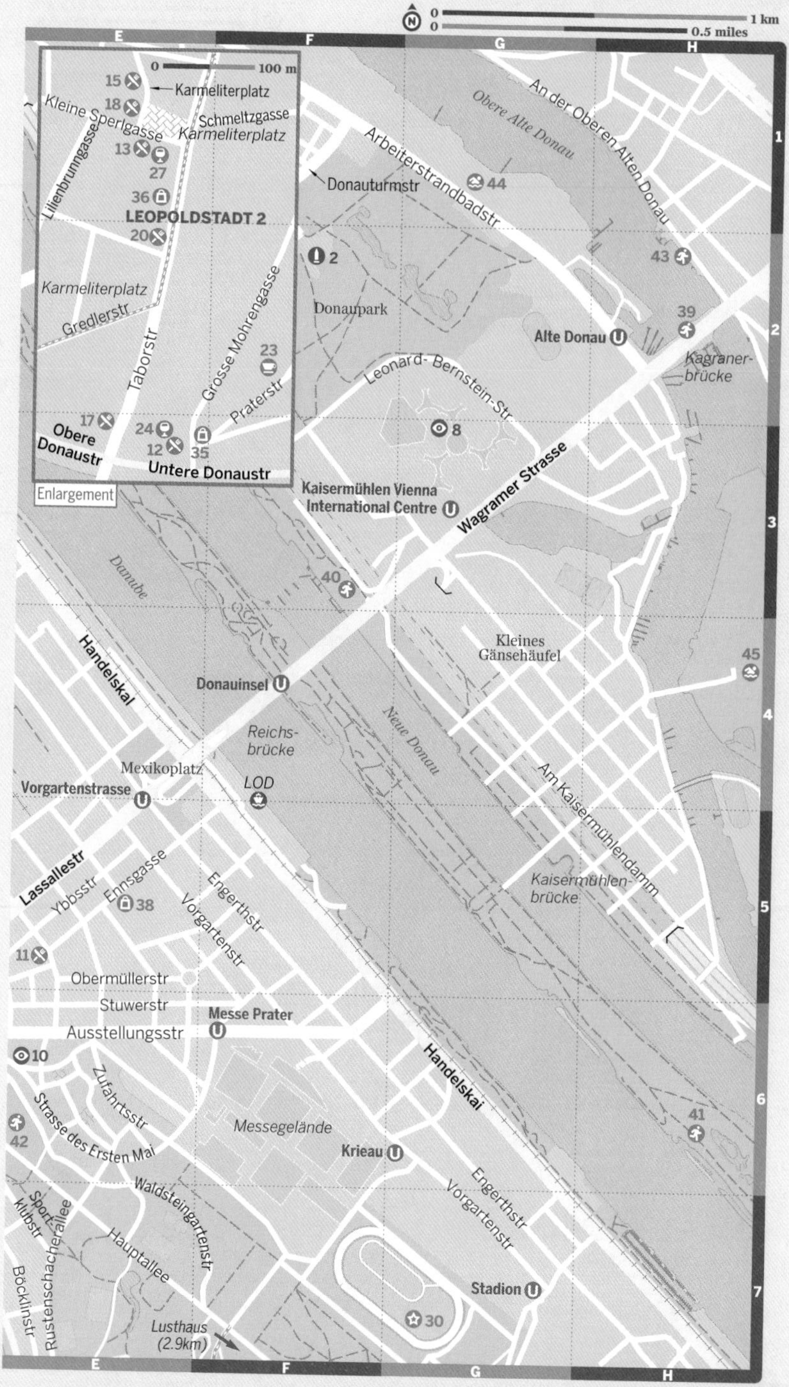
0
1 km
0
0.5 miles
E
F
G
H
1
2
3
4
5
6
7
0
100 m
15
18
Karmeliterplatz
Kleine Sperlgasse
Schmeltzgasse
Karmeliterplatz
13
27
Lilienbrunngasse
36
LEOPOLDSTADT 2
20
Karmeliterplatz
Gredlerstr
Taborstr
Grosse Mohrengasse
23
Praterstr
17
24
Obere Donaustr
12
35
Untere Donaustr
Enlargement
Obere Alte Donau
An der Oberen Alten Donau
Arbeiterstrandbadstr
Donauturmstr
44
2
Donaupark
43
39
Alte Donau
Kagraner-brücke
Leonard-Bernstein-Str
8
Kaisermühlen Vienna International Centre
Wagramer Strasse
Danube
40
Kleines Gänsehäufel
45
Handelskai
Donauinsel
Reichs-brücke
Neue Donau
Mexikoplatz
Vorgartenstrasse
LOD
Am Kaisermühlendamm
Lassallestr
Ybbsstr
Ennsgasse
38
Engerthstr
Vorgartenstr
Kaisermühlen-brücke
11
Obermüllerstr
Stuwerstr
Messe Prater
Ausstellungsstr
10
Zufahrtsstr
Handelskai
Strasse des Ersten Mai
42
Messegelände
Krieau
41
Waldsteingartenstr
Sport-klubstr
Rustenschacherallee
Hauptallee
Engerthstr
Vorgartenstr
Böcklinstr
Stadion
30
Lusthaus (2.9km)

SCHLOSS BELVEDERE TO THE CANAL

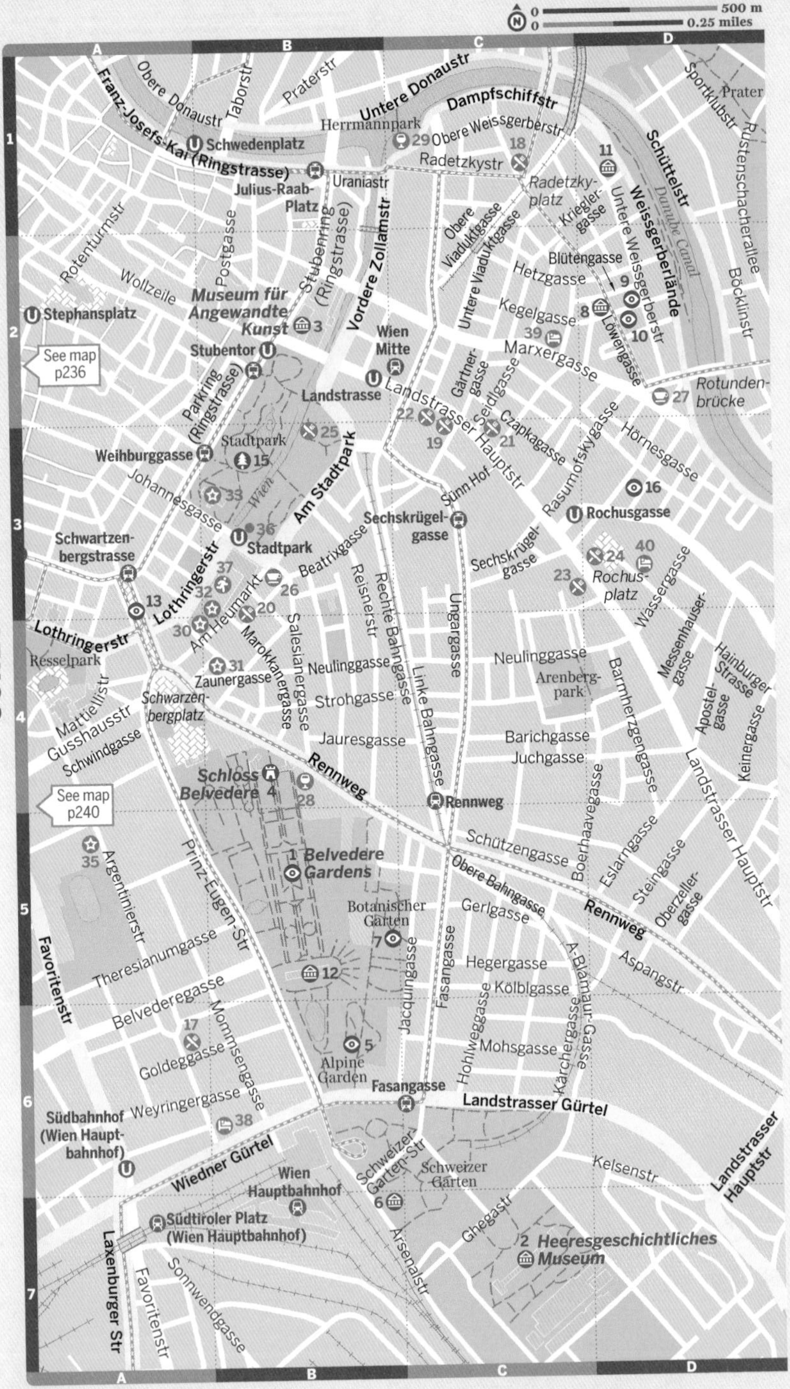

Top Sights (p135)

1 Belvedere Gardens B5
2 Heeresgeschichtliches Museum C7
3 Museum für Angewandte Kunst B2
4 Schloss Belvedere B4

Sights (p144)

5 Alpengarten B6
6 Belvedere 21 .... B7
7 Botanischer Garten B5
8 Fälschermuseum D2
9 Hundertwasser Village D2
10 Hundertwasserhaus D2
11 KunstHausWien D1
12 Oberes Belvedere B5
13 Schwarzenbergplatz A3
14 St Marxer Friedhof E7
15 Stadtpark B3
Unteres Belvedere .... (see 4)
16 Wittgensteinhaus D3

Eating (p144)

17 Café Goldegg A6
18 Cafe Menta C1
19 Colono C3
20 Gmoakeller B3
21 Heunisch & Erben C3
22 Joseph Brot C2
23 Lingenhel C3
Meierei im Stadtpark . (see 25)
24 Rochusmarkt D3
25 Steirereck im Stadtpark B3

Drinking & Nightlife (p147)

26 Café am Heumarkt B3
27 Café Zartl D2
28 Salm Bräu B4
29 Strandbar Herrmann C1

Entertainment (p147)

30 Akademietheater A4
31 Arnold Schönberg Center B4
32 Konzerthaus B3
33 Kursalon B3
34 Marx Halle E6
35 Radiokulturhaus A5

Sports & Activities (p148)

36 Vienna Walks & Talks B3
37 Wiener Eislaufverein B3

Sleeping (p189)

38 Mooons B6
39 Ruby Sofie C2
40 Spiess & Spiess D3

SCHLOSS SCHÖNBRUNN & AROUND

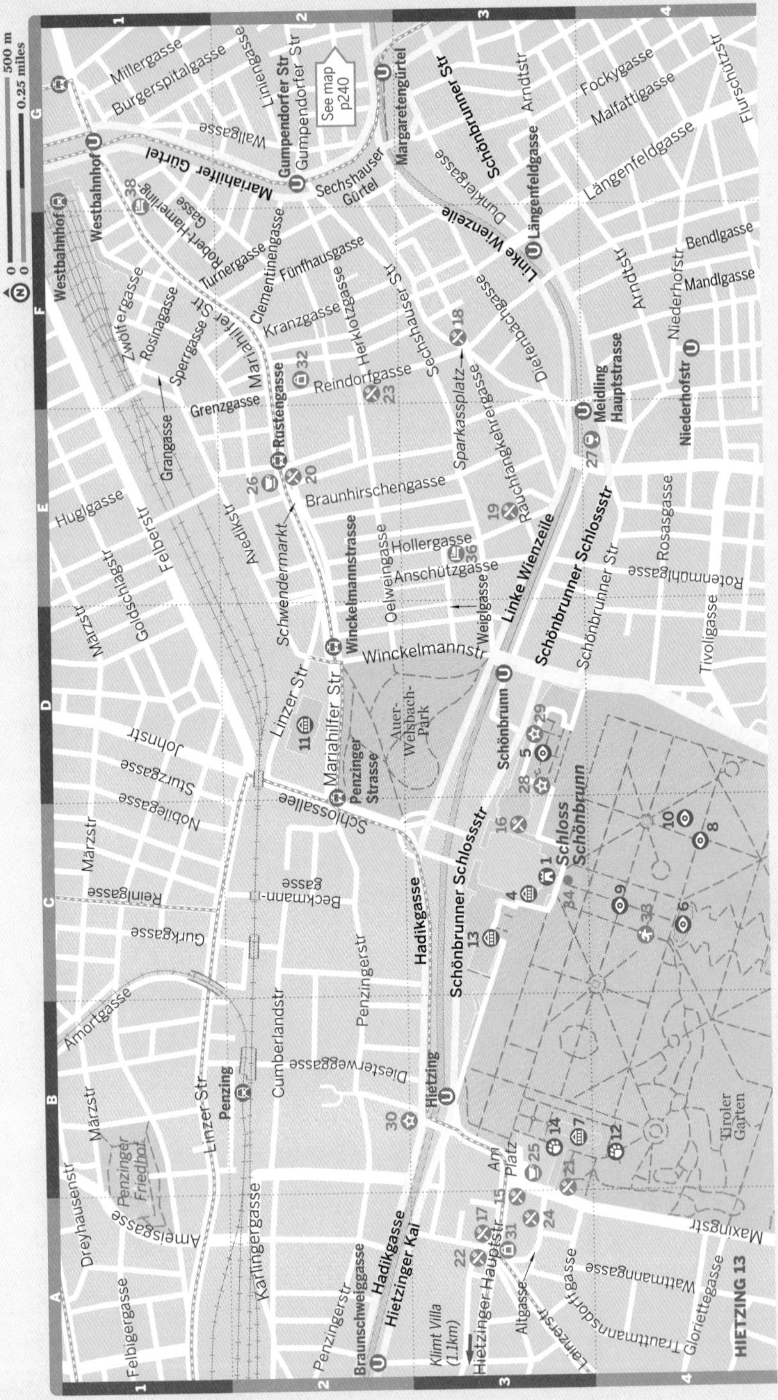